Professional Conduct and Discipline in Psychology

Larry J. Bass, PhD
Stephen T. DeMers, EdD
James R. P. Ogloff, PhD, JD
Christa Peterson, PhD
Jean L. Pettifor, PhD
Randolph P. Reaves, JD
Teréz Rétfalvi, PhD
Norma P. Simon, EdD
Carole Sinclair, PhD
Robert M. Tipton, PhD

AMERICAN PSYCHOLOGICAL ASSOCIATION
WASHINGTON, DC

ASSOCIATION OF STATE AND PROVINCIAL PSYCHOLOGY BOARDS
MONTGOMERY, AL

First printing July 1996
Second printing January 1998

Published by
American Psychological Association
750 First Street, NE
Washington, DC 20002

Association of State and Provincial Psychology Boards
P.O. Box 4389
400 South Union Street
Suite 295
Montgomery, AL 36103

Typeset in Century by EPS Group, Inc., Easton, MD

Printer: Kirby Lithographic Company, Inc., Arlington, VA
Cover designer: Rohani Design, Edmonds, WA
Technical/production editor: Valerie Montenegro

Library of Congress Cataloging-in-Publication Data
Professional conduct and discipline in psychology / Larry J. Bass . . . [et al.].
p. cm.
Includes bibliographical references and index.
ISBN 1-55798-372-0 (pbk. : acid-free paper)
1. Psychologists—Professional ethics—United States. 2. Psychologists—Professional ethics—Canada. 3. Psychology—Standards—United States. 4. Psychology—Standards—Canada. I. Bass, Larry J.
[DNLM: 1. Ethics, Professional. 2. Psychology—standards.
BF76.4 P963 1996]
BF76.4.P76 1996
353.9′383—dc20
DNLM/DLC
for Library of Congress 96-8182
CIP

British Library Cataloguing-in-Publication Data
A CIP record is available from the British Library.

Printed in the United States of America

Contents

Acknowledgments

The writing of this book has been a collegial and collaborative endeavor of 11 people of diverse backgrounds from six states and four provinces. Although individual chapters were assigned to specific authors, every chapter has been enriched and refined through the active participation of all authors.

Appreciation is enthusiastically extended to participants at the 1994 Association of State and Provincial Psychology Boards (ASPPB) Midwinter Meeting in Jacksonville, Florida. Videotapes of their presentations provided the basic content for scripting the videotape that complements this book.[1] Our special thanks go to Norma P. Simon and Stephen T. DeMers for chairing the project. Always the continuing support of the ASPPB Central Office is indispensable, and very special kudos go to Randolph P. Reaves and Emily Bentley. We hope that the reader will find the product as rewarding as we found the process of producing it.

[1]Readers may order the video or obtain information by writing to ASPPB Publications, P.O. Box 4389, Montgomery, AL 36103.

About the Authors

Larry J. Bass, PhD, is a clinical psychologist in private practice in Springfield, Missouri. He received his doctorate in clinical psychology at Washington University in St. Louis. He served two terms on the Missouri State Committee of Psychologists and serves as member at large of the ASPPB Board of Directors. He served on the Association of State and Provincial Psychology Boards (ASPPB) Professional Conduct and Discipline in Psychology Committee and the ASPPB/National Register Joint Designation Committee.

Stephen T. DeMers, EdD, is an associate professor and coordinator of the School Psychology Program, Department of Educational and Counseling Psychology, at the University of Kentucky. He received his doctorate in school psychology from Rutgers University. He has served on the Kentucky Board of Psychology, the ASPPB Board of Directors, and the Committee for the Advancement of Professional Practice (CAPP) of the American Psychological Association (APA). He has served as ASPPB president and as chairperson of the ASPPB's Model Licensure and Professional Conduct and Discipline in Psychology committees.

James R. P. Ogloff, PhD, JD, is an associate professor, associate chair of psychology, and coordinator of the Graduate Program in Law and Psychology at Simon Fraser University. He is also an adjunct professor of law at the University of British Columbia. He has served as a member of the Board of Directors of the Canadian Psychological Association (CPA) and currently is chair of the CPA's Committee on Ethics. He received both his doctorate in psychology and his juris doctor from the University of Nebraska–Lincoln.

Christa Peterson, PhD, is a clinical child psychologist who resides in Las Vegas, Nevada. She received her doctorate from the University of North Carolina at Chapel Hill. She is deputy administrator for the Nevada State Division of Child and Family Services and is an adjunct professor of special education at the University of Nevada, Las Vegas. She has served as president of the Nevada Board of Psychological Examiners and as a member of the ASPPB's Long Range Resource Planning and Professional Conduct and Discipline in Psychology committees.

Jean L. Pettifor, PhD, teaches part-time at the University of Calgary. She received her doctorate in clinical psychology from Wayne State University. She is retired from clinical practice in Alberta Mental Health Services and from management and quality assurance positions with Alberta Family and Social Services. She is a former president of the CPA and has served on the ASPPB's Professional Conduct and Discipline in Psychology

Committee. She is a coauthor of the *Companion Manual to the Canadian Code of Ethics*.

Randolph P. Reaves, JD, is an attorney with broad experience in professional regulation. He received his law degree from the University of Alabama School of Law. He is the author of *The Law of Professional Licensing and Certification* and is executive officer and general counsel of the ASPPB. He has served on the ASPPB's Model Licensure and Professional Conduct and Discipline in Psychology committees.

Teréz Rétfalvi, PhD, serves on the faculty of the Department de Psychologie of the Université de Moncton. She served as a member and president of the College of Psychologists of New Brunswick and serves on the college's Registration Committee. She served as a member of the Professional Conduct and Discipline and Model Licensure committees of the ASPPB. She also served as vice president of the Canadian Register of Health Service Providers in Psychology and as cochair of the Council of Provincial Associations of Psychologists. She received her PhD from the University of Ottawa.

Norma P. Simon, EdD, is director of training for the New Hope Guild Training Programs and is an adjunct professor of psychology at Teachers College, Columbia University, and supervisor at the New York University Postdoctoral Program in Psychoanalysis. She is the chairperson of the Professional Conduct and Discipline Committee of the ASPPB, served as a member of the ASPPB's Model Licensure Committee, and is vice chair of the Ethics Committee of the APA. She is a former president of the ASPPB and former chairperson of the New York State Board for Psychology. She received her doctorate in counseling psychology from Teachers College, Columbia University.

Carole Sinclair, PhD, is director of treatment services at the Dellcrest Children's Centre in Toronto, Ontario. She is cochair of the Committee on Ethics of the CPA and was instrumental in the development of the Canadian Code of Ethics for Psychologists. She has served as member of the CPA's Board of Directors and as a member of the editorial board for *Canadian Psychology*. She cowrote the *Companion Manual to the Canadian Code of Ethics*. She received her PhD from York University.

Robert M. Tipton, PhD, is professor emeritus at Virginia Commonwealth University, where he has served as director of the counseling psychology program and associate chairperson of the Department of Psychology. He received his doctorate from the University of Missouri. He is a past president of the Virginia Psychological Association and has served on the Virginia Board of Psychology.

Introduction

Stephen T. DeMers
University of Kentucky

The purpose of this book is to increase awareness and understanding of the regulation and ethical practice of professional psychology in the United States and Canada. Regulation of the profession of psychology in the United States and Canada is a complex and multifaceted process involving a combination of legislatively mandated credentialing and discipline by regulatory bodies along with voluntary credentialing and discipline associated with an individual's participation in a professional society. The mechanisms of regulation employed either by regulatory bodies or by professional associations or by both include the adoption of standards for professional preparation, credentialing, adoption of codes of professional conduct and ethics, and finally disciplinary procedures. While these aspects of regulation are similar in all professions, psychology regulation has been difficult for many to understand because of the interplay between mandated and voluntary regulation, the diversity and lack of uniformity in the professional preparation of psychologists, and the variety of credentials psychologists obtain to document their competence to practice.

According to Hogan (1979), one of the hallmarks of a profession is the presence of an organization that standardizes and advances the development of the field. Professional societies, such as the American Psychological Association (APA) and the Canadian Psychological Association (CPA), are examples of such entities for psychology in Canada and the United States. These organizations develop standards and criteria that describe the education, training, competencies, scope of practice, and appropriate conduct or behavior for the members of the profession. Such criteria offer the public a means of recognizing competent practitioners and regulating their conduct.

Another hallmark of a profession is the presence of recognized academic programs that offer degrees documenting the specialized training necessary to competently practice the profession. Unlike other well-established professions such as law and medicine, psychology has evolved with a somewhat confusing array of degrees and credentials that makes identifying the competent practitioner difficult. For example, while physicians have largely standardized training and a single degree (i.e., doctorate of medicine) to identify competent practitioners, the methods and models for preparing practicing psychologists vary greatly across institutions and programs, and they culminate in a variety of doctoral and non-doctoral degrees. The public and even many allied professionals have great difficulty understanding why some psychologists have doctorates of philosophy; some, doctorates of education; and others, doctorates of psychology; still other individuals with a variety of master's degrees are credentialed as psychologists in many jurisdictions. Furthermore, psychologists often receive identical degrees (e.g., doctorates of philosophy) despite marked differences in graduate programs intending to prepare practitioners (e.g., clinical, counseling, and school psychology) and those preparing nonpractitioners (i.e., researchers and scholars) in areas such as experimental, developmental, and social psychology.

In addition to academic degrees, competent practitioners in a profession are usually identifiable by a license or certificate issued by a legislatively mandated professional regulatory body. Such regulatory bodies are typically empowered by state or provincial statutes to identify by training, experience, and examination the competent members of the profession and to discipline incompetent or negligent practitioners in order to protect the public from harm. One of the hallmarks of psychology's emergence as a recognized profession was the passage of psychology licensing laws in states and provinces in the United States and Canada.[1] However, unlike medicine or law, many psychology-licensing acts allow for the credentialing of all psychologists with a doctoral degree in psychology. Thus, in most jurisdictions, the term *licensed psychologist* is not restricted to those individuals trained to provide psychological services to the public. The parallel in medicine would be the issuance of a doctorate of medicine degree and a medical license to someone trained at the doctoral level in physiology rather than a doctorate of philosophy degree in physiology. Such a situation leaves the public confused and less able to identify who is competent to provide professional services. Fox, Barclay, and Rodgers (1982) listed the absence of a credential that would clearly identify the psychological practitioner as one of the most serious impediments facing the profession of psychology.

Another aspect of regulation is the process of disciplining members of the profession who violate the public trust. Professional associations and regulatory bodies adopt and promulgate ethical standards and codes of professional conduct in psychology. Both professional associations and psychology regulatory boards adjudicate complaints and impose sanctions on those association members and licensed psychologists found guilty of misconduct. The rationale for this professional self-regulation is based on the belief that the average citizen is not competent to judge appropriate professional behavior, and thus professionals should be regulated by their peers.

The chapters that follow describe the common variations in the educational preparation and credentialing of psychologists as well as the common disciplinary processes employed by psychology regulatory bodies in

---

[1]States and provinces are referred to as *jurisdictions* throughout the text for purposes of brevity. The term *regulatory body* is used throughout the text to refer to the legally appointed, elected, or otherwise constituted agency within a jurisdiction to regulate the profession of psychology. In U.S. jurisdictions, the regulatory body is often called the *board of psychology*. In Canadian jurisdictions, the regulatory body in psychology may be referred to as a *register*, *college*, *association*, *corporation*, or *board*.

the United States and Canada. In addition, the book compares the codes of ethics and professional conduct from the major psychology professional associations, describes the most frequent areas of disciplinary complaints against psychologists, and presents a model for maintaining ethical principles in daily practice. The book also addresses the disciplinary process and the growing concern among practicing psychologists with the civil and criminal liability they may face when presented with a complaint.

The intended audience includes licensed psychologists, graduate students, applicants for licensure, and those participating in the preparation of professional psychologists (e.g., training program faculty, field supervisors, and internship directors). Other potential audiences include new members of psychology regulatory boards, members of state and provincial psychological associations, providers of continuing education for psychologists, attorneys, hearing officers, the public, and other professionals interested in psychology regulation. This book is also intended for practicing psychologists to increase their understanding of the rationale and methodology of psychology regulation and to increase their awareness of common areas of professional misconduct. For all audiences, the goal is to increase knowledge and understanding of the regulatory process and reduce the occurrence of professional misconduct.

To accomplish the intended purposes, each chapter addresses topics related to psychology regulation. Chapter 1 presents a brief history of the development of ethical codes, standards of practice, and professional licensure in psychology. The perceived need to regulate occupations and professions has a long history, but the development of mechanisms for regulating the practice of psychology is barely 50 years old. Regulatory issues related to professional conduct and discipline will be more meaningful when examined in a historical context. Collegial and professional associations such as the APA and the CPA support and advocate for the profession of psychology. In addition to developing ethical standards and determining appropriate professional conduct, they assist in developing standards and criteria that describe the education, training, competencies, and scope of practice. Regulatory bodies such as state and provincial psychology boards regulate entrance to the profession, adopt criteria and standards for competent and ethical practice, and participate in disciplinary procedures for adjudicating complaints. Most of the regulatory boards in the United States and Canada are members of the Association of State and Provincial Psychology Boards (ASPPB), an organization that provides leadership in the effective development of regulatory standards and procedures across jurisdictions.

Competent practice, which is the foundation of ethical conduct, requires sound education and training. Chaper 2 focuses on professional education and training in psychology. The chapter describes various models of professional training and retraining in psychology, including the evolution of the generic core curricula. Training in specialty areas of practice within psychology complement and expand the common skills acquired in the generic core. Chapter 2 includes a rationale for the relationship between training and ethical practice and provides a guide to current structures and issues in the education and training of professional psychologists.

Chapter 3 takes the reader through the intricacies of obtaining legal recognition to offer psychological services to the public. Credentialing is the process by which the professions regulate and control who may obtain and maintain the right or privilege to practice. Typically, boards of psychology are empowered by state and provincial legislation to identify the training, experience, and examination required to establish the competency of candidates to practice.

Chapter 4, "A Comparison of Codes of Professional Conduct and Ethics," describes the similarities and differences among the three major codes (APA, CPA, and ASPPB) governing the ethical practice of psychologists in North America. In addition to these broad codes, psychologists need to be aware of standards of practice and codes of ethics that have been adopted by their jurisdiction and those that pertain to their specialty areas of practice (see Appendix J for a bibliography of selected practice guidelines). These various codes and guidelines are generally consistent on the relevance of specific ethical principles and often consistently proscribe specific behaviors. However, the standards do vary in terms of level of proscription and emphasis on the ethical decision-making process. Ethical decisions may be influenced by the application of ethical principles and rules of conduct in specific situations and by internal and external pressures.

Chapter 5, "Common Problem Areas and Their Causes Resulting in Disciplinary Actions," describes the most common types of professional misconduct and suggests strategies to avoid these pitfalls. The most frequent complaints adjudicated by disciplinary boards relate to incompetence, dual relationships, inadequate record keeping, lack of informed consent, breach of confidentiality, and vague or exploitative financial arrangements.

Chaper 6, "Maintaining Professional Conduct in Daily Practice," provides suggestions for psychologists to enhance the quality of their psychological services for the best interests of consumers. The pursuit of excellence is an aspirational and self-monitoring process that exceeds meeting the minimal requirements to avoid disciplinary violations. This chapter demonstrates an ethical decision-making process, provides an annotated bibliography of practice guidelines, and outlines a comprehensive range of self-evaluation questions with detailed references to the ASPPB Code of Conduct (1991), the APA Ethical Principles of Psychologists and Code of Conduct (1992), and the CPA Canadian Code of Ethics for Psychologists (1991).

The formal regulation of professions is based on state and provincial legislation. The purpose of professional regulation is the protection of the public from incompetent or unethical practices. Chapter 7, "Enforcement of Codes of Conduct by Regulatory Boards and Professional Associations," describes the legal foundation and procedures used to adjudicate, discipline, and if appropriate, rehabilitate members judged guilty of professional misconduct. Chapter 8, "Laws That Affect the Practice of Psychology," summarizes the impact of types of legislation other than psychology licensure or certification acts. Professional misconduct may be adjudicated in the courts as well as within the profession.

Chapter 9, "Liability for Professional Misconduct," defines the legal context and indicates the types of situations in which psychologists and health-care providers may be liable. Such situations include professional negligence, failure to warn, failure to protect, negligent prescription of drugs, sexual relations with clients, and public disclosure of confidential information.

The practice of psychology continues to evolve. Chapter 10, "Future Trends," offers insight into emerging issues, from increased emphasis on addressing the special needs of diverse populations to providing quality care under the constraints of managed health care programs. Structures and funding for the provision of health and educational services are in a process of change, and there are trends suggesting that legislatures may wish to provide easier access to professional credentialing. The public good must be the primary objective in assessing and influencing proposed changes.

Because the focus of this book is on professional conduct and regulatory practices throughout the United States and Canada, the information contained is exemplary but not specific to any jurisdiction. The reader is advised to consult the psychology regulatory act in the relevant jurisdiction for specific information about requirements for credentialing and practice.

Ethical issues related to professional practice are often complex and do not readily lend themselves to predetermined textbook solutions, and in many cases there are numerous ways to view an ethical dilemma. This text presents a strategy for self-assessment that should increase practitioners' self-awareness of ethical behavior. It also suggests a framework for conceptualizing ethical issues when seeking solutions to ethical dilemmas. Some of the chapters include hypothetical vignettes to illustrate potential ethical dilemmas that give the reader an opportunity to think through some of the material presented in the related chapters. Additionally, a companion videotape that presents scenarios illustrating ethical problems related to the issues presented in the text has been developed. The purpose of this videotape is to provide stimulus material for group discussion in the context of a potential real-life situation. The text and videotape work in concert to provide a thoughtful and thought-provoking examination of ethical behavior, regulation, and professional conduct and discipline in psychology.

References

American Psychological Association. (1992). Ethical principles of psychologists and code of conduct. *American Psychologist, 47,* 1597–1611.

Association of State and Provincial Psychology Boards. (1991). *Code of conduct.* Montgomery, AL: Author.

Canadian Psychological Association. (1991). *Canadian code of ethics for psychologists. Revised.* Ottawa, ON: Author.

Fox, R. E., Barclay, A. G., & Rodgers, D. A. (1982). The foundations of professional psychology. *American Psychologist, 37*, 306–312.

Hogan, D. (1979). *Regulation of psychotherapists*. Cambridge, MA: Ballinger.

1

The History of Ethical Codes and Licensure

Carole Sinclair
Dellcrest Children's Centre

Norma P. Simon
Private Practice

Jean L. Pettifor
University of Calgary

The provision of competent and beneficial service to the public requires keen awareness of ethical issues and standards. However, a psychologist in Canada or the United States sometimes feels that, in the name of protecting the public, there has been an over-generation of standards, regulations, and requirements defining how the psychologist may practice. This activity has included the generation of mechanisms for investigation and punishment of psychologists who do not conform, and, in our increasingly litigious society, psychologists' concerns have expanded. A previously perceived straightforward concern about how to provide the most competent, ethical service has grown to include a concern about how to avoid what is perceived to be a plethora of possible complaints and violations. In some areas of practice, psychologists believe that the question is not if but when allegations of professional misconduct will be made, and they are concerned how they will defend themselves. How did all of this come about?

A Historical Perspective on Professions

The concept of profession has developed over time. In previous centuries, the only occupations awarded the status of a profession were theology,

---

The content of this chapter has been borrowed significantly from Sinclair, C. (1993). Codes of ethics and standards of practice. In K. Dobson & D. Dobson (Eds.), *Professional psychology in Canada* (pp. 167–199). Seattle, WA: Hogrefe & Huber Publishers. Copyright 1993 by Hogrefe & Huber Publishers. Adapted with permission of the publisher.

This chapter contains a review of the broad historical context of ethical codes and licensure for professions in general, as well as an outline of the development of ethical codes and licensure for psychology. For a detailed discussion of current codes for psychologists, see chapter 4.

medicine, and law. They were referred to as the learned professions. About a century ago, architecture and engineering were added to the list. However, the present century has seen an explosion in the number of occupations requesting professional status.

Dictionary meanings of a profession include:

> 1: the act of taking the vows that consecrate oneself to special religious service 2: an act of openly declaring or publicly claiming a belief, faith, or opinion 3: a calling requiring specialized knowledge and often long and intensive preparation including instruction in skills and methods as well as in the scientific, historical, or scholarly principles underlying such skills and methods, maintaining by force of organization or concerted opinion high standards of achievement and conduct, and committing its members to continued study and to a kind of work which has for its prime purpose the rendering of a public service. (Adapted from Webster, 1986)

These definitions indicate that the fundamental concept of a profession is derived from religious ideas of commitment, promises, learning, and service. In ancient times, there was less differentiation among members of the three learned professions, because the role of theologian, lawyer, and physician sometimes rested in a single person who often was believed to be divinely chosen to perform public service. The third definition is the one most commonly accepted today.

With the professionalization of society, professions have come under intense sociological study (Kultgen, 1988). The characteristics of a profession that consistently have appeared in the literature (Gross, 1978; Jennings, Callahan, & Wolf, 1987; Newton, 1988; Rychlak, 1984; Sinclair, Poizner, Gilmour-Barrett, & Randall, 1987; Weissman, 1984) are:

1. Members individually and collectively render service to members of the public and to society.
2. Members possess a high degree of generalized and systematic knowledge and skills requiring long and difficult education, extended practice, and continuing education.
3. Members develop and promote a code of ethics and function in accordance with this code.
4. Members function as a community that (a) controls entry requirements; (b) trains new members; (c) socializes new members into the attitudes, values, and accepted practices of the community; (d) regulates and monitors the professional activities of members; and (e) develops its field of knowledge and skill.
5. Members are accountable, willing to subject their activities to scrutiny both from within their own community and from society at large.

The last three characteristics are particularly important in any exploration of professional codes of ethics. They assume that an established profession will have developed a code of ethics, will socialize and regulate its members in the context of that code, and will be both internally and externally accountable for its ethical behavior.

On the other side of the ledger, there is extensive literature arguing that the very existence of professions has a negative impact on society because it involves assigning power and status to a small number of persons who tend to use professional self-regulation primarily to serve their own self-interest (Gross, 1978, 1984; Illich, Zola, McKnight, Caplan, & Shaiken, 1977; Larson, 1977). This sociological perspective on professions was labeled "the conflict perspective" by Kultgen (1988). Those who take this perspective see professionalization as a product of a class struggle that involves the domination of some groups by others with harmful consequences. There is some support for this perspective in the psychological literature itself. For instance, an ad hoc committee of the Committee on Scientific and Professional Responsibility of the American Psychological Association (APA, 1964) expressed the opinion that professions tend to use controls and standards to protect their own members but under the pretense of safeguarding the interests of clients. As another example of support, Zemlick (1980) expressed the opinion that economic and political interests had hindered psychologists from maintaining the highest ethical standards. He suggested that four areas of regulation that should have served the protection of the public had been guided primarily by self-interest, namely: (a) selection and training of graduate students, (b) faculty selection and retention, (c) licensing and credentialing of professionals, and (d) guidelines for protecting consumer welfare in service delivery.

The sociological perspective that emphasizes the socially beneficial characteristics of professions was labeled the "functionalist perspective" by Kultgen (1988). He and several other authors (Bayles, 1989; Beauchamp & Childress, 1988; Camenisch, 1983; Flores, 1988; May, 1975; Newton, 1988; Ravetz, 1971) hold that, because of the tremendous advancement in scientific and technological knowledge, a division of labor, roles, and expertise is essential in today's complex society. However, Kultgen argues that, to avoid a destructive impact on society, all professions—or occupations wishing to be professions—must become true "moral communities"; that is, groups of persons who have a genuine commitment to a clear and socially responsible ethic, who effectively socialize and regulate one another in the context of this ethic, and who are actively accountable to the public for their activities.

Several authors conceptualize the commitment of professions as a contract with society. This contract is based on principles of mutual dependence, respect, and trust (Kohlberg, 1969, 1976). May (1975) states that, in this reciprocal model, professionals acknowledge indebtedness for societal support of their training, of their livelihood, and of the public's active assistance in developing the science that nurtures their profession's field of knowledge. In return for professional autonomy, security, and the ability to work in an atmosphere of public trust, the contract with society requires each profession to pledge that it will develop those structures needed to help it ensure that each member will honor general ethical imperatives, be sensitive to the need for thoughtful and sound decision making when faced with ethical dilemmas, and put the welfare of members of the public ahead of the interests of the profession (Newton, 1988).

A Historical Perspective on Professional Ethics and Practice Standards

From the earliest recorded times to the present, the generation of standards of practice, codes of ethics, and processes for professional regulation has been shaped by the evolution of society and its various values, expectations, and structures. Although the regulation of the professional practice of psychology has a very short history, concern about the regulation of occupational groups, including professions, dates back to prerecorded times, with the articulation of standards of practice appearing to predate the development of codes of ethics.

Egyptian papyri of the 16th century B.C. outlined methods for physicians to establish diagnoses and to make choices on treatment. If followed, the physician was relieved of responsibility if the patient died (American College of Physicians [ACP], 1984). The Code of Hammurabi (about 2000 B.C.) contains the first written evidence of societal concern that occupations should be controlled in some way and accountable to society. In addition to detailing laws governing adultery, alimony, witchcraft, and slavery, the code specified laws and punishments (for poor technical performance) for the occupational behavior of tavern keepers, servants, and those who practiced medicine. Physicians were expected, for example, to set surgical fees according to the social status of the patient, reflecting a very early version of "sliding fees." An additional law stated that the punishment for killing a patient while opening an abscess was to have one's hands cut off unless the patient was a slave (in which case the replacement of the slave would be sufficient), reflecting the values and culture of the civilization that produced the code (ACP, 1984).

The Hippocratic Oath, written about 400 B.C., is believed to have been part of a rite of induction into a specific Greek medical guildlike community and is the first known example of a profession-generated code of ethics. It is still the foundation of codes of ethics for today's physicians. Unlike other oaths of the day, which tended to mention only a member's responsibility to the "art," one's teachers and other members (and perhaps to any standards or rules defined by the members), the Hippocratic Oath was unusual in that it incorporated specific obligations of the physician to members of the public. Because of its current relevance, it is quoted in full:

> The Hippocratic Oath
>
> I swear by Apollo, the Physician, by Aesculapius, by Hygeia, by Panacea, by all the gods and goddesses, that, according to the best of my ability and judgment, I will adhere to this oath and guarantee to hold the one who taught me this art equally precious to me as my parent; to share my assets with him, if need be, to see to his needs; to treat

> his children in the same manner as my brothers and to teach them this art free of charge or stipulation, if they desire to learn it; that by maxim, lecture and every other method of teaching, I will bestow a knowledge of the art to my own sons, to the sons of my teacher and to disciples who are bound by a contract and oath according to the law of medicine, and to no one else; I will adhere to that method of treatment which, to the best of my ability and judgment, I consider beneficial to my patients and I will disavow whatever is harmful and illegal; I will administer no fatal medicine to anyone even if solicited, nor will I offer such advice; I will not provide a woman with an implement useful for abortion.
>
> I will live my art and practice my art with purity and reverence. I will not operate on someone who is suffering from a stone, but will leave this to be done by those who perform this work. Whatever house I enter, I will go therein for the benefit of the sick and I will stand free from any voluntary criminal action and corrupt deed and the seduction of females or males, be they slaves or free. I will not divulge anything that, in connection with my profession or otherwise, I may see or hear of the lives of men which should not be revealed, on the belief that all such things should be kept secret.
>
> So long as I continue to be true to this oath, may I be granted the happiness of life, the practice of my art, and the continuing respect of all men. But if I forswear and violate this Oath, may my fate be the opposite. (Perkin, 1980, p. 1584)

Although the physician's specific obligations to teachers may sound odd to today's professional, they demonstrate the perceived "community" aspect of a profession or occupational group. In addition, not differentiating between slaves and free persons must have been progressive in its day but also reflects an environment in which slavery was an acceptable part of society. Of more importance, however, is the fact that this early ethics code touches on many ethical issues and dilemmas that are current today; namely, determining what might benefit or harm, assisted suicide, euthanasia, abortion, competence, confidentiality, and sexual involvement. Although the positions taken by today's society on some of the specific issues might be different, it is interesting to note that the code advocates ethical principles and values that are keystones to today's ethics codes, including being of benefit, avoiding harm, developing competence, staying within the bounds of one's competence, respecting privacy, and respecting the laws of society.

One can imagine an ethics complaint in ancient Greece might include the following facts:

> An Athenian businessman of some means has a particularly jealous younger wife who is preoccupied with the inheritance of his wealth when he dies. When the businessman impregnates a slave woman working as his wife's personal servant, he seeks the services of the family physician to perform an abortion. Both he and his wife value the slave woman. However, the businessman does not wish to upset his jealous wife. Therefore, he asks the physician to disguise the nature of

the woman's need for medical attention from his wife. He promises to pay the physician handsomely for doing this.

The physician ponders the Hippocratic Oath. He believes that he can meet the request of the businessman and still honor the Oath he had taken. He reasons that the treatment would be beneficial to both the businessman and the slave woman. He has determined that the slave woman is in agreement with the plan, having previously decided that a slave has the right to refuse his services, even if the owner has requested and is paying for them. Although the Oath states that he should not provide a woman with an implement for an abortion, it is silent on whether he can perform an abortion himself. Although he has never performed an abortion before, he believes that his performing the abortion would pose less risk than her doing it herself. He has no problem with maintaining the confidentiality requested by the businessman, believing that the situation is a "secret" that should be kept and that the harmful consequences of the wife learning about the pregnancy would be avoided.

The physician performs the abortion. However, the slave woman bleeds to death. The businessman is very upset and accuses the physician of not being competent. In the end, both agree to maintain secrecy about what caused the woman's death and agree that the loss of a slave is less serious than the loss of a free person. Due to the unfortunate outcome of his services, the physician offers to accept half the fee originally agreed on, and to replace the slave.

Two weeks later, a physician colleague is told the facts of the situation by a friend of the slave woman. The friend had been informed of the circumstances of the impending abortion by the slave woman before her death.

As you can see, many of the questions raised by this vignette are questions that would be raised today as well. One wonders how a hearing panel today would respond if a similar situation were brought to its attention.

Ethics Codes for Psychologists in the United States and Canada

There is little evidence of any serious effort to articulate ethical guidelines for psychologists until the end of World War II. Following this war, there was an upsurge of articles on the ethical responsibilities of and the need for ethics codes for psychologists. One precipitating factor for this increased interest was the increased application of psychology to everyday problems in health, education, and industry. In addition to being an academic discipline, psychology earned the reputation during the war of being a practicing profession. Another factor was the postwar discovery of atrocities performed, in the name of science, on concentration-camp victims and the subsequent 1946 development of the *Nuremberg Code of Ethics in Medical Research* (1964).

In 1947, the APA established a Committee on Ethical Standards for Psychologists (Hobbs, 1948). A 2-year plan for developing a code of ethics for psychologists was proposed (APA, 1949). The plan included a year to collect from members of APA descriptions of incidents that required ethical choices and to classify those incidents. It included a second year for a critical examination of the incidents and to formulate and test ethical principles derived from them. After the publication of a series of articles (APA, 1950, 1951a, 1951b, 1951c, 1951d) and feedback from the membership, a set of provisional ethical standards was adopted by its Council of Representatives on September 4, 1952 (APA, 1953).

The development and adoption of this first APA code of ethics had a significant impact on the international community of psychologists and the interdisciplinary community. Psychologists in France and Germany expressed admiration for the American process and product and began development of their own codes of ethics (Bloom, 1964; Bondy, 1959; Pacaud, 1954). Group workers and sociologists (Hall, 1952; Lee, 1953) also proposed the APA approach as a model for their own codes.

The APA revised its code in 1959, 1963, 1977, 1981, 1989, and 1992. The latest version, titled Ethical Principles of Psychologists and Code of Conduct (APA, 1992), was a major revision of the code and followed a series of legal challenges. The 1992 revision separates what is termed *aspirational principles* from what are described as *enforceable behavioral standards*.

Meanwhile, the Canadian Psychological Association (CPA) had adopted the 1959, 1963, and 1977 revisions of the APA code of ethics. Although the CPA had considered developing a Canadian code of ethics from the time of its inception in 1949, it was not until 1986 that the *Canadian Code of Ethics for Psychologists* was approved and adopted by the CPA Board of Directors. Prior to developing its own code, there was evidence of periodic discontent by CPA members with the APA code. For example, in a 1976 CPA document titled "Alternative Strategies for Revising CPA's Code of Ethics," the statement was made that the 10 APA ethical principles were "clearly designed for the current American social and moral climate and geared to American traditions and law" (Dunbar, 1990, p. 4). However, it was not until the 1977 revision of the APA code that the discontent became serious. Of particular concern was the fact that, in response to U.S. court applications of antitrust law to professional activities (Overcast, Sales, & Polard, 1982), the APA had removed some of its restrictions on advertising. Many Canadian psychologists believed such application of antitrust laws ran the risk of changing the nature of the professional relationship from a primarily fiduciary contract to a commercial one. Although recognizing that the professional relationship has elements of both the fiduciary and the commercial and that both have advantages and disadvantages to the parties involved, Canadian psychologists believed that, among other problems, such a change would make it much more difficult to protect the public from unscrupulous and self-serving professionals. It was at this point that the development of a Canadian code of ethics began in earnest.

After a critical analysis of the interdisciplinary and international research on the purposes and weaknesses of ethics codes, the CPA set four objectives for its own code: (a) to be conceptually cohesive and thereby a more effective educational tool, (b) to be more inclusive of recently developed areas of practice, (c) to give more explicit guidelines for action when ethical principles are in conflict, and (d) to reflect explicitly the most useful decision rules (ethical principles) for ethical decision making (Sinclair et al., 1987). In attempting to meet these objectives, the CPA code used a somewhat empirical methodology in its development and incorporated a number of unique features. Although a revision was approved and adopted in 1991, the structure, principles, and values remained virtually identical to the original 1986 version and reflect a logical structure within a framework of ethical theory. Currently, the Canadian code has been adopted by most provincial jurisdictions and is beginning to receive international attention. (For a comparison of the *ASPPB Code of Conduct*, the APA Ethical Principles of Psychologists and Code of Conduct, and the CPA *Canadian Code of Ethics for Psychologists*, please refer to chap. 4.)

Standards of Practice for Psychology in Canada and the United States

In contrast to ethics codes, standards of practice do not articulate the underlying ethical principles or values of a profession. Rather, they specify indicators of quality practice. As noted above, the existence of standards of practice for occupational groups seems to have predated ethics codes. The articulation of ethical principles, which may have been silently embedded in the standards of practice, came later. However, in today's world there is an expectation that standards of practice will reflect and be consistent with a profession's already articulated ethical principles.

Many early craft guilds, unlike the professions, were established primarily to protect the craft and its members. Generally, they were not held accountable under the law for the quality of their work. However, many had practice standards relating to the quality of work and to business practices. Medicine was the first profession known to establish standards of practice and to be held accountable under the law for maintaining those standards.

The introductory statements to *General Guidelines for Providers of Psychological Services* (APA, 1987) and *Practice Guidelines for Providers of Psychological Services* (CPA, 1989) outline the following objectives for practice standards:

1. To define common expectations for psychologists, users, and organizations.
2. To help define legislative and regulatory requirements for the practice of psychology.
3. To provide an external authority for psychologists working in situations in which others may be minimally knowledgeable about or supportive of quality practice in psychology (e.g., third-party payers and employers).
4. To be incorporated into teaching and training programs, in order to help socialize tomorrow's professionals.

5. To provide specific content and structure to the profession's principles of ethical practice.

If done well, practice standards and guidelines for licensed practitioners help to assure respectful and competent practice for members of the public. They serve as guidelines for practitioners and are also used for the training, screening, and regulation of members of the profession.

However, as the interest in standards has grown, so has the proliferation of documents. In addition to the general practice-guideline documents developed by the CPA and the APA, one can find practice standards and guidelines on such topics as the provision of therapy to women, the elimination of sexual harassment, educational and psychological testing, and custody and access assessments. There are so many that it is difficult to have detailed knowledge of them all. However, today's psychologists need to be particularly knowledgeable of those standards and guidelines that relate to their own areas of practice and of those recommended or formally adopted by their regulatory and voluntary organizations. Of some reassurance to practitioners is the opinion that the many documents are consistent with the underlying ethical principles of the APA and the CPA codes of ethics (Psychologists Association of Alberta, 1990).

A Historical Perspective on Licensure

Although there is evidence that laws were established related to the practice of various professions in the ancient world, there is little evidence that the state was involved in deciding who could practice. (It should be noted, however, that women were excluded, by edict, from certain occupations at various points in time in various nations). There seemed to be an assumption that any practitioner would have been trained within a particular school and that continued membership in the school (guild or professional society) was a sign that the individual was a practitioner in good standing. The various schools or professional communities seemed to have virtual autonomy regarding who was admitted and who was deemed qualified to practice.

As the world became more populated and complex, the population became more mobile. There was an increase in the number of medical schools and in government involvement. In A.D. 931, an examining and licensing board for "healers" was established in Baghdad. In A.D. 1140, Roger II of Sicily proclaimed an edict that persons who practiced medicine without a license would be punished. In A.D. 1225, Holy Roman Emperor Frederick II forbade the practice of medicine without a license and declared that obtaining a license must be preceded by 5 years of academic study (including 3 years of logic), 1 year of practice under the direction of an experienced physician, and the passing of an examination by a teacher of medicine (Gross, 1984). This government-involved self-regulation model for licensing of professionals, in which the state provides a framework but delegates the training and declaration of competence (licensing) to members of the profession, is the model that prevailed in England in the 15th and 16th centuries. It is also the model brought to the New World colonies.

Licensing in the United States and Canada

In Canada and the United States, the first licensed physicians immigrated from France and England. Therefore, at first, there was no perceived need for the various governments to establish their own licensing framework. However, over time, concerns were raised about various practices. For example, Ehrl (1994) reports that there were concerns in 1639 in Virginia that physicians were overcharging. Also, in New France, complaints about the practices of ship physicians with the population led the government to enact a law allowing only physicians from "countries established in the cities of this country and its coasts" to practice, unless the physician had submitted himself to a "serious preliminary examination" (Hamowy, 1984). By 1800, 13 American states had licensing or regulation legislation, and Upper Canada (Ontario) had attempted to pass a licensing act that, after many attempts, was finally passed in 1815 (MacNab, 1970). Lower Canada (Quebec) passed its first act in 1831. Following the imported model established in Europe, the legislation usually delegated the power to examine and license physicians to existing medical societies or to medical schools but sometimes proposed an "independent board" of practitioners selected by a government official (e.g., the governor) or through a government selection process.

In spite of these early efforts, Canada was reluctant to enforce its legislation and, in the United States, many states had repealed their laws by the middle of the 19th century. The reasons differed somewhat in each country. In Canada, the population was scattered, and there was an inadequate supply of qualified physicians. As a result, there was little public support or pressure to ensure that only licensed physicians practiced. In the United States, there had been a public upsurge in distrust of authority, including a distrust of government control.

After the establishment of several Canadian medical schools and extended experience with deregulation in the United States, public opinion began to support reinvolvement of government in the licensing and regulation of the professions. Ontario passed the first modern medical act in Canada in 1869. Texas passed the first modern medical act in the United States in 1873. In 1888, a key decision of the United States Supreme Court opened the floodgates to professional licensure (*Dent v. West Virginia*, 1889). In the decision, the Court reinforced ideas about the desirability of a free-market economy system but made an exception for medical licensure under the doctrine of police powers. This doctrine legitimizes policing powers (including licensing and regulation) when they are exercised to protect the health, welfare, or safety of citizens (Gross, 1984). By 1894, 21 U.S. states had examinations for physicians, and 14 others permitted only graduates of accredited medical schools to practice in their jurisdictions. By 1912, all states had practice acts, including those that had previously repealed their acts (Ehrl, 1994). Meanwhile, both before and after the 1888 decision, similar U.S. regulations were being established for other professions that, after the 1888 decision, went unchallenged. The first law licensing dentists passed in 1868, followed by pharmacy in 1874, accounting and veterinary medicine in 1886, and architecture in 1897. In the early 20th century, the Flexner Report led to the standardization of the education and training of physicians in the United States, setting the standard for professional training for this century (Flexner, 1910). Other professions, including psychology, studied the report and began to standardize their education and training. Similar developments could be found in Canada, where the first dentistry act was passed in 1868, the first pharmacy act in 1869, the first architecture act in 1890, the first optometry act in 1919, and the first nursing and engineering acts in 1922 (Trebilcock, Tuohy, & Wolfson, 1979).

Because standards of practice had been developed in many professions, when legislatures began bringing professions under government regulation, they turned to members of those professions. In most cases, boards of professionals were established to design and implement the details of a governing process for the members of the profession in each jurisdiction. The functions that these self-regulatory boards perform according to Shimberg (1982) are as follows:

> 1. Screening applicants to insure that they possess at least the minimum qualifications for safe practice. Thus, the public is spared the distress and practical hazard of dealing with unqualified practitioners.
> 2. Setting practice standards and codes of conduct for practitioners. These further safeguard the public, which often lacks a basis for judging what constitutes acceptable quality in service or conduct.
> 3. Investigating charges of incompetence or impropriety against licensees and taking appropriate disciplinary action where warranted. Such action helps to rid the profession of incompetent, unethical, and dishonest practitioners. It also serves notice on others that the regulatory agency will not tolerate practitioners whose activities may be contrary to the public interest. (p. 6)

According to Gellhorn (1976), as new professions evolved, including psychology, they have generally sought licensure voluntarily. This was purportedly to safeguard the public against untrained and unscrupulous practitioners. However, all professions have been accused of being self-serving in their licensing efforts, seeking to limit the entrance of members to the profession to keep the number of professionals down and to command higher fees.

Licensure for Psychology in the United States and Canada

During World War II, many psychology academicians were pressed into applied practice to aid the military effort. After the war, these new practitioners continued to practice and to train others, thereby changing the face of psychology. The first licensing law for psychologists in the United States or Canada was passed in Connecticut in 1945. The 50th anniversary of this historical event was celebrated by the Association of State and Provincial Psychology Boards (ASPPB) in April 1995, with the First International Congress of Licensing, Certification, and Credentialing. By 1977, all states in the United States had licensure laws, with Missouri being the last. Canadian provinces followed somewhat later, with Ontario being the first province to have a psychologists' act in 1960, and Prince Edward Island being the last in 1990 (Wand, 1993).

As an increasing number of jurisdictions in the United States and Canada began to license psychologists, the need for a standard examination to evaluate the knowledge of applicants became apparent. The American Association of State Psychology Boards (AASPB; the name was changed in 1992 to Association of State and Provincial Psychology Boards to reflect the organization's Canadian membership) was formed to create such an examination, the Examination for Professional Practice in Psychology (EPPP). The association held its organizing meeting in November 1959, supported by the APA Board of Professional Affairs Committee on State Examination Procedures (Carlson, 1978). The association became official in 1961, with the boards of 21 jurisdictions pledged to membership. The issues of concern to these early leaders were public information; reciprocity; the examination; a common pass point; and the most important concern, the definition of practice (Carlson, 1978). These continue to be important to the association and its members. However, as the association grew, so did its scope and function. In addition to the examination, the association provides education and training for members of licensing boards, develops educational materials, and holds two general educational meetings each year. The ASPPB developed for the use of its members the model licensing law, the code of conduct, and the disciplinary data bank. It conducted a second practice analysis to identify the scope of practice in the 1990s. Over the years, regulatory bodies have increasingly accepted the recommendations of the association regarding standards, such as the doctoral-level entrance criteria and the 70% passing score on the EPPP. While ASPPB has no statutory authority, it has been influential in changing the face of licensure in psychology in the United States and Canada.

With respect to the primary function of regulatory bodies, namely investigating alleged violations and disciplining members where warranted, legislation generally has favored professionals setting the criteria by which their colleagues will be judged. Thus, the codes of ethics and codes of conduct developed by national associations (including the ASPPB) often are incorporated into state and provincial laws and regulations for the profession. The number of psychologists charged by licensing boards with violations has increased dramatically in recent years. With increased public awareness and increased willingness by aggrieved individuals to face the ordeal of bringing charges, licensing boards in many professions have many more cases to adjudicate. The profession is faced with reacting to this increased activity in a manner that ensures justice is done to all parties as well as ensuring that psychologists fulfill their other obligations in a manner that prevents harmful and unethical practices from occurring in the first place.

Concluding Comment

The ethical concerns, principles, and values of professions have expanded since the acceptance of the Hippocratic Oath but have retained the same core. Many professions have incorporated these principles and values into both their codes of ethics, which tend to be aspirational, and their codes of conduct, which are useful in defining the parameters of acceptable behavior. Current codes and standards are much longer and definitive, raising the concern that too much attention to specific rules runs the risk of obscuring the underlying principles and values. In light of increased formal mechanisms for regulation and public accountability, it is sometimes argued that psychology is in danger of exchanging its historical ethical values and principles for a rule-driven, legalistic, and behavioral approach to defining and enforcing acceptable professional practice and to maintaining its contract with society. Specific rules, although helpful, are unlikely to prove sufficient to resolve the many ethical dilemmas of a complex and changing society. As such, psychology may need to find ways of helping psychologists rediscover the broader moral context of the profession's rules and regulatory activity.

References

American College of Physicians, Ad Hoc Committee on Medical Ethics. (1984). Part I: History of medical ethics, the physician and the patient, the physician's relationship to other physicians, the physician and society. *Annals of Internal Medicine, 101*, 129–137.

American Psychological Association, Committee on Ethical Standards for Psychologists. (1949). Developing a code of ethics; a first report of progress. *American Psychologist, 4*, 17.

American Psychological Association, Committee on Ethical Standards for Psychologists. (1950). Ethical Standards for the distribution of tests and diagnostic aids. *American Psychologist, 5*, 620–626.

American Psychological Association, Committee on Ethical Standards for Psychologists. (1951a). Ethical standards in clinical and consulting relationships: Part I. *American Psychologist, 6*, 57–64.

American Psychological Association, Committee on Ethical Standards for Psychologists. (1951b). Ethical standards in clinical and consulting relationships: Section 3, Parts II-V. *American Psychologist, 6*, 145–166.

American Psychological Association, Committee on Ethical Standards for Psychologists. (1951c). Ethical standards for psychologists; Section 2, ethical standards in professional relationships; Section 4, ethical standards in research; Section 5, ethical standards in writing and publishing. *American Psychologist, 6*, 427–452.

American Psychological Association, Committee on Ethical Standards for Psychologists. (1951d). Ethical standards for psychologists; Section 1, ethical standards and public responsibility; Section 6, ethical standards in teaching. *American Psychologist, 6*, 626–661.

American Psychological Association. (1953). *Ethical standards of psychologists*. Washington, DC: Author.

American Psychological Association, Committee on Scientific and Professional Ethics and Conduct, Ad hoc Committee on Ethical Practices in Industrial Psychology. (1964). Ethical practices in industrial psychology: A review of one committee's deliberations. *American Psychologist, 19,* 174–182.

American Psychological Association. (1987). *General guidelines for providers of psychological services.* Washington, DC: Author.

American Psychological Association. (1992). Ethical principles of psychologists and code of conduct. *American Psychologist, 47,* 1597–1611.

Bayles, M. D. (1989). *Professional ethics, Second Edition.* Belmont, CA: Wadsworth Publishing Company.

Beauchamp, T. L., & Childress, J. F. (1988). Virtues and conscientious actions. In A. Flores (Ed.), *Professional ideals.* Belmont, CA: Wadsworth.

Bloom, B. L. (1964). The code of ethics of the French Psychological Society. *American Psychologist, 19,* 183–185.

Bondy, C. (1959). Die ethischen Grenzen psychologischer Arbeit [Ethical limits of psychological investigations]. *Psychologische Rundschau, 10,* 237–250. (From *Psychological Abstracts,* 1960, *34,* Abstract No. 5088.)

Camenisch, P. R. (1983). On being a professional, morally speaking. In B. Baumin & B. Freedman (Eds.), *Moral responsibility and the professions* (pp. 42–61). New York: Haven.

Canadian Psychological Association. (1989). *Practice guidelines for providers of psychological services.* Ottawa, ON: Author.

Canadian Psychological Association. (1991). *Canadian code of ethics for psychologists. Revised.* Ottawa, ON: Author.

Carlson, H. S. (1978). The AASPB story. *American Psychologist, 11,* 487–489.

Dent v. West Virginia, 129 U.S. 114, 9 S.Ct. 231 (1889).

Dunbar, J. N. (1990). *Historical background to the Canadian code of ethics for psychologists.* Paper presented at the Canadian Psychological Association Convention, Ottawa, ON.

Ehrl, D. (1994). Regulating health care professionals: An overview. *Resource Briefs, 4,* 2–3.

Flexner, A. (1910). *Medical education in the United States and Canada.* New York: Carnegie Foundation.

Flores, A. (1988). *Professional ideals.* Belmont, CA: Wadsworth.

Gellhorn, W. (1976). The abuse of occupational licensing. *University of Chicago Law Review, 44,* 6.

Gross, S. J. (1978). The myth of professional licensing. *American Psychologist, 11,* 1009–1016.

Gross, S. J. (1984). *Of foxes and hen houses. Licensing and the health professions.* Westport, CT: Quorum Books.

Hall, L. K. (1952). Group workers and professional ethics. *Group, 15,* 3–8.

Hamowy, R. (1984). *Canadian medicine.* Toronto, ON: The Fraser Institute.

Hobbs, N. (1948). The development of a code of ethical standards for psychology. *American Psychologist, 3,* 80–84.

Illich, I., Zola, I. K., McKnight, J., Caplan, J., & Shaiken, H. (1977). *Disabling professions.* London: Marian Boyars.

Jennings, B., Callahan, D., & Wolf, S. M. (1987). The professions: Public interest and common good. *Hastings Center Report: Special Supplement, 17* (February), 3–10.

Kohlberg, L. (1969). Stage and sequence. The cognitive–developmental approach to socialization. In G. A. Goslin (Ed.), *Handbook of socialization theory and research* (pp. 31–53). Chicago: Rand-McNally.

Kohlberg, L. (1976). Moral stages and moralization. The cognitive-developmental approach. In T. Lickona (Ed.), *Moral development and behavior* (pp. 31–53). New York: Holt, Rinehart, & Winston.

Kultgen, J. (1988). *Ethics and professionalism.* Philadelphia: University of Pennsylvania Press.

Larson, M. S. (1977). *The rise of professionalism.* Berkeley: University of California Press.

Lee, A. M. (1953). Responsibilities and privileges in sociological research. *Sociology and Social Research, 37,* 367–374.

MacNab, E. (1970). *A legal history of health professions in Ontario*. Toronto, ON: Queen's Printer.

May, W. F. (1975). Code, covenant, contract, or philanthropy. *Hastings Center Report, 5,* 29–38.

Newton, L. H. (1988). Lawgiving for professional life: Reflections on the place of the professional code. In A. Flores (Ed.), *Professional ideals*. Belmont, CA: Wadsworth.

Nuremberg code. (1964). *Science, 143,* 553.

Overcast, T. D., Sales, B. D., & Pollard, M. R. (1982). Applying antitrust laws to the professions: Implications for psychology. *American Psychologist, 37,* 517–525.

Pacaud, S. (1954). La déontologie et l'organisation de la profession. *Revue de Psychologie Appliquée, 4,* 13–19. (From *Psychological Abstracts,* 1954, *28,* Abstract No. 6872).

Perkin, R. L. (1980). The Hippocratic Oath in the 1980s. *Canadian Family Physician, 26,* 1584–1592.

Psychologists Association of Alberta. (1990). *Guidelines for the practice of psychology: An annotated bibliography*. Edmonton, AB: Author.

Ravetz, J. R. (1971). *Scientific knowledge and its social problems*. Oxford, England: Oxford University Press.

Rychlak, J. F. (1984). Newtonianism and the professional responsibility of psychologists: Who speaks for humanity? *Professional Psychology: Research and Practice, 15,* 82–95.

Shimberg, B. (1982). Occupational licensing: A public perspective. Princeton, NJ: Educational Testing Service.

Sinclair, C., Poizner, S., Gilmour-Barrett, K., & Randall, D. (1987). The development of a code of ethics for Canadian psychologists. *Canadian Psychology, 28,* 1–8.

Trebilcock, M. J., Tuohy, C. J., & Wolfson, A. D. (1979).
Professional regulation: A staff study of accountancy, architecture, engineering and law in Ontario prepared for the Professional Organizations Committee. Toronto, ON: Ministry of the Attorney General.

Wand, B. (1993). The nature of regulation and entrance criteria. In K. Dobson & D. Dobson (Eds.), *Professional psychology in Canada* (pp. 149–165). Toronto, ON: Hogrefe & Huber.

Webster's third new international dictionary of the English language: Unabridged. (1986). Toronto, ON: Encyclopaedia Britannica.

Weissman, H. N. (1984). Professional standards from the perspective of the sociology of professions. *Professional Psychology: Research and Practice, 17,* 448–453.

Zemlick, M. J. (1980). Ethical standards: Cosmetics for the face of the profession of psychology. *Psychotherapy: Theory, Research, and Practice, 17,* 448–453.

2

Education and Training

Robert M. Tipton
Virginia Commonwealth University

Sound education and training are the foundations of competent and ethical practice in psychology. Although other professions, such as psychiatry, social work, professional counseling, and psychiatric nursing, provide direct services and employ psychological principles in their practices, applied psychology differs from these related professions in that education and training in psychology is more thoroughly grounded in the science of the discipline. This section addresses the unique features of education and training of the professional psychologist.

Models of Training in the United States

There has always been general agreement that training programs in professional psychology should be thoroughly grounded in the science of psychology, although differences have existed as to what the appropriate training model should be. At the time Lightner Witmer (1996) started the first psychological clinic in 1896, thereby formalizing the practice of applied psychology in the United States, he stated "that there is no valid distinction between pure science and an applied science" (p. 249). Early training in professional psychology focused mainly on basic psychology with course work and laboratories in such areas as experimental and physiological psychology; applied training was secondary and emphasized such areas as psychometrics and child development. There was little uniformity in the applied aspects of graduate training, and departments offering professional training varied according to the interests of the faculty.

By the middle of the 20th century, the roles of professional psychologists had expanded, and demands for services had dramatically increased. The impetus for these changes derived from World Wars I and II. Along with this rapid growth in applied psychology came an awareness of the need to develop standards and to formalize training programs. David Shakow was keenly interested in the training of clinical psychologists and played a major role in the early development of a model for the clinical internship, which was described by the subcommittee on Graduate Internship Training to the Committee on Graduate and Professional Training of the APA and the American Association for Applied Psychologists (1945). Among other things, this committee "emphasized particularly the value of a 3rd-year internship with a 4th year spent at the university" (Shakow, 1978, p. 1950). The first major document to address graduate training requirements, known as the Shakow report, endorsed the aforementioned internship requirements and also included recommendations for training in six major areas: general psychology, related disciplines, psychodynamics of behavior, diagnostic methods, research methods, and therapy. It recommended also that training be at the doctoral level and that practicum training be provided as well as the internship (APA, 1947).

At the Boulder Conference in 1949 a group of clinical psychologists adopted the scientist–practitioner model as the appropriate method for training clinical psychologists (Raimy, 1950). This model asserts that applied psychology has its roots in the science of the discipline and that research is integral to the practice of psychology. The scientist–practitioner model has subsequently been accepted by psychologists representing the other three specialty areas in applied psychology: counseling, industrial-organizational, and school psychology.

During the years immediately following the Boulder Conference, the research aspect of the training model was emphasized, with minimal emphasis on applied training. There was a general expectation that students educated in scientist–practitioner programs would pursue research and teaching, and academic positions were readily available. During the 1960s, there was an increased demand for psychologists in a broader range of employment settings. The independent practice of psychology, however, was in its infancy. There was a dramatic growth in the number of psychologists graduated in the 1960s, and it was said that if growth in the profession continued at the same rate, by the year 2000 everybody in the United States would be a psychologist. Fortunately, the growth curve leveled off. As more applied positions became available, academic programs directed more attention to the applied aspects of training. The scientist–practitioner model continued to prevail, however, as the dominant approach to educating applied psychologists.

In 1990, 41 years after the Boulder Conference, a National Conference on Scientist–Practitioner Education and Training for the Professional Practice of Psychology was held in Gainesville, Florida, for the purpose of defining the essential characteristics of the scientist–practitioner model (Belar & Perry, 1992). Conference participants represented a cross section of professional psychology including members of U.S. and Canadian licensing boards and professional associations, heads of psychology departments, and representatives of internship centers and included clinical, counseling, school, community, and social psychologists and health service providers in psychology. Conference delegates determined that such terms as *clinical* and *clinician* should be replaced with *professional* and *practitioner* because the scientist–practitioner model, which had been initially conceived as a training model for clinical psychology, had much broader applications. The delegates viewed the scientist–practitioner model as essential for an evolving discipline because it provides a foundation for the future development of the practitioner. A major conclusion of conference delegates was that the scientist–practitioner model must provide an integrative approach to training, which develops interlocking skills in the areas of research and practice. Another major conclusion was that the scientist–practitioner was not restricted to a specific job or a role, but that he or she might function as a researcher, practitioner, or both. The integration of scientific methods with professional practice was the essence of the model, not whether one formally engaged in research leading to publication (Belar & Perry, 1992).

Ellis (1992) emphasized the critical role that training in the scientific foundation of psychology plays in the education of applied psychologists. He noted that psychologists are uniquely defined by their training in research techniques and basic psychological science and this training differentiates them from other professionals such as counselors and social workers. His "major argument for teaching scientific fundamentals to all Ph.D. graduate students, scientists, practitioners, or scientist–practitioners is that without a strong grounding in scientific fundamentals, it is unlikely that there will ever be effective applications of our science to practical concerns" (Ellis, 1992, p. 573). Training in the science and methodology of psychology provides researchers and practitioners with a model for conceptualizing problems that is broadly applicable to the practice of professional psychology.

During the 1950s when the professional practice of psychology was in its infancy as an employment alternative to teaching or research, academic programs sometimes failed to recognize students' needs for training in applied skills. Ellis (1992) referred to a dissatisfaction among some psychologists with the Boulder training model due in part to a "perceived intractability of those who advocated the traditional scientist–practitioner model and in part because of the perceived inadequacies in professional training offered by existing programs" (p. 571). Such concerns were the impetus for the 1973 training conference held in Vail, Colorado. The Vail Conference (Korman, 1976) supported the scientist–practitioner model, but it also endorsed the professional model as an alternative approach to clinical training. Along with the recognition of a professional model of training, participants at the Vail Conference reaffirmed a commitment to comprehensive psychological science as the substantive and methodological basis of any education or training enterprise in the field of psychology.

In spite of the endorsement of a professional model as an alternative approach to clinical training, the scientist–practitioner model continues to receive strong support among directors of training at doctoral-level clinical training programs and terminal master's programs. Although other models have been considered, the basic scientist–practitioner model has been reaffirmed at all of the major national conferences on graduate education in professional psychology: Boulder Conference in 1949 (Raimy, 1950); Thayer Conference in 1954 (Cutts, 1955); Miami Conference in 1958 (Roe, Gustad, Moore, Ross, & Skodak, 1959); Greystone Conference in 1964 (Thompson & Super, 1964); Chicago Conference in 1965 (Hoch, Ross, & Winder, 1966); Vail Conference in 1973 (Korman, 1976); Utah Conference in 1987 (Bickman, 1987); and Atlanta Conference in 1987 (Meara et al., 1988).

The scientist–practitioner model continues to receive strong support among directors of training at doctoral-level clinical training programs and terminal master's degree programs. In a study conducted by O'Sullivan & Quevillon (1992), 90 directors from APA-approved doctoral training programs and 58 directors of master's programs returned questionnaires (63% overall return rate) addressing this issue. Respondents overwhelmingly endorsed the Boulder (scientist–practitioner) model as the appropriate model for training students in clinical training programs.

Models of Training in Canada

Because of the need created by the U.S. Veterans Administration (VA) for trained professional psychologists, applied psychology in the United States developed earlier than in Canada. The first Opinicon Conference on Canadian psychology, sponsored by the CPA in 1960, like the Boulder Conference, recommended the scientist–practitioner model, which placed primary emphasis on research and secondary emphasis on the teaching of clinical skills (Bernhardt, 1961).

Five years later, the 1965 Couchiching Conference on professional psychology in Canada (Webster, 1967) again addressed the issue of training models. In preparation for the conference, Sydhia (1966) conducted a survey that yielded inconsistent findings with respect to agreement with the scientist–practitioner model. The scientist–practitioner model was reaffirmed at the Couchiching Conference, but, whereas the wording of the first Opinicon Conference was heavily weighted toward emphasis on scientific training, the recommendations of the Couchiching Conference seemed more balanced (Dobson & Dobson, 1993). More recently, the teaching group of the 1984 Opinicon II Conference again recognized the scientific–practitioner model as "the generally accepted model for graduate training of professional psychologists in Canada" (Ritchie, Hogan, & Hogan, 1988, as quoted by Dobson & Dobson, 1993, p. 55).

The CPA in collaboration with eight other psychology-related organizations convened the Mississauga Conference on Professional Psychology in March 1994. Among the conclusions of the conference was the recommendation that the doctorate in psychology be the standard for practice of professional psychology (Dobson & King, 1994). The conference supported training in research as an integral part of professional psychology programs but recognized that training models may vary in emphasis on practice and research.

Professional Schools

The idea of emphasizing professional training in a doctoral program in psychology and awarding a professional degree did not originate with the

Vail Conference. The Université de Montréal, in the late 1940s, was the first university to award the doctor of psychology (PsyD) degree, followed by McGill University in the early 1950s (Ellis, 1992). Both of these Canadian programs were short lived, neither lasting for more than a few years. The Vail Conference and related events ushered in the beginning of a movement in the United States that resulted in a proliferation of professional schools well into the 1980s. Professional schools trained approximately 29% of clinical psychologists in 1979, and this figure had increased to 39% by 1989 (Kohut, Wicherski, & Pion, as cited in Ellis, 1992). The rate of growth has diminished somewhat since the mid-1980s (Ellis, 1992).

The Core Curriculum in Psychology

A core curriculum in psychology was not a major concern to training programs prior to 1960 because applied programs trained students primarily for academic and research positions (Altman, 1990). In the early 1960s, when increasing numbers of applied-program graduates sought clinical positions, the issue of a core curriculum in psychology emerged. The delineation of a core curriculum became more important following the Vail Conference in 1973, which endorsed the professional model of training as well as the scientist–practitioner model.

In 1975, the concept of a conference on Education and Credentialing in Psychology originated between representatives of the ASPPB, which was then known as the American Association of State Psychology Boards, and the Council for the National Register of Health Service Providers in Psychology (CNRHSPP; "the Register"). The two organizations, in collaboration with the APA Board of Professional Affairs and the APA Education and Training Board, formed a steering committee.

Data and information on education and training of psychologists were quickly generated. Two national meetings were held in June 1976 and 1977. A consensus developed on the definition of doctoral education in psychology as well as a proposal to form a National Commission on Education and Training. During this process, 13 national organizations, 7 APA boards and committees, and 18 APA divisions participated.

The proposal for a National Commission never came to fruition. However, the work of the steering committee and other participants was not lost. In fact, the Criteria for Designation of Doctoral Programs in Psychology were a major part of this effort. Those criteria now form the basis for qualification to be listed in "Doctoral Programs Meeting Designation Criteria," published annually as a joint project of ASPPB and the Register.

Designation criteria number 10 speaks to the necessity of the core curriculum. It states:

> The curriculum shall encompass a minimum of three academic years of full time graduate study. In addition to instruction in scientific and professional ethics and standards, research design and methodology,

> statistics and psychometrics, the core program shall require each student to demonstrate competence in each of the following substantive content areas. This typically will be met by including a minimum of three or more graduate semester hours (5 or more graduate quarter hours) in each of these 4 substantive content areas:
> a) Biological bases of behavior: Physiological psychology, comparative psychology, neuropsychology, sensation and perception, psychopharmacology.
> b) Cognitive/affective bases of behavior: Learning, thinking, motivation, emotion.
> c) Social bases of behavior: Social psychology, group processes, organization and systems theory.
> d) Individual differences: Personality theory, human development, abnormal psychology. (ASPPB & CNRHSPP, 1995, inside cover)

These areas of instruction are essentially the same as those adopted by the APA Council of Representatives in January 1979 and revised in 1980, and which are elucidated in the 1986 APA accreditation criteria (APA, 1986). The APA recognizes these content areas as the body of knowledge in the discipline of psychology and asserts that graduate training in these areas form the foundation of the professional practice of psychology. The APA *Accreditation Handbook* (APA, 1986) acknowledges the evolving nature of the body of scientific knowledge that makes up the core of the discipline; however, Matarazzo (1987) pointed out that the broad content and principles have remained the same for more than 100 years. The APA accreditation procedures were revised in 1995 (APA, 1995), and the core content areas used in defining the discipline remained essentially unchanged. The new procedures for accrediting professional programs in psychology will be discussed in a later section.

The CPA in conjunction with the Council of Provincial Associations of Psychology (CPAP) reviewed the criteria for designating programs in psychology developed by the ASPPB, CNRHSPP, and the APA and have adapted them with minor changes to the Canadian context (Dobson & Wand, 1987). Several Canadian jurisdictions have begun using the designation system. As in the United States, Canadian programs accredited by the CPA or the APA are assumed to have met the designation criteria (Dobson & Dobson, 1993).

Levels of Professional Training

From the outset, doctoral-level training has been considered the appropriate academic credential for entry into the independent practice of psychology in the United States. This was clearly stated in the recommendations of the Boulder Conference (Raimy, 1950). In 1977, the APA passed a resolution formalizing its policy that the use of the term *professional psychologist* and its variations *clinical psychologist*, *counseling psychologist*, *school psychologist*, and *industrial–organizational psychologist* should be restricted to those with a doctoral degree, that is, a PhD, PsyD, or EdD. With the exception of training in school psychology, there has been remarkably little debate over the appropriate level of training for psychologists in the United States (Bickman, 1985). The training of school psychologists will be discussed in more detail in a later section.

In Canada, the doctoral degree was endorsed as the "desirable" degree for psychologists employed in applied settings. In spite of the adoption of the doctoral level degree by the CPA as the appropriate academic credential for the practice of psychology, there has been more opposition to the requirement than in the United States. A survey of psychologists by Sydhia (1966) found the psychology community to be almost evenly split in their opinions as to whether the entry level into "professional work in psychology" should be at the doctoral level or the master's level. The lack of agreement on this issue was made clear at the Couchiching Conference (Webster, 1967) where a resolution to restrict the use of the title "psychologist" to individuals trained at the doctoral level was overwhelmingly defeated. The recommendations of the Couchiching Conference were somewhat contradictory because participants reendorsed the doctoral requirement for psychologists and at the same time endorsed the principle of certifying professional competence of individuals at the nondoctoral level.

The teaching group at the Opinicon II Conference recommended that the CPA should continue to promote the doctoral degree "as the appropriate educational requirement for statutory recognition as a psychologist" (Ritchie et al., 1988, p. 131). At the present time, support of doctoral training for entry into the profession is not universally accepted in Canada. Several jurisdictions in Canada still allow for entry into the practice of psychology at the master's level. As in the United States, the greatest controversy regarding the appropriate level of training for professional practice is in the area of school psychology.

Specialty Training in Psychology

The APA currently recognizes four professional specialties: clinical, counseling, school, and industrial–organizational psychology. An APA committee formed to recommend a mechanism for establishing new specialties proposed that any professional specialty area in psychology should require education in the scientific and professional foundations as well as training in the application of professional knowledge to related populations and particular setting (APA, 1993). The four currently recognized specialty areas have evolved over many years and have been formally recognized by APA through the publication of specialty guidelines for service providers in each area. Also, APA has developed guidelines and procedures for accrediting training programs for three of the four specialties: clinical, counseling, and school psychology (to be discussed in a later section).

Clinical Psychology

In the early years of the development of the specialty, clinical psychologists were concerned almost exclusively with psychometric testing. In 1917, the

American Association of Clinical Psychologists was formed by a splinter group of the APA but was dissolved 2 years later when the APA incorporated this group as a Section of Clinical Psychology. In 1921, the APA created the Division of Consulting Psychologists for the purpose of certifying its members for private practice, but, having certified only 24 members, the group was abolished in 1932 (Hilgard, 1987). In 1921, another clinical group, the Association of Consulting Psychologists (ACP) was formed. This was the first professional psychological association to adopt a code of ethics for the practicing psychologist, a major marker in the identification of a profession (Hilgard, 1987). In 1936, the American Association of Consulting Psychology was formed, and soon after it merged with the ACP.

Before World War II, there were few universities offering separate programs in clinical psychology, and most offered little in the way of courses with clinical content. As during the previous war, psychologists during World War II were called on to develop and administer a variety of psychometric instruments for screening and selection purposes (Harrell, 1945). As a result of the need to treat soldiers as soon as possible and to get them back into action, psychologists during World War II for the first time had the opportunity to do psychotherapy, an activity previously considered the exclusive domain of psychiatrists. By the end of the war, the roles of clinical psychologists had expanded to include treatment of individuals with emotional problems as well as intellectual and personality assessment.

Immediately after World War II, the APA was reorganized and the Division of Clinical Psychology was created. The APA bylaws were changed to include the advancement of psychology as a profession as well as a science, and at the same time, membership requirements were modified in a way to encourage the growth of professional psychology (Brems, Thevenin, & Routh, 1991). A strong demand for mental health services after the war led to an unprecedented growth in the clinical specialty. Following the war, the U.S. Veterans Administration (VA) had a major impact on the development of clinical psychology by offering numerous traineeships and internships and by becoming a major employer of clinical psychologists. The National Institute of Mental Health (NIMH) also contributed to the growth and development of clinical psychology during the 1950s and 1960s by awarding grants to graduate training programs.

The APA accredited the first graduate programs in clinical psychology in 1948. In 1949, the Boulder Conference on training in clinical psychology recommended that training in the specialty should follow the scientist–practitioner model (Raimy, 1950). In 1951, the VA introduced the requirement of a doctoral degree as a prerequisite for recognition as a psychologist. Currently, as with counseling psychology, doctoral-level training is the standard for the specialty.

As noted earlier, clinical psychologists began practicing psychotherapy out of necessity during World War II, and they continued to practice after the war. An early survey of clinical practice shows a shift toward greater emphasis on psychotherapy relative to diagnostic testing (Lubin, 1962). A more recent survey showed psychotherapy to be overwhelmingly the most frequent activity engaged in by practicing clinical psychologists (87% of the sample) compared with a relatively modest amount of time spent in the next most frequently occurring professional activity, diagnosis and assessment (16% of the sample; Norcross, Prochaska, & Gallager, 1989). In another study (Tipton, 1983), clinical psychologists rated psychotherapy as the most essential activity for defining their specialty. Although they apparently do not engage in psychological assessment as frequently as in psychotherapy, they rate psychological assessment to be almost as important as psychotherapy in defining their specialty (Tipton, 1983).

Counseling Psychology

Counseling psychology traces its roots to early work in vocational guidance. Division 17 of APA (Division of Counseling Psychology), which was established in 1945, was initially called the Division of Personnel and Guidance Psychologists. Through the course of its history, three major conferences have influenced the identity of this specialty. In 1951, the Northwestern Conference recognized the importance of clearly establishing the specialty as requiring doctoral-level training in psychology as a prerequisite for its practice (APA, 1952a, 1952b). Following this conference the name of the specialty was formally changed from the Division of Personnel and Guidance Psychologists to the Division of Counseling Psychology to avoid confusion with master's level guidance counselors. Criteria for doctoral-level training also were established at that time.

The Greystone Conference in 1964 also addressed training and professional identity among other issues (Thompson & Super, 1964). This conference affirmed the scientist–practitioner model as appropriate for counseling psychology training programs and stressed the importance of working with a normal client population (e.g., vocational counseling) in defining the identity of counseling psychologists.

The third national conference held in Atlanta, Georgia, in 1987 reaffirmed the scientist–practitioner model of training (Meara et al., 1988). The report from the Atlanta Conference reaffirms the traditional perspective of counseling psychology, which employs a developmental perspective to focus on the strengths and adaptive strategies of an individual across the individual's life span (Kagan et al., 1988). The Atlanta Conference report emphasized the importance of traditional roles and employment settings for counseling psychology but recognized that the specialty had evolved to also encompass remedial treatment in hospitals, clinics, and independent practice (Kagan et al., 1988). Two surveys of Division 17 members found that counseling psychologists viewed their professional roles as involving short-term and intermediate-term counseling and psychotherapy with relatively normal and mildly to moderately emotionally disturbed clients with a goal of problem resolution, teaching problem-solving skills and behavior change (Goldschmitt, Tipton, & Wiggins, 1981; Tipton, 1983). Fitzgerald and Osipow (1986) performed an occupational analysis of counseling psychologists and found that they spend more of their professional time performing personal-adjustment counseling and long-term psychotherapy than any other professional activities.

School Psychology

The impetus for school psychological services came from the social-reform movement in the United States in the late 1800s. Emphasis on compulsory education and a greater awareness for the necessity of increasing the quality of children's lives created a need for broadening the scope of professional services offered in public schools. Fagan (1992) divides the historical development of school psychology into two periods: the hybrid years (1890–1969) and the thoroughbred years (1970–present). During the early years, school psychologists often played an ancillary role in the educational system, functioning as "gatekeepers" for special education (Elliott & Whitt, 1986). The development and proliferation of individual ability and achievement tests in the early part of this century facilitated this role (Kehle, Clark, & Jenson, 1993). During the hybrid period, school psychologists lacked a cohesive identity; persons delivering psychological services were not always called school psychologists and rarely had doctoral degrees. Toward the latter part of the early period, there was a rapid expansion in the field of school psychology with the number of school psychologists increasing from 500 in 1940 to 5,000 in 1970 (Fagan, 1988).

When the APA reorganized and created Division 16, the Division of School Psychology, (initially called the Division of School Psychologists), school psychologists had little cohesion as a professional group nationally. The formation of Division 16, and later the Thayer Conference held in 1954 (Cutts, 1955), helped to bring school psychologists together with more group solidarity. The St. Louis Convention in 1969 was the site of the formation of the National Association of School Psychologists (NASP; Fagan, 1993). Another major event helping to solidify the specialty was the passage of Public Law 94-142 in 1975, which called for special education, including psychological services, for all handicapped children. Partially as a result of this legislation and a corresponding increased demand for services, the ranks of school psychologists swelled fourfold from 5,000 in 1970 to 20,000 in 1988 (Fagan, 1988). Although school psychologists have increased dramatically in numbers and have developed a more cohesive professional identity, they continue to be predominately nondoctoral practitioners in school settings. The APA and the NASP have differed with respect to what the appropriate entry level should be in the profession and what the title of nondoctoral practitioners should be, with APA holding that the nonschool practice of school psychology should be restricted to duly licensed practitioners with doctoral degrees. Tensions have eased somewhat between these two national associations as they have worked jointly on common projects.

The number of doctoral-level school psychologists had increased considerably by the late 1980s but still only accounted for about 20% of practicing school psychologists (Fagan, 1988). Smith (1984) and Reschly and Wilson (as cited in Fagan & Wise, 1993) found that psychological testing continues to be the major function of school psychologists. After the passage of Public Law 94-142, it was thought that school psychologists' roles would shift toward the inclusion of more consultation and intervention. However, this has apparently not been the case because a study by Goldwasser, Meyers, Christenson, and Graden (1983) found that professional roles had changed very little "with heavy emphasis on assessment rather than prevention, consultation, or intervention" (p. 163). School psychologists in general appear to be comfortable with the testing role as the survey by Reschly and Wilson (as cited in Fagan & Wise, 1993) found a strong preference for this role.

Industrial–Organizational Psychology

Industrial–organizational psychology differs in a fundamental way from the other applied areas, that is, clinical, counseling, and school psychology, in that practitioners in this area are not concerned with health-care issues. Similar to organizations in other specialty areas, however, the Society for Industrial and Organizational Psychology (SIOP) endorses the scientist–practitioner model of training (SIOP, 1985). In addition to developing competency in the generic areas of psychology (the core curriculum), SIOP recommends 19 other areas of competence to be developed in doctoral-level industrial–organizational programs. Although SIOP recommends the use of supervised field experience and on-the-job training as a means of developing competence, there is no recommendation for an internship requirement. The issue of licensure can be problematic for industrial–organizational psychologists because, although licensure laws are generic in nature, they are primarily designed to regulate health service providers. Industrial–organizational psychologists are not trained in the health care field, but their training often qualifies them to perform services the practice of which is often regulated by state and provincial boards. For example, such general practice areas as behavior modification, psychological evaluation, assessment of aptitudes, abilities and interests—all of which are within the competency domain of industrial–organizational psychologists—are often restricted by state and provincial statutes and regulations to licensed individuals (Fischer, 1991).

The dilemma is that although state and provincial statutes and regulations often restrict areas of practice that industrial and organizational psychologists are qualified to perform, requirements for licensure are designed with health care providers in mind and in many cases, industrial and organizational psychologists do not meet the standards. For example, boards of psychology typically require an internship in a health care setting, which industrial and organizational psychologists do not have. Also, the EPPP, developed by the ASPPB, includes many generic questions but also contains a large number of items designed specifically for psychologists trained to function in health care settings. It should be noted, however, that in spite of this, industrial and organizational psychologists who have taken the EPPP have generally performed well on it (Fischer, 1991).

In 1985, the SIOP took the position that most industrial–organizational psychologists should be exempt from licensure on the basis that they do not offer potentially hazardous services to the public (Fischer, 1991). At the same time, the SIOP supported the adoption of procedures by regulatory boards to eliminate unnecessary barriers to licensure for psychologists engaged in practice not in health care areas.

Similarities and Differences in the Specialty Areas

The four specialty areas in professional psychology have evolved from their unique beginnings. The APA developed *Generic Standards for Providers of Psychological Services*, which were adopted in 1974 and revised in 1977 (APA, 1974, 1977). At the time of the revision, the APA Council of Representatives charged the Committee on Standards for Providers of Psychological Services with the task of developing multiple standards in specialty areas. During a period of 3 years, the committee met with psychologists in the four recognized speciality areas and developed specialty guidelines: "Together with the *Standards*, the *Specialty Guidelines* state the official policy of the Association regarding delivery of services by . . . psychologists in each of the four specialty areas" (APA, 1981a, p. 640). Each specialty has some distinct defining characteristics, but there are a number of overlapping roles and functions, particularly among the clinical and counseling specialties (Tipton, 1983, 1985). Inspection of the *Specialty Guidelines for the Delivery of Services* (APA, 1981b), which have now been withdrawn from circulation but which still provide some historical perspective, illustrates the similarities among these specialties with respect to psychological services offered. Because of the overlap in training and services provided among psychologists trained in the clinical, counseling, and school specialties, the term *clinical* is sometimes used by legislators and policy makers in a generic sense to refer to psychologists trained to provide direct services in a health care setting, regardless of the formal title of their training program. Because psychologists trained in different specialty areas often provide similar services, both the APA and the ASPPB advocate generic licensure, a fact that is reflected in their respective model licensure bills (APA, 1987; ASPPB, 1992).

In recognition that some psychologists are trained to provide direct clinical service, some jurisdictions have legislative provisions for specialty certification or allow for a health service provider designation. This designation may cut across actual formal specialty training. The Register, an independent organization that maintains a registry of psychologists trained to provide health services in psychology, takes a generic approach and evaluates candidates on the basis of their particular course work, internship, and supervised experience rather than the specialty area of their training program. Thus, although the four professional specialties in psychology have unique roots and defining characteristics, in many instances they perform similar functions and provide similar services.

Practicum and Internship

Professional psychology programs in clinical, counseling, and school psychology require practica and applied course work in addition to core content courses and courses in research methodology. The integration of applied training and theory with basic science courses is unique to psychology. The capstone of the training experience for the applied programs in psychology is the predoctoral internship. The internship in psychology cannot substitute for the integrated doctoral program in psychology that precedes it, nor can it simply be an add-on to a doctoral program in a nonapplied area of psychology or even an applied program in some area related to psychology. The internship is the culmination of an integrated sequence of course work that facilitates the development of the psychologist's readiness for independent practice. According to the APA *Accreditation Handbook* (1986), the internship is an essential component of doctoral programs in professional psychology and should be undertaken only after relevant didactic and practicum work has been completed.

In 1987, a National Conference on Internship Training in Psychology held in Gainesville, Florida (Carrington & Stone, 1987), recommended that the core content of internship training should include the following:

1. A variety of methods of assessment and diagnosis across a variety of problems and diverse populations.
2. A variety of methods of intervention and treatment across a variety of problems and populations.
3. Experience with culturally or ethnically diverse populations.
4. Research and its applications.
5. Application of empirical skill and critical thinking to professional practice.
6. Professional, legal, and ethical issues.
7. Introduction to supervision and management of psychological services.

The process by which this core training is accomplished should include supervisory experiences, formal didactic experiences, guided readings, and opportunities for training interaction (Carrington & Stone, 1987). Although internships in different settings naturally emphasize certain areas of training by virtue of the populations they serve and the services they offer, internships are expected to provide as broad a training experience as possible.

Accreditation of Academic Programs in Professional Psychology

The APA in 1995 published new guidelines and principles for accrediting professional programs (APA, 1995). In addition to covering traditional substantive professional areas of clinical, counseling, and school psychology or a combination of these areas, in recognition of the evolving nature of the field, the new guidelines provide for the consideration of programs in emerging substantive areas of professional psychology. The essential purpose of accreditation is "to protect the interests of students, benefit the public, and improve the quality of teaching, learning, research, and professional" (p. 2).

Since the APA began accrediting professional psychology programs in the 1940s, beginning with clinical psychology, the procedures have undergone continual revision. Several changes made when the 1995 procedures were published should be noted. Although previous accreditation standards required programs to define their training models, the new procedures appear to give programs broader latitude in defining their philosophies and models of training, as well as determining their goals, objectives, and methods. Consistent with this, new procedures place greater emphasis on evaluating each program relative to its education and training model, philosophy, objectives, and methods. Although a program is given considerable latitude, its philosophy, model, goals, objectives, and methods must be consistent with those generally accepted as appropriate to the profession.

Probably the greatest difference between the 1995 guidelines and previous versions is the emphasis placed on outcomes or products of the training program. The criteria used in previous years related almost exclusively to process rather than outcome variables (APA, 1986). The new procedures identify domains judged essential for professional psychology training programs as opposed to checklists of criteria (APA, 1995). The program's task is to document how it has been or expects to be successful in these domains, employing its training model.

According to the 1995 guidelines, professional training should be broad and professional as opposed to narrow and technical and should be integrated with the broad theoretical and scientific foundations of the discipline. Although the 1995 guidelines define the discipline in terms of content areas, they seem to give programs more latitude with respect to how students are prepared in these areas. Courses or numbers of credit hours are not specified. Consistent with the "outcome approach to evaluation," programs must document how students demonstrate substantial understanding of and competence in these areas. The core areas of psychology that define the discipline and in which students are expected to show competency are fundamentally the same as in previous years. These areas are as follows:

1. The breadth of scientific psychology including: biological aspects of psychology, cognitive and affective aspects of behavior, social aspects of behavior, history and systems of psychology, psychological measurement, research methodology, and techniques of data analysis.
2. The scientific foundations of professional practice including: individual differences in behavior, human development, psychopathology, and professional standards and ethics.

3. Assessment and intervention including: theories and methods of assessment and diagnosis, effective intervention, consultation and supervision, and evaluating the efficacy of interventions.
4. Issues of cultural and individual diversity relevant to all of the above.

Students are also expected to receive appropriate practical training in the form of practica that should be an integral component of the student's education and training program. In addition to the above knowledge and skill areas, the 1995 guidelines require that students develop attitudes that foster life-long learning, scholarly inquiry, and professional problem solving.

In conclusion, the thrust of the new APA accreditation guidelines (APA, 1995) is to give the programs more leeway as well as more responsibility in defining themselves. Focus is more on outcome as opposed to the previous process-oriented evaluations. Criteria do not include checklists and seem to rely more on qualitative judgments of evaluators. Because content areas are not defined as specific hours in a given course, programs are allowed to integrate certain content areas into various places in the curriculum.

Changes that give programs more latitude in defining their training models and offer more flexibility in determining how students acquire knowledge in the content areas address a criticism occasionally leveled at the accreditation process: that accreditation usurps academic freedom. In fact, the 1995 guidelines cite encouraging institutional freedom as one of its purposes.

In 1984, the CPA created an Accreditation Panel (now the Accreditation Panel in Professional Psychology) for the purpose of accrediting academic programs in applied psychology in Canadian universities. The accreditation standards established by the CPA are essentially the same as those previously used by the APA. In fact, the CPA and the APA have an agreement whereby a joint accreditation review from both associations can occur when accreditation is sought from both associations. It is as yet unclear how the revised APA accreditation guidelines will affect this understanding between the CPA and the APA regarding accreditation.

Postdoctoral Training

Almost all state and provincial boards of psychology require that psychologists have a year of supervised postdoctoral experience before they are licensed. At the present time, this postdoctoral training does not have to be a part of a formal training program, and in many cases, the standards for this training experience are ill defined with the exception that the supervision must be by a licensed psychologist. In October 1992 at the National Conference on Postdoctoral Training in Professional Psychology, in Ann Arbor, Michigan, a set of standards for postdoctoral training in psychology was proposed (Belar et al., 1993). In essence the members of this conference conceive of the postdoctoral program as an organized education and training program designed to foster advanced competency and expertise rather than basic training in new areas.

The postdoctoral programs should offer opportunities for residents to engage in scholarship or research in the area in which the postdoctoral residency services are delivered, as well as develop competency in the professional practice of psychology. The scientist–practitioner model was affirmed with the recommendation that content areas are sequentially organized within a framework that integrates scientific and practice bases of the profession at an advanced level. The following major content areas were recommended (Belar et al., 1993):

- Skill enhancement
- Application of relevant theories, with attention to their limitations
- Legal, ethical, social, and cultural dimensions that impact on professional practice
- Application of advanced knowledge to professional practice, including issue of human diversity
- Generation of scholarship
- Management and administration issues in service delivery and research
- Consultation, supervision, and program development and evaluation
- Limitations of the practice domain and the dimensions of development necessary for its evaluation (p. 1287)

Although these proposed standards do not have any formal status with state and provincial psychology boards, members of this conference recommend their use by these regulatory bodies in evaluating postdoctoral training experiences of prospective licensees.

Training and Scope of Practice

Most graduate programs in professional psychology offer a broad range of training. However, it is impossible for students to develop competence in all practice areas. It is each psychologist's responsibility to limit the practice or supervision of practice to areas of competence in which proficiency has been gained by the psychologist through education and training. Psychologists should maintain proficiency through reading literature, continuing education, consultation, and other means. For further discussion of this issue, the reader is referred to chapter 6 "Maintaining Professional Conduct in Daily Practice."

Adding Areas of Competence

A broad knowledge and skill base gained in a professional psychology doctoral program gives the psychologist the background to develop competency in a new area. This can be accomplished through appropriate education and training, experience, and consultation with other psychologists or relevant professionals.

Retraining

It is possible to retrain in a whole new area for which one was not originally trained. The APA *Accreditation Handbook* (1986) provides procedural guidelines for such a change in emphasis. The *Accreditation Handbook* states that the internship is an essential component for persons seeking to change psychological specialties. It is noted, however, that the internship experience is only one element of training. Before this is undertaken, it should be preceded by appropriate course work and practica.

Continuing Education

Continuing education typically takes the form of brief seminars and workshops usually ranging from one half day to 2 days in duration. Continuing education courses are not vehicles for retraining but offer opportunities for psychologists who have already been trained in the basics of one area to receive additional training to keep up to date. The requirement for psychologists to enroll periodically in continuing-education courses as a condition of maintaining their licenses is a controversial issue among state and provincial licensing boards. On the one hand, continuing-education courses are viewed as excellent vehicles for keeping current in the profession. On the other hand, there is no good way of evaluating what participants learn in these experiences. Also, record keeping for workshop participation is an onerous task. At the present time, boards are split on the issue of continuing education with some boards requiring it and others not. Despite this controversy, in the United States, many state legislatures have imposed continuing education credits as a mandatory requirement for licensure renewal.

Education in Psychology Outside the United States and Canada

Models and curricula in graduate training in professional psychology outside the United States and Canada vary considerably. The length of time typically required to complete training programs in psychology varies in different countries and regions of the world. Nixon (1990) reported the following minimum time periods required to complete the educational requirements necessary to enter the professional practice of psychology in various regions of the world: Western Europe, 5 or 6 years (3 years bachelor degree with major in psychology and 3 years postgraduate work); Latin America, 5 years at the undergraduate level leading to a professional degree in psychology; Australia and New Zealand, 6 years (4 year degree in psychology at the undergraduate level followed by a 2 year master's program or advanced seminars, workshops, and supervised experience); Israel, 6 or 7 years (3 year bachelor's degree with 60 credits plus a master's degree and 2 years postmaster's supervised experience); and the United States, 7 or 8 years (4 year bachelor's degree followed by a doctoral program of 3 or 4 years). Nixon (1990) stressed the point that these were minimum time requirements, noting that the median amount of time taken to complete the doctorate in the United States was 6.9 years after completing the baccalaureate and Australian students typically took from 4 to 5 years to complete doctoral studies following completion of a bachelor's or master's degree.

Nixon (1990) identified the common threads among psychologists across international boundaries as being their "concern for individuals within their social groupings, commitment to empirical inquiry as a means toward problem solutions, and allegiance to practice grounded in high level, publicly recognized training" (p. 1259). In spite of these broad commonalities, differences in professional training exist among the various geographical regions of the world. An obvious difference is the amount of education required in different countries. Additionally, training programs in different geographic regions differ by virtue of their cultural contexts. Most training programs recognize the multicultural nature of today's world and offer courses to sensitize students to these issues. However, major cultural and philosophical differences among populations give rise to different systems of psychology and may affect the nature of psychological training programs at a deeper level (Nixon, 1990).

References

Altman, I. (1990). Centripetal and centrifugal trends in psychology. In L. Bickman & H. C. Ellis (Eds.), *Preparing psychologists for the 21st century: Proceedings of the National Conference on Graduate Education in Psychology* (pp. 39–64). Hillsdale, NJ: Erlbaum.

American Psychological Association, Committee on Training in Clinical Psychology. (1947). Recommended training in clinical psychology. *American Psychologist, 2,* 539–558.

American Psychological Association, Committee on Counselor Training, (1952a). The practicum training of counseling psychologists. *American Psychologist, 7,* 182–188.

American Psychological Association, Committee on Counselor Training, (1952b). Recommended standards for training counseling psychologists at the doctoral level. *American Psychologist, 7,* 175–181.

American Psychological Association. (1974). *Standards for providers of psychological services.* Washington, DC: Author.

American Psychological Association. (1977). *Standards for providers of psychological services* (Rev. ed.). Washington, DC: Author.

American Psychological Association, Committee on Professional Standards. (1981a). Specialty guidelines for the delivery of psychological services. *American Psychologist, 36,* 640–657.

American Psychological Association, Committee on Professional Standards. (1981b). *Specialty guidelines for the delivery of services.* Washington, D.C.: Author.

American Psychological Association, Committee on Accreditation and Accreditation Office. (1986). *Accreditation Handbook* (Rev. ed.). Washington, DC: Author.

American Psychological Association, Office of Professional Affairs. (1987). Model act for state licensure of psychologists. *American Psychologist, 42*, 696–703.

American Psychological Association, Office of Ethnic and Minority Affairs. (1993). Guidelines for providers of psychological services to ethnic, linguistic and culturally diverse populations. *American Psychologist, 48*, 45–48.

American Psychological Association, Office of Program Consultation and Accreditation (1995). *Guidelines and principles for accreditation of programs in professional psychology*. Washington, DC: Author.

Association of State and Provincial Psychology Boards. (1992). *Model act for licensure of psychologists*. Montgomery, AL: Author.

Association of State and Provincial Psychology Boards and the Council for the National Register of Health Service Providers in Psychology. (1995). Guidelines for defining doctoral degree in psychology. *Designated doctoral programs in psychology* (inside cover). Washington, DC: Author.

Belar, C. D., Bieliauskas, L. A., Klepac, R. K., Larsen, K. G., Stigall, T. T., & Zimet, C. N. (1993). National conference on postdoctoral training in professional psychology. *American Psychologist, 48*, 1284–1289.

Belar, C. D., & Perry, N. W. (1992). National conference on scientist-practitioner education and training for the professional practice of psychology. *American Psychologist, 47*, 71–75.

Bernhardt, K. S. (Ed.). (1961). *Training for research in psychology*. Toronto, ON: University of Toronto Press.

Bickman, L. B. (Ed.). (1985). *Issues and concerns: Graduate education in psychology*. Washington, DC: American Psychological Association.

Bickman, L. (1987). Graduate education in psychology. *American Psychologist, 42*, 1041–1047.

Brems, C., Thevenin, P. M., & Routh, D. K. (1991). The history of clinical psychology. In C. E. Walker, (Ed.), *Clinical psychology: Historical and research foundations* (pp. 3–35). New York: Plenum.

Carrington, C., & Stone, G. (1987). Summary of working group eleven—Implementation. In C. D. Belar, L. A. Bieliauskos, K. G. Larson, I. N. Marsh, K. Poly, & H. J. Roehlke (Eds.), *Proceedings: National Conference on Internship Training in Psychology* (pp. 38–39). Baton Rouge, LA: Land and Land Printers.

Cutts, N. E. (Ed.). (1955). *School psychologists at mid-century: A report of the Thayer Conference on the function, qualifications and training of school psychologists*. Washington, DC: American Psychological Association.

Dobson, K. S., & Dobson, D. J. G. (1993). Graduate education in professional education in Canada. In K. S. Dobson & D. J. G. Dobson (Eds.), *Professional psychology in Canada* (pp. 48–76). Toronto, ON: Hogrefe & Huber.

Dobson, K. S., & King, M. (Eds.). (1994). *The Mississauga Conference on Professional Psychology*. Ottawa, ON: Canadian Psychological Association.

Dobson, K. S., & Wand, B. (1987). *Report of the CPA-CPAP Task Force report on designation*. Old Chelsea, QC: Canadian Psychological Association.

Ellis, H. C. (1992). Graduate education in psychology. *American Psychologist, 47*, 570–576.

Elliott, S. N., & Witt, J. C. (1986). Fundamental questions and dimensions of psychological service delivery in schools. In S. N. Elliott & J. C. Witt (Eds.), *The delivery of psychological services in schools: Concepts, processes and issues* (pp. 1–26). Hillsdale, NJ: Erlbaum.

Fagan, T. K. (1988). The historical improvement of the school psychology service ratio: Implications for future employment. *School Psychology Review, 17*, 447–458.

Fagan, T. K. (1992). Compulsory schooling, child study, clinical psychology, and special education: Origins of school psychology. *American Psychologist, 47*, 236–243.

Fagan, T. K. (1993). Separate but equal: School psychology's search for organizational identity. *Journal of School Psychology, 31*, 3–90.

Fagan, T. K., & Wise, P. S. (1993). *School psychology: Past, present and future*. New York: Longman.

Fischer, D. L. (1991). Licensure and I/O psychology: A primer. *The Industrial-Organizational Psychologist, 28*, 33–48.

Fitzgerald, L. F., & Osipow, S. H. (1986). An occupational analysis of counseling psychology. How special is the specialty? *American Psychologist, 41*, 535–544.

Goldschmitt, M., Tipton, R. M., & Wiggins, R. C. (1981). Professional identity of counseling psychologists. *Journal of Counseling Psychology, 28*, 158–167.

Goldwasser, E., Meyers, J., Christenson, S., & Graden, J. (1983). The impact of PL 94-142 on the practice of school psychology: A national survey. *Psychology in the Schools, 20*, 153–165.

Harrell, J. (1945). Applications of psychology in the American army. *Psychological Bulletin, 42*, 453–460.

Hilgard, E. R. (1987). *Psychology in America: A historical survey*. New York: Harcourt Brace Jovanovich.

Hoch, E. L., Ross, A. C., & Winder, C. L. (Eds.). (1966). *Professional Preparation of Clinical Psychologists*. Washington, DC: American Psychological Association.

Kagen, N., Armsworth, M. W., Altmaier, E. M., Dowd, E. T., Hansen, J. C., Mills, D. H., Schlossberg, N., Sprinthall, N. A., Tanney, M. F., & Vasquez, M. J. T. (1988). Professional practice of counseling psychology in various settings. *The Counseling Psychologist, 16*, 347–365.

Kehle, T. J., Clarke, E., & Jenson, W. R. (1993). The development of testing as applied to school psychology. *Journal of School Psychology, 31*, 143–161.

Korman, M. (Ed.). (1976). *Levels and patterns of professional training in psychology*. Washington, DC: American Psychological Association.

Lubin, B. (1962). Survey of psychotherapy training and activities of psychologists. *Journal of Clinical Psychology, 18*, 252–256.

Matarazzo, J. D. (1987). There is only one psychology, no specialties, but many applications. *American Psychologist, 42*, 893–903.

Meara, N. M., Schmidt, L. D., Carrington, C. H., Davis, K. L., Dixon, D. N., Fretz, B. R., Myers, R. A., Ridley, C. R., & Suinn, R. M. (1988). Training and accreditation in counseling psychology. *The Counseling Psychologist, 16*, 366–384.

Nixon, M. (1990). Professional training in psychology. *American Psychologist, 45*, 1257–1262.

Norcross, J. C., Prochaska, J. O., & Gallagher, K. M. (1989). Clinical psychologists in the 1980s: Demographics, affiliations, and satisfactions. *The Clinical Psychologist, 42*, 29–39.

O'Sullivan, J. J., & Quevillon, R. P. (1992). 40 years later: Is the Boulder model still alive? *American Psychologist, 47*, 67–70.

Raimy, V. C. (1950). *Training in clinical psychology*. New York: Prentice Hall.

Ritchie, P., Hogan, T. P., & Hogan, T. V. (Eds.). (1988). *Psychology in Canada: The state of the discipline, 1984*. Old Chelsea, QC: Canadian Psychological Association.

Roe, A., Gustad, J. W., Moore, B. V., Ross, S., & Skodak, M. (Eds.). (1959). *Graduate education in psychology*. Washington, DC: American Psychological Association.

Shakow, D. (1978). Clinical psychology seen some 50 years later. *American Psychologist, 33*, 148–158.

Smith, K. D. (1984). Practicing school psychologists: Their characteristics, activities and populations served. *Professional Psychology: Research and Practice, 15*, 798–810.

Society for Industrial and Organizational Psychology. (1985). Guidelines for education and training at the doctoral level in industrial/organizational psychology. College Park, MD: Author.

Subcommittee on Graduate Internship Training to the Committee on Graduate and Professional Training of the APA and the Association for Applied Psychologists. (1945). Graduate internship training in psychology. *Journal of Consulting Psychology, 9*, 243–266.

Sydhia, D. (1966). A survey of psychologists in Canada. *Canadian Psychologist, 7*, 413–485.

Thompson, A. S., & Super, O. E. (Eds.). (1964). *The professional preparation of counseling psychologists*. New York: Teachers College Press.

Tipton, R. M. (1983). Clinical and counseling psychology: A study of roles and functions. *Professional Psychology: Research and Practice, 14*, 837–846.

Tipton, R. M. (1985). Metareflections on the roles and functions of counseling psychologists. *Professional Psychology: Research and Practice, 16,* 8–10.

Webster, E. D. (Ed.). (1967). *The Couchiching conference on professional psychology.* Montreal, QC: Eagle Publishing.

Witmer, L. (1996). Clinical psychology. *American Psychologist, 51,* 248–251.

3

Licensing, Certification, Registration, Chartering, and Credentialing

Teréz Rétfalvi
Université de Moncton

Norma P. Simon
Private Practice

This chapter is divided into two major sections. The first section addresses the issue of statutory regulation of professional psychology, that is, the purpose of the regulation and how it is carried out. It explains who is legally entitled to the title of psychologist and can thus engage in the practice of psychology. The second section addresses the issue of other forms of professional credentialing. While having no legal status, credentialing by various psychology or other professional organizations bestows on the psychologist a form of recognition based on excellence in one's contribution to the profession or on a special expertise in one's practice.

Purpose and Types of Regulation

Purpose of Regulation

In the United States, Canada, and some other countries, professional psychology is regulated by legislative act. Each state or province has a law that defines the standards for the entry level for the autonomous practice of psychology and thus limits the use of the title of psychologist to those who are judged to be appropriately qualified. Such law may be referred to as the psychologists act or psychology practice act.

The purpose of statutory regulation of the profession is to protect the public from unqualified, incompetent, or unethical practitioners. Thus, one will typically find a statement of purpose or a declaration of policy at the beginning of the statute of each jurisdiction that may read as follows:

> The practice of psychology in (name of jurisdiction) is hereby declared to affect the public health, safety, and welfare, and to be subject to

> regulation to protect the public from the practice of psychology by unqualified persons and from unprofessional conduct by persons licensed to practice psychology. (ASPPB, 1992b, p. 3)

Regulatory Statutes

There are two types of statutes: certification and licensing. Statutory certification refers to a type of statute that protects the title "psychologist" (and other derivatives of the word *psychology*, such as *psychological*) by limiting the use of the title to those who meet the criteria specified by law. This type of statute is described as a title act. As for licensing, it refers to a type of statute that not only protects the title of psychologist but in addition also defines the scope of practice. This form of legislation is described as a practice act.

On examining the two types of psychology statutes, it becomes obvious that licensing is more restrictive than certification. Certification certifies the title. Practically, it means that someone who has not been certified to use the title of psychologist may still offer psychological services as long as this person does not use the title psychologist or associate the word psychological to the services offered.

Licensing, on the other hand, goes beyond certifying the title by also defining the practice of psychology. The ASPPB (1992b), in its *Model Act for Licensure of Psychologists*, has proposed the following definition of the practice of psychology:

> Practice of psychology is defined as the observation, description, evaluation, interpretation, and/or modification of human behavior by the application of psychological principles, methods, or procedures, for the purpose of preventing or eliminating symptomatic, maladaptive, or undesired behavior and of enhancing interpersonal relationships, work and life adjustment, personal effectiveness, behavioral health and mental health. The practice of psychology includes, but is not limited to, psychological testing and the evaluation or assessment of personal characteristics, such as intelligence, personality, abilities, interests, aptitudes, and neuropsychological functioning; counselling, psychoanalysis, psychotherapy, hypnosis, biofeedback, and behavior analysis and therapy; diagnosis and treatment of mental and emotional disorder or disability, alcoholism and substance abuse, disorders of habit or conduct, as well as of the psychological aspects of physical illness, accident, injury, or disability; and psychoeducational evaluation, therapy, remediation, and consultation. Psychological services may be rendered to individuals, families, groups, organizations, institutions and the public. The practice of psychology shall be construed within the meaning of this definition without regard to whether payment is received for services rendered. (pp. 4–5)

Despite the distinction made between the two types of statutes, certification and licensing have in common the fact that the psychologist has the authority to engage in the autonomous practice of psychology. The use of the word *autonomous* reflects the idea that the psychologist has the authority to practice psychology without the statutory or regulatory requirement for supervision. Service extenders, that is, individuals who work for an autonomous practitioner, work under the license of the provider and are responsible to the provider, supervised by the provider, and must conform to regulations stipulated for extenders in the statute.

However, having drawn the distinction and commonality between certification and licensing statutes, it is also important to note that in practice the distinction between the two types of statutes is not always respected. Because of the particularities of the law within each state and province, a scope of practice definition may appear in both types of statutes. Furthermore, the terms *licensing* and *certification* are often used interchangeably, as are other terms such as *registration* and *chartering*. Consequently, for the remainder of this chapter, the term licensure and its derivatives, unless otherwise specified, will be used in the generic statutory sense, encompassing all terms referring to both forms of legislation, that is, title and practice acts.

The Regulatory Body

Establishment of the Board of Psychology

Within each jurisdiction, there is a legally constituted regulatory board that, for the purpose of this text, will be referred to as the Board of Psychology or the board. However, the name of the regulatory body varies considerably from one jurisdiction to the next.

The board of psychology is usually composed of a certain number of licensed psychologists and lay persons, or public members. The number of psychologists constituting the board, the length of their terms, as well as the procedure used for their selection may also vary. For example, in some jurisdictions, as is the case in several Canadian provinces, the psychologists are elected by their peers. In other jurisdictions, psychologist members are appointed by a designated authority, such as the governor of a state or the lieutenant governor in council of a province. Lay members are usually appointed to the board by the appointing authority. The psychologist members of the board usually must reflect a diversity of practice specialities.

Functions of the Board

Promulgating rules and regulations. The board has the authority to adopt rules and regulations to carry out the provisions of the psychologists act or the psychology practice act. These rules and regulations provide details for the terms set forth in statute as well as standards of professional conduct for licensed psychologists in their practice of psychology.

When adopting rules and regulations, the board assesses these in relation to their relevance for the protection of the public.

Evaluating the qualifications of the candidate. When a candidate applies for licensure, the board examines the qualifications of the candidate's credentials including his or her education and supervised professional experience.

Education. In almost all American states and Canadian provinces, the entry level to the profession is a doctoral degree from a program of graduate study in professional psychology awarded by an institution of higher education recognized by the board. However, there are a few states and provinces that accept a master's level degree as the entry level to the profession. Applicants trained in an institution outside the United States or Canada must demonstrate to the satisfaction of the board that their training is substantially similar to the one required by the board.

Practice experience. The most common standard for acceptable experience is 2 years of supervised professional experience, 1 year of which is usually predoctoral (internship) and 1 year postdoctoral. Both years of supervised experience must be acceptable to the board and must comply with the specific guidelines set out in the board's rules and regulations.

Foreign credentials. Because of the complexity of the issue, the evaluation of foreign credentials may pose specific difficulties to the board. Some disciplines that have been around much longer than psychology have developed some semblance of international accreditation for training programs. Committees may be appointed by an international society to evaluate training programs at institutions in different countries. Although international societies, such as the International Union of Psychological Sciences and the International Association of Applied Psychology, exist in the field of psychology, formulating international standards of training would be difficult because of the major differences that now exist among the different training programs. In addition to the differences in the amount of training typically required by training programs in different regions of the world, there are some concerns that requirements for programs to adhere to certain training models could obscure the reality that human behavior may be described in many different ways, using different descriptors and based on different assumptions about human nature and human needs (Nixon, 1990). These cultural, political, and philosophical differences would need to be addressed in any effort toward establishing international standards of training.

In spite of the fact that psychology is in its infancy with respect to developing and agreeing on standards of training that would cut across national boundaries, the world is becoming more multicultural and boards of psychology are increasingly faced with the challenge of evaluating educational credentials of applicants for licensure who have been educated in different countries. Several issues that are particularly salient in the evaluation of applicants who are foreign graduates have been addressed by the ASPPB (Edwards, Reaves, Schauble, & Weeks, 1989). The issue of citizenship of the applicant is controversial. While it might be desirable for a psychologist practicing successfully in a foreign country to know if his or her credentials would be acceptable to the board before emigrating to the United States or Canada, certain statutes or regulations may preclude some boards from considering documents of applicants from some foreign countries. Also, communication about documents presented, often in a foreign language, is extremely difficult at such a distance. Edwards et al. (1989) do not recommend formal review of application of foreign applicants who apply from outside the country but do not discourage informal correspondence.

Evaluation of foreign credentials usually takes longer and often causes delays. Academic transcripts and additional correspondence may need to be translated into the working language of the board. To ensure accuracy and objectivity of the translation, boards usually insist that the translation be provided by professional translators. The ASPPB as well as the Comparative Education Service (affiliated with the University of Toronto, Ontario) offer services that facilitate the evaluation of an equivalency in level between foreign academic credentials and academic degrees conferred by a recognized university within Canada or the United States.

Application for licensure in another state or province. Whereas law might prohibit the acceptance of applications of citizens of foreign countries, accepting applications from applicants of a different state in the United States or a different province in Canada is a different issue. There is legal precedent that prevents jurisdictions in the United States from imposing total bans on nonresident applications from within the United States. Although there is no known case law concerning this issue in Canada, Canadian boards are not known to discriminate on the basis of province or territory in which the person lives at the time of the application (Edwards et al., 1989).

Examining the candidate's general knowledge in psychology. Once the academic qualifications and practice experience have been reviewed and are deemed acceptable, the board has the authority to examine the candidate's general knowledge in psychology as well as judgment on ethical issues. The board has the authority to require a candidate to take and pass such examinations that the board may set or approve.

Examination for professional practice in psychology. The ASPPB has developed a written examination called the Examination for Professional Practice in Psychology (EPPP). The EPPP has become the standard examination for entry into the profession in most of the jurisdictions in Canada and the United States and is considered to measure the knowledge base of psychology. A passing mark reflects the basic level of general knowledge in psychology that the candidate should have to become eligible for licensure. Each jurisdiction sets its passing point. However, delegates at the 1992 Annual Meeting of the ASPPB have recommended that 70% (140) be the passing point on the EPPP, thus setting a national as well as an international standard. A French version of the EPPP is also available.

Oral examination. In addition to the EPPP, the board may require that the candidate pass an oral examination. The purpose of an oral examination is to assess the candidate's knowledge and competence in areas such as jurisdictional and ethical issues, jurisprudence, as well as specialty area of practice.

Examination of the foreign applicant. Foreign applicants are typically required to fill out the application and take all written and oral examinations in the working language of the board. Because the EPPP is considered a power test, the ASPPB recommends allowing foreign applicants additional time on this examination. While it may seem politically incorrect not to allow applicants to take the examinations in their native languages, the fact is that competence in the language of the jurisdiction where one desires to practice may be as important as his or her professional qualifications (Nixon, 1990). For this reason, the requirement of the board for all applicants to take the EPPP in the most commonly used language of the jurisdiction does not render it invalid (Edwards et al., 1989).

Granting licenses. Once the board is satisfied that the candidate has the minimum level of education, training, experience, and knowledge, the board will grant a license to the candidate. The candidate is then entitled to use the title of psychologist and may engage in the practice of psychology. The licensee, in his or her practice, must practice according to the code of conduct and code of ethics adopted by the board through its rules and regulations and limit practice to demonstrated areas of competence.

The board of a jurisdiction may grant a license to any qualified psychologist licensed in another jurisdiction, pursuant to an agreement of reciprocity or endorsement entered into by the board of a given jurisdiction with the board or boards of other jurisdictions.

However, the mobility issue involving licensed psychologists moving from one jurisdiction to another has been frustrating both for licensing boards and for licensees. In 1989, the ASPPB formed a Mobility Committee, which was charged with investigating the feasibility of facilitating reciprocity among jurisdictions. Because a reciprocity agreement would likely take years to develop and implement, the committee recommended that the ASPPB as an organization not pursue reciprocity as an organization at that time. At that midwinter meeting, representatives from the jurisdictions of Texas, New Mexico, and Oklahoma began to discuss the possibility of forming a regional reciprocity agreement.

At the 1991 ASPPB Annual Meeting, the Southwest Regional Reciprocity Agreement was presented to the delegates as a formal agreement with the Texas, New Mexico, and Oklahoma jurisdictions participating

(ASPPB, 1991). Other jurisdictions became interested in joining this agreement, and at the 1994 Midwinter ASPPB Meeting, there were a total of 10 jurisdictions who had signed the agreement. The name was changed to the North American Reciprocity Agreement and included the jurisdictions of Colorado, Iowa, Kentucky, Louisiana, Manitoba, Missouri, New Mexico, Nevada, Oklahoma, and Wisconsin.

One factor that appeared to facilitate the ability to form the reciprocity agreement seemed to be the decision by the delegates to the 1992 ASPPB Annual Meeting to adopt a 70% pass point or a score of 140 on the national EPPP (ASPPB, 1992a). This became one of the criteria required in the North American Reciprocity Agreement.

Membership in the North American Reciprocity Agreement required the following as minimum standards for initial licensure in each jurisdiction: (a) a doctoral degree in psychology; (b) 2 years of supervised experience, one of which must have been completed postdoctorally; (c) the minimum passing score on the EPPP of 70%; (d) in addition to the EPPP, an additional examination to determine practice competence; and (e) an oral procedure that includes an individual face-to-face meeting with the candidate (points a and b may be accomplished together). Under the terms of the agreement, a psychologist licensed and practicing for 5 consecutive years in a member jurisdiction without any adverse action against the license is eligible for licensure by reciprocity.

In 1994, ASPPB reconstituted the Mobility Committee to work toward facilitating reciprocity among member jurisdictions. The committee developed a standard Reciprocity Agreement application and began work reviewing jurisdictions' applications. In 1995, the ASPPB Reciprocity Agreement included four jurisdictions (ASPPB, 1995). The committee's name was changed to the Reciprocity Committee to reflect its focus on encouraging and reviewing applications.

Denying licenses. The board has the power to deny a candidate a license. Such denial is essentially for the protection of the public and is usually based on the fact that the candidate does not meet all the standards required for licensure as set forth by the act and the rules and regulations of the license granting jurisdiction. Other reasons may include failure to demonstrate good moral character and mental competence.

Renewing licenses. In addition to the functions of the board that pertain to the process of granting licenses, the board maintains a list of all psychologists duly licensed and may publish the names of those whose licenses have been suspended or revoked. This information is available to the public. Practicing without a license is illegal. To maintain the right to practice, the licensed psychologist must pay the annual renewal fee established by the board. Failure to do so within a time prescribed by the board will cause the license to lapse.

The psychology licensee has a right to present himself or herself as a licensed psychologist to the public as well as to engage in the practice of psychology as long as he or she has a license.

Controlling continuing-education credits. The move to require continuing-education (CE) credits for renewal of license has been expanding during the past decade. The board has the power to promulgate rules and regulations for regulating acceptable CE credits.

This movement toward more psychology boards requiring CE is an attempt to control some of the learning activities of the holder of a license to practice psychology. The boards vary in the amount of credits required. Boards in some states, such as California and New York, require that certain courses be completed, such as Child Abuse Reporting courses. Other boards require a number of credits in approved CE. This can be from any APA- or CPA-approved CE workshop to a broader state- or provincial-approved course. The ASPPB has considered recommending that if boards require specific courses for CE, that a course in ethics and jurisprudence be included. Even though having CE requirements cannot ensure that a practitioner is able to apply what is learned or even that the practitioner will attend and listen at the workshop he or she signed up to take, it can create the opportunity for the practitioner to gain up-to-date information and techniques to keep one's qualifications current.

Overseeing conduct and competence. The board has the power and the duty under legislation to investigate allegations of incompetence or misconduct of its licensed members and, following a hearing, to place restrictions on the licensee's professional activities.

Fitness to practice. The board has the power and the duty to investigate a complaint that a licensed psychologist may be physically or mentally incapacitated to the extent that he or she is not capable of practicing psychology with reasonable skill and safety to clients. If the psychologist is found to be incompetent and impaired, the board may revoke, suspend, or impose conditions limiting the practice as the board considers appropriate.

Conduct. All licensed psychologists, as well as anyone under their supervision, are required to conduct their professional activities in conformity with the ethical and professional standards promulgated by the board in its rules and regulations (see chap. 4 on codes of professional conduct and ethics).

The board, after due investigation and hearing, has the power and duty to revoke, deny, or suspend a license; to place any licensed psychologist on probation for a specified time; or to require remediation if warranted. Other possible disciplinary actions include reprimands, administrative fines, and the costs of disciplinary actions.

Any psychologist found incompetent or guilty of misconduct and whose license has been denied, limited, suspended, or revoked has the right to appeal the action of the board pursuant to the provisions of the jurisdiction's Administrative Procedures Act.

Other Professional Credentials

Forms of Recognition for Special Qualifications

In addition to licensure, there are a number of other qualifications that recognize a provider's expertise that might be defined in as broad an arena as health service provider or as narrow an arena as forensic psychology. The increased reliance on credentialing has grown with the need not only to explain training and services to various other groups from the public to the insurance industry but also to provide levels of expertise that would be recognized within and without the profession of psychology. In addition, various levels of credentialing are honored by universities, hospitals, and community mental health agencies for advancement purposes. For the future, it is conceivable that third-party payers may recognize only those providers who hold credentials in a special expertise.

The major forms of recognition are: (a) Those that require special qualifications such as the Register, the Canadian Register of Health Service Providers in Psychology (the Canadian Register), and the American Board of Professional Psychology (ABPP); and (b) those that provide recognition by ones peers such as Fellow status of the APA or that of the CPA, or Distinguished Practitioner of the National Academies of Practice (NAP), or other organizations that offer special recognition. An explanation of each follows.

Recognitions that require special qualifications. *The Register.* In 1974 the APA Board of Directors, believing that a national health plan would be in the offing, requested that the ABPP develop a separate organization that would have as its responsibility the development of criteria for identifying health service provider psychologists and publishing a register of such providers. The APA Board of Directors believed this publication would be an aid to psychologists who had the training and experience to qualify for inclusion in the listing of the Register. It was also important that other bodies be able to differentiate which licensed psychologists were health service providers. The Register was the result. The Register would identify psychologists to insurers, government, health services, other organizations, and the public who were not only licensed to practice but also had training and experience in the health services area. This publication became known as *The National Register of Health Service Providers in Psychology*, and was first published in 1975.

The Register has a Board of Directors whose members are chosen by the board from nominations solicited by the board of the Register from the membership of the Register. The board is composed of eight psychologists and three public members. The term of office is 4 years. This is renewable once.

To be listed in the Register, the individual must meet specific criteria (see Appendix A). The definition of a health service provider as determined by the Register (CNRHSPP, 1993) is:

> A Health Service Provider in Psychology is defined as a psychologist, certified/licensed at the independent practice level[1] in his/her jurisdiction, who is duly trained and experienced in the delivery of direct, preventive, assessment and therapeutic intervention services to individuals whose growth, adjustment, or functioning is actually impaired or is demonstrably at high risk of impairment. (p. 1)

The Register is also involved in identifying the work of the health service provider. At the time this is being written, the Register is collecting information from all registrants on many areas of practice. This information will provide the psychological community with the most up-to-date data on the functioning of health service providers on a day-to-day basis in the 1990s. The ASPPB will be doing a broader study—a practice analysis that will identify the practice of psychology both of health service providers and of providers in other specialty areas.

The Canadian Register. The Canadian Register, established in 1985, is a more recent version of the same effort to distinguish health service providers in psychology from generic psychologists. The Canadian Register lists psychologists who, in accordance with their education and training, provide a variety of diagnostic, therapeutic, and consultative health services. The governance structure of the Canadian Register is somewhat different from its American counterpart. The Canadian Register is managed by a Board of Directors consisting of one representative from each of the recognized provincial or territorial psychological organizations, societal or regulatory, and one representative from CPA. The representatives are named by their respective organizations. Presently, the Canadian Register has a board composed of 20 directors (Canadian Register, 1995). Eligibility criteria for listing in the Canadian Register and the definitions of terms are presented in Appendix B.

American Board of Professional Psychology (ABPP). The ABPP provides a different kind of credential. The ABPP Diplomate is the highest form of credential that a psychologist can earn. Unlike the Register, to qualify for the diplomate, the individual psychologist must have the paper credentials, write a work sample, and take a rigorous examination that is devised by the board of the specialty area in which the individual wishes a diplomate. For the Clinical, Counseling, and School Diplomates, the individual must be a graduate of a program in the discipline for which the individual is examined. For example, the individual with training in clinical psychology cannot take the examination in school psychology even if the individual has worked for many years in the schools. The other specialty areas, for example, forensic, neuropsychology, and psychoanalysis (a

[1] "Currently licensed, certified or registered" as a psychologist "at the independent practice level" means currently, actively licensed, certified, or registered for psychology practice generally, with no material limitations, conditions or restrictions (e.g., supervision or other conditions or limitations on practice) required by a state, provincial, or territorial board or government body.

newly formed specialty for the ABPP), require the individual to meet various criteria; however, because doctorates are not offered in these specialty areas, the candidate may hold a doctorate in clinical, counseling, or school psychology. In some instances, such as psychoanalysis, postdoctoral training is required. A number of people take the ABPP's examinations in more than one specialty. This means taking the examination and passing the work sample in each specialty area. The ABPP Diplomate has become recognized as a very important credential for a psychologist to have. The VA even decided to pay a salary differential to those holding the diplomate (though this has not happened to date). The ABPP has a national board that governs all of the ABPP Diplomates, and each specialty area has its own governing body that sets the criteria for the diplomate in that area. Each specialty area also has an academy of all psychologists holding the diplomate in that specialty. A great effort has been made in the past 2 years to standardize ABPP examinations so as to ensure that the credential has the same meaning wherever the examination is given.

College of Professional Psychology. In February 1994, the APA Council of Representatives authorized the establishment of the College of Professional Psychology (the College). The College is charged with developing criteria for credentialing specific proficiencies in psychology. The first such credential is in the treatment of alcohol and other psychoactive substance–abuse disorders. Requirements for certification include state or provincial psychology licensure at the independent practice level, evidence of provision of health services in psychology, documentation of experience in the treatment area, and passing of an examination.

Recognitions by one's peers. *Fellow of the APA, the CPA, and other organizations.* The second type of credential, the recognition by one's peers, takes a number of forms. Fellow status in the APA, the CPA, or other similar associations, such as the American Psychological Society (APS), is also a credential for which an individual must be chosen. In the United States, individuals can be nominated for Fellow through the Divisions of the APA. The criteria for Fellow (see Appendix C) are for all of the APA, but each division can interpret the standards as it sees fit. The Division Fellows committee decides on those individuals it wishes to propose for Fellow to the APA membership committee. The membership committee then makes its decisions, and the final list is sent to the APA Council for approval.

In Canada, the procedure is somewhat similar. Individuals can be nominated through national and provincial organizations or the CPA sections. The Committee of Fellows of CPA makes its decisions and submits the list to the CPA board. To be considered for a Fellow, the member must have made a distinguished contribution to the advancement of the science or profession of psychology or have given exceptional service to their national or provincial associations.

This honor, for it is more that than a credential, is understood within the profession to acknowledge individuals who have earned recognition in their area of specialty or in psychology in general. This is different from the credentials for special qualifications because, even though the Fellow undoubtedly has many qualifications, the acceptance for fellow is based on a different set of criteria. Being a member of a collegial professional association or a Fellow is not an appropriate credential for licensing purposes.

National Academies of Practice. A fairly new credential based on recognition by a peer group is the National Academies of Practice (NAP). This organization, founded by a psychologist and former president of the APA, Nicholas Cummings, is modeled on the American Academy of Science. Only 100 members in each of the nine professions recognized by the federal government (i.e., dentistry, medicine, nursing, optometry, osteopathic medicine, podiatric medicine, psychology, social work, and veterinary medicine) can be members of the Academy. The NAP was created to be the advisor to Congress in matters of health care delivery. Senator Daniel K. Inouye, who has led the movement to make the NAP the advisor to Congress, called our Distinguished Practitioners "the crème de la crème of health care practice in the United States" (N. Cummings, personal communication, June 1991).

The NAP has a board of directors made up of the chairs of each Academy. In addition, each Academy of the NAP has an executive body. A number of committees are formed to cover areas that cross over disciplines. A major conference is held biannually stressing crucial health care issues. None of the Academies has as yet a full 100 members. To be chosen for the Academy of psychology, an individual must be nominated and backed by the nominator and three other members of the Academy. The credentials of the nominee are reviewed by a committee of the Psychology Academy and passed by the board of the NAP. Recognition by NAP is an honor and a credential but not one that is recognized for licensing purposes.

In the future, there will undoubtedly be more credentialing bodies that will fill a need to recognize excellence in psychology or to identify psychologists with special expertise.

References

Association of State and Provincial Psychology Boards. (1991). *Minutes of the Annual Meeting of Delegates, October 4–6, 1991.* Montgomery, AL: Author.

Association of State and Provincial Psychology Boards. (1992a). *Minutes of the Annual Meeting of Delegates, October 1–4, 1992.* Montgomery, AL: Author.

Association of State and Provincial Psychology Boards. (1992b). *Model act for licensure of psychologists.* Montgomery, AL: Author.

Association of State and Provincial Psychology Boards. (1995). *Minutes of the Annual Meeting of Delegates, October 11–15, 1995.* Montgomery, AL: Author.

The Canadian Register of Health Service Providers in Psychology (1995). *Canadian register of health service providers in psychology/Répertoire canadien des psychologues offrant des services de santé.* Ottawa, ON: Author.

Council for the National Register of Health Service Providers in Psychology (1993). *The national register of health service providers in psychology.* Washington, DC: Author.

Edwards, H., Reaves, R., Schauble, P., & Weeks, H. (1989). *Evaluation for licensure: Applicants who submit unusual credentials or who are foreign graduates*. Montgomery, AL: American Association of State Psychology Boards.

Nixon, M. (1990). Professional training in psychology. *American Psychologist, 45*, 1257–1262.

4

A Comparison of Codes of Professional Conduct and Ethics

Carole Sinclair
Dellcrest Children's Centre

The behavior and regulation of psychologists are guided by codes of professional conduct and ethics developed at the national levels in addition to requirements made by local jurisdictions. In some jurisdictions, one or more of these national codes have been formally adopted or integrated into statutes by the local regulatory or collegial bodies; in other jurisdictions, these codes, although not formally adopted, are used to help define the standard of practice of the profession of psychology. The codes are often used additionally to guide the development of local written standards or regulations and to help train candidates for membership in the profession of psychology.

There are three major national codes governing the practice of psychology within Canada and the United States:

1. *ASPPB Code of Conduct*. (ASPPB, 1991); see Appendix D.
2. Ethical Principles of Psychologists and Code of Conduct. (APA, 1992); see Appendix E.
3. *Canadian Code of Ethics for Psychologists*. (CPA, 1991); see Appendix F.

The ASPPB code is the newest of the three codes, having been first adopted in 1991. The need for the ASPPB code became apparent when the regulatory boards found the codes of ethics difficult to enforce because they were heavily aspirational in nature rather than specifically defining appropriate conduct. The APA code is the latest of many revisions, with the first version of the code having been adopted in 1952. The CPA code is the second version of a code that was first adopted in 1986.

The purpose of this chapter is to outline, compare, and contrast the underlying purposes; philosophy; ethical principles; and specific requirements, rules, and standards of the three national codes. How do they differ? Do the differences present a problem for the profession in defining its standards of practice? Do they give consistent or conflicting messages to psychologists? What can be learned from such a comparison?

A First-Glance Comparison

An obvious difference in the three codes is their length. The CPA code is the longest (about 10,000 words), the APA code moderately shorter (about 8,000 words), and the ASPPB code much shorter (about 2,500 words).

Of more significance is the obvious difference in the structure of the three codes. Each code contains one or more introductions, variously called "Foreword," "Introduction," or "Preamble." These introductions provide information about the scope, purposes, and intended uses of the particular code, reveal some of the underlying philosophy, and in two codes, provide definitions of some of the terms used. However, organization of the remaining contents of the codes varies strikingly. The ASPPB code launches right into its specific requirements (Rules of Conduct), with no discussion of the ethical principles that the developers of the code espouse or that the contents of the Rules of Conduct reflect. The 48 rules are grouped under 10 headings that are a mixture of ethical concepts (e.g., Competence, Client Welfare, and Violations of Law) and professional activities (e.g., Fees and Statements, and Assessment Procedures). In contrast, the APA code devotes a special section, General Principles, to listing and explaining the six ethical principles that underlie and are reflected in the 108 Ethical Standards that follow. These standards are organized under eight different headings, only one of which is an ethical concept (Privacy and Confidentiality). Of the other seven headings, one is called General Standards and contains those standards that "are potentially applicable to the professional and scientific activities of all psychologists" (APA, 1992, General Standards); one is called Resolving Ethical Issues; the other five relate to particular activities of psychologists (e.g., Therapy, and Advertising and Other Public Statements).

In contrast to both the ASPPB and the APA codes, the CPA code organizes all of its 152 Ethical Standards around four ethical principles. Each of these four sections begins with an explanation (Values Statement) of the particular ethical principle and then is followed by those Ethical Standards that "illustrate the application of the specific principle and values to the activities of psychologists" (CPA, 1991, Preamble: Structure and Derivation of Code). The CPA code is the only code to provide an Index in addition to a Table of Contents. This Index allows the reader to find standards that specifically mention a particular topic (e.g., students, and fees and financial arrangements).

Comparison of Purposes and Philosophy

The one or more introductions to each of the codes provide information about each code's scope, purposes, and intended uses and allow some comparisons of their underlying philosophy. Table 1 contains excerpts from each of the codes relating to these issues.

Table 1. Statements About General Scope, Purposes, and Uses

ASPPB (1991)	APA (1992)	CPA (1991)
The psychologist shall be governed by this Code of Conduct whenever providing psychological services in any context. (Introduction, B. *Scope*.)	This Ethics Code provides a common set of values upon which psychologists build their professional and scientific work. (Preamble, para. 1.)	This Code articulates ethical principles, values, and standards to guide all members of the Canadian Psychological Association, whether scientists, practitioners, or scientist–practitioners. (Preamble, *Introduction*.)
The rules within this Code of Conduct constitute the standards against which the required professional conduct of a psychologist is measured. (Introduction, A. *Purpose*.)	This Code is intended to provide both the general principles and the decision rules to cover most situations encountered by psychologists. (Introduction, para. 4)	This Code is intended to guide psychologists in their everyday conduct, thinking and planning, and in the resolution of ethical dilemmas. (Preamble. *Uses of the Code*.)
They assure the creation/existence/retention of appropriate information with which the regulatory body can judge compliance with or deviation from its requirements. (Foreword, no. 5)	The Ethics Code is intended to provide standards of professional conduct that can be applied by the APA and by other bodies that choose to adopt them. (Introduction, para. 4.)	A third use of the Code is to assist in the adjudication of complaints against psychologists . . . judge whether unacceptable behaviour has occurred, and determine what corrective action should be taken. (Preamble, *Uses of the Code*.)
	Whether or not a psychologist has violated the Ethics Code does not by itself determine whether he or she is liable in a court action, whether a contract is enforceable, or whether other consequences occur. These results are based on legal rather than ethical rules. However, compliance with or violation of the Ethics Code may be admissible as evidenced in some legal proceedings, depending on the circumstances. (Introduction, para. 4.)	The Code is also intended to serve as an umbrella document for the development of codes of conduct or other more specific codes. (Preamble. *Uses of the Code*.)

Scope and Purpose

Although the concept of a contract with society (to protect and act in the best interests of society) is implied in both the ASPPB and the APA codes, only the CPA code states explicitly that such a contract is the foundation of any ethics code or code of conduct.

> Every discipline that has relatively autonomous control over its entry requirements, training, development of knowledge, standards, methods, and practices does so only within the context of a contract with the society in which it functions. This social contract is based on attitudes of mutual respect and trust, with society granting support for the autonomy of a discipline in exchange for a commitment by the discipline to do everything it can to assure that its members act ethically in conducting the affairs of the discipline within society; in particular, a commitment to try to assure that each member will place the welfare of the society and individual members of that society above the welfare of the discipline and its own members. (CPA, 1991, Preamble)

The ASPPB code is clearly presented as governing the behavior of psychologists and providing the standard against which the behavior of a psychologist will be measured, particularly in any situation in which a regulatory body must judge compliance with or deviation from its requirements. There is no mention of the rules being intended to guide the behavior of psychologists, although they could be used this way. On the other hand, both the APA and CPA codes use phrases such as "guide," "values," and "decision rules" that are to be used in "everyday thinking" and in building the "professional and scientific work" of psychologists. However, both the APA and the CPA codes, like the ASPPB code, present themselves as useful for the adjudication of complaints. The APA document is the only one that contains a warning that the contents of the code could be used in legal matters outside the jurisdiction of the profession (presumably, malpractice suits); the CPA code is the only one that presents itself as "an umbrella document" that can serve as a framework for the development of codes of conduct or other specific standards documents (e.g., guidelines for specific areas of practice).

Aspirational Goals Versus Minimum Requirements

The introduction to the ASPPB code states that the Rules of Conduct "are nonoptional and always pertain. They are coercive, not advisory or aspirational. They are nontrivial, to the extent that any violation is basis for formal disciplinary action, including loss of licensure" (ASPPB, 1991, Foreword, no. 7).

On the other hand, the introduction to the APA (1992) code states that "The Preamble and General Principles are aspirational goals to guide psychologists toward the highest ideals of psychology. The Ethical Standards set forth enforceable rules for conduct as psychologists." In this way, the

APA code is presented as being both aspirational and mandatory. The aspirational requirements are contained in the section called General Principles. The enforceable, coercive requirements are contained in the section called Ethical Standards. This is a departure from previous versions of the APA code in which each standard appeared as a subsection of 1 of 10 Principles whose labels were a mixture of ethical concepts (e.g., Principle 5: Confidentiality) and areas of practice (e.g., Principle 8: Utilization of Assessment Techniques; APA, 1981). In the 1992 version of its code, APA has ensured that the titles given to its General Principles are ethical in nature; however, the content under each of the General Principles has been classified as "aspirational" rather than "enforceable." It is interesting to note that the 1992 APA code is called "Ethical Principles of Psychologists and Code of Conduct," instead of the traditional "Ethical Standards of Psychologists" (used until 1979) or "Ethical Principles of Psychologists" (used in the 1981 code and its 1989 revision). The new title demonstrates the change in thinking reflected in the 1992 APA code.

The CPA code differs from both the ASPPB code and the APA code, insofar as "the standards range from minimal behavioural expectations . . . to more idealized, but achievable, attitudinal and behavioural expectations" (CPA, 1991, Preamble: Structure and Derivation of Code); that is, the standards themselves are seen to be differentially coercive or enforceable. The CPA code is presented as an overall ethical framework for psychologists that, in addition to other uses, could be used "for the identification of behaviours which would be considered enforceable in a certain jurisdiction, the violation of which would constitute misconduct" (CPA, 1991, Preamble: Uses of the Code). Therefore, it is evident that the CPA code makes no claim to be a code of conduct. Rather, it is presented as an ethics code whose standards may overlap with a code of conduct but that has a broader and more inclusive purpose than a code of conduct.

Behaviors Not Specifically Covered by the Codes: What to Do About Them

Although the ASPPB code states that each Rule of Conduct is "nontrivial, to the extent that a violation is basis for formal disciplinary action" (ASPPB, 1991, Foreword, no. 7), the code seems to contain somewhat contradictory statements about what a psychologist or regulatory body should do if a particular behavior does not seem to be covered by one of its rules. In the opinion of the committee that developed the ASPPB code, effective rules of conduct are, among other things, "sufficient unto themselves, without dependence for interpretation or additional explanatory materials" (ASPPB, 1991, Foreword, no. 6). However, the ASPPB code also states that "Ethics codes and standards for providers promulgated by the American Psychological Association, the Canadian Psychological Association, and other relevant professional groups shall be used as an aid in resolving ambiguities that may arise in the interpretation of this Code of Conduct" (ASPPB, 1991, Introduction, section E).

In contrast, both the APA and the CPA codes are presented as being nonexhaustive. The APA code states: "The Ethical Standards are not exhaustive. The fact that a given conduct is not specifically addressed by the Ethics Code does not mean that it is necessarily either ethical or unethical" (APA, 1992, Introduction). The CPA code is presented as an umbrella document that can be used "for the development of codes of conduct or other more specific codes" (CPA, 1991, Preamble: Uses of the Code), thereby also presenting itself as nonexhaustive. In addition, both the APA and the CPA codes refer to the importance of proactive ethics, which includes engaging in an ethical decision-making process when the most ethical course of action is not clear. Both codes assume that there will be situations that present ethical questions not covered by the code and view engaging in an ethical decision-making process and obtaining consultation as ethical responses to such questions. In addition, the CPA code provides a seven-step ethical decision-making model and orders its Ethical Principles according to the priority each principle generally should be given in resolving ethical dilemmas. For examples of how this seven-step model can be applied see Appendix K.

In addition to the above, both the APA and the CPA codes acknowledge that, when the codes or other guidelines or laws and regulations are not sufficient for resolving ethical dilemmas, personal conscience can play a role in ethical decision making; as follows:

> If neither law nor the ethics code resolves an issue, psychologists should consider . . . the dictates of their own conscience. (APA, 1992, Introduction)
>
> In some cases, resolution may be a matter of personal conscience. However, decisions of personal conscience are also expected to be the result of a decision-making process which is based on a reasonably coherent set of ethical principles and which can bear public scrutiny. If the psychologist can demonstrate that every reasonable effort was made to apply the ethical principles of this Code and resolution has had to depend on the personal conscience of the psychologist, such a psychologist would be deemed to have followed this Code. (CPA, 1991, Preamble)

The ASPPB code makes no mention of a role for personal conscience.

Relationship of the Codes to Law

The codes also differ with respect to whether the law or the particular code is seen to provide the higher or more binding standard. The ASPPB code specifies that the law provides the more binding standard: "This Code shall not supersede state, federal or provincial statutes" (ASPPB, 1991, Introduction, section B). On the other hand, both the APA and the CPA codes seem to allow for the possibility of some civil disobedience:

> If the Ethics Code establishes a higher standard of conduct than is required by law, psychologists must meet the higher ethical standard.

> . . . If psychologists' ethical responsibilities conflict with law, psychologists make known their commitment to the Ethics Code and take steps to resolve the conflict in a responsible manner. (APA, 1992, Introduction)
>
> Although it is necessary and important to consider responsibility to society in every ethical decision, adherence to this principle must be subject to and guided by Respect for the Dignity of Persons, Responsible Caring, and Integrity in Relationships. (CPA, 1991, Preamble)

Paralleling APA's inclusion of the concept that ethics provides a higher standard than law, the CPA code states the following as one of its standards:

> Abide by the laws of society in which they [psychologists] work. If those laws seriously conflict with the ethical principles contained herein, psychologists would do whatever they could to uphold the ethical principles. If upholding the ethical principles could result in serious personal consequences (e.g., jail or physical harm), decision for final action would be considered a matter of personal conscience. (CPA, 1991, Standard IV.15)

The Role of a Professional Association Ethics Code

The three codes also differ with respect to their view of the primary purpose of a professional association ethics code. The ASPPB code states the opinion that the primary purpose of a professional association ethics code "is to protect the welfare and integrity of the profession" (ASPPB, 1991, Foreword, p. 3) and that the primary purpose of a regulatory body's code of conduct is "to protect the public interest" (ASPPB, 1991, Foreword, no. 2). The APA code directly contradicts this ASPPB viewpoint by stating that the APA code, a professional association ethics code, "has as its primary goal the welfare and protection of the individuals and groups with whom psychologists work" (APA, 1992, Preamble). The CPA code also contradicts the ASPPB viewpoint, in so far as it presents itself as a partial fulfillment (through the articulation and promotion of ethical principles, values, and standards) of each discipline or profession's contract with society to "assure that each member will place the welfare of the society and individual members of that society above the welfare of the discipline and its own members" (CPA, 1991, Preamble: Introduction).

Responsibility to Regulatory Bodies

The ASPPB code seems to present the view that a psychologist's first responsibility, after the law, is to the rules of conduct of the regulatory body or, at least, to the Rules of Conduct in the ASPPB code: "this Code of Conduct shall prevail whenever any conflict exists between this Code and any professional association standard" (ASPPB, 1991, I. Introduction, Section E).

The APA code is silent on a psychologist's responsibility to the regulatory body's requirements and on how a psychologist should respond to any conflict between a regulatory body requirement and the APA Ethics Code (although a psychologist's responsibility when the Code conflicts with the law is described in the Introduction and in Ethical Standard 1.02). On the other hand, the CPA code states that psychologists are expected to "respect the requirements of their provincial/territorial regulatory bodies" (CPA, 1991, Preamble: Relationship of Code to Provincial Regulatory Boards). However, Standard III.34 of the CPA code qualifies this requirement, "unless abiding by them would be seriously detrimental to the rights or well-being of others as demonstrated in the Principles of Respect for the Dignity of Persons or Responsible Caring. (See Standard IV.6 for guidelines regarding the resolution of such conflicts.)" (CPA, 1991, Standard III.34).

Purposes and Philosophy: Summary and Conclusions

All three codes provide introductions that are clear about their purposes. In my opinion, it is evident that the differences in purpose that can be found from code to code are consistent with the nature, responsibilities, and experiences of the organizations producing them. Through generation of a code of conduct, the ASPPB's primary concern is to provide statements of unacceptable conduct that are legally definable and defensible. Insofar as breaking such rules can lead to losing one's license to practice, the legal forum is much more important to the ASPPB than to either the APA or the CPA. In contrast, consistent with their collegial nature and experience, the APA and the CPA try to provide aspiration, guidance, and education to their members, as well as "bottom lines." [1]

Taking into account these differences in purpose, there appear to be only two philosophical differences that result in potential sources of conflict between the three codes. In each case, the difference is found between the regulatory code of conduct and the two professional association ethics codes. The first such difference is found in the ASPPB assertion that obeying the law is the top requirement of a psychologist, followed by the code of conduct, followed by any ethics code; whereas, both the APA and the CPA codes specify that the ethics code may sometimes provide a higher standard than the law and that psychologists are expected to demonstrate a commitment to the ethics code if there is a conflict between the law and the ethics code. Although this philosophical difference is striking and could lead to serious conflicts for a psychologist, the next two sections of this chapter will explore how likely it would be that such conflicts would surface.

The second philosophical difference that could lead to conflict is the ASPPB assertion, mentioned above, that its code is primarily concerned with protecting the public interest, whereas the professional association

[1]This is not to suggest that the APA and CPA codes do not provide legally definable and defensible guidance.

codes are primarily for the protection of the profession. Both the APA and the CPA codes make statements that indicate strong disagreement with this assertion. The CPA code, in particular, argues that the public cannot be given an adequate level of protection only through assurance that minimum requirements are met; rather, such protection is given only if the entire discipline of psychology promotes aspiration toward standards of excellence.

Comparison of Underlying Ethical Principles

Both the APA and the CPA codes delineate and define specific ethical principles. Although the ASPPB code groups its Rules of Conduct under some headings that could be considered primarily ethical in nature, it does not delineate or define any specific ethical principles. This section will explore and compare the explicitness of each of the voluntary association codes about their ethical principles and will analyze and compare the differential attention given by all three codes to specific ethical principles.

Explanations of the Ethical Principles

Although the CPA code is longer than the APA code, this difference can be attributed primarily to the amount of explanation given to each of the ethical principles. The CPA code, consistent with one of the objectives for its development (Sinclair, Poizner, Gilmour-Barrett, & Randall, 1987), is much more explicit about its underlying principles. As one example of this difference in explicitness, the following comparison can be made of how these two codes explain the importance of respecting the rights of individuals and of possible limitations on those rights.

First, the APA example: "They respect the rights of individuals to privacy, confidentiality, self-determination, and autonomy, mindful that legal and other obligations may lead to inconsistency and conflict with the exercise of these rights" (APA, 1992, Principle D: Respect for People's Rights and Dignity).

Next, the CPA example:

> Adherence to the concept of moral rights is an essential component of respect for the dignity of persons. Rights to privacy, self-determination, personal liberty, and natural justice are of particular importance to psychologists, and they have the responsibility to protect and promote these rights in all of their activities. As such, psychologists have a responsibility to develop and follow procedures for informed consent, confidentiality, fair treatment, and due process that are consistent with those rights.
>
> As individual rights exist within the context of the rights of others and of responsible caring (see Principle II), there may be circumstances in which the possibility of serious detrimental consequences to themselves or others, or a diminished capacity to be autonomous, or a

> court order, might disallow some aspects of the rights to privacy, self-determination, and personal liberty. Indeed, such circumstances might be serious enough to create a duty to warn others (see Standards I.40 and II.36). However, psychologists still have a responsibility to respect the rights of the person(s) involved to the greatest extent possible under the circumstances, and to do what is necessary and reasonable to reduce the need for future disallowances. (CPA, 1991, Principle I: Respect for the Dignity of Persons)

Attention to Various Ethical Principles

A line-by-line comparison of the three codes prepared for the ASPPB by Sinclair (1993) classified each standard and rule of conduct or, if necessary, each subsection of a standard or rule of conduct (requirement), as reflecting one of the four ethical principles delineated by the CPA code. Emphasis on various ethical principles was measured by simply counting the number of requirements under each of the four ethical principles for each of the three codes and calculating percentages based on the total number of requirements in each of the codes. Table 2 summarizes the findings of this study.

Although it is evident that all three codes place least emphasis on Responsibility to Society (ranging from 9% to 18%), only the CPA code places about equal emphasis (ranging from 25% to 29%) on the other three ethical principles. Also of interest is the fact that both the APA and the ASPPB codes place their greatest emphasis on the principle of Integrity in Relationships.

The more uneven emphasis placed by the ASPPB and the APA codes on the four ethical principles and, in particular, their placement of highest emphasis on Integrity in Relationships would suggest that these two codes have been more influenced than the CPA code by the content of complaints against psychologists and the concomitant development of case law based on decisions reached when such complaints are adjudicated. This is supported by the observation in many quarters (e.g., APA, 1991) that a majority of complaints against psychologists fall under the rubric of Integrity in Relationships (e.g., dual relationships, conflicts of interest and misleading public statements). In contrast to this observation, Pope and Vetter (1992) found that the ethical concerns and dilemmas faced by psycholo-

Table 2. Percentage Occurrence of CPA's Four Ethical Principles in Each of Three Codes

Ethical principle	CPA	APA	ASPPB
I. Respect for the dignity of persons	27 (n = 42)	24 (n = 55)	29 (n = 23)
II. Responsible caring	29 (n = 45)	28 (n = 63)	21 (n = 17)
III. Integrity in relationships	25 (n = 38)	38 (n = 87)	41 (n = 33)
IV. Responsibility to society	18 (n = 28)	10 (n = 23)	9 (n = 7)
Total	99 (n = 153)	100 (n = 228)[a]	100 (n = 80)[a]

[a]Some requirements reflected more than one ethical principle.

gists in their day-to-day activities are distributed across a wider range of ethical issues than the content of complaints against psychologists would indicate. The more-even emphasis in the CPA code would therefore suggest that the development of this code has been more strongly influenced by its primary intent to educate and guide psychologists in ethical practice and decision making than by specific case law.

The influence of case law on the development of the APA code of ethics, in spite of the fact that the APA is a voluntary association, may partially be explained by the APA's long-term involvement in the investigation and adjudication of complaints. Unlike the CPA, which yields the adjudication of complaints to provincial and territorial regulatory bodies when the complaint concerns a registered or licensed psychologist (Sinclair & Pettifor, 1992), the APA accepts and adjudicates complaints even if a regulatory body is also doing so. In addition, the APA code of ethics until recently has been the primary code of behavioral standards used by regulatory bodies for adjudication purposes. As such, it could be expected that case law established through state adjudications and appeals of decisions has influenced the development of the APA code. In this context, criticism by state lawyers and judges about the applicability of the APA code in legal forums (ASPPB, 1991) could be expected to influence the APA's decision to alter the structure of its code in the latest revision, separating the more aspirational General Principles from the more enforceable Ethical Standards and changing the name of the revised code to include the phrase "Code of Conduct."

Ethical Principles: Summary and Conclusions

Although the ASPPB code does not delineate or explain the ethical principles that underlie its rules of conduct, it is possible to discern them for each rule or subsection of a rule. Similarly, although the APA code does not group its Ethical Standards under ethical principles, it is possible to discern the ethical principles underlying each of its standards or subsections. With the four ethical principles of the CPA code as a framework for analysis and comparison, it is clear that all three codes reflect all four of the ethical principles, although moderate differences can be found in the emphasis placed on each principle. The differences in emphasis seem to be related, at least in part, to the amount of involvement each organization has had in the adjudication of complaints and to the stated purposes of each code.

Comparison of Rules and Standards

Comparison of the specific rules and standards of the three codes reveals two differences; the first difference is in the language used, and the second is in the actual content covered.

Differences in Language

The ASPPB code uses primarily the mandatory *shall* for each of its rules. The APA code generally uses descriptive active verbs (e.g., "the psychologist discusses X with Y") in its standards. The CPA code, with the exception of one passive verb, uses an auxiliary form of each verb through the use of the word *would* (e.g., "adhering to the Principle of Z, psychologists would discuss X with Y"). This difference in language is consistent with the different purposes and philosophy of each code. *Shall* is consistent with the idea that rules of conduct are coercive, not advisory. Descriptive active verbs (as in the APA code) not only do not sound as coercive but also do not sound totally advisory. An auxiliary form of each verb (as in the CPA code) is consistent with the behavior or attitude described being both advisory and educational in intent.

A second difference in language is in the three codes' differential use of prohibitive verbs (e.g., *shall not, do not, would not*). Table 3 presents the results of calculations performed by Sinclair (1993) and indicates that the CPA code is the least prohibitive (16%) of the three codes. It also indicates that the APA code is closer (23%) to the CPA code than to the ASPPB code (33%) in prohibitiveness. On the other hand, the results also indicate that all three codes are more positive than prohibitive.

A third difference in language that helps to identify similarities and differences among the three codes is their differential use of softer, attitudinal verbs (e.g., *promote, strive, uphold,* and *acknowledge*) versus harder, behavioral verbs (e.g., *provide, make known, clarify,* and *obtain*). By using the same process as that used for measuring prohibitiveness, each verb in the three codes was classified as *attitudinal* or *behavioral*. Table 4 presents the results.

As expected, the ASPPB code contains the highest percentage (91%) of harder, behavioral verbs, followed by the APA code (72%), and then by the CPA code (68%). What is not expected, perhaps, is that the ASPPB code contains some softer, attitudinal verbs in its rules and that the APA and the CPA codes are so similar, in spite of the claim by APA that its ethical standards are all enforceable and in spite of the general perception that the requirements of the CPA code are much more aspirational than those of the APA code.

Table 3. Percentage of Verbs in Three Codes Classified as "Prohibitive" or "Positive"

Classification	CPA	APA	ASPPB
Prohibitive	16 (n = 30)	23 (n = 57)	33 (n = 23)
Positive	84 (n = 158)	68 (n = 169)	64 (n = 45)
Passive	1 (n = 1)	10 (n = 24)	3 (n = 2)
Total	101 (n = 189)	101 (n = 250)	100 (n = 70)

Table 4. Percentage of Verbs in the Three National Codes Classified as "Behavioral" or "Attitudinal"

Classification	CPA	APA	ASPPB
Behavioral	68 (n = 129)	72 (n = 180)	91 (n = 64)
Attitudinal	30 (n = 56)	18 (n = 46)	6 (n = 4)
Passive	1 (n = 1)	10 (n = 24)	3 (n = 2)
Total	99 (n = 189)	100 (n = 250)	100 (n = 70)

Specific Content of Rules and Standards

Appendix G allows comparison of the specific requirements of the three codes' rules and standards. It cites the major content of each Rule of Conduct of the ASPPB code. Beside each ASPPB Rule of Conduct are quotations from the APA and the CPA ethical standards that relate to the same or similar issues as the specific rule. Appendix G, then, allows for a direct comparison of specific issues addressed in the ASPPB, APA, and CPA codes.

Comparison of Specific ASPPB Rules of Conduct With APA and CPA Standards

Appendix G indicates that although the APA and the CPA codes speak to most of the issues covered in the ASPPB code, they sometimes deal with the issues in different ways and with different amounts of detail and scope. These differences will be explored by considering each of the major rule categories used in the ASPPB code.

Competence. The first rule of conduct in the ASPPB code (limiting work to one's areas of competence) and its comparators in the APA and the CPA codes demonstrate some of the major differences that can be found among the statements. Two of these differences are the scope of application and the provision of indicators. The CPA code contains a high proportion of standards that are worded in such a way that they can be applied to all activities in which a psychologist engages (e.g., services, teaching, and research). The CPA code tends not to give specific indicators for judging whether or not the rule or standard is being honored, whereas the ASPPB code tends to limit its statements to a specific area of activity (e.g., practice) and to provide details that can be used as indicators. The APA code tends to fall between the other two in these characteristics. These differences are demonstrated in the wording of the first ASPPB rule of conduct, which limits its application to "practice and supervision" (A.1.), whereas both the APA and CPA codes refer to a broader set of activities. The differences are also demonstrated in both the ASPPB and the APA codes' tendency to provide more frequently a set of indicators (e.g., education, training, and experience), whereas the CPA code refers only to "established their competence" (II.6.). There is also a tendency for the APA code, in contrast to the other two codes, to mention many more specific applications of a requirement. This is demonstrated by the additional APA standard cited as a comparator (2.04.a) to ASPPB's first rule of conduct. This APA standard lists specific competencies needed to perform interventions or use assessment techniques.

Proceeding through the other ASPPB rules of conduct related to competence, other general observations can be made:

1. All three codes agree that psychologists should keep up to date in their areas of practice, should refer clients to others if they are not competent to meet the clients' needs, should assess competently, should maintain adequate records, and should make sure records are adequately protected.
2. Both the ASPPB and the APA codes make special mention of taking care to be as competent as possible when techniques are new or not fully developed; the CPA code makes no special mention of this.
3. Only the ASPPB code explicitly requires that records of professional supervision be kept. Neither of the other two codes explicitly require this; however, there is nothing in the other two codes that would discourage or prohibit such records. In fact, in the CPA code, there is a specific requirement to familiarize oneself with the discipline's rules and regulations and abide by them "unless abiding by them would be seriously detrimental to the rights or well-being of others" (CPA, 1991, Standard III.34). Because it is difficult to imagine how the specific ASPPB requirement to keep records of professional supervision would be "seriously detrimental," the CPA code would support adherence to such a requirement. (A similar comment can be made about the ASPPB requirement that records be kept for a specific number of years.)

Impaired objectivity and dual relationships. All three codes require, either explicitly or implicitly, that a psychologist not engage in an activity if he or she is impaired in some way and that the psychologist assist a client to find another appropriate resource if necessary. Both the APA and the CPA codes mention potential harm to the client as the criterion against which to judge whether or not the level of impairment is such that activities should be limited or terminated. Both the APA and the CPA codes mention seeking consultation or assistance for impairments. The ASPPB code does not. Demonstrating the APA's more proactive nature, the APA code urges psychologists to be alert to early signs of impairment and seek assistance at an early stage; similarly proactive, the CPA code urges psychologists to engage in self-care activities that will prevent impairment.

The ASPPB code prohibits dual relationships. Both the APA and the CPA codes suggest that dual relationships are not always avoidable but that they should be avoided where possible. However, all three prohibit a specific kind of dual relationship, namely sexual intimacy, with certain kinds of current clients. All three agree that current therapy clients are one kind of client with whom sexual intimacy is prohibited. However, the ASPPB code goes beyond use of the term "therapy client" to include any client receiving services related to "the treatment or amelioration of emotional distress or behavioral inadequacy" (B.2.b.). On the other hand, both the APA and the CPA codes, in standards under other sections, extend the prohibition of sexual intimacy to include persons other than those that would be included in the ASPPB code. The CPA code extends the prohibition through a specific standard that mentions sexual intimacy as a possible form of prohibited exploitation (e.g., of students, employees, and industrial and organizational clients). The APA code extends the prohibition through adding a specific mention of sexual intimacy with persons "over whom they have supervisory, evaluative, or other authority" (1.19.a.). All three codes extend the prohibition of sexual intimacy with therapy and psychotherapeutic clients indefinitely if the client is vulnerable; however, only the ASPPB and the APA codes specifically mention a 2-year posttermination prohibition, regardless of vulnerability. As with record keeping, the CPA code avoids drawing specific lines. (See earlier discussion of the CPA's Standard III.34 and its implications with regard to this matter.)

Client welfare. The most interesting difference in this set of rules and standards is the way in which each of the codes deal with the concept of informed consent. Although all three seem to agree that clients should be informed and should be kept informed and contain numerous rules and standards on this matter, the ASPPB code never uses the phrase "informed consent," and the APA code mentions it only in the context of therapy, release of information, and research. On the other hand, in the CPA code, the section labeled Informed Consent contains more standards than any other section of the code.

With respect to other requirements regarding client welfare, all three codes agree that clients need to be terminated carefully and sensitively. They also agree that discrimination or the use of stereotypes is unacceptable. However, on this latter point, the APA and CPA codes extend the concept of discrimination into the realm of needing to be sensitive and responsive to individual differences and vulnerabilities.

Welfare of supervisees and research subjects. One of the most striking differences between the ASPPB code and the two voluntary association codes is the amount of attention paid to the responsibility of psychologists to students and supervisees and to research participants. Whereas the two voluntary association codes contain numerous standards related to both types of persons, the ASPPB code contains only one Rule of Conduct for each. The first Rule of Conduct states that students are not to be exploited. The second states that the dignity and welfare of research participants are to be respected and promoted and that statutes and administrative rules regarding research participants are to be honored.

Protecting confidentiality of clients. There is almost total agreement in the three codes' treatment of the issues of confidentiality. All three with the need for informed consent for release of confidential information, exceptions to this need (including exceptions related to the "duty to protect"), and how to relay information and yet respect confidentiality.

Representation of services. Although the three codes deal with the topic slightly differently, and the two professional codes expand the scope of representation to include a much wider variety of activities in which psychologists are involved, all agree that dishonesty, misrepresentation, falsification, and misleading statements are not acceptable. They also agree that psychologists have a responsibility to correct others who have misrepresented their services, qualifications, affiliations, and activities, whether intentionally or unintentionally. The only significant point of difference would appear to be the ASPPB requirement that psychologists display their current license to practice. Neither of the professional association codes require this; however, once again, there would be nothing in either of these two codes that would prohibit or discourage such a requirement.

Fees and statements. All three codes make strong statements against the use of any form of misrepresentation or dishonesty in charging fees. All three codes also seem to go beyond this basic prohibition, however, in so far as they all speak of the need to "be clear and straightforward" (CPA, III.14.), to not "withhold . . . information" (ASPPB, G.I.), or "to reach an agreement" (APA, 1.25.a.). Both the ASPPB and the APA codes specifically mention exploitation as it relates to fees and specifically mention bartering as a problem. In addition to prohibiting exploitive bartering (as does the ASPPB code), the APA code prohibits bartering if it is "clinically contraindicated" (1.18). Although the CPA code prohibits exploitation of a client (as well as students or research participants), fees and bartering are not given as specific examples of possible exploitation.

Assessment procedures. Once again, there seem to be few differences among the three codes. Although both of the voluntary association codes speak to requirements regarding assessment, the standards that do so tend to go beyond just the area of assessment. All three codes expect psychologists to consider assessment results as confidential, to give adequate feedback about results, to acknowledge limitations of their findings, to protect the validity of assessment procedures, and to communicate clearly and completely about any assessment techniques developed.

Violations of law. The purpose of the two rules of conduct included in this ASPPB section are related primarily to laws that impinge directly on the practice of psychology (e.g., using fraud to obtain a psychology license). Neither the APA nor the CPA code specifically mention such laws, although adherence to the law (with the possibility of some exceptions) is expected by both codes. A discussion of the philosophical differences between the three codes with respect to the law can be found above.

Aiding illegal practice. Once again, there is substantial agreement among the three codes. Psychologists should not help someone else to misrepresent themselves as psychologists, should not delegate to unqualified persons (the APA and the CPA codes, however, emphasize competence over qualifications), should exercise appropriate levels of supervision, and should act when violations or unethical behaviors occur. This last item indicates some disagreement among the codes, insofar as the two voluntary association codes express concern not just about violations of rules but also of potentially harmful unethical acts (even where there is no standard or rule that mentions the specified act) and, unlike the ASPPB code, suggest that informal resolutions are sometimes possible.

Issues Covered in the APA and CPA Codes Exclusively

It is interesting to note the more proactive and aspirational nature of the two voluntary association codes. A few of the major requirements that can be found in both of the voluntary association codes, but not the ASPPB code, are as follows:

1. Attend to issues of due process and fairness in dealing with others.
2. Limit information collected or recorded to what is needed, to avoid invasions of privacy.
3. Teach with reasonable objectivity and careful preparation.
4. Bring perceived ethical violations to the professional involved, discuss, and seek resolution, if appropriate.
5. Protect the welfare of animals used in teaching or research.
6. Take and give credit only for and in proportion to work done.
7. Honor promises and commitments.
8. Not conceal the status of a trainee.
9. Seek consultation from colleagues or competent others when faced with difficult situations.

Overall Summary and Conclusions

In spite of concern about the possibility of confusion and conflict resulting from having three national codes that guide or govern the behavior of psychologists in the United States and Canada, the differences among the codes are ones of purpose, structure, and underlying philosophy rather than ones of ethical principles or requirements. It is my opinion that, rather than conflicting with one another, the three codes complement one another, serving different purposes and providing both overlapping and singular examples of psychologists' responsibilities. The current versions are attempts by three different bodies of psychologists in Canada and the United States, at similar points in time, to define the obligations of psychologists. Each has its own strengths and weaknesses.

The ASPPB code is helpful in the precision of its language, including the many definitions it provides. Its weakness is in its lack of articulation of an overall ethical framework; however, this weakness is consistent with its purpose. The APA code is helpful in the detailing of applications of its standards, giving psychologists more examples of what to do in particular situations than either of the other two codes. Its weakness is in sometimes not giving examples of applications of all of its underlying ethical principles to all of its areas-of-practice headings, thus appearing to exclude some activities of psychologists from some of its ethical principles. The CPA code is helpful in its provision of an explicit ethical framework and its emphasis on ethical decision making, resulting in the code being a more valuable educational tool than the other codes. Its weakness is its comparative lack of examples and detail and potential difficulty with enforceability.

Consistent with their stated purpose as codes of ethics, the two professional association codes reflect and promote an increased understanding of the ethical framework of the profession's responsibilities and standards. This is demonstrated in their proactive stance compared with previous codes of ethics, in their willingness to include and define aspirational concepts as well as enforceable standards, in their attention to issues involving vulnerability, and in their attention to the role of self-knowledge and self-care in protecting the public and in enhancing the profession's ability to benefit society.

The fact that there are three major national codes is a product of the complexity and multiple responsibilities and stresses of psychology in the United States and Canada. The codes are the product of a natural and ongoing evolutionary process. As part of this process, future development of each of the codes will be influenced by the others. For the moment, psychologists would be wise to keep and refer to all three codes as part of their effort to be a responsible community of professionals.

References

American Psychological Association. (1981). Ethical principles of psychologists. *American Psychologist, 36,* 633–638.

American Psychological Association. (1991). Report of the Ethics Committee, 1989 and 1990. *American Psychologist, 46,* 750–757.

American Psychological Association. (1992). Ethical principles of psychologists and code of conduct. *American Psychologist, 47,* 1597–1611.

Association of State and Provincial Psychology Boards. (1991). *ASPPB code of conduct.* Montgomery, AL: Author.

Canadian Psychological Association. (1991). *Canadian code of ethics for psychologists. Revised.* Ottawa, ON: Author.

Pope, K., & Vetter, V. (1992). Ethical dilemmas encountered by members of the American Psychological Association. *American Psychologist, 47,* 397–411.

Sinclair, C. (1993). *Comparison of CPA, APA, and ASPPB codes.* Ottawa, ON: Canadian Psychological Association.

Sinclair, C., & Pettifor, J. (1992). *Companion manual to the Canadian code of ethics for psychologists, 1991.* Ottawa, ON: Canadian Psychological Association.

Sinclair, C., Poizner, S., Gilmour-Barrett, K., & Randall, D. (1987). The development of a code of ethics for Canadian psychologists. *Canadian Psychology, 28,* 1–11.

5

Common Problem Areas and Their Causes Resulting in Disciplinary Actions

Christa Peterson
Division of Child and Family Services, Las Vegas, Nevada

Available data clearly indicate that there has been a significant increase in disciplinary and legal actions against psychologists for unprofessional and unethical conduct. Disciplinary actions by state and provincial regulatory boards have increased by 500% over the past 10 years for some types of unethical conduct as documented in the Disciplinary Data Bank (Reaves, 1993) of the ASPPB. The Ethics Committee of the APA reported that the number of complaints filed with the APA against psychologists more than doubled in a 5-year period (1984–1989), with a similar increase in the number of sanctions by the association (APA, 1991). Malpractice claims against psychologists through the APA Insurance Trust (APAIT) have also risen in recent years (APAIT, personal communication, May 4, 1993).

A wide range of behaviors and practices may lead to disciplinary or legal action before a regulatory board, professional association, or court of law. The purpose of this chapter is to describe the problem areas that most frequently result in disciplinary or legal action. Common problem areas include: (a) competence, (b) informed consent and confidentiality, (c) dual relationships, and (d) financial arrangements.

Competence

As professionals, psychologists have an ethical and legal responsibility to provide competent care to their clients. However, competence in the practice of psychology is a complex and multifaceted concept. Competence may be defined as having the requisite knowledge to understand a particular issue, the necessary skills to apply this knowledge effectively, and the judgment and objectivity to know when and to whom those skills should be applied (Bennett, Bryant, VandenBos, & Greenwood, 1990; Haas & Malouf, 1989).

Competent practice is usually associated with meeting a "reasonable" standard of care for the profession. Regulatory boards and professional associations also offer many guidelines useful in specifying competent practice. At times, regional and cultural factors may play a role in defining an "adequate" standard of care.

Section II.6-23 of the *Canadian Code of Ethics for Psychologists* of the CPA (1991), Principle A and Sections 1.04-1.07, 1.23, 1.24, 2.02-2.10 of the Ethical Principles of Psychologists and Code of Conduct of the APA (1992), and Section III A of the *ASPPB Code of Conduct* of the ASPPB (1991) provide guidance on standards for competence.

Scope of the Problem

The most common problems that psychologists encounter under the broad area of competence are: (a) practicing outside the limits of training; (b) misuse of tests; (c) practicing while physically or mentally impaired; (d) failure to diagnose, treat, or refer; and (e) failure to warn. In the past 10 years, 47% of reported disciplinary actions by state and provincial psychology boards were related to problems in these areas. In addition, these issues accounted for 34% of the cumulative total malpractice claims (as of January 1, 1991) submitted by psychologists to their primary insurer and 33% of the total costs of these claims (APAIT, personal communication May 4, 1993). Finally, 42% of cases opened by APA for complaint investigation from 1990 to 1993 resulted from psychologists' failure to practice competently (APA, 1993b, 1994).

In a study of self-reported behaviors of psychologists (Pope, Tabachnick, & Keith-Spiegel, 1987), 24.6% of psychologists reported practicing outside their area of competence. In another study, psychologists rated issues surrounding their own competence to be one of the most frequent problems encountered in practice. In addition, psychologists presented with ethical dilemmas surrounding competence issues had the lowest consensus on appropriate ways to solve such issues as compared with other ethical dilemmas (Haas, Malouf, & Mayerson, 1986).

Practice Dilemmas

Practicing outside limits of competence. Pope and & Vasquez (1991) discuss some common reasons psychologists develop problems in this area. A client who holds exaggerated beliefs about a psychologist's competence may make it difficult for that psychologist to refer him or her to a more appropriately trained professional. Fear of alienating a valued referral source may motivate the psychologist to accept a client who presents challenges beyond the psychologist's level of training. Psychologists working in rural areas may feel compelled to provide treatment to clients with problems they are not competent to handle because of an absence of nearby referral sources. In any setting, new issues raised by the client may arise midway during therapy and fall outside the psychologist's area of competence. All of these situations require psychologists to monitor their own ability to provide competent treatment (see Exhibit 1).

Psychologists may incorrectly assume that a license to practice authorizes them to provide treatment in areas outside their competence or that adherence only to legal requirements is sufficient to guarantee competent practice. Psychologists must be careful to seek out additional education and training when adding new services or techniques. In addition, some codes of conduct require that clients be informed if techniques are new to the therapist or to the profession (ASPPB, 1991).

Professional organizations such as the APA also provide guidelines for those who wish to develop new areas of competence. In addition, the *ASPPB Code of Conduct* (1991) Section III A.3 requires that:

> The psychologist, when developing competency in a service or technique that is either new to the psychologist or new to the profession, shall engage in ongoing consultation with other psychologists or relevant professionals and shall seek appropriate education and training in the new area. The psychologist shall inform clients of the innovative nature and the known risks associated with the services, so that the client can exercise freedom of choice concerning such services. (p. 8)

Psychologists sometime use "vanity" credentials to extend their area of competence or seek employment for which they are not qualified (Woody, 1988). For example, the psychologist who displays a certificate of completion from a weekend workshop may incorrectly do so to imply competency to practice in this new specialty area. Psychologists viewing their practices as only businesses may risk practicing outside their area of competence for financial gain, thus increasing the likelihood of harm to the client.

Psychologists who conduct isolated practices or do not regularly seek supervision and consultation from other psychologists may drift away from

---

Exhibit 1

Dr. Thomas is a psychologist who has been practicing for 20 years, primarily working with adults in a small rural community. Mr. Adams is receiving psychotherapy from Dr. Thomas. Dr. Thomas evaluates Mr. Adams' 3-year-old daughter who is exhibiting sleeping problems following a dog bite. Dr. Thomas has recently attended a continuing education workshop on posttraumatic stress disorders in children and adults. Dr. Thomas later prepares a report to be used in court, because Mr. Adams is suing the owner of the dog who bit his daughter. After the jury returns a verdict unfavorable to Mr. Adams, Mr. Adams sues Dr. Thomas for incompetence.

All vignettes are composite or hypothetical scenarios.

an acceptable standard of care. Also, psychologists who are not diligent in maintaining current knowledge and awareness of professional standards and legal requirements, including case law, may risk a practice that violates the standard of care. Psychologists must be aware that standards of care are constantly evolving because of new areas of practice and new technologies. For example, psychologists unaware of the developments in child-custody assessment and treatment and in the area of forensic psychology are likely to practice incompetently in these areas. Professional organizations such as the APA have recently drafted guidelines to suggest appropriate interventions in these problematic areas.

Test misuse. Psychologists who are poorly trained do not have a systematic approach to diagnosis and assessment and are likely to encounter problems in this area. For example, psychologists may misuse tests by administering under nonstandard conditions such as abbreviating the instructions, allowing the client to take the test home, or providing supervision of a paper-and-pencil test by an untrained person (Pope & Vasquez, 1991).

Lack of knowledge and skill in the application of statistics, especially with regard to test reliability and validity, can result in the misuse of tests. Psychologists can experience difficulty in this area when they use tests on client populations not included in the test validation process. Similarly, utilization of test versions with outdated norms or procedures is an unacceptable standard of practice for the psychologist.

In addition, psychologists may use faulty decision making during the diagnostic process, such as failure to consider low base rates of certain phenomenon (e.g., probabilities of assaultive behavior in predicting client risk or assumptions about past abuse based on observing symptoms common in victims). Psychologists may ignore potential physical causes of symptoms or fail to consider the client's past medical history prior to initiating assessment, treatment, or both.

Psychologists should also be aware that their own biases may affect the assessment process and should take care in monitoring and ensuring objectivity in the context of the client interview.

Physical or mental impairment. Pope et al. (1987) reported that 59.6% of a national sample of psychologists reported working when too distressed to be effective. In the same study, 5.7% of psychologists reported they had conducted therapy under the influence of alcohol. Common causes of impairment include drug or alcohol abuse, mental illness, physical or mental disability, and grief over loss or separation of a loved one (Bouhoutsos, 1983). Problems in this area may develop when impaired psychologists are unable to monitor their own condition or are reluctant to seek therapy. Deutsch (1985) surveyed mental health professionals and found many reluctant to seek therapy because of lack of resources, concern about confidentiality, and fear of professional judgement. This study of members of several APA divisions found that a substantial number of impaired psychologists (22.9%) had not received therapy.

Psychologists may be vulnerable to mental distress or impairment following such stressful events as a marital separation, suicide of a client, or a financial loss. As with other life stress, psychologists who do not seek social or professional support (through therapy, supervision, and consultation) risk practicing incompetently (see Exhibit 2).

Burnout and fatigue may also impair the psychologist's ability to practice competently. Psychologists must be alert to signs of burnout and fatigue as inattention to or impatience with a client during a session.

Poor record keeping. As Bennett et al. (1990) point out, psychologists face one of their greatest challenges in record keeping. While client records must support the treatment of the client, they must also fulfill record-keeping requirements of insurance companies, governmental agencies, legal entities, and other organizations to whom the psychologist may have some obligation. With increased reporting requirements, it has become more difficult for the psychologist to maintain client confidentiality, which will be discussed later.

A psychologist who does not have clearly thought out and established record-keeping practices is at risk for disciplinary action, legal action, or both. Psychologists most often have record-keeping problems when there is insufficient case documentation. In one study of self-reported behavior, 50.9% of psychologists indicated they limited chart notes to the date, name, and fee only (Pope et al., 1987). However, the psychologist should be aware that recording every statement of the client verbatim will not prevent problems related to record-keeping issues (Haas & Malouf, 1989). If subpoenaed, a psychologist may be held liable for any factual information represented in case records. In addition, psychologists who "embellish" their records with more than factual information (i.e., subjective impressions or hypotheses not substantiated by client data) may be accused of violating standards of care, of harming the client, or of both. Content of records should be relevant to client care and administrative requirements.

Exhibit 2

Dr. Brown is a psychologist in practice treating individuals and couples. His wife is suing him for divorce, and he is being forced to sell his home and move to a condominium. Dr. Brown frequently calls his receptionist and cancels appointments with his clients at the last minute. Dr. Brown's receptionist notices that when his clients come in for appointments, Dr. Brown is short-tempered with them and makes sarcastic comments.

After Dr. Brown is particularly rude with Mrs. Cook, a client, Mrs. Cook files a complaint alleging incompetent practice.

Record keeping may become a problem unless the psychologist has documented the following: (a) client history, (b) explanation of presenting problems, (c) foundation for developing a diagnosis, and (d) a plan of treatment, based on sound theoretical principles. Psychologists should also take care to document all aspects of the informed consent process, including: (a) risks and benefits of treatment; (b) reasons why alternative treatments were rejected; (c) instructions on exceptions to confidentiality; and (d) instructions to the patient regarding billing, insurance, and so forth. Hall (1988) suggests that psychologists keep financial records separate from treatment records. Because financial records are frequently accessed by office staff and third-party payers, this procedure may help to preserve the confidentiality of treatment records and avoid problems in terms of liability.

During the course of treatment, psychologists should also be diligent in recording each client session. Ideally, these contact notes should contain not only client behavior and progress but also any interventions used and contacts made as a result of the session. Tests given as well as their results should be included. Consultations with other professionals or attempts to refer should be noted. Any information on medications being taken should be included. There should be a record of the termination process.

In the case of suicidal patients, it is important that the psychologist document the assessment of suicide risk, the options considered for the prevention of suicide, and the treatments undertaken. The psychologist should note any special precautions such as informing others of the risk, contracting with the patient to give up lethal weapons, or increasing the frequency of therapy sessions.

Mental health providers who work in treatment facilities should be doubly cautious to avoid problems with record keeping. Oftentimes local, state, provincial, or federal regulations may dictate the scope of record keeping, particularly in school, government, and military settings.

Psychologists may also be vulnerable to disciplinary action, legal action, or both if they are careless about records security, storage, and disposal. Psychologists should be aware of the specific ethical and legal guidelines in their jurisdictions and their practice setting (i.e., hospital or other accredited health care facility), especially with regard to the length of time that records should be maintained. Hall (1988) suggests some consideration be given to storing a separate set of abbreviated records designed for an unforeseen emergency, such as an office fire. This type of record would only contain a minimal amount of information, such as names of the clients, their addresses, and phone numbers.

Although no one can fully anticipate what client record information may be needed, the psychologist should keep records, anticipating that they may be: (a) used in malpractice suits, criminal actions, or some form of civil action such as divorce or custody; (b) used by third-party payers; and (c) used by other clinicians and professionals who may treat the client at present and in the future (Haas & Malouf, 1989).

Providers should also note the growing number of jurisdictions that have passed laws regarding client access to medical records. Psychologists may be subjected to successful civil actions based on refusal to provide client access to records. Charging exorbitant rates for copies of records may be construed as an illegal business practice.

Guidelines outlining the content and control of records can be found in the *ASPPB Code of Conduct* (1991), Section III A.6.:

> a. The psychologist rendering professional services to an individual client (or a dependent), or services billed to a third party payor, shall maintain professional records that include:
> 1) the presenting problem(s) or purpose or diagnosis,
> 2) the fee arrangement,
> 3) the date and substance of each billed or service-count contact or service,
> 4) any test results or other evaluative results obtained and any basic test data from which they were derived,
> 5) notation and results of formal consults with other providers,
> 6) a copy of all test or other evaluative reports prepared as part of the professional relationship.
>
> b. To meet the requirements of this rule, so as to provide a formal record for review, but not necessarily for other legal purposes, the psychologist shall assure that all data entries in the professional records are maintained for a period of not less than five years after the last date that service was rendered. The psychologist shall also abide by other legal requirements for record retention, even if longer periods of retention are required for other purposes.
>
> c. The psychologist shall store and dispose of written, electronic and other records in such a manner as to insure their confidentiality.
>
> d. For each person professionally supervised, the psychologist shall maintain for a period of not less than five years after the last date of supervision a record of the supervisory session that shall include, among other information, the type, place, and general content of the session.

More recently, the APA has developed record-keeping guidelines (APA, 1993a). These guidelines were developed for providers of health care services. The APA guidelines are aspirational in nature and require the individual psychologist's professional judgement for specific applications (see Appendix H).

Informed Consent and Confidentiality

The psychologist has a duty to respect the autonomy and dignity of the client through the process of informed consent. Because the psychologist occupies a unique position of power and trust with the client, ethical and legal standards are designed to protect the client from abuse. Power to initiate and terminate the professional relationship is given to the client, while the psychologist is clearly obliged to clarify the nature of treatment, including potential risks and benefits.

Haas and Malouf (1989) outline components of informed consent:

1. Client is competent: The client, or guardian, has the ability (i.e., mental, emotional) to initiate a voluntary action.
2. Consent is informed: The clients are given sufficient information, in a manner they comprehend, to make a decision about participation in assessment or treatment. Sufficient information is often defined as the level of information a reasonable person would want to know (CPA, 1991, Standard I.16) before making a decision.
3. Consent is voluntary: Informed consent from the client must be obtained without coercion, except in exceptional circumstances where the client may be judged incompetent to render such a decision.

The psychologist also has an ethical obligation to ensure that information obtained during the professional relationship with the client is used only for the benefit of the client. Confidentiality not only protects the client's fundamental right to privacy but also facilitates the maintenance of client trust so essential to the professional relationship (Haas & Malouf, 1989).

Whereas maintaining confidentiality is the ethical obligation of the psychologist, it should not be confused with the client privilege, which is a legal right belonging to the patient. Psychologist–patient privilege guidelines are legally established in most U.S. jurisdictions and allow the client to withhold communications with the psychologist from the court during legal proceedings. If the privilege is waived by the client or abrogated by court order, disclosure is required. However, under ethical requirements of confidentiality, psychologists are obligated to protect and maintain other aspects of the client's confidentiality even when permission has been given for the release of selected information. For example, the client may specifically authorize release of diagnostic information to third-party payers, but the psychologist has an obligation to protect other confidential information in the treatment record from disclosure to third-party payers. Some third-party payers now ask for detailed information, and clients may need to be informed of that possibility. For an in-depth discussion of confidentiality, see Canter, Bennett, Jones, and Nagy (1994).

The most common causes of disciplinary actions, legal actions, or both related to informed consent and confidentiality are: (a) failure to obtain adequate informed consent, (b) failure to warn, (c) breach of confidentiality without informed consent, and (d) breach of confidentiality in family therapy and child-custody cases.

Informed consent and confidentiality are addressed in Section III.E of the *ASPPB Code of Conduct* (1991), in Sections I.11-23 of the *Canadian Code of Ethics for Psychologists* (CPA, 1991), and in Section 5 of the Ethical Principles of Psychologists and Code of Conduct (APA, 1992).

Scope of the Problem

In the past 10 years, 2% of the reported disciplinary actions by state and provincial psychology boards were related to improper breaches of confidentiality (Reaves, 1993). Failure to preserve confidentiality was the fourth most frequent ethics complaint reported to APA over a 5-year period (APA, 1988). Problems in breaching confidentiality accounted for 10% of the cases opened for investigation by the Ethics Committee of the American Psychological Association from 1990 to 1993 (APA, 1993b, 1994). In addition, problems with confidentiality accounted for 6.7% of the total cumulative malpractice claims (as of January 1, 1991) submitted against psychologists to their primary insurer (APAIT, personal communication, 1993). Failure to warn, failure to protect, and failure to prevent suicide accounted for another 3.6% of all such malpractice claims.

In a study of self-reported behaviors, 61.9% of psychologists surveyed reported that they had unintentionally breached confidentiality (Pope et al., 1987). In another study, senior, prominent psychologists reported the most frequent intentional acts they committed in violation of the law or ethics involved confidentiality, with 21% breaching confidentiality in violation of the law, and another 21% refusing to break confidentiality to make mandated child-abuse reports (Pope & Bajt, 1988). In a survey of APA Division 29 members, confidentiality and informed consent were rated as two of the most frequent ethical dilemmas encountered in practice (Haas et al., 1986). In another survey of 679 APA members, confidentiality was reported as the most frequently occurring ethical dilemma faced in their work (Pope & Vetter, 1992).

Practice Dilemmas

Poor informed-consent process. Psychologists must understand that informed consent is both an ethical obligation and a technical skill (Haas & Malouf, 1989). Psychologists who assume they are informing the client through use of a written form as a substitute for the process of informed consent may experience difficulties in this area. In one study (Grundner, 1980), five informed-consent forms were analyzed and found to be written at a college-upper-division or graduate reading level. Other studies have shown that recall for informed-consent material in written form is poor (Pope & Vasquez, 1991).

Psychologists have an obligation to ensure that the clients understand not simply the risks and benefits of treatment, or the lack thereof, but other aspects of the professional relationship as well. Psychologists often fail to clarify the following important aspects of the professional relationship through the informed-consent process:

1. How and when treatment will begin.
2. How and when treatment will be terminated.
3. Access to the psychologist in emergencies.

4. Policy for beginning and ending sessions.
5. Access between sessions, during therapist's illness.
6. Nature of fees and billing practices.
7. Limits of confidentiality.
8. The client's right to withdraw consent and terminate treatment at any time.

The possibility that the client may fail to improve with treatment or may improve without treatment should be part of the informed-consent process, whenever relevant. The psychologist who enters into a treatment contract guaranteeing a desired outcome risks legal action, disciplinary action, or both for breach of contract should the client fail to improve (Bennett et al., 1990).

Breach of confidentiality. An ethical approach to issues of confidentiality also necessarily involves the concept of informed consent (APA, 1988). Psychologists who obtain the client's written consent to release confidential information but do not inform the patient of the exact nature of the information to be released and of the potential consequences of sharing such information may be subject to legal sanctions, disciplinary sanctions, or both. For example, the client must be informed of the implications of releasing diagnostic information to third-party insurers. The patient may well want to reconsider the release of such information and bear the cost of treatment once informed of the potential consequences. Similarly, the psychologist who evaluates an individual for employment purposes must ensure that the employee understands the potential consequences of and consents to limitations on confidentiality.

Written release forms should include several key elements, including: (a) name of the person to whom the records are to be released, (b) which records are to be released, (c) intended use of released records, (d) date the form was signed, (e) expiration date, (f) any limitations on data to be provided, and (g) name of person authorizing the release (in relationship to client; Keith-Spiegel & Koocher, 1985).

Similarly, psychologists must be extremely cautious to release only relevant information on receipt of a signed release form and to inform the client of the nature of the release. Psychologists who do not inform the patient as to the limits of confidentiality prior to entering a professional relationship will increase the likelihood that the patient will seek legal action, disciplinary action, or both should the psychologist later find it necessary to breach confidentiality (see Exhibit 3). In general, ethical standards and legal requirements allow such disclosure of confidential information if the client presents an imminent danger to self or others. Disclosure is often mandated by law in cases of child or elder abuse. However, psychologists often experience problems with mandated reporting because they do not follow the correct procedures outlined in the legal standards of their jurisdiction or they release more information than necessary by law.

Psychologists face special complications in protecting confidentiality

---

Exhibit 3

Dr. White provides treatment to the children of Mr. and Mrs. Baxter. Dr. White occasionally sees the parents in collateral treatment. Dr. White explains to the parents that the issues discussed during therapy will be confidential except in cases of suspected child abuse.

During therapy, Mr. and Mrs. Baxter's children report they're often anxious when Mr. and Mrs. Baxter argue, and especially after Mr. Baxter drinks too much and threatens violence. Six months following the termination of treatment, Mrs. Baxter sues Mr. Baxter for divorce. Mrs. Baxter asks Dr. White to write a report about the children's therapy, including their issues with Mr. Baxter's drinking behavior. Dr. White agrees to write the report.

After Mr. Baxter loses custody of his children, he sues Dr. White for violating confidentiality.

---

when it is difficult to define who is the client. For example, when the client is a child, the psychologist must be sensitive to the parents' legal right and obligation to know what is going on in treatment, while offering the child enough confidentiality to facilitate the development of a trusting and honest therapeutic relationship (Haas & Malouf, 1989). The psychologist may want to obtain written consent from the parents or guardians waiving their legal right to information if necessary to protect the child's confidentiality, well-being, or both. The psychologist who does not use the informed-consent process to clarify who has access to confidential information may also experience difficulties in other situations where the identified "client" is ill-defined, such as in family therapy or forensic work. Similarly, when dealing with couples in therapy, psychologists should ensure that the clients understand the potential problems with maintaining confidentiality should they later be involved in divorce litigation.

Finally, psychologists violate confidentiality of the clients when they inadvertently discuss cases with colleagues, gossip, or fail to ensure that case records are secured and disposed of in a confidential manner. Psychologists who are careless with phone messages, cellular phones, answering machines, or office soundproofing may also be inadvertently violating client confidentiality (Pope & Vasquez, 1991).

Dual Relationships

A dual relationship may occur whenever a therapist interacts with a client in more than one capacity, that is, as a therapist and a business partner, as a therapist and a teacher, and so on (Bennett et al., 1990). As will be described later, not all dual relationships are inherently unethical or illegal. However, such relationships should be avoided if they: (a) affect the client's ability to develop an open, trusting relationship with the psychologist; (b) impair the psychologist's objectivity in providing treatment; or (c) cause harm or exploit the client. Sexual intimacies with clients meet all three criteria above and are specifically prohibited by ethical and legal standards in all jurisdictions.

Dual relationships are addressed in Section III.B of the *ASPPB Code of Conduct* (ASPPB, 1991), Section II.26 and Section III.32-33 of the *Canadian Code of Ethics for Psychologists* (CPA, 1991), and Section I.17-19 and Section 4.05-4.07 of the Ethical Principles of Psychologists and Code of Conduct (APA, 1992).

Scope of the Problem

Dual relationships are by far the most frequent cause for disciplinary action, legal action, or both against psychologists; most of these actions involve dual relationships of a sexual nature. Over the past 10 years, 46% of disciplinary actions against psychologists by state or provincial psychology boards involved dual relationships with clients (Reaves, 1993). Dual relationships were a problem in 43% of the cases opened for investigation by the APA Ethics Committee from 1990 to 1993, nearly 50% more than filed for this reason in 1988 (APA, 1993b, 1994). In cases adjudicated by the APA's Ethics Committee in 1994, sexual misconduct was the largest single category of unethical behavior resulting in loss of APA membership (APA, 1995). Sexual dual relationships with patients account for 21.1% of the total cumulative claims against psychologists with the APAIT (APAIT, personal communication, May 4, 1993) and 50.8% of the claims costs.

Although most psychologists view sexual relationships with clients as a serious ethical violation, most seldom rate it as a concern in their own daily practice (Haas et al., 1986). Nonetheless, in a recent survey of APA Division 29 psychologists, 1.9% self-reported sexual contact with clients and 2.6% self-reported erotic activity with clients (Pope et al., 1987). Early studies have estimated that between 6.5% (Pope, Levenson, & Schover, 1979) and 7.9% (Holroyd & Brodsky, 1977) have engaged in sexual contact with clients. Recent decreases in the self-reporting of this behavior by psychologists are most likely due to increased penalties (sex with clients is a felony in some states) for this behavior. More alarming are the results of a recent study by Stake and Oliver (1991) in which 43.6% of Missouri psychologists responding to a survey reported receiving client reports of sexual contact with a previous therapist.

In contrast to the small yet significant proportion of psychologists reporting dual relationships of a sexual nature, nearly one third of APA Division 29 psychologists surveyed in Pope et al. (1987) reported engaging in nonsexual dual relationships. A total of 28.3% provided therapy to friends and 15.6% provided therapy to employees. In a survey of 679 APA members, dual-relationship issues were reported as the second most frequently occurring dilemma in daily practice (Pope & Vetter, 1992). These data are surprising as most ethical codes discourage this type of behavior.

Practice Dilemmas

Surveys indicate that male therapists engage in sexual misconduct with their clients at much higher rates than female therapists; for example, in one study, 85% of self-reported incidents of therapist–patient sex involved male therapists (Holroyd & Brodsky, 1977). Ninety percent of sexual-misconduct complaints filed with the APA Ethics Committee involved male therapists (APA, 1993b). The research also indicates that psychologists who have had sexual contact with a patient are likely to have continuing problems in this area (Bates & Brodsky, 1989).

It should also be noted that 87% of all psychologists feel sexually attracted to their clients at times, and 63% of these professionals feel confused about such feelings (Pope et al., 1987). The psychologist who does not acknowledge, monitor, or address these feelings promptly is at risk of harming the client (Pope & Vasquez, 1991).

A large survey of mental health professionals found that male psychologists rated examples of social and financial dual relationships as more ethically appropriate than did female respondents. This study also showed that male therapists are more likely to engage in nonsexual dual relationships with clients of the opposite sex than their female counterparts (Borys & Pope, 1989). Finally, these investigators demonstrated that nonsexual dual relationships accurately predicted therapist–client sexual involvement in 78.3% of cases studied (APA, 1988). On the basis of these findings, psychologists who frequently engage in what they consider to be innocuous dual relationships may be vulnerable to difficulties with more significant dual relationships such as sexual contact with patients. The psychologist should never agree to treat a former sexual partner, see a client in a social setting, or direct comments or actions toward a client that might be interpreted as sexual in nature.

Those psychologists who consistently violate role boundaries in the professional relationship may also be particularly likely to have dual-relationship difficulties with patients (see Exhibit 4). Warning signs of role-boundary problems include: (a) a high level of self-disclosure to patients; (b) anticipation of a session with a particular client; (c) a desire to prolong the session; (d) a consistent desire to please, impress, or punish the client; and (e) failure to refer or terminate therapy when otherwise appropriate (Haas & Malouf, 1989).

Psychologists should use particular care in the use of nonsexual touching with patients (Pope & Vasquez, 1991). In one study, a therapists' preference for nonsexual touching of the opposite gender during therapy was associated with erotic contact (Brodsky, 1989).

A psychologist engaging in nonsexual dual relationships of a social or financial nature must similarly take great care to avoid the three problems of dual relationships outlined above: (a) harm to the client (e.g., exploi-

Exhibit 4

Dr. Smith is seeing Mrs. Casper, a realtor, in therapy for depression and marital problems. After several therapy sessions, Mrs. Casper offers to show Dr. Smith some houses that are for sale. Dr. Smith purchases a home through Mrs. Casper, while she continues in therapy.

One night, she calls Dr. Smith in crisis. She is distraught because her husband has left her. She asks Dr. Smith to make a home visit. Several months later, Mrs. Casper's husband files a complaint with the state licensing board against Dr. Smith, alleging sexual misconduct.

---

tation), (b) impaired objectivity, and (c) harm to the professional relationship. Bennett et al. (1990) cautions against initiating therapy or even giving casual advice to friends, colleagues, and acquaintances, thereby avoiding even the appearance of conflict of interest.

Psychologists working in isolated rural areas may face unique challenges in avoiding dual relationships. In many rural areas, psychologists participate in community activities along with their clients. These relationships are not sought by the psychologist or the client but derive from their common membership in a given group. In many cases, lack of alternative professional resources may prevent the psychologist from referring a client when there is a nonsexual dual-relationship issue. Similarly, the psychologist may not be able to avoid doing business with a client who may be the rural community's sole provider of certain goods or services. For example, in a small community, the client's auto-repair shop may be the only resource available to the psychologist who has car trouble. The psychologist placed in these situations should seek consultation from colleagues and other professionals to avoid the potential problems of dual relationships outlined above.

Financial Arrangements

Psychologists are frequently ill-trained to manage the financial aspects of their practice. Psychologists must balance the ethical obligation to the client inherent to the professional relationship with the need to maintain a financially sound and successful practice. Setting and collecting fees, dealing with delinquent accounts, splitting fees or other reciprocal arrangements, bartering, and pro bono work are frequent financial issues for the professional psychologist.

Ethical guidelines regarding the financial aspects of the professional relationship are provided in the Section III.G of the *ASPPB Code of Conduct* (ASPPB, 1991), Section I.19 of the *Canadian Code of Ethics for Psy-*

chologists (CPA, 1991), and Sections I.25-27 of the Ethical Principles of Psychologists and Code of Conduct (APA, 1992).

Scope of the Problem

Between 1986 and 1988, more than 11% of disciplinary actions by psychology boards involved improper billing practices. Insurance and fee problems were involved in 15% of the cases opened for investigation by the APA Ethics Committee from 1990 to 1993 (APA 1993b, 1994). A total of 3.8% of claims to date filed with the APAIT against psychologists involved counter suits for fee collection (APAIT, personal communication, May 4, 1993).

In a survey of APA Division 29 psychologists (Pope et al., 1987), a large number of those surveyed reported use of several high-risk financial practices such as: (a) altering a diagnosis to meet insurance-reimbursement criteria (61%), (b) bartering with the client (25%), and (c) lending money to a client (25.7%). In a survey of 679 APA members, financial arrangements were reported as one of the top three ethical dilemmas faced in daily practice (Pope & Vetter, 1992).

Practice Dilemmas

Setting and collecting fees. Psychologists who neglect the financial aspects of their practices or delegate money matters to a secretary or untrained office manager risk operating at a standard well below acceptable business and accounting standards. Psychologists who operate using substandard business practices risk violating the ethics of the professional relationship. Psychologists who do not seek out the expertise of specialists, such as accountants and business lawyers, may unknowingly perpetuate faulty business practices that also increase the risk of liability.

Psychologists have an ethical obligation to inform fully clients of fee-setting and payment options on initiating the professional relationship (see section on Informed Consent). Psychologists are vulnerable to complaints and sanctions if they do not develop clearly established policies for setting and collecting fees that are shared with the client before charges are incurred. When the psychologist offers a sliding-scale fee or discounted fee, the basis for the fee variance must be consistently established, communicated to the client, and collected (Keith-Spiegel & Koocher, 1985). Ideally, to meet requirements for informed consent, psychologists should clarify the potential limitations of insurance reimbursements (i.e., diagnostic and procedural exclusions, deductibles, and copayments).

More disciplinary actions, legal actions, or both against psychologists arise from billing practices than from any other type of financial arrangements encountered in practice. As stated previously, the most common cause of disciplinary and legal actions for billing practices involves altering a diagnosis to maximize third-party reimbursements. For example, a psychologist may assign a superfluous diagnosis (i.e., depression) so that a

Exhibit 5

Dr. Washington is seeing Mr. and Mrs. Denver and their children for family therapy. Mr. and Mrs. Denver's insurance does not cover family therapy sessions. Mr. and Mrs. Denver request that Dr. Washington bill the sessions under individual psychotherapy, which is covered under their insurance plan. Dr. Washington agrees to do so.

After Mr. and Mrs. Denver divorce, Mr. Denver files a complaint against Dr. Washington, alleging fraud and unprofessional conduct.

---

client's marital-therapy session will be eligible for insurance payments (see Exhibit 5). This type of unethical billing practice may very well result in a revocation of the psychologist's license. With the development of managed care, contracts with health-plan providers increasingly require psychologists to collect the copayment from the client when they accept the third-party payment. Practitioners who write off the client's required copayment are at risk for accusations of fraudulent billing.

Failure to properly acknowledge the actual provider of the services rendered, billing third-party payers for missed sessions, or misrepresenting couple, family, or group services as individual psychotherapy are likely causes for disciplinary or legal action against a psychologist.

Poor management of delinquent accounts. Psychologists have the right to use fee-collection agencies in the collection of delinquent accounts. However, psychologists who do not clarify this practice with their clients on initiation of the professional relationship may increase the likelihood of later disciplinary action, legal action, or both. Similarly, psychologists who do not give clients adequate notice or seek to negotiate a solution to delinquent accounts may be faced with a complaint from a disgruntled client. The psychologist who is not familiar with the practices of the designated collection agency may later become responsible for harm to the client based on aggressive collection methods by the agency that exploit the client's vulnerability.

There is also ample evidence that as the client accrues a large deficit in payment to the psychologist the probability of malpractice claims also increases (Woody, 1988). Psychologists have an ethical obligation to determine with clients whether the latter have the means to pay for services at the onset of treatment. The psychologist should also be knowledgeable about community resources should referral be necessary at that time. Psychologists who manage effectively their clients' delinquent payments before large balances accumulate will reduce their liability risk.

Psychologists who terminate treatment prematurely because of lack of payment or insurance limitations may be charged with abandoning their clients. Appropriate referral of these clients, including follow-up to ensure linkage with other treatment resources, will reduce the likelihood of disciplinary action for client abandonment.

Fee splitting. In fee splitting (often called a kickback), part of the fees received for professional services are returned or paid out because of a prearranged agreement between the professional and another individual. One example of fee splitting occurs in a group practice where a portion of the fees collected by one professional is returned to another professional for referral services. Generally speaking, these arrangements do not violate ethical codes in all jurisdictions. The APA code allows fee splitting in an employer–employee relationship or as long as payment is based on psychological services provided rather than on the referral itself (Section 1.27). In Canadian jurisdictions, it may be illegal to engage in fee splitting with respect to certain services, such as health services covered by provincial health insurance. Nonetheless, psychologists should be extremely cautious of fee-splitting arrangements and should be aware of specific regulations in their jurisdictions that may affect the legality of such arrangements.

Psychologists who refer their clients to other professionals with whom they have fee-splitting arrangements must ensure that such referrals are in the best interest of their client and are not motivated by their own financial gain. Psychologists who engage in this practice must ensure that such a referral is necessary for the treatment of their client and is made to a professional best qualified to treat their client.

Psychologists who engage in fee-splitting practices increase the likelihood of complaints based purely on the appearance of a conflict of interest. Psychologists who profit from such fee-splitting arrangements should inform the client and any third-party payer of the proprietary relationship between the service provider and the person making the referral as a part of the informed-consent process (Keith-Spiegel & Koocher, 1985).

Other questionable financial arrangements. Bartering is one solution to the financial problems faced by some clients in paying for professional services. The client may offer to provide goods or services in exchange for psychotherapy or other professional services offered by the psychologist. Bartering exposes the psychologist to all of the potential problems of any nonsexual dual relationship. Psychologists who barter with clients risk exploitation of the client by accepting goods and services that may be worth an undetermined amount or much more than the market value of the therapy.

Bartering arrangements should be considered only when the market value of the goods or services traded are clarified prior to the initiation of the professional relationship and the psychologist is confident that the welfare of the client will be preserved. Bartering may be particularly problematic in cases where the client offers to trade a service (i.e., house painting) and the psychologist is not satisfied with the end product. If such problems are not anticipated and resolved prior to initiating therapy, disruption in the therapeutic relationship may become the unfortunate result.

Pro bono or free services may also be provided to the client who has insufficient resources to pay for psychological services. Psychologists have an ethical obligation to provide some pro bono services to clients. As in other financial arrangements, pro bono services should be determined by the psychologist prior to charges being incurred. Unpaid accounts treated as pro bono work leave the psychologist open to sanctions (Bennett et al., 1990).

Providing pro bono services does not relieve the psychologist of the responsibility to meet all the ethical and legal standards of practice.

Conclusion

In conclusion, psychologists risk legal or disciplinary actions whenever they stray from reasonable standards of competent practice. In addition, the complexity of ethical decision making with regard to informed consent and confidentiality places particular demands on the psychologist for awareness, caution, and prudence in daily practice. Finally, the ambiguity and the lack of specific practice guidelines in the areas of dual relationships and financial arrangements require of the psychologist to be particularly cautious in these areas. Psychologists can best avoid disciplinary or legal actions by becoming skillful in the ethical decision-making process.

References

American Psychological Association. (1987). *General guidelines for providers of psychological services*. Washington, DC: Author.

American Psychological Association, Ethics Committee. (1988). Trends in ethics cases, common pitfalls and published resources. *American Psychologist, 43*, 564–572.

American Psychological Association, Ethics Committee. (1991). Report of the Ethics Committee, 1989 and 1990. *American Psychologist, 46,* 750–757.

American Psychological Association. (1992). Ethical principles of psychologists and code of conduct. *American Psychologist, 47*, 1597–1611.

American Psychological Association. (1993a). Record keeping guidelines. *American Psychologist, 48*, 984–986.

American Psychological Association, Ethics Committee. (1993b). Report of the Ethics Committee, 1991 and 1992. *American Psychologist, 48*, 811–820.

American Psychological Association, Ethics Committee. (1994). Report of the Ethics Committee. *American Psychologist, 49*, 659–666.

American Psychological Association, Ethics Committee. (1995). Report of the Ethics Committee. *American Psychologist, 50*, 706–713.

Association of State and Provincial Psychology Boards. (1991). *ASPPB Code of Conduct*. Montgomery, AL: Author.

Bates, C. M., & Brodsky, A. M. (1989). *Sex in the therapy hour: A case of professional incest*. New York: Guilford.

Bennett, B. E., Bryant, B. K., VandenBos, G. R., & Greenwood, A. (1990). *Professional liability and risk management*. Washington, DC: American Psychological Association.

Borys, D. S., & Pope, K. S. (1989). Dual relationships between therapist and client: A national study of psychologists, psychiatrists and social workers. *Professional Psychology: Research and Practice, 20,* 283–293.

Bouhoutsos, J. C. (1983, August). *Programs for distressed colleagues: The California model.* Symposium presented at the annual meeting of the American Psychological Association, Anaheim, CA.

Brodsky, A. M. (1989). Sex between patient and therapist: Psychology's data and response. In G.O. Gabbard (Ed.), *Sexual exploitation in professional relationships* (pp. 15–25). Washington, DC: American Psychiatric Press.

Canadian Psychological Association. (1991). *Canadian code of ethics for psychologists. Revised.* Ottawa, ON: Author.

Canter, M. B., Bennett, B. E., Jones, S. E., & Nagy, T. F. (1994). *Ethics for psychologists: A commentary on the APA Ethics Code.* Washington, DC: American Psychological Association.

Deutsch, C. (1985). A survey of therapists' personal problems and treatment. *Professional Psychology: Research and Practice, 16,* 305–315.

Grundner, T. M. (1980). On the readability of surgical consent forms. *New England School of Medicine, 302,* 900–902.

Haas, L. J., & Malouf, J. L. (1989). *Keeping up the good work: A practitioner's guide to mental health ethics.* Sarasota, FL: Professional Resource Exchange.

Haas, L. J., Malouf, J. L., & Mayerson, N. H. (1986). Ethical dilemmas in psychological practice: Results of a national survey. *Professional Psychology: Research and Practice, 17,* 316–321.

Hall, J. E. (1988). Records for psychologists. *Register Report, 14,* 3–4.

Holroyd, J. C., & Brodsky, A. M. (1977). Psychologists' attitudes and practices regarding erotic and nonerotic physical contact with clients. *American Psychologist, 32,* 843–849.

Holroyd, J. C., & Brodsky, A. M. (1980). Does touching patients lead to sexual intercourse? *Professional Psychology, 11,* 807–811.

Keith-Spiegel, P., & Koocher, G. P. (1985). *Ethics in psychology: Professional standards and cases.* New York: Random House.

Pope, K. S., & Bajt, T. R. (1988). When laws and values conflict: A dilemma for psychologists. *American Psychologist, 43,* 828.

Pope, K. S., Levenson, H., & Schover, L. R. (1979). Sexual intimacy in psychology training: Results and implications of a national survey. *American Psychologist, 34,* 682–689.

Pope, K. S., Tabachnick, B. G., & Keith-Spiegel, P. (1987). Ethics of practice: The beliefs and behaviors of psychologists as therapists. *American Psychologist, 42,* 993–1006.

Pope, K. S., & Vasquez, M. J. T. (1991). *Ethics in psychotherapy and counseling.* San Francisco: Jossey-Bass.

Pope, K. S., & Vetter, V. A. (1992). Ethical dilemmas encountered by members of the American Psychological Association. *American Psychologist, 47,* 397–411.

Reaves, R. (1993). *Disciplinary data bank. 8th Midwinter Meeting, Feb. 20, 1993.* Montgomery, AL: Association of State and Provincial Psychology Boards.

Stake, J., & Oliver, J. (1991). Sexual contact and touching between therapist and client: A survey of psychologists' attitudes and behavior. *Professional Psychology: Research and Procedure, 22,* 297–307.

Woody, R. H. (1988). *50 ways to avoid malpractice.* Sarasota, FL: Professional Resource Exchange.

6

Maintaining Professional Conduct in Daily Practice

Jean L. Pettifor
University of Calgary

Psychologists have a responsibility to provide competent and ethical services for the benefit or best interests of consumers. This responsibility goes beyond doing no harm and beyond mere avoidance of negligence and misconduct.

In the regulation of the practice of psychology, many approaches are used to assure, or at least attempt to assure, the public that newly licensed or registered psychologists will practice competently and ethically. These measures include establishing entrance criteria through evaluation of academic credentials, supervised practice, written examinations, oral examinations, and review of work samples. Between the point of admission to the profession and the infrequent circumstance of disciplinary action, professional psychologists generally have no mechanisms for ensuring compliance with professional standards or ensuring quality services. Respect for the privacy of clients requires that the majority of psychological services are undertaken behind closed doors.

Many jurisdictions require continuing-education credits as a condition for psychologists to maintain their licenses to practice. It is doubtful that mandatory continuing education is sufficient in itself to maintain the competence of practitioners. Disciplinary committees have an important role in investigating complaints of misconduct and in imposing sanctions against a small number of erring psychologists. However, disciplining professionals is no substitute for individual psychologists' accepting the responsibility to maintain competent and ethical services on a daily basis. There are philosophical differences between those who believe that mandatory measures are necessary to assure a minimum level of continuing competency and those who believe that only voluntary measures can inspire psychologists to enhance their practice to optimum levels of caring.

It is the thesis of this chapter that psychologists who maintain high levels of professional conduct are encouraged by aspirational ethics to practice appropriately and that the measures they take to maintain competence are voluntary and targeted to specific professional needs. Aspirational ethics are based on moral principles that always place the well-being of the other, the consumer, above self-interest, as opposed to codes of conduct that define minimal levels of acceptable behavior. I believe that it is the rare psychologist who does not want to provide good service for clients. Therefore, it is also argued that regulatory and professional bodies should spend more energy and resources supporting psychologists in maintaining quality services and that such a proactive approach would increase the likelihood of the public being well-served.

There are societal changes that influence the nature of presenting problems, technological changes that affect the way psychologists conduct their work, and philosophical changes that affect the nature of ethical concerns and there is a rapid acceleration and proliferation of documents defining ethics and standards to guide psychological practice. Psychologists need training in ethics and ethical decision making to behave ethically in complex and confusing situations. They need continuing education to meet new challenges and changing conditions in society. Without denying the individual responsibilities of psychologists to be competent and ethical, professional organizations often provide assistance for psychologists to teach and monitor their own practices. Psychologists also need assistance in managing new modes of service delivery and funding, of which managed care is a recent and dramatic example.

Maintaining competent services that protect consumers and care for their best interests requires an attitude of constant problem solving and self-evaluation. Individual practitioners need to be able to evaluate and monitor their own performance and to consider various alternatives for maintaining and expanding their competence. The professional responsibility of practitioners is to protect the well-being of clients and of themselves.

This chapter emphasizes the positive aspiration of psychologists to provide optimal quality services. It also describes some of the practical strategies which may be used. In recent years there has been an abundance of psychological literature on ethics and standards. Three publications are outstanding for their practicality and self-help. *Ethics in Psychology: Professional Standards and Cases* (Keith-Spiegel & Koocher, 1985) covers a broad range of ethical issues with abundant use of vignettes. *Professional Liability and Risk Management* (Bennett, Bryant, VandenBos, & Greenwood, 1990) provides a wealth of information and self-evaluation questions on maintaining good practices with a view to reducing risk and protecting against liability suits. *Companion Manual to the Canadian Code of Ethics for Psychologists, 1991* (Sinclair & Pettifor, 1992) is invaluable for teaching, learning, and practicing an ethical decision-making process based on moral principles, as is *Ethics for Psychologists: A Commentary on the APA Ethics Code* (Canter, Bennett, Jones, & Nagy, 1994).

Following are some suggestions to enhance the maintenance of professional conduct in daily practice. The state or provincial, collegial or regulatory body, could implement a coordinated plan to provide positive support to psychologists in order to increase the confidence of psychologists in their own practice, to assure and protect the public, and to protect the integrity of the profession. There are a number of specific activities and resources that might be considered.

Self-Evaluation

Self-evaluation seems highly relevant for independent practitioners who wish to monitor their own practices and to determine their own continuing-education needs. It is also useful for psychologists working as employees, although large organizations are more likely to have their own quality assurance and management systems, and psychologists within a department are more likely to have colleagues with whom they can discuss issues. Self-evaluation instruments may also provide professional training departments with practical strategies to assist graduates in obtaining a systematic overview of the requirements of practice.

The purpose of a self-evaluation questionnaire (see Appendix I) is to provide a comprehensive list of questions directed to the self-evaluation of practice and to reference each question to principles in the major standards documents (Pettifor, Bultz, Samuels, Griffin, & Lucki, 1994). The questions may be generic to any type of practice where there is a psychologist–client relationship, or questions may address details of various specialty areas. The advantage of the generic approach is the acknowledgement that the generic standards do cover all types and specialties of practice. The disadvantage of developing only specialty self-evaluation questionnaires is that it is impossible to cover every special area of practice. It also may be impossible to obtain consensus on operational definitions in fields where professional judgments of complex situations and collaboration with consumers is the essence of competent and respectful practice. Although the questions and the ethical standards referenced will not necessarily identify specific behaviors, they provide psychologists the opportunity to check their specific behaviors against the articulated standards of the profession. The self-evaluation will assist individuals to identify areas where they are confident of their competency, as well as areas where they should take measures to ensure their competency or refrain from practice.

Professional associations may serve and support their members by developing such instruments. Although individual practitioners may feel pressed for time, it may still be a useful exercise for individuals, or groups, to develop questionnaires and references to serve their own specific needs. It would also be a useful exercise for graduate students in psychology.

The major standards referenced in developing a self-evaluation questionnaire are the appropriate codes of ethics, codes of conduct, and guidelines for providers of psychological services. For U.S. jurisdictions, these will usually be Ethical Principles of Psychologists and Code of Conduct (APA, 1992), *ASPPB Code of Conduct* (ASPPB, 1991), or a code of professional conduct of the local regulatory jurisdiction and *General Guidelines for Providers of Psychological Services* (APA, 1987). For Canadian provincial jurisdictions, the major references will usually be *Canadian Code of*

Ethics for Psychologists (CPA, 1991), a code of professional conduct of the local regulatory jurisdiction, and *Practice Guidelines for Providers of Psychological Services* (1989). If one wishes to develop self-evaluation questions for specialty areas of practice, one can find many interdisciplinary references on treatment modalities or special guidelines in problem areas such as custody and access and visitation assessments.

Some suggestions can be made on the format of self-evaluation questionnaires, whether they be generic or for specialty areas. It is important that questionnaire items be referenced to standards and guidelines that have evolved to delineate good practice. Where no standards have been developed there may be a lack of consensus within the profession. Questions should begin with first-person action verbs such as "Do I inform, provide, ensure, maintain?" and so on. One should avoid passive verbs, such as "Am I aware, cognizant, knowledgeable, sensitive?" and so on.

There is some advantage in separating a self-evaluation checklist for business practice from other questions and guidelines for direct services. Business practices can usually be defined in operational terms that are appropriate for a checklist format, for example: "Do I keep records?" "Do client records for which I am responsible contain the following information?" "Do I inform my clients of fees and billing practices prior to providing service?" and "Does my work environment ensure privacy between the client and myself?" The business section might be expected to address such areas as record keeping, service fees, service environment, representation, referral to other professionals, confidentiality, and supervision.

A major section affecting consumers, which cannot be fully defined in operational terms, would be professional client services. The quality of psychological practice requires sound professional judgment in assessing and treating complex human problems. Although such judgments are difficult to operationalize, there are a number of guidelines and principles that generally help to define good practice. The following kinds of questions require thoughtful consideration and self-awareness to make meaningful responses: "Do I use only assessment procedures (or intervention procedures) that are appropriate to the client and to the client's problems?" and "Do I use only assessment procedures (or intervention procedures) for which I am adequately trained and in which I have demonstrated my competence?" The underlying issue is whether I can justify what I am doing professionally in terms of quality and competence of practice for the benefit of the recipients of services. A professional client services section might address assessment procedures, intervention procedures, use of other professional services, coverage during absences, service evaluation, supervision, administration, professional and employer relationships, continuing education, self care, and scope and limitations of practice.

A section may be included on self-evaluation guidelines for research activities, primarily because practitioners may engage in research outside of an institutionalized research setting and may not have the benefit of research consultation and ethics review. This section might include the research plan, risks, benefits, informed consent, deception, privacy and confidentiality, and supervision.

A section on self-evaluation guidelines for teaching may be beneficial for practitioners who engage in some teaching activities, as well as for full-time teaching psychologists. This section might address information taught and relationships with students.

A Central Resource Library (Manual or Computerized)

Individual practitioners may check whether their state or provincial psychology regulatory boards or collegial associations maintain a resource library (manual, computerized, or both) of professional standards, regulations, and guidelines. They may also maintain an up-to-date bibliography of publications on professional standards and ethics. Whether maintained by the voluntary or regulatory organization, it is helpful to have a central source of available standards documents. Many psychologists are not aware of how many standards documents have been created.

Guidelines for Establishing Peer Mutual-Support Networks

Practitioners can take responsibility to establish guidelines for peer support groups and to meet periodically to share experiences that will help reduce their isolation and maintain the competency of their practices. A peer support group is likely to consist of members interested in a particular area of practice. It needs to be a voluntary group of practitioners who have mutual respect for each other. There should be a regular place and time to meet to discuss whatever is of current interest. They may wish to deal with issues that arise in emerging areas of practice, such as managed care, recovered memories, therapy via the Internet, dual relationships, or they may discuss new literature in their field or difficulties they have encountered in their practice. Rules need to be established regarding confidentiality. Personal information about colleagues as well as about clients must be kept confidential. Client names should never be used, and identifying information must be kept to the minimum required for a professional consultation. Information shared about a colleague's practice must not be used by others to gain a competitive advantage. Peers can be mutually supportive in enhancing competency and in providing role models. It takes minimal effort to establish such groups.

Ethics Workshops

Both regulatory bodies and voluntary professional associations may provide workshops to address current issues of concern to local psychologists. A group of practitioners can also organize workshops to meet their needs. Topics may include problems in newer areas of practice, topics on which psychologists express uncertainty, and issues about which there are frequent complaints of misconduct or unethical behavior. Current topics might include competency in addressing recovered memories, managing managed care, setting up a private practice, being an expert witness, child custody assessments, and the "slippery slope" of dual relationships. The use of real-life dilemmas and steps for an ethical decision-making process is invaluable in empowering psychologists to navigate among conflicting pressures.

A collegial or regulatory body of a state, province, or territory may wish to establish a roster of approved consultants—representing different specialty areas and geographical areas—who can provide on request confidential expert advice to psychologists. Psychologists may be uncertain of what is proper conduct in a specific situation, or they may want advice on what to do about undue personal stress. Such a program would require clear guidelines regarding confidentiality, appropriate documentation of consultations, and liability protection for the consultants. Practitioners would generally be more comfortable about confidentiality if the consultation were available from the voluntary association whose mandate is to support psychologists rather than from the regulatory body whose mandate is to protect the public from incompetent and unethical practice. However, any consultation that enhances the quality of services protects the public.

Voluntary Practice or Peer Reviews

A psychological association may establish a system whereby an individual, instead of depending solely on the self-evaluation, may request a committee of peers to review his or her individual practice and make useful recommendations on enhancing that practice. Such a system requires some administrative structure and needs to address issues such as selection of reviewers, confidentiality, records, and liability. A questionnaire or checklist similar to the self-evaluation questionnaire may be used as a review guide. This type of peer review is internal, voluntary, and initiated by the psychologist, in contrast to external peer review accountability required by regulatory boards, insurance carriers, or employer organizations. Included in this process could be reviews of selected protocols, review and discussion of "difficult clients," discussion or demonstrations of techniques or strategies, review of current literature, evaluation of experimental strategies, and ongoing discussion of ethical concerns. Reviews of individual practices by a trusted small group of colleagues using a self-evaluation questionnaire could also provide valuable discussion and feedback.

Guidelines for the Practice of Psychology: An Annotated Bibliography

Psychologists are often surprised to discover how many articulated standards and guidelines have been developed. Generic codes of ethics and guidelines for providers of psychological services have general applicability to practice. Additional standards and guidelines, although consistent with the general documents, provide specific applications to special areas of practice. The major standards may be national and supplemented by other standards adopted by the local state or provincial jurisdiction. It is not possible or necessary to have detailed knowledge of every standards document, but psychologists should pay special attention to standards that are adopted by their own state or provincial regulatory organization as well as to other standards that address their specialty area of practice (Pettifor, Bultz, Samuels, Griffin, & Lucki, 1990).

An annotated bibliography of documents that details major standards in psychology is a helpful aid in listing documents and providing dates, names of approving bodies and addresses (see Appendix J for annotated bibliography of standards). Standards are living documents continually in a process of change, and, therefore, it is necessary to keep up-to-date. Any bibliography of standards and guidelines should be revised at least every 2 years to keep it current and relevant. Standards may be grouped under categories, such as:

1. General standards for competent and ethical practice
2. Psychological testing
3. Special treatment interventions
4. Special populations
5. Research with human subjects.

Steps in an Ethical Decision-Making Process

An explicit ethical decision-making process is helpful to psychologists in resolving ethical dilemmas that involve complex relationships found in today's society and reflected in psychological practice (see Appendixes K and L for examples that use the ethical decision-making process). An ethical dilemma exists when one does not know what is the right decision or action to take in a given situation. One may not know because there are no standards to specifically address this situation, there are standards or principles that seem to be in conflict, or the apparent best interests of different parties are in conflict. When the right answer is difficult to find, psychologists may feel anxious or guilty about any decision, especially when there are pressures from different sources to make different decisions. Internal pressures may occur when the situation touches on personal beliefs, biases, attitudes, or self-interest. As one works through the steps, one needs to be aware of personal feelings and beliefs that may compromise one's objectivity. For example:

1. You discover that your client is HIV positive and is having unprotected sex with several persons without revealing her condition. Does confidentiality of client information (respect for the client) take priority over attempting to protect others from potential dan-

ger? What degree of risk to the public justifies breaking confidentiality? Is there a course of action that will serve both the client and potential victims?

2. You discover that your client has physically abused his two children. The law requires you to report it to the authorities. However, the offenses occurred 2 years ago, your client is remorseful, and he is making good progress in therapy. You believe it would cause great harm to the client, his family, and to the therapeutic relationship for charges to be laid. Must you choose between obeying the law and your perception of serving the client, or is there a way of serving both?
3. A renowned elderly professor continues to teach unacceptable outdated material. As chairperson of the department, you are uncertain how to resolve the situation since the professor insists that her course material is important. You have a responsibility to students to provide appropriate instruction; you have a responsibility to the department to retain a scholar whose name still provides external credibility and prestige; and you have compassion and respect for an aging professor who in the past has made major contributions to the field of psychology. The ethical decision-making process involves the attempt to meet all these responsibilities. The chair has a primary responsibility to the students. However, making a decision also involves the reputation of the department and the well-being of the professor.

When in an ethical dilemma one's perception often narrows to two unacceptable options with each option having some ethical merit but also doing harm to someone. The ethical decision-making process helps to clarify principles, to gain objectivity, to envisage more than two options, and to develop a plan of action that will serve the best interests of as many involved parties as possible.

There are several references on ethical decision making. The *Canadian Code of Ethics for Psychologists* (CPA, 1991) is more specific than other codes in defining typical steps for ethical decision making. The steps are quoted below as a guide for psychologists who wish to empower themselves in making ethical decisions.

1. Identification of ethically relevant issues and practices.
2. Development of alternative courses of action.
3. Analysis of likely short-term, ongoing, and long-term risks and benefits of each course of action on the individual(s) and group(s) involved or likely to be affected (e.g., client, client's family or employees, employing institution, students, research participants, colleagues, the discipline, society, self).
4. Choice of course of action after conscientious application of existing principles, values, and standards.
5. Action, with a commitment to assume responsibility for the consequences of the action.
6. Evaluation of the results of the course of action.

7. Assumption of responsibility for consequences of action, including correction of negative consequences, if any, or re-engaging in the decision-making process if the ethical issue is not resolved. (Preamble: The Ethical Decision-Making Process)

Summary of Action a Psychologist Might Take Subsequent to Self-Evaluation of Practice

Suppose that the practitioner has systematically reviewed all aspects of the practice and reviewed the relevant standards. The practitioner may feel reassured that on the whole the practice is competent, of high quality, and consistent with professional standards. However, there may be concerns that should be addressed. What does the psychologist do about them?

1. Some matters may be easily remedied, such as making confidential files less accessible, clarifying billing procedures, revising the content of consent forms, or clarifying limitations on confidentiality. These matters require a decision and action.
2. The practitioner may identify some specific topics for self study that require investigation, review, or study to determine the current status of knowledge in the field.
3. With a little initiative, practitioners who feel isolated can reduce their isolation by developing peer support systems and arranging to meet colleagues on a regular basis to share strategies, techniques, concerns, and information.
4. Practitioners in the midst of excessive stress are wise to seek trusted colleagues to consult and to assist in self-monitoring. In addition, practitioners who recognize danger to their own health and the risk to competent practice may need to change their life style or obtain treatment to attend to both self-care and client care.
5. When psychologists are tempted to practice beyond the limits of competence or wish to expand or to change the scope of practice, it is necessary to develop a plan of action. Psychologists should not undertake independent practice outside of the limits of their competence. There are several other options. It is possible to consult and to assess whether adequate supervision can be obtained to enable the practitioner to provide competent service while still learning. It is possible to assess whether short workshops or summer sessions are sufficient to provide the necessary knowledge and skills, such as new testing or treatment techniques. Psychologists may wish to consider external training programs that allow the practitioner to continue working while studying, but it will be important to know whether the training is acceptable to the regulatory body and whether it provides the quality of training sought. They may wish to assess whether they have the motivation and

resources to return to school full time for what amounts to a mid-career change. It is important to determine whether there is any financial assistance available to support such endeavors. A personal evaluation may indicate that further training is not worth the cost and effort, and the better choice is to restrict practice to present knowledge and skills.

Maintaining professional conduct in daily practice requires an ongoing commitment of psychologists to an ethic of caring, self-evaluation, and validation of practice against effectiveness of client outcome.

References

American Psychological Association. (1987). *General guidelines for providers of psychological services*. Washington, DC: Author.

American Psychological Association. (1992). Ethical principles of psychologists and code of conduct. *American Psychologist, 47*, 1597–1611.

Association of State and Provincial Psychology Boards. (1991). *ASPPB Code of conduct*. Montgomery, AL: Author.

Bennett, B., Bryant, B., VandenBos, G., & Greenwood, A. (1990). *Professional liability and risk management*. Washington, DC: American Psychological Association.

Canadian Psychological Association. (1989). *Practice guidelines for providers of psychological services*. Ottawa, ON: Author.

Canadian Psychological Association. (1991). *Canadian code of ethics for psychologists. Revised*. Ottawa, ON: Author.

Canter, M. B., Bennett, B. E., Jones, S. E., & Nagy, T. F. (1994). *Ethics for psychologists: A commentary on the APA Ethics Code*. Washington, DC: American Psychological Association.

Keith-Spiegel, P., & Koocher, G. (1985). *Ethics in psychology: Professional standards and cases*. New York: Random House.

Pettifor, J., Bultz, B., Samuels, M., Griffin, R., & Lucki, G. (1990). *Guidelines for the practice of psychology: An annotated bibliography*. Edmonton: Psychologists Association of Alberta.

Pettifor, J., Bultz, B., Samuels, M., Griffin, R., & Lucki, G. (1994). *The professional practice of psychology: Self-evaluation*. Edmonton: Psychologists Association of Alberta.

Sinclair, C., & Pettifor, J. (1992). *Companion manual to the Canadian code of ethics for psychologists, 1991*. Ottawa, ON: Canadian Psychological Association.

7

Enforcement of Codes of Conduct by Regulatory Boards and Professional Associations

Randolph P. Reaves
Association of State and Provincial Psychology Boards

Enforcement of Codes of Conduct by Regulatory Boards

The psychology regulatory boards in the various U.S. and Canadian jurisdictions typically have the legal authority to revoke, suspend, or otherwise sanction a psychologist's license when the psychologist is found guilty of illegal, unethical, or inappropriate behavior. In some jurisdictions, that authority rests with a Department of Professional Regulation or some other administrative agency. In some Canadian jurisdictions, this authority is held by provincial psychological associations. Regardless of which U.S. entity holds the authority, the parameters of such authority will derive from the same statute. In Canada the authority will be vested by statute, but reference to the association's bylaws may also be required.

The statute referred to, typically the jurisdiction's "practice act," may contain a reference to a code of conduct or a code of ethics. Violation of the referenced code may be a reason for disciplinary action. Examples include:

> *Code of Alabama* (1975):
> "Violation of the code of ethics adopted in the rules and regulations of the board."
> *Idaho Code* (1995):
> "The board of psychologist examiners shall have the following powers . . . (b) To adopt, and, from time to time, revise such rules and regulations not inconsistent with the law as may be necessary to carry into effect the provisions of this act. Such rules and regulations shall include, but not be limited to, (1) a code of ethics for psychologists in the state consistent with the current, and as future amended, ethical standards for psychologists of the American psychological association."
> Bylaw No. 1 under the Manitoba Psychologists Registration Act (1981):
> "Article XII. Standards of Conduct and Procedure for Expulsion and Withdrawal of Members

> 1. The Association hereby adopts the Ethical Standards of the Canadian Psychological Association as amended from time to time which upon registration of the member shall be binding upon each and every member of the Association."

As these provisions demonstrate, psychologists are often legally required to conform their behavior to the dictates of such codes. In many jurisdictions, the relevant code is repeated in full in the board's rules and regulations. However, in others it is simply incorporated by reference. In either case, psychologists must know and understand the relevant code because a violation can be a reason for disciplinary action.

The Complaint Process

Virtually all jurisdictions require that complaints concerning psychologists' behavior be in writing. Unless a complaint is determined to be frivolous or made in bad faith, an investigation ensues. In some jurisdictions, trained investigators are employed to perform this task. In smaller jurisdictions, a board member may be assigned as an investigating officer. The method used to investigate a complaint varies with the type or substance of the complaint. For example, an allegation that a licensee has been convicted of a felony would involve obtaining documentation from the court where the conviction occurred, whereas an allegation of sexual intimacies with a client would likely involve interviews and possibly collection of other evidence.

Constitutional and Statutory Protections

Enforcement of these codes involves the application of constitutional and statutory protections. A license to practice is a "property" right that cannot be taken away without due process of law. Therefore, U.S. agencies or disciplinary authorities must provide any licensee charged with an infraction at least the following:

1. Adequate notice of the charges.
2. An opportunity for a hearing.
3. A fair and impartial hearing panel.
4. The opportunity to confront and cross-examine adverse witnesses.
5. A decision based on the evidence.
6. A record of the proceedings.
7. Some form of judicial review.

These requirements are mandated by either the U.S. Constitution, most state constitutions, or state statutes. Similar protections are guaranteed by the Canadian Constitution and provincial constitutions.

In an effort to standardize procedures among administrative agencies, most of the requirements set out above have been incorporated in each jurisdiction's administrative procedures act.

Contested and Uncontested Cases

Most administrative procedure acts distinguish between cases in which the accused professional admits the charges and those in which the charges are denied. With the former, typically referred to as uncontested cases, there are provisions that allow the professional to waive his or her constitutional rights and consent to an informal disposition of the charges. Informal dispositions usually involve consent agreements entered into by the agency and the professional. Readers should not assume that informal dispositions involve only minor infractions. Often the most egregious infractions are involved because the professional may be overwhelmed by the damaging evidence and simply plead guilty and accept the resulting consequences.

Contested cases are quite different and proceed in a manner that is similar to civil trial–type proceedings. Often the actual hearing is preceded by a discovery phase that may involve interrogatories and depositions. The agency typically is required to subpoena witnesses for both the prosecution and the defense.

Actual hearings in disciplinary cases are conducted in different manners depending on the model utilized. There are three principal models. With the first, and more historical, the hearing is conducted entirely by the regulatory board members themselves. In such a model, the chair of the board sits as the hearing officer and rules on procedural and evidentiary issues.

In the second model, an attorney assists the regulatory board members by serving as the hearing officer and rules on motions and the various evidentiary issues that arise. The agency members in this model sit as a jury and determine the facts proven and the conclusions that should be drawn by applying the relevant law to the facts. The hearing officer then puts agency members' findings of fact and conclusions of law in the proper legal form prior to the issuance of the final order.

In the third model, adopted by many departments of professional regulation, an attorney conducts the entire hearing without the assistance of agency members. The attorney hears the evidence, determines both the facts and the conclusions, and issues a recommended order. That order is then reviewed by the agency members who must accept the recommendation, reject it, or modify it. Rejection or modification will be upheld only if there is evidence in the record of the proceeding to support the agency's decision.

The penalties available to psychology boards are diverse. They range from a simple written reprimand to permanent revocation of the psychologist's license. Between these two extremes other possibilities include continuing education, therapy, passage of examination(s), period of suspension, probation, restrictions on practice, supervised practice, administrative fines, and restitution to an injured client.

It is rare that a single sanction is imposed once a psychologist is found guilty of misconduct. More often, a punitive sanction is accompanied by a sanction designed to educate or rehabilitate.

Decisions in all such cases are also subject to judicial review. Whether the review occurs in a court of general trial jurisdiction, an appellate court, or both depends on the relevant statutes of the various jurisdictions. In some jurisdictions, the professional may be entitled to a new trial on appeal. In the majority of jurisdictions, however, the appeal only amounts to a review of the record of the hearing.

The Impact of Disciplinary Action on a Psychologist's License

There are a number of consequences when sanctions are imposed on a psychologist's license following a disciplinary hearing before a state or provincial regulatory board. If the discipline is serious enough, the practitioner may be removed from practice or his or her practice may be restricted. The jurisdiction that imposes the disciplinary sanction will also notify the Disciplinary Data System managed by the ASPPB. If the sanction is stronger than a reprimand, the information will be included in the next regularly scheduled disciplinary data report and transmitted to all other jurisdictions within North America. The sanction will also be permanently included in the association's data bank.

If the disciplined practitioner holds a license in another jurisdiction, it is highly likely that this (these) jurisdiction(s) also will take steps to impose disciplinary action based on the proceedings that occurred earlier. The notice will also be sent to entities such as the Registers in the United States and Canada, the ethics committees of the APA and the CPA, and the ABPP. These entities may take action to delist an individual whose license has been impaired or begin proceedings to remove the individual from membership in the organization or revoke the diploma issued to the practitioner.

The U.S. Department of Health and Human Services is also notified, and other sanctions may be imposed on the individual's practice by the U.S. government. Such sanctions include removal from Medicaid/Medicare programs. Many such sanctions will affect a practitioner's ability to obtain hospital privileges and approved status from health maintenance organizations and other third-party payers. It also is likely that disciplinary sanctions will affect the ability to obtain malpractice insurance and certainly the amount of the premium, if coverage can be obtained.

Applicable Case Law

There have been a number of cases in which appellate courts have reviewed the legal viability of requiring professionals to follow various ethical canons or codes of conduct. When courts have considered challenges to such requirements, they have usually been upheld. A good example is

State Board of Psychological Examiners v. Hosford (1987). Here the Supreme Court of Mississippi held that the Mississippi State Board of Psychological Examiners acted within its authority when it suspended the license of a clinical psychologist for 90 days, on a finding that he had violated Principle 5 of the APA's Ethical Principles of Psychologists and Code of Conduct (APA, 1992). The psychologist, after having counseled a couple with marital difficulties, submitted an affidavit during the ensuing divorce proceeding in which he recommended that custody of the couple's 6-year-old child be placed with the husband. Principle 5, which then required that information obtained in clinical or consulting relationships be held in confidence, encompassed not only the patient's words but also communications from the psychologist himself and opinions or impressions formed on the basis of the patients' communications.

The court also held that the board acted reasonably in ruling that the principle's "clear and present danger" exception should be read narrowly and that the psychologist's actions were not justified by the danger that the child might not be placed with the more suitable of the two parents.

Likewise is *Johnson v. Board of Examiners in Psychology* (1991). Here, the Arkansas Supreme Court upheld the use of the APA Code of Ethics for psychologists and rejected several constitutional challenges. The court upheld the board's rule against sexual dual relationships between psychologists and their patients, finding that the rule was not ambiguous.

However, these cases should be compared to *White v. North Carolina Board of Practicing Psychologists* (1990). This case involved a psychologist who was charged with 34 violations to the preambles to and the ethical principles contained within the Code of Ethics adopted by the North Carolina State Board of Examiners of Practicing Psychologists. Following the decision of the board to revoke his license for such violations, the respondent appealed, and a trial court affirmed the action of the board. The Court of Appeals of North Carolina considered the issues involved, including the challenge that the ethical principles utilized by the board were vague and unconstitutional under the North Carolina and U.S. constitutions. The court ultimately held that the preambles to the ethical principles would not place reasonably intelligent members of the psychological community on notice that any particular conduct was forbidden, and thus they were unconstitutionally vague and could not be used as the basis for disciplinary action against a psychologist.

At the same time, the court held that the actual ethical principles were not unconstitutionally vague and could be used as a basis for disciplinary action. The court eventually held that the evidence presented supported only six of the 34 charged violations and remanded the case to the board to consider whether, in view of the violations actually proven and affirmed, the psychologist's license should be revoked or suspended or any other appropriate action taken under North Carolina law.

This case gave a great deal of impetus to the ASPPB to formulate its Code of Conduct, a document that is quite specific in nature. It should also be noted that in 1992, the APA adopted a new version of its Ethical Principles, including a Code of Conduct.

Enforcement of Codes of Conduct by Professional Associations

Membership in a professional association is voluntary. Most professional associations provide important benefits to their members, ranging from opportunities to obtain continuing-education credits to various insurance programs. Other benefits may include opportunities to publish and forums in which to exchange information and ideas. In many ways, membership in professional associations is desirable and should be encouraged.

With the benefits of membership in professional associations come certain responsibilities. These include obvious responsibilities, such as the obligation to pay membership dues or otherwise provide financial support. One not-so-obvious responsibility is the requirement that members adhere to the code of ethics or code of conduct adopted by the association.

An explanation of this responsibility can be found in Frances B. Thomas' foreword to *Codes of Professional Responsibility* (1990). She writes:

> The professions have long carried distinct moral obligations with respect to public and private decisionmaking and behavior. What we do as professionals and how we do it, whether in commercial or nonprofit contexts, our sense of integrity, and our regard for self and others, affect the lives of everyone. There is no individual or group who is not touched—directly or indirectly, for better or worse—by how we deal with increasingly difficult and varied ethical matters. To address these matters is our task, our charge, and the highest order of professional responsibility to those around us. (p. v)

Failure to conform professional conduct to the expectations of the relevant code may result in the revocation of membership status. And many professionals belong to more than one professional organization, thus requiring conformance to multiple codes of ethics.

Recently, the California Court of Appeal considered the legal propriety of disciplinary actions within voluntary associations of psychologists. In *Budwin v. American Psychological Association* (1994), this court held that such an association could discipline a member for improper professional behavior.

Major Professional Associations in Psychology

The two largest professional associations in the United States and Canada are the APA and the CPA. These are not the only associations of interest to many psychologists. Examples of others include the American Association of Behavioral Therapy, American Psychological Society, Canadian Association of School Psychologists, National Association of School Psychologists, the Society for Child Development, and the Society for Industrial-Organizational Psychology.

APA Ethical Principles and Code of Conduct

APA has more than 142,000 members and affiliates. Its ethical code, now known as the APA Ethical Principles of Psychologists and Code of Conduct, was originally approved in 1952. Its most recent revision occurred in 1992. The full text of the APA code can be found in Appendix E.

The APA's bylaws establish an Ethics Committee, and the APA assigns certain full-time employees to staff the committee's activities. There are written procedures that dictate how the committee manages complaints made against current members.

Discipline by an association ethics committee can take various forms, the most serious being expulsion from the association. However, there are many other sanctions that can be rendered that are as nonpunitive as an "educative advisory." Other common sanctions include reprimands and censures.

Canadian Code of Conduct

The CPA (1991) created and maintains its *Canadian Code of Ethics for Psychologists*, which is used by some Canadian provincial regulatory bodies. Complaints against member psychologists that are received by the CPA are generally referred to the provincial psychological association for investigation and disciplinary action, if warranted (J. Service, personal communication, September 1995).

State and Provincial Associations' Ethics Committee Proceedings

Just as the American and Canadian psychological associations exist on the national level, in all North American jurisdictions there is at least one state or provincial psychological association. Also voluntary in nature, these associations operate under written bylaws that typically include provisions adopting a particular code of ethics and establishing procedures for disciplinary action.

Proceedings at the state or provincial level are dictated by those bylaws; however, most create an ethics committee made up of a small number of association members. Those members are empowered to hear complaints regarding members' conduct and to issue sanctions when necessary against a psychologist's membership status. A psychologist adversely affected by such a sanction on his or her membership is usually allowed to appeal the ethics committee's decision to the association's board of directors.

Conclusion

The enforcement of codes of conduct by regulatory agencies and by professional associations can provide a deterrent to professional misconduct.

For the desired deterrent effect to be realized, however, psychologists must remain aware of the ethical behavior that is expected of them and of the potential consequences of professional misconduct.

References

American Psychological Association. (1992). Ethical principles of psychologists and code of conduct. *American Psychologist, 47*, 1597–1611.

Budwin v. American Psychological Association, 29 Cal.Rptr.2d 453 (Cal. App. 1994).

Canadian Psychological Association. (1991). *Canadian code of ethics for psychologists. Revised.* Ottawa, ON: Author.

Code of Alabama 1975, Section 34-26-46(a)(17).

Idaho Code, Chapter 23, 54-2305 (1995).

Johnson v. Board of Examiners in Psychology, 808 S.W.2d 766 (Ark. 1991).

Manitoba Psychologists Registration Act, Bylaw Number 1 (1981).

State Board of Psychological Examiners v. Hosford, 508 So.2d 1049 (Miss. 1987).

Thomas, F. B. (1990). *Code of Professional Responsibility (2nd ed.)*. Washington, DC: BNA Books.

White v. North Carolina Board of Practicing Psychologists, 388 S.E.2d 148 (N.C. App. 1990).

8

Laws That Affect the Practice of Psychology

Randolph P. Reaves
Association of State and Provincial Psychology Boards

James R. P. Ogloff
Simon Fraser University

The statute that regulates the practice of psychology or use of the title psychologist in each jurisdiction is of obvious importance to psychologists. This statute authorizes a state or provincial body to promulgate administrative regulations. Together, the statute and regulations form the structure or legal framework for the regulation of the profession in each state and province.

However, these "practice acts," as they are commonly known, are not the only statutes relevant to the profession. In fact, in any jurisdiction, there are many more laws, some with attendant regulations, that are important for psychologists to know and understand.

Were we to attempt to identify and discuss all such statutes, as well as the differences between jurisdictions, this chapter would never end. In fact, the APA is publishing a series of books titled *Law and Mental Health Professionals* that will include a volume on the laws affecting the professional practice of psychology in each state and province. Our purpose here is to simply identify the types of statutes that affect psychological practice, with some explanation of the purpose and scope of each type.

Federal Compared With State or Provincial Laws

In the United States and Canada there are statutory schemes at both the federal and the state or provincial level. At the federal level, laws are made by the Canadian Parliament and the U.S. Congress. State and provincial laws are made by their various legislatures.

Both federal and state or provincial statutes can and do affect the practice of psychology. In the United States, most federal laws that have an impact on psychologists involve reimbursement for services rendered under federally funded programs. However, there are other laws at the federal level that can affect practice. Some of these would include the confidentiality laws that relate to drug and alcohol rehabilitation facilities, the myriad federal criminal provisions, and statutes that relate to the trial of many types of cases in U.S. federal courts.

In Canada, as in the United States, the laws relating to psychologists are more likely to be found at the provincial level. It is at that level that laws affecting child and family services, schools, health-care implementation, and the like are found. Federal laws rarely relate specifically to psychologists, with the exception of the Criminal Code of Canada (1985) and laws affecting federal employees, including psychologists.

The majority of statutes that affect psychologists on a regular basis have been or will be created at the state or provincial level of government. Consequently, most of the remainder of this chapter refers to those types of laws.

Laws That Involve the Legal System

There are literally hundreds of laws in every jurisdiction that may affect psychologists or the practice of the profession. Many of these involve the legal system and the trial of criminal or civil cases.

In the criminal-justice system, there are statutes that relate to the competency—or often in Canada, the "fitness"—of defendants to stand trial and the mental capacity to commit crimes. Defenses to certain acts of violence such as battered-wives syndrome, insanity, or even self-defense may require expert psychological testimony. The effect of violence on victims, such as rape trauma, may also require such testimony. There may be particular statutes that affect who may provide such testimony or put limitations on its use.

It is not unusual for psychologists to testify in civil cases, meaning cases involving the resolution of disputes between private individuals or corporations, and in many instances there are statutes that relate to expert testimony and production of records in such cases. Psychologists may become involved in issues such as the capacity of individuals to enter contracts or execute wills and the extent of injuries that follow accidents and intentional torts.

In Canada and the United States there are thousands of state and federal administrative agencies that hold hearings involving expert witnesses (e.g., workers compensation or parole hearings). Psychologists can and do participate in such hearings.

Regardless of whether the litigants are in civil or criminal court or before an administrative agency, psychologists also may be involved in issues relating to jury selection and decision making, polygraph evidence, hypnosis, and so forth. Often there are individual statutes that dictate which professionals may offer testimony on these matters.

Laws Relating to Liability

All psychologists should know that in each jurisdiction there are laws that affect the liability of various professionals. Examples include statutes addressing informed consent, the right to refuse treatment, malpractice liability, and quality assurance for hospital care. Most of these statutes are designed to place limits on liability for professionals who act in the line and scope of their duties as state or provincial or federal employees. Psychologists serving on regulatory boards, administrative tribunals, or peer-review committees are often protected by laws that relate to their liability for acts done in "good faith" in furtherance of regulation or quality assurance. Again, these statutes are typically designed to protect those professionals that serve as quasi-governmental officials.

Statutes That Protect Children and the Elderly

Virtually every U.S. and Canadian jurisdiction has a statute that requires individuals, including either explicitly or implicitly mental health professionals, to report suspected instances of child abuse or neglect to appropriate legal authorities. In most jurisdictions, these statutes are known as "child-abuse reporting acts," although they may bear differing names. Some jurisdictions in the United States and all the Atlantic provinces protect the elderly through the same or similar statutes, known as "elder-abuse reporting laws." Recently, some jurisdictions have passed similar statutes to protect adults in abusive relationships.

The purpose of these laws is obvious. They provide some guarantee of legal protection from physical or mental abuse of those too young to know or understand the abuse and too young or too old to protect themselves from such abuse.

Such statutes differ. For several reasons, every psychologist should know and understand the reporting requirements and specific conditions under which a report of abuse must be made in his or her jurisdiction. First, there is a need to protect those persons in society who may be unable to protect themselves. Second, there is the clear need to assist law-enforcement personnel in the investigation and possible prosecution of abusers. Finally, there can be serious criminal, civil, and license-related liability for a psychologist who fails to follow the mandates of such statutes. Most such statutes also provide protection from civil liability for those who report suspected abuse so long as the report is made in good faith.

Laws Relating to Families and Juveniles

There are a host of statutes in every jurisdiction that specifically address issues of the family. Some that may affect the practice of psychology include guardianship statutes; conservatorship laws; and the myriad statutes involving separation, divorce, and child custody.

In the United States, all states have a set of statutes that relate to juveniles, many of which may affect psychology practice. These statutes relate to such matters as juvenile neglect, dependency, and delinquency. Some such statutes involve the termination of parental rights, adoption, foster care, and conservatorship.

In Canada, the law pertaining to juvenile delinquents is found in the Young Offenders Act (1985), an act of Parliament separate from the Criminal Code of Canada (1985). Statutes pertaining to child abuse, neglect, and dependency as well as those relating to parental rights, custody, adoption, foster care, and conservatorship are all provincial acts that vary from one province to the next.

There are many other statutes that involve such issues as education for gifted and handicapped children, consent for health care (including abortion), capacity to marry, and the like. All may have some effect on psychological practice.

Civil Commitment Statutes

During the course of many psychologists' practice, situations will arise where a patient requires hospitalization. If such a patient is competent to consent to voluntary admission and does so, admission can be easily accomplished. However, if the patient is not competent to consent, or is competent and refuses, the psychologist may have to confront the involuntary civil commitment system. These laws are by nature complex and distressing. Knowledge of their scope is essential when the loss of a patient's freedom may be the end result.

Courts in the United States generally have ruled that a finding of danger to self or others is required for involuntary commitment. So in the United States, psychologists should be prepared to ask how substantial and how immediate is the risk of danger. In Canada, civil commitment laws vary considerably from province to province, with some requiring a finding of imminent danger and others permitting commitment for the more general protection of the patient or others. Some jurisdictions specify that a person be committed involuntarily only if he or she has refused voluntary commitment.

Laws That Relate to Psychologist–Patient Relationships

Ideally, every psychologist practicing today will have a solid understanding of the reasons for, and the parameters of, psychologist–patient confidentiality. The paramount legal provision that recognizes the confidentiality of communications between psychologists and patients in U.S. jurisdictions is typically found in the state practice act. This statute often likens these communications to those between attorneys and clients and creates a legally recognized privilege from disclosure. Although psychologist–patient communication is not in Canada a legally recognized privilege from disclosure, psychologists are nonetheless required to maintain patient confidentiality under most normal circumstances, as dictated by their professional ethics codes and by statute.

It is just as important, however, for psychologists to know the exceptions to confidential communications, which were referred to in chapter 5. There are others that can be found in a variety of ethics codes and statutes as well as other laws that can affect other aspects of the relationship between the provider and the patient.

Laws Involving Forms of Business Practice

All private practitioners will have to adopt some form of business practice. Some examples include sole proprietorships, partnerships, professional associations and professional corporations, and limited-liability companies. There may be others depending on the jurisdiction.

Choosing the appropriate form will likely require the assistance of an accountant, lawyer, or financial adviser. It is important to note that some jurisdictions have professional association or corporation laws that prohibit professionals from different licensed fields from owning stock in the same professional association or corporation.

All mental health professionals in private practice should obtain competent advice regarding responsibilities for state or provincial and federal taxes. Often these statutes require employers to withhold payments for their employees, including social security in the United States or pension-plan contributions in Canada, unemployment compensation insurance, and workers compensation. Tax laws are often complex and contain serious civil and criminal penalties for violations.

Statutes Involving Insurance and Third-Party Payers

Psychologists, particularly those in private practice, should be aware that there are a growing number of state and provincial statutes and attendant regulations that have an important effect on the financial operation of a psychologist's practice. Some statutes, such as "freedom of choice" laws, which exist in most states and the District of Columbia, require third-party payers to reimburse psychologists in the same manner as psychiatrists. Others, such as Medicare and Civilian Health and Medical Program for the Uniformed Services (CHAMPUS) statutes, dictate what a governmental plan will cover. A rudimentary knowledge of some of the statutes is crucial to successful practice as a psychologist. Psychologists should also understand the interrelationship of state and federal laws in this area. For example, many state freedom of choice laws have been severely affected by the federal Employer's Retirement Insurance Security Act (ERISA).

Medicare

In the United States, Medicare is a federally financed health-benefits program primarily for persons age 65 or older (Medicare Act, 1965). Medicare also covers certain disabled individuals. Medicare is administered by the states; however, the Health Care Finance Administration (HCFA), which is part of the U.S. Department of Health and Human Services, establishes the relevant rules and regulations. Reimbursement for psychologist's services provided to Medicare beneficiaries is severely restricted, although some recent changes allow for reimbursement on a limited basis.

In Canada, there is universal medical coverage for all citizens. At this time, psychologists in private practice are not included in the payment system, although psychological services may be provided as part of medical care in a hospital or outpatient clinic. Health-care delivery in Canada is governed by the Health Act (*Canada Health Act*, 1984) and is administered separately by each province. Psychological services also are provided to people under a variety of federal or provincial programs, and psychologists working within such programs need to be aware of the rules and regulations governing their respective program.

Medicaid

Medicaid is a medical-assistance program for certain low-income people in the United States. The Medicaid program is administered by individual states under broad federal guidelines (Medicaid Act, as amended 1984). Unlike Medicare, which is a federally financed and regulated program, Medicaid is financed by a combination of federal and state funds. The rules governing eligibility; the coverage of treatments, services, and procedures; and the method and amount of reimbursement vary widely from jurisdiction to jurisdiction.

The importance of Medicaid to psychologists can vary greatly as well, depending on their practice location and their ability to serve the indigent population.

Commercial Insurers

While it is uncertain what health care reform will mean to psychologists in the United States, more than two thirds of insured persons in the United States now rely exclusively on private insurance because most of the nonmilitary population is ineligible for Medicaid, Medicare, or other governmental health care programs. Laws that relate to the health-insurance industry are constantly changing at both the state and the federal level. In Canada, psychologists need to be familiar with regulations regarding extended health care and employee-assistance plans that may provide for the delivery of psychological services.

CHAMPUS

CHAMPUS provides nonmilitary health benefits to active-duty military personnel, retired personnel and their dependents, and dependents of deceased military personnel. Under CHAMPUS, a psychologist can obtain reimbursement for certain services by meeting qualifications and conditions.

Freedom of Choice

About 40 states and the District of Columbia have freedom of choice laws that prohibit health insurers from restricting the licensed providers from whom an individual may obtain certain psychological services. These laws are important to the practice of psychology because they assure the patient the right to see nonphysician as well as physician mental health care providers. Some of these laws also are referred to as "direct recognition" laws because they afford the consumer the right to have reimbursed services of a specified professional without a prior physician referral. Freedom of choice and direct recognition are distinct concepts, however, and some state laws provide freedom of choice only after physician referral, that is, without direct recognition of psychologists. And at least one federal statute complicates this area. The Employee Retirement Insurance Security Act (ERISA) preempts such state statutes and makes them inapplicable to health plans covered by this law.

Laws Regulating Health-Benefits Plans

Some states, such as Missouri, require that health-insurance policies offered for sale in their jurisdiction provide specific benefits, including mental health coverage. However, the scope of mandated benefits is the subject of litigation and legislative modification. In *Metropolitan Life Ins. Co. v. Massachusetts* (1985), the U.S. Supreme Court ruled that states can impose mandated benefits on insured health plans. However, this case did not decide whether such mandated benefits apply to self-insured employers' plans.

Laws Prohibiting Certain Billing Practices

There are statutes that prohibit certain types of billing practices. These include federal laws against fraud and abuse in the Medicaid and Medicare programs and state laws against kickbacks, fee-splitting, fraud, and similar activities. Health care fraud has been identified as a significant contributor to rising health costs in the United States, and therefore, these fraud and abuse laws have been enacted in many jurisdictions as well as at the federal level.

Conclusion

As this chapter shows, there are many statutes that affect the practice of psychology. The matter is further complicated by the fact that state and federal acts in the United States and provincial and federal acts in Canada vary considerably across jurisdictions. The intent of this chapter was to outline the nature of statutes that pertain to the practice of psychology. Individual psychologists must make themselves familiar with statutes and regulations that are relevant in their respective jurisdictions and that relate to their practice of psychology.

References

Canada Health Act, R.S.C., C. 6 (1984).

Civilian Health and Medical Program for the Uniformed Services (CHAMPUS), 10 U.S.C.A. 1072, 1079.

Criminal Code of Canada, R.S.C. C. C-46 (1985).

Employee Retirement Income Security Act, 29 U.S.C.A. 1001, et seq. (1982).

Medicaid Act, 42 U.S.C.A. Section 1396, et seq. (as amended 1994).

Medicare Act, 42 U.S.C.A. Section 1395, et seq. (1965).

Metropolitan Life Ins. Co. v. Massachusetts, 471 U.S. 724 (1985).

Young Offenders Act, R.S.C., C. Y-1 (1985).

9

Liability for Professional Misconduct

Randolph P. Reaves
Association of State and Provincial Psychology Boards

James R. P. Ogloff
Simon Fraser University

Introduction

The amount of ongoing litigation in the United States has reached appalling proportions, and although the growth in litigation has not been as severe in Canada, often the response to problems or differences among people is the initiation of a lawsuit. Although many people seem to abhor this growing trend, the fact remains unaltered. Although mental health professionals may enter practice concerned that they may someday be a defendant in a civil lawsuit, most never consider the possibility that they may face criminal charges or loss of their licenses. Although there are more professionals sued civilly, criminal and license-related cases are far more serious. Even more important is the possibility that inappropriate professional behavior may result in all three types of lawsuits.

This chapter is designed (a) to enlighten the reader as to types of legal liability, (b) to explore each type in depth, (c) to educate the reader regarding how to avoid such liability, and (d) to make suggestions about appropriate conduct if a psychologist is sued. Most of the general principles of civil liability in the United States and Canada emanate from English common law and are therefore similar. Differences exist, however, and such differences will be noted as necessary.

Civil Liability

Introduction

Every year, more and more civil lawsuits are filed against psychologists. Some rudimentary understanding of the causes should prove useful to all practitioners. The first part of this chapter discusses *theories of liability* and *causes of action*. The terms are used interchangeably, although *theory of liability* is more accurate. When a civil lawsuit is drafted, it must state a cause of action to meet the sufficiency requirements of the rules of civil procedure. The cause of action is thus the theory of the liability—the legal explanation of how the plaintiff was harmed and why he or she should recover damages in accordance with the principles of civil law. Malpractice includes a number of subtypes, such as failure to warn, sexual relationships with patients, and public disclosure of confidential information. These are not the only theories of liability that may form the basis for a civil suit, and although others are reviewed, they are less important. Suits on contract or fraud counts occur, but they are few compared with those brought for negligent conduct.

Malpractice, or Professional Negligence

Malpractice can be referred to as *professional negligence*. The term *malpractice* is frightening to most practitioners; however, it results in a legal advantage as compared with a regular negligence claim. To prove that a layperson involved in ordinary, everyday pursuits negligently caused him or her harm, a plaintiff must show the following:

1. That the defendant owed the plaintiff a duty recognized by law requiring him or her to exercise reasonable care not to harm him or her; and
2. That the defendant breached the duty of care; and
3. That the defendant's actions were the cause of the harm done to the plaintiff; and
4. That indeed the plaintiff suffered an injury.

With a malpractice case, the plaintiff's burden is much the same with respect to (3) and (4) above. However, in proving (1) and (2), the plaintiff is no longer dealing with the average, reasonable person standard. The plaintiff in a malpractice action must establish a duty recognized by law requiring the professional to exercise the degree of care, skill, and diligence ordinarily possessed and used by those in the same general line of practice under similar circumstances. Furthermore, they must prove breach of that duty.

To meet his or her burden of proof in a malpractice case, the plaintiff must establish the standard of care and the breach of the standard through an expert witness, a task more difficult than the proof of simple negligence (*Grote v. J. S. Mayer & Co., Inc.,* 1990; *Hubbard v. Laurelwood Hospital,* 1993; *Rudy v. Meshores,* 1985). In states where a "locality" rule exists (and there are a few left[1]), in the United States, the expert must be

[1]In Canada, the locality rule still has its devotees. Courts generally have continued to hold that a doctor's standard of skill is measured against doctors in similar locations under similar circumstances (see *Mang v. Moscovitz*, 1982; *McBride v. Langton*, 1982; *Neufeld v. McQuitty*, 1979).

knowledgeable or practice in the same locality with the defendant. That type of cooperation is difficult for the plaintiff to obtain. With most professions, it is much easier to find willing professionals to testify as experts for the defendant.

The "tort reform" movement of the late 1980s also was helpful to professionals. Several states imposed limits on malpractice damages. And there are a number of states that passed other statutes to lessen the impact of civil liability on health care professionals. In those states where courts have upheld the constitutionality of such legislation, insurance premiums should have been positively affected. (However, not all mental health professionals are included in the definition of health care provider found in some tort reform statutes; *Groth v. Weinstock*, 1992.) In Canada, traditionally, the amount of damages awarded in civil liability cases is far less than the amounts awarded in the United States.

Despite tort reform efforts in the United States and lower damages awards in Canada, there are many successful malpractice cases and more on the way. Why does a professional fall victim to such a suit? Often it is human error, occasionally ignorance, and—sadly—sometimes, intentional malice. A review of different types of malpractice actions may help answer that question more fully.

Failure to warn. There are probably few members of the psychological community who are not familiar with the name Tarasoff. Tatiana Tarasoff was a California teenager killed by a young man (Poddar) who was a patient at Cowell Memorial Hospital at the University of California at Berkeley. The killer was examined before the crime by a psychologist, who recommended that he be involuntarily committed; by two psychiatrists, who concurred with this evaluation and recommendation; and by another psychiatrist, chief of the department, who countermanded the psychologist's recommendation and directed the staff to take no action to confine him.

Poddar eventually carried out a previously expressed threat and killed the unknowing victim. One other important fact is that the psychologist warned campus police. Three officers took Poddar into custody but released him because they considered him rational.

For the purpose of this text, the importance of the *Tarasoff* case is in the conclusions reached by the Supreme Court of California (*Evans v. Morehead Clinic*, 1988; *Tarasoff v. Regents of the University of California*, 1976) regarding the liability of the psychologist and psychiatrists. The court held that under some circumstances, psychologists and psychiatrists may have a duty to protect third parties from the actions of their patients.

The court said that when such a professional determines, or pursuant to the standards of the profession should determine, that a patient presents a serious danger of violence to another, he or she incurs an obligation to use reasonable care to protect the intended victim from such danger. The court held that "the discharge of this duty may require the therapist . . . to warn the intended victim or others . . . to notify police, or to take whatever steps are necessary" (*Tarasoff*, 1976, p. 340). Thus, the Tarasoff doctrine imposes on therapists a duty to protect third parties from foreseeable harm by the therapist's client. The duty may also extend to other foreseeable persons who may be injured if the threat is carried out, such as a young child of the intended victim.

Mental health professionals need not be in practice long to understand how difficult such decisions can be. Practitioners recognize that predicting violent acts is unreliable, but this is rarely understood by laypeople. Moreover, the problems with confidential communications are clear and compelling, although both of these defenses were rejected in a Vermont decision, *Peck v. Counseling Service of Addison County* (1985).

There is no simple solution to the problem, and the usefulness of this theory of liability is not limited to California (see Fulero, 1988, for a review of the duty to protect doctrine in the United States). At least 15 states enacted "Tarasoff statutes" following that decision, including Alaska, California, Colorado, Florida, Indiana, Kansas, Kentucky, Louisiana, Massachusetts, Minnesota, Montana, New Hampshire, Ohio, Utah, and Washington (Smith, 1991). Furthermore, at least five or six other jurisdictions, in different parts of the United States, have embraced the theory. These now include Colorado (*Perreira v. Colorado*, 1989); Michigan (*Davis v. Lhim*, 1983/1988); Kansas (*Durflinger v. Artiles*, 1983); Georgia (*Bradley Center, Inc. v. Wessner*, 1982); and Kentucky (*Evans v. Morehead Clinic*, 1988). In other states, such as Wisconsin, significant settlements have been reached on the basis of such theories (*Lindsey v. Rousseau*, 1993). Most recently, the Arizona Supreme Court adopted a "zone of danger" test as the scope of a psychiatrist's duty to protect third parties. In that case, the foreseeability of the victim was the key (*Hamman v. County of Maricopa*, 1989). However, it is not a theory that will be easily accepted by many courts in our present conservative era. Similar cases have been lost in Indiana (*Webb v. Jarvis*, 1990); Iowa (*Matter of Estate of Votteler*, 1982); Minnesota (*Cairl v. State*, 1982); and South Carolina (*Ellis v. U.S.*, 1978).

Several courts have approved of a variety of defenses to such suits. A line of cases holds that there can be no liability when the patient has not made specific threats against readily identifiable victims (*Brady v. Hopper*, 1983; *Cairl v. State*, 1982; *Doyle v. U.S.*, 1982). At least two cases have held that the cause of action is not available when the foreseeable victim is aware of the danger (*Hinkleman v. Kalamazoo*, 1987; *Matter of Estate of Votteler*, 1982). And some cases immunize providers using a "psychotherapist judgment" rule, under which a court considers the good faith, independence, and thoroughness of a psychotherapist's decision in determining whether liability should be imposed (*Currie v. United States*, 1986; *Smith v. Fishkill*, 1991).

In any event, providers should be aware of the problem and prepare to face it someday. Readers may wish to refer to Monahan (1993) or Ogloff (1995) for a discussion of strategies for dealing with Tarasoff-type situations. In practice, therapists are more likely to experience the dilemma of warning or failing to warn the parents or other relatives of a potentially suicidal patient. Should the therapist breach the confidential nature of the relationship, lose the patient, and perhaps only frighten relatives and friends? Or in situations in which other options are available, what is the best choice?

Some of the options available to therapists confronted with this problem include therapeutic management of patient; discussing the matter with the patient; warning potential victims; calling police; seeking involuntary commitment of the patient consistent with state law; referring patient to a physician or another provider for prescription of medication; seeking assistance of other providers, clergy, or friends of the patient; and trying to involve the patient, family, or others in confronting and resolving the threatening situation.

Do not make the mistake that an emergency room physician made in *Tabor v. Doctors Mem. Hospital* (1986). There, the plaintiffs' son was brought to the emergency room after he was found to have taken 10 to 13 Quaaludes. He was denied admission on financial grounds because the emergency room physician refused to certify the case as an emergency. The young man killed himself the following day. Later at trial, a psychiatrist testified that issuance of an emergency certificate was required in cases where a patient was suicidal, and emergency room nurses testified that they were very concerned for the patient's safety and had urged the physician to issue the certificate. The Louisiana Court of Appeals held that reasonable men would likewise have found that the young man's suicide was causally connected to refusal of treatment. Nor is it advisable to leave a patient in the same room in which he tried to hang himself from the sprinkler pipes. The New York courts in *Kerker by Kerker v. Hurwitz* (1990) held that allowing the patient a second opportunity to do the same thing to himself was actionable as ordinary negligence and readably determinable based on common knowledge, and, thus, there was no need for expert testimony.

Most lawyers suggest that the conservative approach is best. If, in a provider's professional opinion, the person is a threat to himself or herself or another, the provider should take steps to warn someone if the individual cannot or will not be committed, and document efforts to do so. Clinicians can take some comfort in knowing that if they make an honest error in diagnosing the situation and the client, they may not necessarily be held liable for damages so long as they can demonstrate that they exercised reasonable care in their work (*Haines v. Bellissimo*, 1977).

Failure to protect. Closely akin to failure-to-warn cases are those referred to as *failure to protect*. They also are similar to negligent release cases, and both causes of action are typically alleged.

A failure-to-protect case differs from a failure-to-warn case in that the victim in the former is rarely identified or identifiable. Liability is predicated upon the negligence of the provider, which allows the patient access to the victim.

A good example is *Tamsen v. Weber* (1990, see also *Schuster v. Altenberg*, 1988), in which a patient escaped from the Arizona State Hospital and later abducted a passerby and beat her severely. The litigation later revealed that Traham (the patient) was admitted to the hospital as a danger to himself. While there he attempted suicide. Records that were ultimately produced indicated he was suffering from major depression recurrent with psychotic features and, as one expert testified, was "thinking of killing people."

Nevertheless, the attending psychiatrist granted Traham unsupervised ground privileges. During an unsupervised period on the hospital grounds, he escaped and assaulted Tamsen the next day. The Arizona Court of Appeals held that the psychiatrist owed a duty to protect Tamsen from the violent acts of Traham although Tamsen was not an identifiable victim. Therefore, the alleged negligence in granting unsupervised ground privileges should have gone to a jury on the issue of causation.

Some cases that involve harm done by one patient to another might logically fall in this area. A good example is *Halverson v. Pikes Peak Family Counseling and Mental Health Center, Inc.* (1991). Here a patient was sexually assaulted by another patient with a history of violent behavior while she was an inpatient at the facility.

Whether or not such victims have the legal standing to sue a provider or facility is often an issue. In *Santa Cruz v. N. W. Dade Com. Health Ctr.* (1991), the District Court of Appeals of Florida held that there was no duty on the part of the psychiatrist or mental health center to detain a voluntary patient or to have him involuntarily committed, and they were not liable for failing to do so to those subsequently injured by the patient.

Whenever a provider is dealing with a potentially dangerous patient, adequate record keeping is a must. The practitioner should document everything done to comply with professional standards.

Before leaving this area of liability, it would be prudent to explore the duty to warn or protect foreseeable victims from patients with sexually transmittable diseases. The problem of confidentiality and AIDS poses a dilemma for practitioners. Already a number of physicians have been sued by patients on such theories as negligent infliction of emotional distress when treated by an HIV-positive practitioner who failed to reveal the condition and obtain consent (*Faya v. Almaraz*, 1993; *Howard v. Alexandria Hospital*, 1993). Many therapists are concerned with the notion that they might be put in the position of having to advise an individual that should the presence of HIV be revealed to them, they would have no choice but to warn foreseeable victims. That concern is understandable. However, viewing that situation from a purely legal point of view, it easily fits into the failure-to-warn/protect doctrines.

There is no doubt that an individual who is HIV positive could do considerable harm to an unknowing spouse or sexual partners. Already there have been numerous successful suits against sexual partners (*Duke v. Housen*, 1979; *Kathleen K. v. Robert B.*, 1984; *Long v. Adams*, 1985). In many cases, those spouses or partners would be known to the provider and therefore foreseeable victims who could be notified. Arguably, courts will find it easier to uphold a failure to warn (protect) theory in this situation than with a potentially violent person.

For an example of such a case involving Rocky Mountain spotted fever, a noncontagious disease, the reader should be aware of *Bradshaw v. Dan-*

iel (1993). There, the Supreme Court of Tennessee held that a physician–patient relationship is not necessary to maintain a negligence suit. The court went on to hold, citing *Tarasoff* at length, that the existence of the physician–patient relationship is sufficient to impose on a physician an affirmative duty to warn identifiable third persons in the patient's immediate family against foreseeable risks emanating from a patient's illness.

A working group on HIV confidentiality at Creighton University's Center for Health Policy and Ethics, Omaha, Nebraska, after conducting a national study on confidentiality in maternal and pediatric HIV, also citing *Tarasoff*, suggested a formula for decision making relative to such disclosures: "When the risk of infection is significant, the identity of the third party is known, warning is likely to be effective in preventing infection, and every reasonable measure to convince the patient to disclose has failed, professionals have a strong ethical obligation to warn those at risk" (Center for Health Policy and Ethics, 1992).

Tarasoff in Canada. To date, the Tarasoff doctrine creating a duty to warn/protect third parties has not been directly expanded into Canadian case law. However, an Alberta court noted that a mental health professional or hospital might be liable for resulting damages if a therapist knew a client was going to harm an identified third party and did not take steps to protect that party (*Wenden v. Trikha*, 1991; see also Birch, 1992). In *Wenden*, a psychiatric patient who was in the hospital on a voluntary basis left the hospital and drove his car recklessly into another car, injuring the other driver. The driver sued the patient's psychiatrist and hospital, arguing that the psychiatrist did not exercise reasonable care to prevent the patient from driving. However, in holding the hospital and psychiatrist not liable, the judge held that reasonable care was exercised because the doctor had warned the patient that to drive while he was still ill would be dangerous. In distinguishing the case from *Tarasoff*, the court noted that it would have been impossible for the psychiatrist to warn or protect all potential accident victims because they were unidentifiable.

It should be noted that although courts in Canada have not recognized the duty to protect or warn third parties from the actions of psychiatric patients generally, there is little doubt that hospitals are responsible for protecting patients and others in the hospital. In *Lawson v. Wellesley Hospital* (1975), a psychiatric patient struck and injured another patient. The injured patient sued the hospital, arguing that the hospital was liable for her injuries because the hospital had known that the patient was dangerous. The court held that the hospital owed a duty of care to patients to protect them from the reasonably foreseeable actions of patients in the hospital's care. In *Lawson*, the psychiatric patient had a history of assaultive behavior, both in and out of the hospital, that was known to the hospital.

It is important for psychologists in Canada to note that although the law has not recognized a general duty to warn or protect third parties as to the actions of their patients, the *Canadian Code of Ethics for Psychol-*

ogists (Canadian Psychological Association, 1991) clearly imposes such a duty (see chap. 4 in this volume). Because provincial statutes that regulate the professional practice of psychology require psychologists to act in accordance with their code of ethics, it would appear that psychologists have a legal duty to prevent clients from seriously harming or killing third parties.

As in the United States, psychologists in Canada can be found liable for patients' suicides if they are negligent in not preventing them (*Haines v. Bellissimo*, 1977). In *Haines*, a clinical psychologist evaluated a patient to assess his potential for suicide. The psychologist concluded that the patient was not suicidal and decided to continue to treat him on an outpatient basis rather than to hospitalize him. The next day, though, the patient killed himself, and the patient's widow sued the psychologist for malpractice. The court held that the psychologist owed the patient the degree of reasonable skill, care, and knowledge possessed by the average psychologist. The court held that the psychologist used reasonable care and was not negligent, although he did make a mistake. Thus, a psychologist who failed to exercise reasonable care in conducting a suicide assessment may be found negligent and may be liable for damages.

Failure to properly supervise hospitalized patients. Because of a special relationship that exists between a therapist and a patient, a recognizable duty often arises to protect the patient from himself or herself. Breach of the duty occurs when the therapist does, or more often fails to do, something that allows the patient to harm himself or herself.

A good example of such a case is *Smith v. Rush Presbyterian St. Luke's Medical Center* (1980), in which a young male with "paranoid personality" was admitted to a psychiatric hospital. Following futile attempts to cut his wrists with a pop top, the patient was put on a "suicide risk" list, which required observation every 15 min. The patient also was placed in a room with an electrically operated bed and, while unobserved, lowered the bed onto his neck and head. The jury verdict was $75,000.

There are a host of such cases and a variety of negligent acts or omissions involved. For instance, there is *Abille v. United States* (1980), where a psychiatric patient jumped from an Air Force hospital window. Not only was the patient unattended, but the window had no security device, such as a detention screen. Similar to *Abille* are *Peterson v. Roosevelt Hospital* (1982), *Radzikowski v. Metcalfe* (1979), and *Stanisci v. New York Hosp.* (1992).

In *Pisel v. The Stamford Hospital* (1979), the patient, again unattended, wedged his head into the rails of his bed resulting in brain damage. With *Roesler v. Menorah Medical Center* (1978), the patient used a pillowcase to strangle herself, and in *Herndobler v. Riveredge Hospital* (1979), an unrestrained patient suffocated herself with a plastic garbage can liner. In *Campbell v. United States* (1980, see also *Vattimo v. Lower Bucks Hosp., Inc.*, 1983), a woman with a diagnosis of paranoid schizophrenia with an active psychosis and a history of suicide attempts was admitted to a Navy hospital with a gun in her purse. No one bothered to search the purse or take it from her. She later attempted to kill herself, sustaining severe brain damage. And in a more recent case, a New York jury awarded substantial damages to a boy who suffered blindness after repeatedly rubbing his eyes and striking his head while hospitalized at a state psychiatric center. The case was tried on an inadequate supervision theory (*Jones v. State of New York*, 1991).

There has been a flurry of cases (*Baher v. State*, 1989; *Donson v. Baez*, 1991; *Halverson v. Pikes Peak*, 1991; see also the Canadian case of *Lawson v. Wellesley Hospital*, 1975) recently in which courts have predicated liability on negligent supervision that resulted in injury to other patients. Almost all of these cases involve either rape or other serious physical injuries. Some were perpetrated by other patients, and some involved employees of institutions.

Negligent release of dangerous patients. Similar to the failure-to-protect type of negligence action is the suit brought for the negligent release of a dangerous patient. Take for instance *Davis v. Lihm* (1983/1988), a Michigan case in which the deceased's 25-year-old son was originally admitted to a state hospital with a diagnosis of paranoid schizophrenia and a history of suicide attempts. Over a 3-year period, the patient was admitted and released five more times. His records indicated not only his suicidal tendencies, but the fact that he committed himself to avoid problems at home. Two weeks after the patient's last discharge, his mother was shot and killed by him while trying to prevent his suicide attempt. The case was tried on both theories, negligent release and failure to warn, and resulted in a jury verdict of $500,000. The case was reversed 5 years later, but on the ground of governmental immunity rather than failure to warn.

Another case of this type is *Durflinger v. Artiles* (1983, see also *Petersen v. State of Washington*, 1983), a Kansas suit brought by the estate of a woman and her son, killed by another son who had been released from a state psychiatric hospital. The young man had been committed after he was found holding an ax over both grandparents and he admitted he intended to kill and rob them. He was diagnosed as having a passive–aggressive personality with sociopathic tendencies. For reasons relating to time and the expense of keeping or transferring him to another facility, he was released after 3 months. Less than a week after his release, he killed both his mother and brother to get the family car to visit a friend at the hospital from which he had been released. The case resulted in judgments of more than $117,000.

Negligence in failing to admit suicidal patients or prematurely releasing such patients has also given rise to liability. An example is *Dunn v. Howard University Hospital* (1983), in which a 28-year-old woman was released from an emergency room after a short period of observation. She had been brought to the emergency room by a friend and complained of severe anxiety, depression, and guilt feelings. She also expressed a desire for suicide and self-maiming. The woman had a history of hospitalizations and was previously diagnosed as a manic-depressive psychotic. After her release, she jumped to her death. A court later awarded her parents $500,000.

Failure to prevent a patient from escaping from a mental institution can also give rise to liability, particularly if others are injured apprehending the patient. A classic example is *Santangelo v. State* (1993), in which two police officers were injured. Evidence in the case revealed that the patient had many previous successful escapes from the institution and that three of those escapes had been accomplished in the same manner. The court agreed that these facts indicated an unreasonable and careless attitude on the part of the state toward the safety of the public as it related to the custody and supervision of the patient. Additionally, the state also violated its regulations by marking the patient as "discharged" 30 days after his escape.

If a provider is required to defend a claim of negligent release of dangerous patients, there is helpful case law. Some courts have simply decided that no such duty is owed to the members of the general public (*Leonard v. State*, 1992). Some rely on the "psychotherapist judgment rule" referred to earlier (*Ellis v. United States*, 1978). Other courts hold, in appropriate factual situations, that the passage of time breaks the causal connection between the alleged negligence and the victim's injury (*Barnes v. Dale*, 1988). And some find immunity for providers employed by governmental entities (*Novak v. Rathnam*, 1987).

A number of states have passed legislation to reduce liability in this area, particularly where the victim is not readily foreseeable. This is a double-edged sword, because the passage of such a law is statutory recognition of the civil cause of action.

Canadian readers are reminded that the court in *Haines v. Bellissimo* (1977) requires them to exercise the reasonable skill, care, and knowledge possessed by the average psychologist when conducting assessments of suicidal patients.

Negligent prescription of contraindicated drugs. Another cause of action that should be of particular interest to psychiatrists and psychiatric clinics, and in the future to prescribing psychologists, is the negligent prescription of contraindicated drugs. This cause of action includes the same elements as other types of professional negligence. It goes without saying that almost every practitioner has a duty to act in a manner that does not cause the patient's condition to worsen. Breach of that duty occurs when the contraindicated drugs—those liable to cause the patient harm rather than effectuate a cure—are prescribed. Doctors are obligated to warn patients about the possible side effects associated with medication (*Crichton v. Hastings*, 1972). Then the doctor must determine at the earliest possible time whether adverse side effects are present and must act to stop the harm.

A good example of this type of action is *Webb v. Lightburn* (1980), a Colorado suit settled for $100,000. In this case, the decedent was diagnosed as having a passive–aggressive personality disorder with depressive and hysterical features and a history of drug overdoses. Despite such, and only days after an attempted suicide, the defendant psychiatrist renewed two prescriptions for Seconal. The patient took them all a few days later and died.

Another $100,000 settlement was reached in a New York case styled *Haggerty v. New York* (1985). In this case, the deceased had been hospitalized previously for suicidal tendencies. On the occasion of his last commitment, Tofranil was prescribed for him, even though his medical records reflected the fact that Tofranil exacerbated his suicidal tendencies. While the ward attendant was asleep, the patient hanged himself with his belt. A similar but more recent case is *Greene v. Guarino* (1992), which involves a substantial settlement for the estate of a man who allegedly committed suicide by ingesting a 30-day supply of an antidepressant. The psychiatrist who prescribed the drug was sued on the theory that he negligently provided a suicidal patient with a toxic amount of the drug.

These are the obvious types of cases, but when dealing with medication of the mentally ill, a number of other areas of potential liability arise. They include the failure to prescribe adequate antipsychotic medication, allowing individuals to cause injury to themselves, an example of which is *Jansen v. University Hospital* (1983). Another area is the potential for creating a drug dependency. A large verdict resulted in a case styled *Badger v. Greenfield* (1981), where a plaintiff produced sufficient proof that his psychiatrist negligently created a drug dependency, which later resulted in the loss of significant income when the patient became unable to work.

Excessive administration of Antabuse has also resulted in large verdicts (*Sawyer v. Tauber*, 1985), but the main area of liability, with the largest verdicts, occurs with the improper use of medication like Mellaril, Penothiazine, Stelazine, Haldol, and Triavil. A trilogy of cases arising in Iowa (*Clites v. State of Iowa*, 1981); Colorado (*Collins v. Cushner*, 1982); and Michigan (*Faigenbaum v. Oakland Medical Center*, 1982) indicate that confined patients who develop tardive dyskinesia are the patients who will obtain the most staggering settlements and verdicts. However, for a case involving significant liability when a patient's Haldol dosage was suddenly reduced and damages occurred, see *Leal v. Simon* (1989).

Counsel defending cases involving negligent prescribing should review a number of cases in which the plaintiff's evidence proved insufficient to support a cause of action (*Allen v. Kaiser Foundation Hospital Inc.*, 1985; *Speer v. United States*, 1981).

Psychologists, particularly in rural areas, are often put in a position of giving opinions to physicians such as general practitioners regarding certain medications. Under the general rule, no duty arises until a provider actually undertakes the patient's care and treatment (*Bankston v. Alexandria Neurosurgical Clinic*, 1991; *Flynn v. Bausch*, 1991; *Rainer v. Grossman*, 1973). However, serious thought should be given to the type of response, if any, to such questions, especially in the light of ethical requirements that a psychologist confine his or her practice to areas in which the psychologist is competent.

Negligence of auxiliaries. Before concluding this section on negligence, it should be noted that often the person at fault in such cases is not the primary provider but the staff or clinic auxiliary. The laws of agency and respondeat superior require a principal to accept responsibility for the actions of his or her agents so long as the agent is acting within the scope of his or her employment. Canadian courts have made clear that a doctor may rely on hospital staff to aid in properly carrying out the doctor's duties; however, the doctor cannot delegate his or her own duties to the staff (see *Cosgrove v. Gaudreau*, 1981). The doctor–patient, or, for that matter, psychologist–client, relationship imposes duties on the professional that cannot be delegated away (*Crichton v. Hastings*, 1972). Therefore, a psychologist may be liable for the acts of other staff employees if the psychologist knows, or reasonably should know, that the employees are performing their duties in a careless or negligent manner and the psychologist does not take reasonable steps to safeguard the patient.

If the primary provider hires any personnel to assist in his or her practice, he or she must be aware that any negligent acts committed by these assistants will, more than likely, be imputed to him or her. This situation can be exacerbated if the assistant is not properly qualified, trained, or supervised by the primary provider. A classic example is *Andrews v. United States* (1984), where a physician's assistant engaged in sexual relations with a female patient under the guise of treatment. Another example is *Doe v. Belmont College* (1992), where a patient sued the counselor's partner, a licensed psychologist, for inadequate supervision and the college that employed both for negligent hiring.

An even better example is *Huntley v. State of New York* (1984), in which a patient at a state psychiatric hospital was permitted to leave the hospital premises and attempted to commit suicide by jumping from the roof of a nearby parking garage. Evidence later revealed that the patient had disclosed her specific suicide plans to a hospital staff member the day before the incident, and the staff member had failed to transmit such information to the staff psychiatrist who controlled the patient's privileges to leave the hospital premises.

Another common mistake that can lead to harmful publicity and liability is the careless misrepresentation of the credentials of staff personnel. The practitioner should pay close attention to the legal requirements for titles or designations of unlicensed personnel and closely observe any published standards for supervision.

Careful attention to prospective employees' past job performance is also important. There is a growing body of case law involving negligent hiring of unqualified, incompetent, or unethical providers in the mental health fields (*Pickle v. Cums*, 1982; *Richter v. Northwestern Memorial Hospital*, 1988).

Sexual Relations With Clients

Sexual intimacies with clients or patients are forbidden by recognized codes of conduct for psychologists. The harm such conduct does to victims has been studied and clearly documented (Council on Ethical and Judicial Affairs, 1991). Similar to the reactions of women who have been sexually assaulted, female patients tend to feel angry, abandoned, humiliated, mistreated, or exploited by their therapists (Council on Ethical and Judicial Affairs, 1991). The largest civil judgments have been reserved for those professionals that engage in such heinous conduct. (See Exhibit 1 for a discussion on avoiding sexual misconduct charges.)

With such a case, the practitioner must consider the possibility that punitive damages will be awarded (*MacClements v. Lafore*, 1991; *Marston v. Minneapolis Clinic*, 1982). In fact, between 1976 and 1986, "sexual re-

---

Exhibit 1

The majority of practitioners are ethical and would never engage in sexual misconduct. How can the innocent mental health professional avoid such a claim of sexual misconduct? Unfortunately, he or she can't avoid the possibility entirely, but steps can be taken to reduce vulnerability.

First of all, never engage in such activities with a current or former client. Conversely, never agree to treat a former sexual partner. Never make sexual overtures to a client and avoid comments and actions that might be interpreted as sexual in nature. Other than shaking hands, do not touch a patient. Don't see clients in social settings and try to avoid self-disclosure. Recognize and respect professional boundaries. Psychologists must be aware of their own emotions, vulnerabilities and stresses, and guard against allowing them to compromise objectivity and professional judgment.

If concerned about objectivity toward a client, a therapist should seek consultation with a trusted colleague or mentor. If uncomfortable with a relationship, refer the client to another provider.

Also remember that a plaintiff's verdict is the result of a series of successfully created images paraded before a sympathetic jury. Beware of the patient who tries to schedule sessions at odd hours or reschedules appointments for hours when the office is normally closed. Again, avoid self-disclosure and never disclose things about your own body, such as scars, that can be seen only when unclothed.

Schedule staff personnel to ensure that someone, preferably a secretary or female assistant, is always near. The presence of an auxiliary within the office area or clinic will tend to discredit the untruthful plaintiff. Be cautious about waiving fees without considering the potential misinterpretation by a sympathetic jury. If a mental health professional becomes involved with a patient, he or she has no alternative but to terminate the therapist–patient relationship immediately, refer the patient to another therapist, and document both.

---

lations with clients was the most frequent cause of suits against psychologists insured under the American Psychological Association's policy; the suits accounted for 44.8% of all monies ($7,019,165) paid in response to claims" (Jorgenson, Randles, & Strasburger, 1991, footnote 15). How much will it take to punish a therapist making $200,000 a year? A La Jolla, California jury (*Walker v. Parzan*, 1981) set the figure at $4,500,000, whereas a Pensacola, Florida, jury (*Rotenberry v. Wilhoit*, 1980) assessed it at $375,000. When sexual abuse was coupled with improper drug treatment, a Maryland jury returned a verdict of $700,000 (*DiLeo v. Nugent*, 1991). And many of these verdicts will not be covered by malpractice insurance (no coverage—*Hirst v. St. Paul*, 1984; *Smith v. St. Paul*, 1984; coverage—*St. Paul v. Love*, 1989; *St. Paul v. Mitchell*, 1982; *Vigilant Ins. Co. v. Kambly*, 1982). In some cases, the lawsuit is actually brought by the spouse of the actual victim, when both are in therapy and such a relationship evolves (*Richard H. v. Larry D.*, 1988).

At least one state's highest court has held that a psychologist who initiates sex with a patient can be liable for negligent infliction of emotional distress. And in *Corgan v. Muchling* (1991), the Illinois Supreme Court also held that the patient need not allege or prove physical injury to pursue liability under this cause of action. Additionally, some cases find that employment facilities are also liable when such conduct occurs. A good example is *Doe v. Samaritan Counseling Center* (1990; see also *Marlene F. v. Affiliated Psychiatric Medical Clinic*, 1989).

Public Disclosure of Confidential Information

A special relationship exists between therapists and their patients. Confidentiality of communication is the base on which this relationship exists. Public disclosure of confidential communications can give rise to liability if the substance of the facts revealed is offensive, embarrassing, objectionable, or harmful to the patient's reputation (*Crippen v. Charter Southland Hosp.*, 1988; *Horne v. Patton*, 1973).

Any practitioner would be well advised to make certain that the privilege exists before advising a potential client. The circumstances surrounding the manner in which the information was obtained may destroy the privilege (*People v. District Court*, 1990). Changing statutes and emerging case law make this a real concern. A good example of this dilemma is *State ex rel. v. Ashley* (1990), in which the Oregon Court of Appeals ruled that the psychotherapist–patient privilege did not apply to communications made during drug counseling (see also *In the Interest of Doe*, 1990).

It should be emphasized that in Canada, the law does not formally recognize a therapist–client, psychologist–client, or even a physician–patient privilege. On a case-by-case basis, courts have recognized a "limited privilege" for psychologists and counselors who protect against the disclosure of confidential information (*Porter v. Porter*, 1983). The Supreme Court of Canada approved the criteria set out by Wigmore (*Slavutych v. Baker*, 1976):

1. The communications must originate in a confidence that they will not be disclosed.
2. This element of confidentiality must be essential to the full and satisfactory maintenance of the relation between the parties.
3. The relation must be one which, in the opinion of the community, ought to be sedulously fostered.
4. The injury that would enure to the relation by the disclosure of the communications must be greater than the benefit thereby garnered for the correct disposal of litigation.

Thus, in a case where a claim of psychologist–client privilege is being made, these four criteria must be satisfied.

Patients obviously should be informed of limitations on confidentiality, for example, when a patient becomes a danger to herself or others. Suits occasionally are brought for wrongful disclosure in such situations. However, at least two courts have recognized the provider's responsibility to warn intended victims and have dismissed suits against providers under the "dangerous patient" exception to the privilege (*Mendendez v. Superior Court*, 1992).

In the area of child custody disputes, psychologists should act cautiously. Do not evaluate a minor without the custodial parent's consent. Know your state or provincial laws as regards confidentiality, advise the parent(s) correctly, and document the advice carefully.

It would also be an excellent idea to review related case law. Several courts have ruled favorably on plaintiff's claims for invasion of privacy and intentional infliction of emotional distress (*Crippen v. Charter Southland Hosp.*, 1988; *Horne v. Patton*, 1973). Psychologists treating patients suffering from AIDS should be especially careful and know not only case law but also antidiscrimination laws where such exist (*Behringer Estate v. Princeton Medical Center*, 1991). Counsel defending such a claim should review the cases resolved in favor of defendants, such as *Werner v. Kliewer* (1985), *Jordan v. Kelly* (1984), and *Williams v. Congdon* (1979).

Another case of great significance is *Snow v. Koeppl* (1990), which involved the revelation of allegedly confidential information in a family court case. In this case, the Wisconsin Court of Appeals upheld a trial court's decision to dismiss claims for invasion of privacy and breach of confidentiality. The suit was brought against a psychologist who obtained and delivered to the court excerpts from the plaintiff's earlier counseling records pursuant to a court-ordered psychological evaluation of the plaintiff in a family court action. The appellate court agreed that the psychologist was entitled to absolute immunity.

The reviewing court concluded that a judicial order creating official duties, directly and closely connected to court proceedings, should be broadly construed in favor of the person required to act. Thus, a directive to perform a psychological evaluation would be construed to protect the court official from liability for the examination and use of reports of earlier psychological counseling or therapy, because such information bore a general frame of reference and relation to the subject matter of the court's order.

A similar case is *Guity v. Kandilakis* (1991), where a psychologist was ordered by a trial court judge to testify about matters arising during joint counseling sessions with a husband and wife. When the husband later sued the psychologist, the court held that he was immune from suit because the court had ordered him to disclose. Just as important is *Howard v. Drapkin* (1990), in which a disgruntled parent sued a psychologist hired by both parties to evaluate allegations of sexual abuse for a custody proceeding. The trial and appellate courts agreed that (a) the psychologist was entitled to common-law immunity as a quasi-judicial officer participating in the judicial process and (b) the psychologist was entitled to a statutory privilege for publication in a judicial proceeding.

In an important 1994 case (*Bird v. W. C. W.*, 1994; see also *Health Law Digest*, 1994), the Texas Supreme Court held that a mental health professional does not owe a duty to a parent not to negligently misdiagnose a child's condition. The court decided that although a risk of harm to a parent accused of sexual abuse was foreseeable, it was outweighed by the need to allow mental health professionals dealing with the sensitive issue of child abuse to exercise their professional judgment in diagnosing abuse "without the judicial imposition of a countervailing duty to third parties."

However, also note the case of *Awai v. Kotin* (1993), in which the Colorado Court of Appeals held that court-appointed psychologists were not entitled to absolute immunity from claims that they negligently treated a parent referred to them for evaluation in a divorce/child custody proceeding. The court held that absolute immunity for quasi-judicial functions applied only to those functions intimately related and essential to the judicial decision-making process.

Before leaving this area of potential liability, it would be prudent to review recent case law abrogating the statutory privilege in parental rights termination cases and divorce litigation. In Alabama, for example, there have been three such cases (*Harbin v. Harbin*, 1986; *Matter of Von Goyt*, 1984; *Wallace v. Jefferson Co.*, 1986) that give cause for much concern. These cases recognize that privileged communication exists; however, the courts have ruled that the welfare of the child outweighs the need for confidentiality (*In the interest of Bender*, 1987; *Matter of Adoption of Embick*, 1986; *Perry v. Fiumano*, 1987).

Also, practitioners should read their state or provincial statute on child abuse reporting and, furthermore, research applicable case law because some potential for liability exists (*Montoya by Montoya v. Bebensee*, 1988). In fact, for a case involving a licensed social worker, the reader should review *Olson v. Ramsey County* (1993). Here, the Court of Appeals of Minnesota held that a social worker's implementation of a child protection plan was not a policy decision. Therefore, the doctrine of discretionary immunity (similar to sovereign immunity) did not apply to protect the county and social worker from liability in an action for the wrongful death of the child that was the subject of the plan. Again, err on the conservative side. There are many statutes and much case law protecting those who are concerned enough to report suspected child abuse (*Brown v. Pound*, 1991; *E. S. by D. S. v. Seitz*, 1987; *Thomas v. Chadwick*, 1990).

Record Keeping and Liability

The primary purpose of building a patient record is to document that treatment occurred and to facilitate coordination of services for the patient (Vandecreek, 1986). Appropriate record keeping is not necessarily proof of quality care, but inadequate records are certainly evidence of inadequate treatment, particularly in a hospital setting (Reaves, 1995). A number of cases recognize this fact (e.g., *Donaldson v. O'Connor*, 1974; *Whitree v. State*, 1968).

There even have been cases in which inadequate record keeping was the cause of the patient's harm:

1. *Gasperini v. Manginelli* (1949), where a psychologist inadvertently omitted the suffix "Jr." from a written diagnosis, and request for hospitalization resulting in a libel suit by the patient's father;
2. *Jablonski v. U.S.* (1983), where a federal court held that a psychiatrist should have known that a patient had a history of violence toward his lovers and that the psychiatrist had failed to obtain proper treatment records, which documented the patient's violent behavior.

Inappropriate or Negligent Release

Practitioners should consult local counsel regarding their responsibility to respond to requests for patient records. In some jurisdictions, an untested subpoena is not the binding type of court order that obligates a provider to release patient records (*Allen v. Smith*, 1988; *Cutter v. Brownbridge*, 1986). Particular care should be given to mental health records that are specifically protected from disclosure by state or federal statute (*Matter of W. H.*, 1993).

Practitioners should also be very careful when dealing with patients infected with HIV. A number of courts have addressed patients' rights to confidentiality. In fact, the Maryland Court of Special Appeals acknowledged in a 1991 decision the presumption of confidentiality of medical records (*Doe v. Shady Grove Adventist Hospital*, 1991).

Informed Consent

Given the plethora of release forms that clutters the office of many practitioners, it may seem unnecessary to mention the necessity for obtaining an informed consent from an individual or a patient or guardian before certain procedures are performed. Nonetheless, cases are filed alleging uninformed consent. And care must be taken to ensure that informed-consent forms are written so they will be understood by clients (Ogloff & Otto, 1991).

In virtually every jurisdiction in the United States, the law now recognizes a duty that a physician or therapist owes to the patient to inform him or her generally of all of the possible serious collateral hazards associated with any type of treatment. Liability on such theories has resulted from electroshock and insulin therapy, and in this day and time, one would expect written releases and consent forms to be standard office practice.

The practitioner cannot be too careful, however. Before initiating a treatment program, some attention should be given to explaining possible consequences to the patient or family. Psychologists should not overlook this step in dealing with groups or in clinic-type settings involving weight loss or smoking cessation. And when dealing with patients who someday may find themselves in divorce litigation, be sure patients understand the potential problems with maintaining confidentiality. A written consent form outlining the limits of confidential communication is a must. Even if failure to obtain such consent does not give rise to civil litigation, it could be the basis for license-related liability.

The Supreme Court of Canada has held that doctors (and presumably psychologists) have a duty to disclose to their patients the nature of the procedure or treatment, its gravity, and any associated risks (*Hopp v. Lepp*, 1976). Only when patients are made aware of the procedures and agree to them can informed consent be deemed to have been given.

Duty to Inform

At least one court has recognized that mental health professionals have a duty to inform subsequent providers of a patient's past attempts at suicide and the present risk of such recurrent behavior. In the California case of *Gross v. Allen* (1994; see also *Health Law Digest*, 1994), the failure of two psychiatrists to inform another physician who sought to obtain a patient's prior psychiatric history resulted in liability for all providers involved.

Assault and Battery

It seems unnecessary to suggest that therapists avoid not only sexual contact with patients but other physical contact as well. Nevertheless, there are documented cases in which mental health professionals have been sued for assault and battery (*Rains v. Superior Court of Los Angeles County*, 1984; *Roy v. Hertogs*, 1976).

Other Possible Areas of Liability

Psychologists must not overlook the fact that there are other areas of legal liability that relate to the business aspects of providing services to the public. Some general categories of liability include employer–employee claims and suits involving charges of sexual harassment and age and gender discrimination.

Malpractice Insurance

There is support for the idea that the best protection from liability is no insurance at all. The absence of insurance coverage certainly changes the complexion of settlement possibilities. However, there are too many successful lawsuits to suggest that such a course of action would be sound or responsible business practice.

Psychologists should be concerned with whether they are covered when they do have insurance. First of all, every provider should read his or her policy carefully and note the *exclusions* it contains. Exclusions are areas or actions for which the carrier will not provide coverage, like exclusions for skydiving or piloting aircraft in a life insurance policy. Only professional services are covered and not all of those. A policy may not cover electroshock therapy, sexual relationships with patients, or punitive damages. It is unlikely to cover dishonest or fraudulent acts. When in doubt, therapists should ask their agents or carriers for written clarification.

When obtaining coverage, complete the application carefully. Be certain to list all staff persons if such information is required. The increased premium is minor compared with the problems that may occur if the carrier later denies coverage. When in a partnership or office-sharing arrangement, make sure all counterparts are covered adequately. When a lawsuit is filed, everyone may be named, and additional coverage may be a real benefit.

Most policies written in recent years are *claims-made* policies. That means that in order to be covered, the provider must be insured by the same carrier at the time the incident occurred and when the claim is made. When switching carriers, the provider may need to purchase a rider to cover prior years of practice. And when providers retire or leave private practice, they should continue their policies in force until the applicable statute of limitation has run or purchase riders to provide this protection.

Another point to note is the policy requirement for notice. The carrier is obligated to cover a provider only if the company receives timely notice of the incident giving rise to liability. The incident is not the filing of the lawsuit; that may be too late. Providers should exercise good judgment and discuss this with their attorneys. If an incident occurs that involves the serious potential for liability, for example a suicide, the provider should put the carrier on notice.

A few other admonitions to practitioners: If a suit is filed, the provider's agent or carrier, or both, should be notified immediately; do not let a summons and complaint sit on your desk while the time for response is running. A provider who has been sued should not contact the opposing party and should not talk to them if contacted. All such communications should be referred to an attorney, not an insurance agent.

Also, beware of requests involving other litigation. It is a favorite ploy of successful plaintiffs' lawyers to file an action against a rather innocuous defendant, such as a state, county, or hospital, and then take a series of depositions from individuals who readily submit because they are not defendants. Following the series of depositions, chances are the pleadings will be amended and unknowing deponents added as parties defendant. A provider should not go to such a deposition alone, even if this means he or she has to retain his or her own counsel. The same admonition applies to records. Providers should not respond to a subpoena without consulting counsel.

Criminal Liability

Criminal liability is rarely associated with the practice of psychology. However, there are activities that can result in arrest and incarceration. The two major causes of criminal liability are sex with clients and fraudulent billing practices.

Sexual Abuse of Patients

A number of states, including California, Colorado, Florida, Georgia, Maine, Minnesota, New Hampshire, New Mexico, North Dakota, Texas, and Wisconsin, have statutes that make it a crime for a therapist to engage in sex with a client. Michigan has a statute that allows prosecution for sexual intercourse under the pretext of medical treatment. And a number of cases, for such offenses as rape and sexual assault, have been successfully prosecuted.

Wisconsin was the first state to pass a law to criminalize sex between therapist and client, in 1984. Its original law made such activity a Class A misdemeanor. In 1985, Wisconsin upgraded its statute to make sex between therapist and client a felony. That same year, Minnesota passed a law making such conduct a felony.

The Wisconsin statute reads as follows:

> Sexual Exploitation by Therapist; Duty to Report.
> (2) Sexual contact prohibited. Any person who is or who holds himself or herself out to be a therapist and who intentionally has sexual contact with a patient or client during any ongoing therapist–patient or therapist–client relationship, regardless of whether it occurs during any treatment, consultation, interview or examination, is guilty of a Class D felony. Consent is not an issue in an action under this subsection. (W.S.A. § 940.22, 1985)

The version passed by the Minnesota legislature reads as follows:

> Criminal Sexual Conduct in the Fourth Degree.
> Subdivision 1. Crime defined. A person who engages in sexual conduct with another person is guilty of criminal sexual conduct in the fourth degree if any of the following circumstances exist:
> . . . (h) the actor is a psychotherapist and the complainant is a patient of the psychotherapist and the sexual conduct occurred during the psychotherapy session. Consent by the complainant is not a defense;
> (i) the actor is a psychotherapist and the complainant is a patient or former patient of the psychotherapist and the patient or former patient is emotionally dependent upon the psychotherapist;
> (j) the actor is a psychotherapist and the complainant is a patient or former patient and the sexual contact occurred by means of therapeutic deception. Consent by the complainant is not a defense . . . (M.S.A. § 609.345, 1985)

According to Schoener et al. in *Psychotherapists' Sexual Involvement With Clients*, the first case to be tried in Wisconsin under the 1984 statute involved a doctor of divinity and psychotherapist who allegedly engaged in sex with a female client. The defendant died prior to trial, however, and the case became moot.

However, in 1991, a physician in Minnesota was convicted of sexually assaulting 11 patients. He was sentenced to 18 years, which was later reduced to 12.

In 1992, the Supreme Court of Colorado considered a constitutional challenge to Section 18-3-405.5(1), 8 B C.R.S. (1988 Supp.), a Colorado statute making sexual penetration of a client by a psychotherapist a class four felony. The psychotherapist who was convicted of four counts of aggravated sexual assault under the statute raised a First Amendment challenge.

Colorado's highest court noted that although certain private activities and intimate relationships may qualify for an elevated status of fundamental constitutional rights, the law has never allowed consenting adults, simply because they are adults and consent, to engage in any type of sexual behavior of their choice under all circumstances. The court then held that neither a treating psychotherapist nor a client has a fundamental constitutional right to engage in sexual intercourse with the other during the existence of the psychotherapist–client relationship and the statute was therefore not unconstitutional.

The court pointed out the special circumstances inherent in the relationship between psychotherapist and his or her client(s) and held that the state could legitimately protect not only nonconsenting victims of sexual assault but also consenting clients. Due process and equal protection claims also were rejected (*Ferguson v. People*, 1992).

Several individuals have been successfully prosecuted under the California statute. There are a number of other criminal charges that can result from inappropriate or unlawful sexual contact with patients and colleagues. *Saenz v. Alexander* (1991) is an example of a Florida case in which both criminal and civil liability arose from such conduct.

Fraud and Inappropriate Billing Practices

Fraud and inappropriate billing practices may also result in criminal liability for psychologists. Many have been convicted of fraud or other theft-related charges incident to inappropriate or illegal billing practices.

Virtually every jurisdiction in the United States and Canada has laws that prohibit this type of activity. Some are routine criminal statutes that prohibit simple theft, theft by deception, fraud, embezzlement, and the like. Other criminal statutes, designed to alleviate the abuse within the health care delivery system, were specifically designed for this purpose.

Note that such activities may involve use of the mail and bring other statutes into play. A number of health care professionals have been convicted of mail fraud for submitting fraudulent reimbursement claims to insurance companies and health plans (*United States v. Harpster*, 1991).

Also note the decision of a New York federal district court, *United States v. Willis* (1990). Here, the court refused to dismiss a securities fraud indictment against a psychiatrist, arising from insider trading on a tip from a patient.

Mandatory Reporting Laws

All psychologists should be aware that most mandatory reporting laws include criminal penalties for violators. The possibility of criminal prosecution makes it imperative that every mental health professional become familiar with these statutes and understand the reporting requirements.

Criminal Procedure

Criminal cases begin in a different fashion than civil cases. The initiation of such a legal action depends on whether the defendant is charged with a misdemeanor or a felony. If the charge is a misdemeanor, the defendant is apprised of the misdemeanor through either an affidavit and summons, a warrant issued by the complaining party, or an indictment handed down by a grand jury. The defendant is typically arrested, required to post bond, and may be required to participate in some pretrial procedures. Even in misdemeanor cases, the defendant is afforded a right to a jury trial, although that right may have to be exercised on an appeal from a lower court decision. Misdemeanor cases can result in incarceration and significant fines.

In felony cases, defendants are formally apprised of the charge after a grand jury has issued an indictment. Again, the defendant will be arrested, required to post a bond, and may well participate in pretrial proceedings, such as a preliminary hearing or other evidentiary proceeding designed to determine whether there is sufficient probable cause to require a trial on the merits. In felonies, defendants are afforded jury trials unless this right is waived by the defendant.

In Canada, the right to a trial by jury is restricted to those cases in which the potential sentence for the crime is 5 years or longer. Also, a grand jury system is not used for either summary convictions (less severe offenses) or indictable offenses (more serious offenses). Rather, a pretrial hearing is held before a provincial court judge who, among other things, makes a determination of whether there is enough evidence against the accused to proceed to trial.

In any criminal case, and particularly in felonies (or, in Canada, indictable offenses), the costs are high, and the penalties can be severe. Incarceration would not be unusual following a conviction on a felony charge. If a defendant is convicted but not incarcerated, it is likely that he or she will be placed on probation, and any number of restrictions will be imposed on his or her liberty. Defendants convicted in criminal cases can expect their licenses to be acted against as well, and the potential for civil suits based on the criminal charges is high.

Other Possible Ramifications

One possible ramification of either a conviction or a disciplinary sanction that is often overlooked by health care professionals and their attorneys is exclusion from reimbursement through Medicare, Medicaid, and other federal health programs and debarment from participation in federal employee health insurance programs. An excluded professional may not be employed by any entity that accepts Medicare, Medicaid, Civilian Health and Medical Program for the Uniformed Services (CHAMPUS), and so on, reimbursement.

References

Abille v. United States, 482 F. Supp. 703 (1980).
Allen v. Kaiser Foundation Hospital Inc., 707 P.2d 1289 (Or. Ct. App. 1985).
Allen v. Smith, 368 S.E.2d 924 (W.Va. 1988).
Andrews v. United States, 732 F.2d 366 (1984).
Awai v. Kotin, 872 P.2d 1332 (Colo. Ct. App. 1993).
Badger v. Greenfield, 24 ATLA L. Rep. 43 (1981, Feb.).
Baher v. State, No. A039654, slip op. (Calif. Ct. App. 1989).
Bankston v. Alexandria Neurosurgical Clinic, 583 So.2d 1148 (La. Ct. App. 3rd Cir. 1991).
Barnes v. Dale, 530 So.2d 770 (Ala. 1988).
Behringer Estate v. Princeton Medical Center, 592 A.2d 1251 (N.J. Super. L. 1991).
Birch, D. (1992). Duty to protect: Update and Canadian perspective. *Canadian Psychology*, *33*, 94–101.
Bird v. W.C.W., 868 S.W.2d 767 (Tex. 1994).
Bradley Center, Inc. v. Wessner, 296 S.E.2d 693 (Ga. 1982).
Bradshaw v. Daniel, 854 S.W.2d 865 (Tenn. 1993).
Brady v. Hopper, 570 F. Supp. 1333 (1983).
Brown v. Pound, 585 So.2d 885 (Ala. 1991).

Cairl v. State, 323 N.W.2d 20 (Minn. 1982).
Campbell v. United States, 23 ATLA L. Rep. 474 (1980, Dec.).
Canadian Psychological Association. (1991). *Canadian code of ethics for psychologists. Revised.* Ottawa, ON: Author.
Center for Health Policy and Ethics. (1992). Confidentiality and its limits: Ethical guidelines for maternal/pediatric HIV infection. (1992). *Creighton Law Review, 25*, 1439–1460.
Clites v. State of Iowa, 24 ATLA L. Rep. 43 (1981, Feb.).
Collins v. Cushner, 25 ATLA L. Rep. 185 (1982, July).
Corgan v. Muchling, 574 N.E.2d 602 (Ill. 1991).
Cosgrove v. Gaudreau (1981), 33 N.B.R. (2d) 523 (Q.B.).
Council on Ethical and Judicial Affairs, American Medical Association. (1991). Sexual misconduct in the practice of medicine. *Journal of the American Medical Association, 266*(19), 2741–2745.
Crichton v. Hastings (1972), 3 O.R. 859, 29 D.L.R. (3d) 692 (C.A.).
Crippen v. Charter Southland Hosp., 534 So.2d 286 (Ala. 1988).
Currie v. United States, 644 F.Supp. 1074 (M.C. N.C. 1986).
Cutter v. Brownbridge, 228 Cal. Rptr. 545 (Cal. Ct. App. 1986).
Davis v. Lihm, 335 N.W.2d 481 (Mich. Ct. App. 1983), *rev'd*, 422 N.W.2d 688 (1988).
DiLeo v. Nugent, 592 A.2d 1126 (Md. Ct. App. 1991).
Doe v. Belmont College, 35 ATLA L. Rep. 148 (1992, May).
Doe v. Samaritan Counseling Center, 791 P.2d 344 (Alaska 1990).
Doe v. Shady Grove Adventist Hospital, 598 A.2d 507 (Md. Ct. App. 1991).
Donaldson v. O'Connor, 493 F.2d 507 (1974).
Donson v. Baez, No.89-365-CMW, U.S.D.C. for the Dist. of Delaware (Feb. 21, 1991).
Doyle v. United States, 530 F.Supp. 1278 (1982).
Duke v. Housen, 589 P.2d 334 (Wyo. 1979).
Dunn v. Howard University Hospital, 26 ATLA L. Rep. 232 (1983, June).
Durflinger v. Artiles, 673 P.2d 86 (Kan. 1983).
E. S. by D. S. v. Seitz, 413 N.W.2d 670 (Wis. Ct. App. 1987).
Ellis v. United States, 484 F.Supp. 4 (D.C. S.C. 1978).
Evans v. Morehead Clinic, 749 S.W.2d 696 (Ky. Ct. App. 1988).
Faigenbaum v. Oakland Medical Center, 25 ATLA L. Rep. 473 (1982, July).
Faya v. Almaraz, 620 A.2d 327 (Md. 1993).
Ferguson v. People, 824 P.2d 803 (Colo. 1992).
Flynn v. Bausch, 469 N.W.2d 125 (Neb. 1991).
Fulero, S. (1988). Tarasoff: 10 years later. *Professional Psychology, 19*, 184–194.
Gasperini v. Manginelli, 92 N.Y.S.2d 575 (NY Sup. Ct. 1949).
Greene v. Guarino, 35 ATLA L. Rep. 29 (1992, Feb.).
Gross v. Allen, 27 Cal. Rptr. 2d 429 (Cal. Ct. App. 1994).
Grote v. J. S. Mayer & Co., Inc., 570 N.E.2d 1146 (Ohio Ct. App. 1990).
Groth v. Weinstock, 610 So.2d 477 (Fla. Ct. App. 1992).
Guity v. Kandilakis, 821 S.W.2d 595 (Tenn. Ct. App. 1991).
Haggerty v. New York, 23 ATLA L. Rep. 285 (1985, Sept.).
Haines v. Bellissimo (1977), 18 O.R. (2d) 177 (C.A.).
Halverson v. Pikes Peak Family Counseling and Mental Health Center, Inc., 795 P.2d 1352 (Colo. Ct. App. 1991).
Hamman v. County of Maricopa, 775 P.2d 1122 (Ariz. 1989).
Harbin v. Harbin, 495 So.2d 72 (Ala. Ct. Civ. App. 1986).
Herndobler v. Riveredge Hospital, 23 ATLA L. Rep. 139 (1979, April).
Hinkleman v. Kalamazoo College and Borgess Medical Center. (1987). *Health Law Digest, 15*(6), 31.
Hirst v. St. Paul Fire & Marine Ins. Co., 683 P.2d 440 (Idaho Ct. App. 1984).
Hopp v. Lepp, 2 S.C.R. 192 (1976).
Horne v. Patton, 287 So.2d 824 (Ala. 1973).
Howard v. Alexandria Hospital, 429 S.E.2d 22 (Va. 1993).
Howard v. Drapkin, 271 Cal. Rptr. 893 (Cal. Ct. App. 1990).
Hubbard v. Laurelwood Hospital, 620 N.E.2d 895 (Ohio Ct. App. 1993).
Huntley v. State of New York, 464 N.E.2d 467 (N.Y. 1984).

In the interest of Bender, 531 A.2d 504 (Pa. Super. Ct. 1987).
In the interest of Doe, 795 P.2d 294 (Hawaii Ct. App. 1990).
Jablonski v. United States, 712 F.2d 391 (9th Cir. 1983).
Jansen v. University Hospital, 26 ATLA L. Rep. 138 (1983, April).
Jones v. State of New York, 34 ATLA L. Rep. 266 (1991, Sept.).
Jordan v. Kelly, 728 F.2d 1 (1984).
Jorgensen, L., Randles, R., & Strasburger, L. (1991). The furor over psychotherapist–patient sexual contact: New solutions to an old problem. *William and Mary Law Review, 32*, 645–730.
Kathleen K. v. Robert B., 198 Cal. Rptr. 273 (Cal. Ct. App. 1984).
Kerker by Kerker v. Hurwitz, 558 N.Y.S.2d 388 (A.D.4 Dept. 1990).
Lawson v. Wellesley Hospital (1975), 9 O.R. (2d) 677 (C.A.).
Leal v. Simon, 542 N.Y.S.2d 328 (A.D.2 Dept. 1989).
Leonard v. State, 491 N.W.2d 508 (Iowa 1992).
Lindsey v. Rousseau, 36 ATLA L. Rep. 220 (1993, Aug.).
Long v. Adams, 333 S.E.2d 852 (Ga. Ct. App. 1985).
MacClements v. Lafore, 408 S.E.2d 878 (N.C. Ct. App. 1991).
Mang v. Moscovitz (1982), 37 A.R. 221 (Q.B.).
Marlene F. v. Affiliated Psychiatric Medical Clinic, 770 P.2d 278 (Cal. 1989).
Marston v. Minneapolis Clinic of Psychiatry & Neurology, Ltd., 329 N.W.2d 306 (Minn. 1982).
Matter of Adoption of Embick, 506 A.2d 455 (Pa. Super. Ct. 1986).
Matter of Estate of Votteler, 327 N.W.2d 759 (Iowa 1982).
Matter of W. H., 602 N.Y.S.2d 70 (N.Y. Fam. Ct. 1993).
Matter of Von Goyt, 461 So.2d 821 (Ala. Civ. Ct. App. 1984).
McBride v. Langton (1982), 22 Alta. L.R. (2d) 174 (Q.B.).
Mendendez v. Superior Court, 834 P.2d 786 (Cal. 1992).
Monahan, J. (1993). Limiting therapist exposure to Tarasoff liability: Guidelines for risk containment. *American Psychologist, 48*, 242–250.
Montoya by Montoya v. Bebensee, 761 P.2d 285 (Colo. Ct. App. 1988).
M.S.A. § 609.345 (1985).
Neufeld v. McQuitty (1979), 18 A.R. 271 (T.D.).
Novak v. Rathnam, 505 N.E.2d 773 (Ill. Ct. App. 1987).
Ogloff, J. R. P. (1995). Navigating the quagmire: Legal and ethical guidelines. In D. Martin & A. Moore (Eds.), First steps in the art of intervention (pp. 347–376). Pacific Grove, CA: Brooks/Cole.
Ogloff, J. R. P., & Otto, R. K. (1991). Are research participants truly informed? Readability of informed consent forms. *Ethics and Behavior, 1*, 239–252.
Olson v. Ramsey County, 497 N.W.2d 629 (Minn. Ct. App. 1993).
Peck v. Counseling Service of Addison County, 499 A.2d 422 (Vt. 1985).
People v. District Court, County of Adams, 797 P.2d 1259 (Colo. 1990).
Perreira v. Colorado, 768 P.2d 1198 (Colo. 1989).
Perry v. Fiumano, 403 N.Y.S.2d 382 (A.D.4 Dept. 1987).
Petersen v. State of Washington, 671 P.2d 230 (Wash. 1983).
Peterson v. Roosevelt Hospital, 25 ATLA L. Rep. 326 (1982, Sept.).
Pickle v. Curns, 435 N.E.2d 877 (Ill. Ct. App. 1982).
Pisel v. The Stamford Hospital, 23 ATLA L. Rep. 138 (1979, April).
Porter v. Porter, 40 O.R.2d417, 32 R.F.L.2d413 (1983).
Psychotherapists' Sexual Involvement with Clients: Intervention and Prevention (1989). Schoener, G. R., Milgrom, J. H., Gonsiorek, J. C., Luepker, E. T., & Conroe, R. M. Minneapolis, MN: Walk-In Counseling Center.
Radzikowski v. Metcalfe, 22 ATLA L. Rep. 89 (1979, March).
Rainer v. Grossman, 107 Cal. Rptr. 469 (1973).
Rains v. Superior Court of Los Angeles County, 198 Cal. Rptr. 249 (Cal. Ct. App. 1984).
Reaves, R. P. (1995). *Avoiding Liability in the Mental Health Professions*. Montgomery, AL: Publications For Professionals.
Richard H. v. Larry D., 243 Cal. Rptr. 807 (Cal. Ct. App. 1988).
Richter v. Northwestern Memorial Hospital, 532 N.E.2d 269 (Ill. Ct. App. 1988).

Roesler v. Menorah Medical Center, 21 ATLA L. Rep.. 327 (1978, Sept.).
Rotenberry v. Wilhoit, 3 ATLA L. Rep. 476 (1980, Dec.).
Roy v. Hertogs, 366 N.Y.S.2d 297 (N.Y. Ct. App. 1976).
Rudy v. Meshores, 706 P.2d 1234 (Ariz. Ct. App. 1985).
Saenz v. Alexander, 584 So.2d 1061 (Fla. Ct. App. 1991).
Santa Cruz v. N. W. Dade Com. Health Ctr., 590 So.2d 444 (Fla. Ct. App. 1991).
Santangelo v. State, 601 N.Y.S.2d 305 (A.D.2 Dept. 1993).
Sawyer v. Tauber, 23 ATLA L. Rep. 277 (1985, Aug.).
Schuster v. Altenberg, 424 N.W.2d 159 (Wis. 1988).
Slavutych v. Baker, 1 S.C.R. 254 (1976).
Smith, S. R. (1991). Mental health malpractice in the 1990s. *Houston Law Review, 28*, 209–253.
Smith v. Fishkill Health-Related Center, 572 N.Y.S.2d 762 (A.D.3 Dept. 1991).
Smith v. Pust, 23 Cal. Rptr. 364 (Cal. Ct. App. 1993).
Smith v. Rush Presbyterian St. Luke's Medical Center, 23 ATLA, L. Rep. 44 (1980, Feb.).
Smith v. St. Paul Fire & Marine Ins. Co., 353 N.W.2d 130 (Minn. 1984).
Snow v. Koeppl, 464 N.W.2d 215 (Wis. Ct. App. 1990).
Speer v. United States, 512 F. Supp. 670 (Tex. 1981).
St. Paul Fire & Marine Ins. Co. v. Love, 447 N.W.2d 5 (Minn. Ct. App. 1989).
St. Paul Fire & Marine Ins. Co. v. Mitchell, 296 S.E.2d 126 (Ga. Ct. App. 1982).
Stanisci v. New York Hosp., 35 ATLA L. Rep. 142 (1992, May).
State ex rel. Juvenile Dept. of Lincoln County v. Ashley, 790 P.2d 547 (Or. Ct. App. 1990).
Tabor v. Doctors Mem. Hospital, 501 So.2d 243 (La. Ct. App. 1986).
Tamsen v. Weber, 802 P.2d 1063 (Ariz. Ct. App. 1990).
Tarasoff v. Regents of the University of California, 551 P.2d 334 (1976).
U.S. v. Harpster, 759 F. Supp. 735 (Kan. 1991).
U.S. v. Willis, 737 F. Supp. 269 (S.D. N.Y. 1990).
Vandecreek, L. (1986, Winter). Patient records as evidence in malpractice litigation. *Psychotherapy Bulletin, 21*, 6–8.
Vattimo v. Lower Bucks Hosp., Inc., 465 A.2d 1231 (Pa. 1983).
Vigilant Ins. Co. v. Kambly, 319 N.W.2d 382 (Mich. Ct. App. 1982).
Walker v. Parzan, 24 ATLA L. Rep. 295 (1981, Sept.).
Wallace v. Jefferson Co. Dept. of Pensions and Security, 501 So.2d 473 (Ala. Civ. Ct. App. 1986).
Webb v. Jarvis, 553 N.E.2d 151 (Ind. Ct. App. 1990).
Webb v. Lightburn, 23 ATLA L. Rep. 285 (1980).
Wenden v. Trikha (1991), 116 A.R. 81 (Q.B.).
Werner v. Kliewer, 710 P.2d 1250 (Kan. 1985).
Whitree v. State, 290 N.Y.S.2d 48 (1968).
Williams v. Congdon, 257 S.E.2d 677 (N.C. Ct. App. 1979).
W.S.A. § 940.22 (1985).

10

Future Trends

Larry J. Bass
Private Practice

The world is changing fast for psychology. As this book goes to print, there are many challenges facing psychology. This chapter provides an overview of several emerging trends that may change the way psychology is defined and practiced. For example, there are many people both within and outside professional psychology who are interested in psychologists with certain training adding the expertise of prescribing certain medications to the professional services provided by psychologists. With the passage of laws like the North American Free Trade Agreement (NAFTA, 1993) there are several implications on the practice of psychology that are unclear at this time. Other laws, such as the Americans with Disabilities Act (1990), also present certain challenges to psychology, but it is again unclear exactly how these laws will affect the practice of psychology. Managed-care concerns have renewed discussions of the appropriateness of master's level training for professional psychologists.

With cuts in federal funding in the United States and the high cost of training in Canada and the United States, many training opportunities both at the predoctoral internship and postdoctoral supervision levels have been deleted. Consequently, it is becoming increasingly difficult for applicants for licensure to find acceptable training experiences. All of these and other changes are indications as to how the world of psychology is evolving.

Psychological Services for Vulnerable Populations

In recent years, there has been an increased presence of ethnically, linguistically, and culturally diverse populations both within the psychologist community and within the society at large. Accompanying this trend is a growing awareness among psychologists of the need to understand factors related to culture and ethnicity in order to provide competent psychological services (American Psychological Association [APA], Office of Ethnic and Minority Affairs, 1990; Canadian Psychological Association [CPA], 1986, 1991). The APA (1986) recognized the need for sensitivity to multicultural diversity in the training of psychologists by requiring accredited programs to provide appropriate training in this area. Although the need for training has been established, multicultural training is still in the embryonic stage, and there is no consensus on the most appropriate training models (Ridley, Mendoza, & Kanitz, 1994). In early 1994, Massachusetts became the first state to require applicants for psychology licensure to have multicultural education and training (DeAngelis, 1994). Effective in July 1996, psychology doctoral students will be required to take at least 4 hr of training in multicultural issues. Effective in July 1999, applicants for licensure will be required to have at least one graduate course in race and ethnicity.

The Feminist Therapy Ethical Code (Feminist Therapy Institute, 1987) particularly emphasizes the importance of addressing issues relevant for disadvantaged or vulnerable populations. The professional therapist should be cognizant of the following areas: cultural diversities and oppression, power differentials, overlapping relationships, therapist accountability, and social change to eliminate the oppressive aspects of society.

Codes of ethics over time have exhorted respect and caring for the welfare of all recipients of psychological services. Recipients of services who belong to special population groups were identified in various ways (e.g., women, the elderly, gays and lesbians, ethnic minorities, persons with disabilities, prisoners, and survivors of abuse). Fairness in many codes basically meant that people were treated the same, without bias or discrimination on the basis of special characteristics. However, recent developments in codes of ethics require professionals to take precautions to protect the rights and well-being of special populations. This reflects a more genuine respect for diversity and commitment to reduce power differentials between providers and consumers of services. A proactive respect for others requires increased self-awareness by professionals of their own socialization, attitudes, and biases, as well as increased cross-cultural awareness and recognition of the limitations of their knowledge and skills. When psychologists choose to work in areas of diversity in which they have limited knowledge, their role must be more that of facilitator, mediator, and assistant in empowering others to have choices rather than that of an expert in diagnosis and intervention.

There are several reasons for these changes in attitude among professionals. Consumer groups and disadvantaged groups have become more vocal about perceived discrimination and lack of access to services. Nations are becoming increasingly diverse culturally as immigrants and refugees are admitted into various countries from many parts of the world. The feminist movement brought to society's attention abuses of power as well as strategies for empowerment. Persons with disabilities are visible and vocal, and consumers are more discriminating about outcomes. Today's professionals are expected to be proactive in providing equal opportunities for disadvantaged persons.

In response to increased awareness concerning the need for psychological services in culturally diverse populations, APA's Board of Ethnic and Minority Affairs (BEMA) in 1990 established a task force on the delivery of services to ethnic and minority populations. The knowledge and skills required for multicultural assessment and intervention are identified as the abilities to do the following:

> - recognize cultural diversity;
> - understand the role that culture, ethnicity/race play in the sociopsychological and economic development of ethnic and culturally diverse populations;
> - understand that socioeconomic and political factors significantly impact the psychosocial, political, and economic development of ethnic and culturally diverse groups;
> - help clients understand, maintain, and resolve their own sociocultural identification; and
> - understand the interaction of culture, gender, and sexual orientation on behavior and needs. (APA, 1990, p. 1)

The nine principles contained in the guidelines and their elaboration are designed to be aspirational in nature and to provide suggestions to psychologists in providing competent and ethical services for ethnically, linguistically, and culturally diverse populations, whether they are native Americans, immigrants, or refugees.

The Ethical Principles of Psychologists and Code of Conduct (APA, 1992) states proactively in Principle D, Respect for People's Rights and Dignity:

> Psychologists are aware of cultural, individual, and role differences, including those due to age, gender, race, ethnicity, national origin, religion, sexual orientation, disability, language, and socioeconomic status. Psychologists try to eliminate the effect on their work of biases based on those factors, and they do not knowingly participate in or condone unfair discriminatory practices. (APA, 1992, pp. 3–4)

Standard 2.04 Use of Assessment in General and With Special Populations (c) states the following:

> Psychologists attempt to identify situations in which particular interventions or assessment techniques or norms may not be applicable or may require adjustment in administration or interpretation because of factors such as individuals' gender, age, race, ethnicity, national origin, religion, sexual orientation, disability, language, or socioeconomic status. (APA, 1992, p. 7)

The *Canadian Code of Ethics for Psychologists* (CPA, 1986, 1991) is one of the earliest ethical codes to take a proactive stance in addressing psychologists' responsibility to safeguard and protect the rights and well-being of vulnerable populations. The code emphasizes both knowledge of others and competency, and self-knowledge and awareness of personal attitudes, as illustrated by the following examples from it:

> Principle I. Respect for the Dignity of Persons Values Statement . . . Psychologists recognize that as individual, family, or group or community vulnerabilities increase and/or as the power of persons to control their environment or their lives decreases, psychologists have an increasing responsibility to seek ethical advice and establish safeguards to protect the rights of the persons involved. (CPA, 1991, p. 2)
>
> Principle II. Responsible Caring Values Statement . . . Psychologists recognize the need for competence and self-knowledge. . . . They also engage in self-reflection with the purpose of determining how their own values . . . and social context (e.g., culture, ethnicity, colour, religion, gender, sexual orientation, physical and mental ability level, age, and socio-economic status) influence their actions, interpretations, choices, and recommendations. (CPA, 1991, p. 9)
>
> Principle III. Integrity in Relationships. Standard 10. Evaluate how their personal experiences, attitudes, values, social context, individual differences, and stress influence their activities and thinking, integrating this awareness into all attempts to be objective and unbiased in their research, service and other activities. (CPA, 1991, p. 19)
>
> Principle IV. Responsibility to Society. Standard 13. Acquire an adequate knowledge of the culture, social structure, and customs of a community before beginning any major work there.
>
> Standard 14. Convey respect for and abide by prevailing community mores, social customs, and cultural expectations in their scientific and professional activities, provided that this does not contravene any of the ethical principles of this Code. (CPA, 1991, p. 27)
>
> Standard 23. Exercise particular care when reporting the results of any work regarding vulnerable groups, ensuring that the results are not likely to be misinterpreted or misused in the development of social policy, attitudes, and practices (e.g., encouraging manipulation of vulnerable persons or reinforcing discrimination against any specific population). (CPA, 1991, p. 28)

Appropriate concern for the well-being of disadvantaged or vulnerable populations is needed in all of the following areas affecting the practice and delivery of psychological services: in offering direct service, in dealing with a community network of services, in addressing policies of government and other funding sources, in performing research and evaluation, and in teaching and supervision.

Hospital and Prescription Privileges

Hospital Privileges

Some psychologists are interested in acquiring privileges to practice within a hospital setting. In inpatient facilities, these privileges allow psychologists to admit, treat, and discharge patients. Some jurisdictions, such as California, have statutes that allow psychologists to have hospital privileges under certain circumstances. The National Register of Health Service Providers in Psychology in 1992 began listing psychologists who currently hold staff privileges in hospital settings. The number listed more than doubled in 1994 from the previous year (J. Hall, personal communication, November 2, 1994).

In October 1994, the U.S. Congress passed a law clarifying that clinical psychologists can oversee psychological treatment of a patient covered by Medicare "as long as the arrangement complies with state law" (Sleek, 1994, p. 29). As of the end of 1994, at least 10 states and the District of Columbia explicitly allowed hospitals to include psychologists on their medical staffs. As of the time this chapter was written, no Canadian jurisdiction provided hospital privileges for psychologists, and there was little lobbying effort devoted to this issue.

Prescription Privileges

In addition to hospital privileges, some psychologists are interested in gaining the ability to prescribe psychotropic medication. If it continues, this recent trend will significantly expand the scope of practice of psychology. Psychologists wishing to prescribe medication as part of their practice will have to meet stringent course and supervised experience requirements. The movement to allow psychologists to prescribe medications is controversial. Some psychologists think that gaining prescription privileges will detract from psychology's distinct focus on understanding and treating human behavior. Other psychologists think that prescribing and monitoring medications are natural extensions of psychological care. This may be especially relevant in rural areas where physicians are scarce.

A few jurisdictions (e.g., Hawaii and California) are currently mobilizing efforts to pass legislation to allow licensed psychologists with special training to prescribe specified medications (Clark, 1995; "Psychology Moves," 1995). The Department of Defense demonstration project on prescription privilege for psychology was implemented in 1992 ("Psychology Moves," 1995; Wright, 1995). The first two graduates from this program completed a 3-year curriculum in 1994 and began prescribing for armed services personnel. On the basis of the experiences of this trial group, in the future the curriculum will be shortened, with less medical school course work required (Sammons, 1995). Much controversy has surrounded the continuation and expansion of this program, although two graduates are currently prescribing at military facilities in the United States (Wright, 1995).

The APA's Board of Educational Affairs formed the Psychopharmacology Working Group in 1994. This group is developing a psychopharmacology curriculum that would help prepare psychologists to prescribe medications. Other groups are also proposing and developing curricula to prepare psychologists to prescribe medications. As with hospital privileges, there has not been any significant effort in Canada to establish prescription privileges for psychologists.

Health Service Provider Certification

Because licensure is generic, not every licensed psychologist is qualified to provide psychological health services. The National Register of Health Service Providers in Psychology was established in 1974, and a similar Canadian organization, the Canadian Register of Health Service Providers in Psychology (CRHSPP), was established in 1984. These organizations have established specific training and education criteria that must be met by licensed psychologists to be listed in the register. Health service provider (HSP) certification also has been developed in several jurisdictions, to identify those psychologists qualified to deliver psychological services in a health care setting. The qualifications necessary to be certified as a HSP in a certain jurisdiction are similar but not identical to those criteria established by the National Register and the Canadian Register. In 1994, nine U.S. jurisdictions had established their own HSP criteria. The HSP certificate identifies psychologists who are qualified to provide clinical or other psychological health services as different from psychologists who function in academic settings, consult with agencies, or are engaged in research or test construction but do not deliver direct psychological health services. This distinction may be helpful for third-party payers and individuals in identifying psychologists trained to provide psychological health services to the public. All jurisdictions that offer HSP certification require that the person already hold a generic license to practice psychology (see chap. 3 in this volume).

Health Care Reform

Health Care Reform in the United States

Health care reform in the United States is likely to evolve over several years, and there are many unanswered questions on how health care reform will impact the practice of psychology in the future. A summary of some of the health care reform issues emerging at the federal level in the United States can be found in an article by Frank and VandenBos (1994) and at the state level in an article by Frank, Sullivan, and DeLeon (1994). Shusterman and Shusterman (1994) encourage psychologists to remain open-minded to changes in the health care delivery system and not be locked out.

Similarly, Cummings (1995a) urges psychologists to consider thoughtfully how they can work with the changes in health care instead of reacting or, worse, ignoring the changes in health care delivery. He makes some predictions as to how the future practice of psychology will look. For example, he predicts that in the future, master's-level technicians will do routine psychotherapy and "doctoral-level psychologists will become managers, researchers and supervisors of therapy in the integrated behavioral care systems that will dominate our field by the end of the century" (Cummings, 1995a, p. 31). Another prediction is that Community Accountable Healthcare Networks will be the delivery systems of the future. "These networks will be comprehensive and provide *all* health services: outpatient, inpatient, and partial care" (Cummings, 1995a, p. 31).

The impact of managed care on the delivery of psychological services is multifaceted. Concerns arise over perceived third-party interference with professional autonomy and external constraints affecting professionals' ability to provide competent and ethical services. Managed care may present problems in assuring client-oriented treatment planning and maintaining confidentiality. The objectives of managed-care organizations may be incompatible with psychology's standards of practice and the profession's primary commitment to the well-being of consumers of services.

In Canada, where all people are provided with medical coverage by provincial health care plans, there is pressure to contain or reduce costs. In some cases, this may mean closing hospitals or downsizing them. As a result, more psychologists may be pressured to move to private-practice settings, where they will be dependent on direct client payment and third-party payer agreements. Given the relative savings in health care that can be realized by increasing psychological services—through preventative health psychology and cost savings compared with psychiatry—it seems timely to some to increase lobbying efforts to provide for coverage of psychological services by Canadian provincial health care plans.

One effect of managed care on the practice of psychology involves changes in the business aspects of psychology practice. It no longer may be sufficient for a psychologist to become licensed and establish a solo practice. Psychologists may need to establish or join groups or networks of health care professionals. Psychologists must be more cognizant of wise business practices to compete in the health care marketplace (Yenny & APA Practice Directorate, 1994).

Health care reform and managed care have prompted a resurgence of discussions about master's-level training for psychologists. Whether or not persons can be adequately trained to practice psychology independently at the master's level has been hotly debated for decades. Managed-care companies operate as a business and seek to contain costs of health care. They may employ master's-level professionals such as licensed professional counselors and social workers instead of psychologists. Consequently, persons with less training may be hired by managed-care companies to provide mental health services when psychologists are better trained to provide these services.

Psychologists are concerned about the impact by managed care on client confidentiality, treatment goals, and the focus of treatment. Can the confidential boundaries of therapy be maintained when treatment must be discussed with a case manager for the managed-care company? If a managed-care company will approve only brief treatment protocols, should a therapist agree to treat complicated, multifaceted, and involved mental health problems? (See Exhibit 1.) Discussion relevant to these concerns can be found in Simon (1994).

Some psychologists have encouraged colleagues to look for ways to

Exhibit 1

A 20-year-old single male college student named Steven was referred to Dr. Gardner, a licensed psychologist, by a managed-care company. Steven's father had died suddenly 6 months before of a heart attack. At the time of the referral, Steven was experiencing difficulties in concentration, poor appetite with weight loss, sleeping disturbances, decreased energy, problems relating socially, and, furthermore, he had recently broken up with his girlfriend. He refused medication and requested individual psychotherapy. Dr. Gardner saw him for 6 months in weekly individual psychotherapy. Steven had made significant progress. However, both he and Dr. Gardner believed that continued therapy would help him maintain the gains he had made and thus help him successfully complete the academic year. His grades had improved and he recently had started dating a new girlfriend. The managed-care company repeatedly pushed for medication, which Steven continued to refuse. Despite the gains Steven had made, the managed-care company's psychiatrist said that appropriate care for patients with these depressive symptoms involved medication as part of the treatment. The psychiatrist called Dr. Gardner again and insisted that Steven be referred for antidepressant medication and threatened to cease authorization for additional psychotherapy unless Dr. Gardner complied with "acceptable practice."

---

integrate psychological services within the broader health care delivery system and to coordinate services with primary-care physicians and other physicians from a wide variety of specialties. This approach views psychology as making contributions to the treatment of the "whole" person and suggests that psychology should not be viewed as a totally separate treatment modality (Belar, 1995; Bray & Rogers, 1995; Cummings, 1995a, 1995b; Hersch, 1995; McDaniel, 1995; Pace, Chaney, Mullins, & Olson, 1995).

Concerns about the future have mobilized psychologists to become active in local, state, and national professional associations to ensure that the voice of psychology is heard by those who will be making the decisions regarding health care reform.

Health Care Reform in Canada

Canada's national health care system is based on five principles: public administration, accessibility, comprehensiveness, universality, and portability. The system is administered and partially funded by the provincial governments, who also receive transfer payments from the federal government on the condition that they adhere to the nationally established criteria. Major concerns in health care reform in Canada are the containment or reduction, or both, of costs (Health Action Lobby [HEAL], 1994; "Health care," 1995; Hurley & Ritchie, 1995; "Paul Martin's budget," 1995), as well as regionalization of services and the implementation of new administrative models.

Controversy surrounds many proposals for change in Canada, especially the possibility of a two-tier system in which basic care is covered by a public system but those who can afford it may receive additional or total care from private sources. Hurley and Ritchie (1995) foresee four major changes affecting psychologists: (a) public-sector health care funding will be capped; (b) health care services will be required to demonstrate quality service at competitive cost; (c) community-based care in low-overhead settings will be preferred, with a larger number of professions defined as primary-care providers; and (d) quality at competitive cost will force evaluation of care provided by institutions, by programs, and by individual practitioners. Wedding, Ritchie, Kitchen, and Binner (1993) addressed potential lessons to be drawn by American psychology from the profession's Canadian experience.

In Canada, health care reform has an impact on psychologist providers, even though the Canadian system has not reimbursed psychologists in private practice. The number of salaried positions for psychologists in public health care facilities is diminishing as budgetary restraints and administrative reorganizations are implemented. These changes result in increasing numbers of psychologists engaging in private practice by either choice or necessity ("Training Psychologists," 1995). All three subgroups (Training, Funding, and Advocacy) at the Mississauga Conference on Professional Psychology (Dobson & King, 1995) emphasized the increased need for entrepreneurial skills, responsiveness to the marketplace, and ethics for independent practitioners. As governments look for cost-effective measures, the question reemerges of whether academic degrees are indicators of competency and whether subdoctoral training is sufficient for the provision of health care services.

The Canadian government exempted health services provided by psychologists who are listed in the CRHSPP from paying the Goods and Services Tax (Goods and Services Tax Legislation, 1991). Negotiations on the Canadian Agreement on Internal Trade are under way with the purpose of removing restrictions on the interprovincial flow of goods and services. The CRHSPP is providing leadership in expanding practice opportunities for psychologists by increasing the public awareness of psychological services and in providing continuing education to address the changes occurring in the delivery of health care. As the range of third-party payers of psychological services expands in Canada, psychologists may be faced with ethical problems similar to those experienced by psychologists working with managed-care systems in the United States.

Canadian psychology enjoys a high degree of interorganizational cooperation and collaboration in dealing with major policy issues. There are close working relationships among the CPA, the Council of Provincial Associations of Psychology, the CRHSPP, the National Professional Psychology Consortium, and HEAL. The various psychological organizations have combined resources to achieve understanding and implementation of the North American Free Trade Agreement as it affects psychologists in Canada, the United States, and Mexico. It is expected that NAFTA and increased collaboration with the European Federation of Professional Psychology Associations will continue to be important initiatives well into the foreseeable future.

Clinical Practice Guidelines

The Agency for Health Care Policy and Research (AHCPR), an agency of the U.S. Public Health Service, has as its missions the enhancement of the quality of health care services and access to such services. These missions are, in part, carried out through the facilitation of the development of clinical guidelines, performance measures, standards of quality, and dissemination of research findings and clinical guidelines (Clinton, McCormick, & Besterman, 1994).

To date, AHCPR-supported clinical guidelines have been developed for the detection, diagnosis, and treatment of major depression (Schulberg & Rush, 1994). Since 1992, the AHCPR has published 6 clinical guidelines for various health care issues and is supporting the development of more than 20 others, 2 of which are clinical practice guidelines in smoking prevention and cessation and diagnosis and treatment of anxiety and panic disorder.

The AHCPR-supported guidelines are developed by selected researchers and practitioners in the particular practice area addressed by the guidelines. These AHCPR guidelines provide information to practitioners regarding what AHCPR believes constitutes the best practices in specific circumstances.

These guidelines are considered controversial by some practitioners. Munoz, Hollow, McGrath, Rehm, and VandenBos (1994) expressed concerns that in some of the published guidelines a "consistent biomedical bias appears evident that is likely to lead patients and their physicians to opt for pharmacological interventions to the exclusion of other alternative treatments" (p. 43). These authors also identified additional concerns as well as areas of agreement with the guidelines. In this article, they concluded that "the AHCPR guidelines overstate the efficacy of pharmacotherapy for patients with less severe depression and understate the efficacy of psychotherapy for the more severe depressions" (Munoz et al., 1994, p. 57). In addition, they "question the wisdom of setting up federal guidelines that imply that [primary care physicians] should be the preferred source of treatment" (Munoz et al., 1994, p. 57).

Concluding Comments

Professional psychology has had 50 years in which to develop standards of practice and regulatory mechanisms to provide protection for the public.

Changes in attitudes toward special populations are positive. We do not know what the human consequences will be of major changes that are occurring in society on the funding and delivery of health and educational services. There is also some public concern that self-regulating professions may at times be more self-serving than public-serving in their maintenance of standards and regulations. As a consequence, there are periodic legislative attempts to reduce the influence of the profession of psychology on professional regulation. Because other professions requiring less training assert that they can provide mental health services comparable to those provided by psychologists, it is increasingly important for the psychology profession to educate legislators and the public as to the value of the education, training, and professional ethics required of licensed psychologists. Consequently, it behooves the profession to keep an open dialogue with legislators to keep the importance of these distinctions in view.

None of us has a crystal ball to see the future, but it seems prudent to retain a strong commitment to using psychological knowledge and skills for the public good. The public good must be the primary objective in assessing proposed changes and in influencing change. Psychologists have knowledge, skills, and moral commitment to navigate in new and uncharted waters of social change and to make positive use of the knowledge and structures that have been established. Certainly, issues such as NAFTA may impact on the future practice of psychology, since NAFTA will introduce variance in education and training requirements for licensure or certification in the participating countries, and the impact of that variance has not yet been gauged.

Psychology is a relatively young profession, and its practitioners are certainly not isolated either as psychologists practicing in the United States or Canada or as psychologists practicing in isolation from other professions. In April 1995, the First International Congress on Licensure, Certification, and Credentialing of Psychologists was held in New Orleans, Louisiana, hosted by the Association of State and Provincial Psychology Boards (ASPPB). Psychologists from 25 different countries were represented. General interest was expressed in working more cooperatively as psychologists around the world to collaborate in the training, credentialing, and regulating of professional psychologists. It is exciting to consider where further dialogues may lead as the education, training, practice, and regulation of psychology continue to evolve.

References

American Psychological Association. (1986). *Accreditation handbook*. Washington, DC: Author.

American Psychological Association, Office of Ethnic and Minority Affairs. (1990). *Guidelines for providers of psychological services to ethnic, linguistic, and culturally diverse populations*. Washington, DC: Author.

American Psychological Association. (1992). Ethical principles of psychologists and code of conduct. *American Psychologist, 47,* 1597–1611.

Americans with Disabilities Act, 42 U.S.C. § 12101, et seq. (1990).

Belar, C. D. (1995). Collaboration in capitated care: Challenges for psychology. *Professional Psychology: Research and Practice, 26,* 139–146.

Bray, J. H., & Rogers, J. C. (1995). Linking psychologists and family physicians for collaborative practice. *Professional Psychology: Research and Practice, 26,* 132–138.

Canadian Psychological Association. (1986). *Canadian code of ethics for psychologists.* Old Chelsea, Quebec: Author.

Canadian Psychological Association. (1991). *Canadian code of ethics for psychologists. Revised.* Ottawa, ON: Author.

Clark, J. H. (1995, Summer). Report released on prescription privileges training needs. *Advance,* pp. 3, 16.

Clinton, J. J., McCormick, K., & Besterman, J. (1994). Enhancing clinical practice: The role of practice guidelines. *American Psychologist, 49,* 30–33.

Cummings, N. A. (1995a). Behavioral health after managed care: The next golden opportunity for professional psychology. *Register Report, 20*(3) & *21*(1), 1, 30–33.

Cummings, N. A. (1995b). Impact of managed care on employment and training: A primer for survival. *Professional Psychology: Research and Practice, 26,* 10–15.

DeAngelis, T. (1994, March). Massachusetts now requires multicultural training. *APA Monitor,* p. 41.

Dobson, K., & King, M. (1995). *The Mississauga conference on professional psychology.* Ottawa, ON: Canadian Psychological Association.

Feminist Therapy Institute. (1987). *Feminist therapy ethical code.* San Francisco: Author.

Frank, R. G., Sullivan, M. J., & DeLeon, P. H. (1994). Health care reform in the states. *American Psychologist, 49,* 855–867.

Frank, R. G., & VandenBos, G. R. (1994). Health care reform: The 1993–1994 evolution. *American Psychologist, 49,* 851–854.

Goods and Services Tax Legislation, Bill C-62 (1991).

Health Action Lobby (HEAL). (1994). *Pre-budget submission to the House of Commons standing committee on finance.* Ottawa, ON: Author.

Health care: no cash, no clout! (1995, Spring). *Psynopsis Bulletin,* p. 8. Ottawa, ON: Canadian Psychological Association.

Hersch, L. (1995). Adapting to health care reform and managed care: Three strategies for survival and growth. *Professional Psychology: Research and Practice, 26,* 16–26.

Hurley, G., & Ritchie, P. (1995). The challenge of tomorrow anticipated today: CRHSPP considers strategic options. *Rapport, 3*(1), 2, 4–7.

McDaniel, S. H. (1995). Collaboration between psychologists and family physicians: Implementing the biopsychosocial model. *Professional Psychology: Research and Practice, 26,* 117–122.

Munoz, R. F., Hollow, S. D., McGrath, E., Rehm, L. P., & VandenBos, G. R. (1994). On the AHCPR depression in primary care guidelines: Further considerations for practitioners. *American Psychologist, 49,* 42–61.

North American Free Trade Agreement Between the Government of the United States of America, the Government of Canada and the Government of the United Mexican States, 1993, T.I.A.S. No.

Pace, T. M., Chaney, J. M., Mullins, L. L., & Olson, R. A. (1995). Psychological consultation with primary care physicians: Obstacles and opportunities in the medical setting. *Professional Psychology: Research and Practice, 26,* 123–131.

Paul Martin's budget: Redefining relationships (1995, Spring). *Psynopsis Bulletin,* p. 1. Ottawa, ON: Canadian Psychological Association.

Psychology moves for prescriptive privilege. (1995, Summer). *Advance,* pp. 1, 14–15.

Ridley, C. R., Mendoza, D. W., & Kanitz, B. E. (1994). Multicultural training: Re-examination, operationalization, and integration. *The Counseling Psychologist, 22,* 227–289.

Sammons, M. T. (1995, Summer). Prescription privileges and psychology's debt to psychiatry. *Advance,* pp. 7, 18.

Schulberg, H. C., & Rush, J. A. (1994). Clinical practice guidelines for managing major depressions in primary care practice. *American Psychologist, 49,* 34–41.

Shusterman, L. R., & Shusterman, A. J. (1994). Preparing the practitioner: The psychologist's role in managed care. *The Independent Practitioner, 14,* 265–267.

Simon, N. P. (1994). Ethics, psychodynamic treatment, and managed care. *Psychoanalysis and Psychotherapy: The Journal of the Postgraduate Center for Mental Health, 11,* 119–129.

Sleek, S. (1994, December). New Medicare rule benefits psychology. *APA Monitor,* p. 29.

Training psychologists as entrepreneurs. (1995). *Rapport, 3*(1), 1, 12.

Wedding, D., Ritchie, P., Kitchen, A., & Binner, P. (1993). Mental health services in a single-payer system: Lessons from Canada and principles for an American plan. *Professional Psychology: Research and Practice. 24,* 387–393.

Wright, R. H. (1995, Summer). Psychiatry wages all-out war on psychologists' prescription demonstration project. *Advance,* pp. 1, 9, 12–15, 18, 20.

Yenney, S., & American Psychological Association Practice Directorate. (1994). *Business strategies for a caring profession.* Washington, DC: American Psychological Association.

Appendix A

Criteria for Listing in The National Register of Health Service Providers in Psychology

1. Currently licensed, certified, or registered by a state/provincial board of examiners of psychology at the independent practice level of psychology.

2. A doctoral degree in psychology from a regionally accredited educational institution.

3. Two years (3,000 hours) of supervised experience in health services in psychology, of which one year (1,500 hours) is in an internship or organized health service training program and one year (1,500 hours) is postdoctoral supervised experience.

From "Criteria for The National Register of Health Service Providers in Psychology." In *The National Register of Health Service Providers in Psychology* (13th ed., pp. 1–2), 1995, Washington, DC: The National Register of Health Service Providers in Psychology.

Appendix B

Criteria for Listing in the Canadian Register of Health Service Providers in Psychology

Eligibility Criteria

1. Section 1
   (1) Eligibility for listing with the Register requires that a person meet all the following criteria:
      a) Be registered, certified, or licensed for the independent practice of psychology in the province or territory in which the person practices.
      b) Have a doctorate degree acceptable to the regulatory organization in the province or territory in which the psychologist practices.
      c) Have two (2) years of supervised experience in health service, of which at least one (1) year is postdoctoral and one (1) year (may be postdoctoral year) is in an organized health service setting. (total min. 3,000 hrs)

   (2) Notwithstanding Subsection 1(1) (a), persons who practice in a province or territory which does not have statutory provisions for the registration, certification or licensing of psychologists, may be listed in the Register provided:
      a) They hold a doctorate degree acceptable to the Register.
      b) Meet the requirements of Subsection 1(1)(c).
2. Section 2
   (1) Notwithstanding Section 1 above, during a period of fifteen (15) years from the date of incorporation of the Register, the following criteria for listing may be substituted for those in Section 1:
      a) Be registered, certified, or licensed for the independent practice of psychology in the province or territory in which the person practices, and
      b) Have a doctorate degree acceptable to the regulatory organization in the province or territory in which the psychologist prac-

---

tices and have attained four (4) years of experience in a health service setting,

(total min. 6,000 hrs.)

or

c) Have a master's degree acceptable to the regulatory body of the province or territory in which the psychologist practices and have attained two (2) years of supervised experience in an organized health service setting, of which at least one (1) year is postgraduate,

(total min. 3,000 hrs.)

or

d) Have a master's degree acceptable to the regulatory body of the province or territory in which the psychologist practices and have attained six (6) years of experience in a health service setting.

(total min. 9,000 hrs.)

(2) Notwithstanding Subsection 2(1), persons who practice in a province or territory which does not have statutory provisions for the registration, certification or licensing of psychologists, may be listed in the Register provided they:

a) Hold a doctorate degree acceptable to the Register and have attained four (4) years of experience in a health service setting;

(total min. 6,000 hrs).

or

b) Have a master's degree acceptable to the Register and have two (2) years of supervised experience in an organized health service setting of which at least one (1) year is postgraduate;

(total min. 3,000 hrs.)

or

c) Have a master's degree acceptable to the Register and six (6) years of experience in a health service setting.

(total min. 9,000 hrs).

3. Section 3

(1) Notwithstanding Sections 1 and 2, a person who

a) is registered, certified or licensed for the independent practice of psychology in the province or territory in which this person practices, and

b) is engaged in the provision of psychological health services in an organized health service setting or a health service setting within the meaning of those terms in this by-law but who has not yet accrued the experience necessary for permanent listing may be temporarily listed in the Register for a period not to exceed six years from the date of initial temporary listing.

(2) As a condition of temporary listing, the listee shall be required to provide such information regarding her/his program of practice in health service settings as the Register may from time to time require.

(3) Temporary listees shall acknowledge that temporary listing does not give them any other rights beyond those of temporary listing and that they must satisfy all requirements established by the register before permanent listing is granted.

Definitions

1. An **"Organized Health Service Setting"** is an organization, institution or agency, or part thereof, established to provide health and/or mental health care services, with defined health service programs and a defined system of supervision. They could include a general hospital, a mental/psychiatric hospital or a rehabilitation hospital, an auxiliary hospital, a mental health rehabilitation clinic or centre local de services communautaires, centre de services sociaux, and psychology services of school boards, colleges and universities, as well as others as may from time to time be designated by Council.

   "Experience obtained within a private practice setting may be considered as experience in an organized service setting. Applicants who wish to submit such experience in support of their application must satisfy the Council that the practice meets the following criteria: (1) The practice consists of three or more psychologists who are themselves (1) listed in CRHSPP or the National Register or (b) eligible for listing in CRHSPP or the National Register. (2) The practice provides and offers the opportunity in a range of psychological health or mental health services. (3) The practice offers a defined and documented program of supervision in psychological health services. (4) Clause 1b will expire as of December 31st, 1994."

2. A **"Health Service Setting"** is an institution or organization or part of an institution or organization established and clearly identified as existing for the provision of health services, or an office or equivalent facility from which a health service provider in psychology offers a psychological service to a client or clients for a fee.

3. **"Supervised experience"** means an acceptable experience under the supervision of a person acceptable to Council.

4. **"Registered," "Certified," "Licensed"** means registered, certified, licensed by providence/territory regulatory organization for individual practice of psychology in providence or territory.

5. **Independent practice** means practice as a psychologist without the statutory or regulatory requirement for supervision.

6. **Four years of post-doctoral experience (without the qualifier "supervised")** means a minimum of 1500 hours per year of acceptable experience in the practice of psychology accrued over a period of not less than four years.

7. **Six years of post-Master's experience (without the qualifier "supervised")** means a minimum of 1500 hours per year of acceptable experience in the practice of psychology accrued over a period of not less than six years. ***This definition applies to section 2(1)D and 2(2)C.**

8. i) **One year of supervised experience** means a minimum of 1500 hours of acceptable experience which includes at least 100 hours of direct individual supervision, accrued over a period of not less than 12 months.
   ii) In the case of group supervision, 2 hours shall count as 1 hour in calculating the aggregate total.
   iii) Acceptable supervised experience refers to direct, format contact with a senior person who is responsible for the educational development and guidance of the supervisee. **Acceptable supervised experience does not include classwork, or other course related experiences.**
   iv) Acceptable supervised experience is that in which health services in psychology are directly provided by the applicant to individuals or groups of patients/clients. The applicant's own personal growth experience, i.e. personal therapy, encounter groups, is not acceptable. Supervision of others is not acceptable.

   ***The four definitions of the preceding paragraph 8 apply to sections 1(1)c, 2(1)c, and 2(2)b of the present criteria for listing.**

9. Some "applied" graduate teaching can at times be construed as health service experience if this teaching is designed to provide students with health service **skills** such as diagnostic abilities, interviewing skills, therapeutic intervention skills. Direct face-to-face supervision of clinical cases is a prime example. Such teaching, however, can never comprise more than 75% of the aggregate hours of health service experience necessary to qualify under the chosen applying criterion.

Appendix C

Criteria for Fellow of the APA

The most difficult judgment that must be made in connection with nominees for Fellow status is to determine whether or not there has been "unusual and outstanding contribution or performance in the field of psychology. . . .

Number of publications, grade-level of an administrative position, academic rank, and number of public addresses or committee memberships are not automatic determiners. The contribution to the science or to the profession of psychology should be original, and perhaps also a contribution to society as a whole.

The following criteria are by no means intended to be exhaustive; divisions develop their own more specialized criteria:

1. the existence of relevant publications is not enough—they must report impressive work, have impact upon the work of others, and have been refereed appropriately;
2. the impact of innovations must be documented;
3. citation of the nominee's work by others may be an important indicator of the impact of his/her contribution;
4. conducting and organizing workshops is not an automatic criterion, but frequent workshop leadership with positive evaluations and evidence of impact over time can be good evidence of contribution;
5. offices held in psychological associations, political and legislative activity, and the like, while relevant, are rarely enough in themselves to prove contribution—endorsers must show impact beyond the local level;
6. accumulation of impact and performance over time must be demonstrated;
7. evidence of steady and continuing competence does not in itself meet the criteria of "outstanding and unusual."

There can be no single criterion upon which to base nomination for Fellow status. Operational definitions of "unusual and outstanding contribution to performance" differ from division to division. The relative

---

weight given to individual criteria and to combinations of criteria shall be carefully examined by divisions and by the APA Membership Committee when they assess the impact the nominee has had on the field of psychology. Criteria may include, but shall not be limited to, the following: publications, innovations, workshop activity, professional service, demonstrated leadership, journal editorship, and awards.

Appendix D

ASPPB Code of Conduct

TABLE OF CONTENTS

Foreword
ASPPB Code of Conduct

Enclosed is the ASPPB Code of Conduct which was approved by the Delegates to the Annual Meeting in October, 1990. Since that meeting several suggestions for minor revisions were incorporated by the Model Licensure Committee which was responsible for the previous draft versions.

It is important to note that this version of the Code of Conduct began with the review and distillation of similar codes from fourteen (14) U.S. and Canadian jurisdictions. These fourteen were selected as representative from twenty-seven (27) U.S./Canadian regulatory codes. The rules contained in the Code reflect suggestions of many jurisdictions and many concerned individuals following the review of former drafts of the Code. The rules contained in the Code also reflect much debate and scrutiny by the Model Licensure Committee, which spent approximately two years in the drafting stage.

The committee that prepared the various drafts, as well as the approved version of the Code, represented considerable geographic and professional diversity, yet was able to reach an essentially enthusiastic consensus on nearly all of the rules contained in the Code. Generally favorable reaction by many boards and board members, as well as the vote of the delegates, supports the impression that a consensus Code of Conduct is possible.

Certain concepts should be kept in mind while reviewing and applying the rules contained in the Code. Regulatory rules of conduct protect the

---

public welfare by assuring that the client of a licensed psychologist can have a reasonable, legally protected, understanding of the rules that will govern the professional's behavior in the professional relationship. Effective rules of conduct, in the opinion of the committee, have several characteristics of note:

1. They pertain to the process or "mechanics" of the professional relationship, not to the content of the professional judgment itself. They set the boundaries within which the professional relationship functions and are not intended to determine or dictate professional judgment as such.
2. They primarily protect the public interest. They secondarily protect the interests of the profession only as they assure public confidence and trust in the predictability of the professional relationship.
3. They are as nonintrusive as possible, interfering as little as possible with professional work while still accomplishing their necessary function of protecting the public from exploitation secondary to particular characteristics of the professional relationship.
4. They are essentially unambiguous concerning what behavior is acceptable and what is not.
5. Among other functions, they assure the creation/existence/retention of appropriate information with which the regulatory board can judge compliance with or deviation from its requirements.
6. They are sufficient unto themselves, without dependence for interpretation on additional explanatory materials, since they will be applied in a judicial/legal context interpreting the regulatory code which they are a part, and the explanatory materials would not be an incorporated part of the regulatory code.
7. They are nonoptional and always pertain. They are coercive, not advisory or aspirational. They are nontrivial, to the extent that any violation is basis for formal disciplinary action, including loss of licensure.

Rules of conduct differ in function in critical ways from a professional association ethics code, with which they are sometimes confused. The professional association ethics code is the profession's own standards and guidelines to its own professionals about how to handle the professional–client relationship. Its ultimate purpose is to protect the welfare and integrity of the profession, although it accomplishes these functions partially by structuring professional behavior such as to build confidence in the profession, by much the same process as do the rules of conduct. It may, and usually does, incorporate the basic concepts or structure of regulatory rules of conduct as those are herein conceptualized. Rules of conduct in a professional association ethics code may be dealt with in less detail or specificity, however, than is desirable for a regulatory code. They also often address aspirational or advisory issues as well as coercive ones, and professional matters as well as regulatory matters.

At least one recent court ruling, *White v. N.C. State Bd. of Examiners*, 388 S.E.2nd 148 (N.C. App. 1990), highlights some distinctions between aspirational ethics code language and enforceable regulatory code of conduct language. In this case, which involved the utilization of the American Psychological Association's "Ethical Principles of Psychologists," a reviewing court held that the preambles to the various ethical principles could not be used as the basis for disciplinary action against a psychologist. At the same time, this court upheld the use of certain specific principles in such disciplinary proceedings. The questionable use of principles adopted by a professional association was one of the reasons that the ASPPB Executive Committee directed the development of this Code of Conduct. Board members and attorneys involved in disciplinary proceedings based on codes of conduct or ethical principles should review *White v. N.C. State Bd. of Examiners*, supra for its most instructive language.

The primary work in drafting the Code was done by the ASPPB Model Licensure Committee consisting of David Rodgers, OH (Chair); Stephen DeMers, KY; Teréz Rétfalvi, NB; Norma Simon, NY; Robert Tipton, VA; Randolph P. Reaves, AL.

ASPPB views this Code as one which may change over time as opinion regarding the proper conduct of psychologists evolves. We trust that it will be a useful and productive document for boards, board members, staff and board attorneys. As always we welcome your comments and suggestions.

Gerald T. Jorgensen, PhD
President

ASPPB Model Code of Conduct

I. Introduction

A. *Purpose*. The rules within this Code of Conduct constitute the standards against which the required professional conduct of a psychologist is measured.

B. *Scope*. The psychologist shall be governed by this Code of Conduct whenever providing psychological services in any context. This Code shall not supersede state, federal or provincial statutes. This Code shall apply to the conduct of all licensees and applicants, including the applicant's conduct during the period of education, training, and employment which is required for licensure. The term "psychologist," as used within this Code, shall be interpreted accordingly.

C. *Responsibility for own actions*. The psychologist shall be fully responsible for his/her own professional decisions and professional actions.

D. *Violations*. A violation of this Code of Conduct constitutes unprofessional conduct and is sufficient reason for disciplinary action or denial of either original licensure or reinstatement of licensure.

E. *Aids to interpretation*. Ethics codes and standards for providers promulgated by the American Psychological Association, the Canadian

Psychological Association, and other relevant professional groups shall be used as an aid in resolving ambiguities which may arise in the interpretation of this Code of Conduct, except that this Code of Conduct shall prevail whenever any conflict exists between this Code and any professional association standard.

II. Definitions

A. *Client*. "Client" means a receiver of psychological services. A corporate entity or other organization can be a client when the professional contract is to provide services of benefit primarily to the organization rather than to individuals. In the case of individuals with legal guardians, including minors and legally incompetent adults, the legal guardian shall be the client for decision making purposes, except that the individual receiving services shall be the client for:

1. Issues directly affecting the physical or emotional safety of the individual, such as sexual or other exploitive dual relationships, and
2. Issues specifically reserved to the individual, and agreed to by the guardian prior to rendering of services, such as confidential communication in a therapy relationship.

B. *Confidential information*. "Confidential information" means information revealed by a client or clients or otherwise obtained by a psychologist, where there is reasonable expectation that because of the relationship between the client(s) and the psychologist, or the circumstances under which the information was revealed or obtained, the information shall not be disclosed by the psychologist without the informed written consent of the client(s). When a corporation or other organization is the client, rules of confidentiality apply to information pertaining to the organization, including personal information about individuals when obtained in the proper course of that contract. Such information about individuals is subject to confidential control of the organization, not of the individual, and can be made available to the organization, unless there is reasonable expectation by such individual that such information was obtained in a separate professional relationship with that individual and is therefore subject to confidentiality requirements in itself.

C. *Court order*. "Court order" means the written or oral communication of a member of the judiciary, or other court magistrate or administrator, if such authority has been lawfully delegated to such magistrate or administrator.

D. *Licensed*. "Licensed" means licensed, certified, registered, or any other term when such term identifies a person whose professional behavior is subject to regulation by the Board.

E. *Professional relationship*. "Professional relationship" means a mutually agreed upon relationship between a psychologist and a client(s) for the purpose of the client(s) obtaining the psychologist's professional expertise.

F. *Professional service*. "Professional service" means all actions of the psychologist in the context of a professional relationship with a client.

G. *Supervisee.* "Supervisee" means any person who functions under the extended authority of the psychologist to provide, or while in training to provide, psychological services.

III. Rules of Conduct

A. Competence

1. *Limits on practice.* The psychologist shall limit practice and supervision to the areas of competence in which proficiency has been gained through education, training, and experience.

2. *Maintaining competency.* The psychologist shall maintain current competency in the areas in which he/she practices, through continuing education, consultation, and/or other procedures, in conformance with current standards of scientific and professional knowledge.

3. *Adding new services and techniques.* The psychologist, when developing competency in a service or technique that is either new to the psychologist or new to the profession, shall engage in ongoing consultation with other psychologists or relevant professionals and shall seek appropriate education and training in the new area. The psychologist shall inform clients of the innovative nature and the known risks associated with the services, so that the client can exercise freedom of choice concerning such services.

4. *Referral.* The psychologist shall make or recommend referral to other professional, technical, or administrative resources when such referral is clearly in the best interests of the clients.

5. *Sufficient professional information.* A psychologist rendering a formal professional opinion about a person, for example about the fitness of a parent in a custody hearing, shall not do so without direct and substantial professional contact with or a formal assessment of that person.

6. *Maintenance and retention of records.*

a. The psychologist rendering professional services to an individual client (or a dependent), or services billed to a third party payor, shall maintain professional records that include:

1) the presenting problem(s) or purpose or diagnosis,
2) the fee arrangement,
3) the date and substance of each billed or service-count contact or service,
4) any test results or other evaluative results obtained and any basic test data from which they were derived,
5) notation and results of formal consults with other providers,
6) a copy of all test or other evaluative reports prepared as part of the professional relationship.

b. To meet the requirements of this rule, so as to provide a formal record for review, but not necessarily for other legal purposes, the psychologist shall assure that all data entries in the professional records are maintained for a period of not less than five years after the last date that service was rendered. The psychologist shall also abide by other legal requirements for record retention, even if longer periods of retention are required for other purposes.

c. The psychologist shall store and dispose of written, electronic and other records in such a manner as to insure their confidentiality.

d. For each person professionally supervised, the psychologist shall maintain for a period of not less than five years after the last date of supervision a record of the supervisory session that shall include, among other information, the type, place, and general content of the session.

7. *Continuity of care.* The psychologist shall make arrangements for another appropriate professional or professionals to deal with emergency needs of his/her clients, as appropriate, during periods of his/her foreseeable absences from professional availability.

B. Impaired objectivity and dual relationships

1. *Impaired psychologist.* The psychologist shall not undertake or continue a professional relationship with a client when the psychologist is, or could reasonably be expected by the Board to be, impaired due to mental, emotional, physiologic, pharmacologic, or substances abuse conditions. If such a condition develops after a professional relationship has been initiated, the psychologist shall terminate the relationship in an appropriate manner, shall notify the client in writing of the termination, and shall assist the client in obtaining services from another professional.

2. *Prohibited Dual Relationships.*

a. The psychologist shall not undertake or continue a professional relationship with a client when the objectivity or competency of the psychologist is, or could reasonably be expected by the Board to be, impaired because of the psychologist's present or previous familial, social, sexual, emotional, financial, supervisory, political, administrative, or legal relationship with the client or a relevant person associated with or related to the client.

b. The psychologist, in interacting with a client or former client to whom the psychologist has at any time within the previous 24 months rendered counseling, psychotherapeutic, or other professional psychological services for the treatment or amelioration of emotional distress or behavioral inadequacy, shall not:

1) engage in any verbal or physical behavior toward him/her which is sexually seductive, demeaning, or harassing; or
2) engage in sexual intercourse or other physical intimacies with him/her; or
3) enter into a financial or other potentially exploitive relationship with him/her.

c. The prohibitions set out in (b.) above shall not be limited to the 24-month period but shall extend indefinitely if the client is proven to be clearly vulnerable, by reason of emotional or cognitive disorder, to exploitive influence by the psychologist.

C. Client welfare

1. *Providing explanation of procedures.* The psychologist shall give a truthful, understandable, and appropriate account of the client's condition to the client or to those responsible for the care of the client. The psychologist shall keep the client fully informed as to the purpose and nature of any evaluation, treatment, or other procedures, and of the client's right to freedom of choice regarding services provided.

2. *Termination of services.* Whenever professional services are terminated, the psychologist shall offer to help locate alternative sources of professional services or assistance if indicated. The psychologist shall terminate a professional relationship when it is reasonably clear that the client is not benefiting from the relationship, and shall prepare the client appropriately for such termination.

3. *Stereotyping.* The psychologist shall not impose on the client any stereotypes of behavior, values, or roles related to age, gender, religion, race, disability, nationality, sexual preference, or diagnosis which would interfere with the objective provision of psychological services to the client.

4. *Sexual or other dual relationship with a client.* The psychologist shall not enter into a sexual or other dual relationship with a client, as specified in Section III, B. of this Code of Conduct.

5. *Solicitation of business by clients.* The psychologist providing services to an individual client shall not induce that client(s) to solicit business on behalf of the psychologist.

6. *Referrals on request.* The psychologist providing services to a client shall make an appropriate referral of the client to another professional when requested to do so by the client.

D. Welfare of supervisees and research subjects

1. *Welfare of supervisees.* The psychologist shall not exploit a supervisee in any way—sexually, financially or otherwise.

2. *Welfare of research subjects.* The psychologist shall respect the dignity and protect the welfare of his/her research subjects, and shall comply with all relevant statutes and administrative rules concerning treatment of research subjects.

E. Protecting confidentiality of clients

1. *In general.* The psychologist shall safeguard the confidential information obtained in the course of practice, teaching, research, or other professional services. With the exceptions set forth below, the psychologist shall disclose confidential information to others only with the informed written consent of the client.

2. *Disclosure without informed written consent.* The psychologist may disclose confidential information without the informed written consent of the client when the psychologist judges that disclosure is necessary to protect against a clear and substantial risk of imminent serious harm being inflicted by the client on the client or another person. In such case,

the psychologist shall limit disclosure of the otherwise confidential information to only those persons and only that content which would be consistent with the standards of the profession in addressing such problems. When the client is an organization, disclosure shall be made only after the psychologist has made a reasonable and unsuccessful attempt to have the problems corrected within the organization.

3. *Services involving more than one interested party*. In a situation in which more than one party has an appropriate interest in the professional services rendered by the psychologist to a client or clients, the psychologist shall, to the extent possible, clarify to all parties prior to rendering the services the dimensions of confidentiality and professional responsibility that shall pertain in the rendering of services. Such clarification is specifically indicated, among other circumstances, when the client is an organization.

4. *Multiple clients*. When service is rendered to more than one client during a joint session, for example to a family or a couple or a parent and child or a group, the psychologist shall at the beginning of the professional relationship clarify to all parties the manner in which confidentiality will be handled. All parties shall be given opportunity to discuss and to accept whatever limitations to confidentiality adhere in the situation.

5. *Legally dependent clients*. At the beginning of a professional relationship, to the extent that the client can understand, the psychologist shall inform a client who is below the age of majority or who has a legal guardian, of the limit the law imposes on the right of confidentiality with respect to his/her communications with the psychologist.

6. *Limited access to client records*. The psychologist shall limit access to client records to preserve their confidentiality and shall assure that all persons working under the psychologist's authority comply with the requirements for confidentiality of client material.

7. *Release of confidential information*. The psychologist may release confidential information upon court order, as defined in Section II of this Code, or to conform with state, federal or provincial law, rule, or regulation.

8. *Reporting of abuse of children and vulnerable adults*. The psychologist shall be familiar with any relevant law concerning the reporting of abuse of children and vulnerable adults, and shall comply with such laws.

9. *Discussion of client information among professionals*. When rendering professional services as part of a team or when interacting with other appropriate professionals concerning the welfare of the client, the psychologist may share confidential information about the client provided the psychologist takes reasonable steps to assure that all persons receiving the information are informed about the confidential nature of the information and abide by the rules of confidentiality.

10. *Disguising confidential information*. When case reports or other confidential information is used as the basis of teaching, research, or other published reports, the psychologist shall exercise reasonable care to ensure that the reported material is appropriately disguised to prevent client identification.

11. *Observation and electronic recording*. The psychologist shall ensure that diagnostic interviews or therapeutic sessions with a client are observed or electronically recorded only with the informed written consent of the client.

12. *Confidentiality after termination of professional relationship*. The psychologist shall continue to treat as confidential information regarding a client after the professional relationship between the psychologist and the client has ceased.

F. Representation of services

1. *Display of license*. The psychologist shall display his/her current (name of jurisdiction) license to practice psychology, on the premises of his/her professional office.

2. *Misrepresentation of qualifications*. The psychologist shall not misrepresent directly or by implication his/her professional qualifications such as education, experience, or areas of competence.

3. *Misrepresentation of affiliations*. The psychologist shall not misrepresent directly or by implication his/her affiliations, or the purposes or characteristics of institutions and organizations with which the psychologist is associated.

4. *False or misleading information*. The psychologist shall not include false or misleading information in public statements concerning professional services offered.

5. *Misrepresentation of services or products*. The psychologist shall not associate with or permit his/her name to be used in connection with any services or products in such a way as to misrepresent (a) the services or products, (b) the degree of his/her responsibility for the services or products, or (c) the nature of his/her association with the services or products.

6. *Correction of misrepresentation by others*. The psychologist shall correct others who misrepresent the psychologist's professional qualifications or affiliations.

G. Fees and statements

1. *Disclosure of cost of services*. The psychologist shall not mislead or withhold from the client, a prospective client, or third party payor, information about the cost of his/her professional services.

2. *Reasonableness of fee*. The psychologist shall not exploit the client or responsible payor by charging a fee that is excessive for the services performed or by entering into an exploitive bartering arrangement in lieu of a fee.

H. Assessment procedures

1. *Confidential information*. The psychologist shall treat an assessment result or interpretation regarding an individual as confidential information.

2. *Communication of results*. The psychologist shall accompany com-

munication of results of assessment procedures to the client, parents, legal guardians or other agents of the client by adequate interpretive aids or explanations.

3. *Reservations concerning results.* The psychologist shall include in his/her report of the results of a formal assessment procedure, for which norms are available, any deficiencies of the assessment norms for the individual assessed and any relevant reservations or qualifications which affect the validity, reliability, or other interpretation of results.

4. *Protection of integrity of assessment procedures.* The psychologist shall not reproduce or describe in popular publications, lectures, or public presentations psychological tests or other assessment devices in ways that might invalidate them.

5. *Information for professional users.* The psychologist offering an assessment procedure or automated interpretation service to other professionals shall accompany this offering by a manual or other printed materials which fully describe the development of the assessment procedure or service, the rationale, evidence of validity and reliability, and characteristics of the normative population. The psychologist shall explicitly state the purpose and application for which the procedure is recommended and identify special qualifications required to administer and interpret it properly. The psychologist shall ensure that the advertisements for the assessment procedure or interpretive service are factual and descriptive.

I. Violations of law

1. *Violation of applicable statutes.* The psychologist shall not violate any applicable statute or administrative rule regulating the practice of psychology.

2. *Use of fraud, misrepresentation, or deception.* The psychologist shall not use fraud, misrepresentation, or deception in obtaining a psychology license, in passing a psychology licensing examination, in assisting another to obtain a psychology license or to pass a psychology licensing examination, in billing clients or third party payors, in providing psychological service, in reporting the results of psychological evaluations or services, or in conducting any other activity related to the practice of psychology.

J. Aiding illegal practice

1. *Aiding unauthorized practice.* The psychologist shall not aid or abet another person in misrepresenting his/her professional credentials or in illegally engaging in the practice of psychology.

2. *Delegating professional responsibility.* The psychologist shall not delegate professional responsibilities to a person not appropriately credentialed or otherwise appropriately qualified to provide such services.

3. *Providing supervision.* The psychologist shall exercise appropriate supervision over supervisees, as set forth in the rules and regulations of the Board.

4. *Reporting of violations to Board.* The psychologist who has sub-

stantial reason to believe that there has been a violation of the statutes or rules of the Board shall so inform the Board in writing, except that when the information regarding such violation is obtained in a professional relationship with a client, the psychologist shall report it only with the written permission of the client. Nothing in this Code shall relieve a psychologist of the duty to file any report required by applicable statutes.

Appendix E

Ethical Principles of Psychologists and Code of Conduct

CONTENTS

3.04 Media Presentations
3.05 Testimonials
3.06 In-Person Solicitation

4. Therapy

4.01 Structuring the Relationship
4.02 Informed Consent to Therapy
4.03 Couple and Family Relationships
4.04 Providing Mental Health Services to Those Served by Others
4.05 Sexual Intimacies With Current Patients or Clients
4.06 Therapy With Former Sexual Partners
4.07 Sexual Intimacies With Former Therapy Patients
4.08 Interruption of Services
4.09 Terminating the Professional Relationship

5. Privacy and Confidentiality

5.01 Discussing the Limits of Confidentiality
5.02 Maintaining Confidentiality
5.03 Minimizing Intrusions on Privacy
5.04 Maintenance of Records
5.05 Disclosures
5.06 Consultations
5.07 Confidential Information in Databases
5.08 Use of Confidential Information for Didactic or Other Purposes
5.09 Preserving Records and Data
5.10 Ownership of Records and Data
5.11 Withholding Records for Nonpayment

6. Teaching, Training Supervision, Research, and Publishing

6.01 Design of Education and Training Programs
6.02 Descriptions of Education and Training Programs
6.03 Accuracy and Objectivity in Teaching
6.04 Limitation on Teaching
6.05 Assessing Student and Supervisee Performance
6.06 Planning Research
6.07 Responsibility
6.08 Compliance With Law and Standards
6.09 Institutional Approval
6.10 Research Responsibilities
6.11 Informed Consent to Research
6.12 Dispensing With Informed Consent
6.13 Informed Consent in Research Filming or Recording
6.14 Offering Inducements for Research Participants
6.15 Deception in Research
6.16 Sharing and Utilizing Data
6.17 Minimizing Invasiveness
6.18 Providing Participants With Information About the Study
6.19 Honoring Commitments
6.20 Care and Use of Animals in Research
6.21 Reporting of Results
6.22 Plagiarism
6.23 Publication Credit
6.24 Duplicate Publication of Data
6.25 Sharing Data
6.26 Professional Reviewers

7. Forensic Activities

7.01 Professionalism
7.02 Forensic Assessments
7.03 Clarification of Role
7.04 Truthfulness and Candor
7.05 Prior Relationships
7.06 Compliance With Law and Rules

8. Resolving Ethical Issues

8.01 Familiarity With Ethics Code
8.02 Confronting Ethical Issues
8.03 Conflicts Between Ethics and Organizational Demands
8.04 Informal Resolution of Ethical Violations
8.05 Reporting Ethical Violations
8.06 Cooperating With Ethics Committees
8.07 Improper Complaints

Introduction

The American Psychological Association's (APA's) Ethical Principles of Psychologists and Code of Conduct (hereinafter referred to as the Ethics Code) consists of an Introduction, a Preamble, six General Principles (A–F), and specific Ethical Standards. The Introduction discusses the intent, organization, procedural considerations, and scope of application of the Ethics Code. The Preamble and General Principles are *aspirational* goals to guide psychologists toward the highest ideals of psychology. Although the Preamble and General Principles are not themselves enforceable rules, they should be considered by psychologists in arriving at an ethical course of action and may be considered by ethics bodies in interpreting the Ethical Standards. The Ethical Standards set forth *enforceable* rules for conduct as psychologists. Most of the Ethical Standards are written broadly, in order to apply to psychologists in varied roles, although the application of an Ethical Standard may vary depending on the context. The Ethical Standards are not exhaustive. The fact that a given conduct is not specif-

---

This version of the APA Ethics Code was adopted by the American Psychological Association's Council of Representatives during its meeting, August 13 and 16, 1992, and its effective beginning December 1, 1992. Inquiries concerning the substance or interpretation of the APA Ethics Code should be addressed to the Director, Office of Ethics, American Psychological Association, 750 First Street, NE, Washington, DC 20002-4242.

This Code will be used to Adjudicate complaints brought concerning alleged conduct occurring on or after the effective date. Complaints regarding conduct occurring prior to the effective date will be adjudicated on the basis of the version of the Code that was in effect at the time the conduct occurred, except that no provisions repealed in June 1989, will be enforced even if an earlier version contains the provision. The Ethics Code will undergo continuing review and study for future revisions; comments on the Code may be sent to the above address.

The APA has previously published its Ethical Standards as follows:

American Psychological Association. (1953). *Ethical standards of psychologists.* Washington, DC: Author.

American Psychological Association. (1958). Standards of ethical behavior for psychologists. *American Psychologist, 13*, 268–271.

American Psychological Association. (1963). Ethical standards of psychologists. *American Psychologist, 18*, 56–60.

American Psychological Association. (1968). Ethical standards of psychologists. *American Psychologist, 23*, 357–361.

American Psychological Association. (1977, March). Ethical standards of psychologists. *APA Monitor*, pp. 22–23.

American Psychological Association. (1979). *Ethical standards of psychologists.* Washington, DC: Author.

American Psychological Association. (1981). Ethical principles of psychologists. *American Psychologist, 36*, 633–638.

American Psychological Association. (1990). Ethical principles of psychologists (Amended June 2, 1989). *American Psychologist, 4*, 390–395.

Request copies of the APA's Ethical Principles of Psychologists and Code of Conduct from the APA Order Department, 750 First Street, NE, Washington, DC 20002-4242, or phone (202) 336-5510.

ically addressed by the Ethics Code does not mean that it is necessarily either ethical or unethical.

Membership in the APA commits members to adhere to the APA Ethics Code and to the rules and procedures used to implement it. Psychologists and students, whether or not they are APA members, should be aware that the Ethics Code may be applied to them by state psychology boards, courts, or other public bodies.

This Ethics Code applies only to psychologists' work-related activities, that is, activities that are part of the psychologists' scientific and professional functions or that are psychological in nature. It includes the clinical or counseling practice of psychology, research, teaching, supervision of trainees, development of assessment instruments, conducting assessments, educational counseling, organizational consulting, social intervention, administration, and other activities as well. These work-related activities can be distinguished from the purely private conduct of a psychologist, which ordinarily is not within the purview of the Ethics Code.

The Ethics Code is intended to provide standards of professional conduct that can be applied by the APA and by other bodies that choose to adopt them. Whether or not a psychologist has violated the Ethics Code does not by itself determine whether he or she is legally liable in a court action, whether a contract is enforceable, or whether other legal consequences occur. These results are based on legal rather than ethical rules. However, compliance with or violation of the Ethics Code may be admissible as evidence in some legal proceedings, depending on the circumstances.

In the process of making decisions regarding their professional behavior, psychologists must consider this Ethics Code, in addition to applicable laws and psychology board regulations. If the Ethics Code establishes a higher standard of conduct than is required by law, psychologists must meet the higher ethical standard. If the Ethics Code standard appears to conflict with the requirements of law, then psychologists make known their commitment to the Ethics Code and take steps to resolve the conflict in a responsible manner. If neither law nor the Ethics Code resolves an issue, psychologists should consider other professional materials[1] and the dic-

---

[1]Professional materials that are most helpful in this regard are guidelines and standards that have been adopted or endorsed by professional psychological organizations. Such guidelines and standards, whether adopted by the American Psychological Association (APA) or its Divisions, are not enforceable as such by this Ethics Code, but are of educative value to psychologists, courts, and professional bodies. Such materials include, but are not limited to, the APA's *General Guidelines for Providers of Psychological Services* (1987), *Specialty Guidelines for the Delivery of Services by Clinical Psychologists, Counseling Psychologists, Industrial / Organizational Psychologists, and School of Psychologists* (1981), *Guidelines for Computer Based Tests and Interpretations* (1987), *Standards for Educational and Psychological Testing* (1985), *Ethical Principles in the Conduct of Research With Human Participants* (1982), *Guidelines for Ethical Conduct in the Care and Use of Animals* (1986), *Guidelines for Providers of Psychological Services to Ethnic, Linguistic, and Culturally Diverse Populations* (1990), and *Publication Manual of the American Psychological Association* (3rd ed., 1983). Materials not adopted by APA as a whole include the APA Division 41 (Forensic Psychology)/American Psychology–Law Society's *Specialty Guidelines for Forensic Psychologists* (1991).

tates of their own conscience, as well as seek consultation with others within the field when this is practical.

The procedures for filing, investigating, and resolving complaints of unethical conduct are described in the current Rules and Procedures of the APA Ethics Committee. The actions that APA may take for violations of the Ethics Code include actions such as reprimand, censure, termination of APA membership, and referral of the matter to other bodies. Complainants who seek remedies such as monetary damages in alleging ethical violations by a psychologist must resort to private negotiation, administrative bodies, or the courts. Actions that violate the Ethics Code may lead to the imposition of sanctions on a psychologist by bodies other than APA, including state psychological associations, other professional groups, psychology boards, other state or federal agencies, and payors for health services. In addition to actions for violation of the Ethics Code, the APA Bylaws provide that APA may take action against a member after his or her conviction of a felony, expulsion or suspension from an affiliated state psychological association, or suspension or loss of licensure.

Preamble

Psychologists work to develop a valid and reliable body of scientific knowledge based on research. They may apply that knowledge to human behavior in a variety of contexts. In doing so, they perform many roles, such as researcher, educator, diagnostician, therapist, supervisor, consultant, administrator, social interventionist, and expert witness. Their goal is to broaden knowledge of behavior and, where appropriate, to apply it pragmatically to improve the condition of both the individual and society. Psychologists respect the central importance of freedom of inquiry and expression in research, teaching, and publication. They also strive to help the public in developing informed judgments and choices concerning human behavior. This Ethics Code provides a common set of values upon which psychologists build their professional and scientific work.

This Code is intended to provide both the general principles and the decision rules to cover most situations encountered by psychologists. It has as its primary goal the welfare and protection of the individuals and groups with whom psychologists work. It is the individual responsibility of each psychologist to aspire to the highest possible standards of conduct. Psychologists respect and protect human and civil rights, and do not knowingly participate in or condone unfair discriminatory practices.

The development of a dynamic set of ethical standards for a psychologist's work-related conduct requires a personal commitment to a lifelong effort to act ethically; to encourage ethical behavior by students, supervisees, employees, and colleagues, as appropriate; and to consult with others, as needed, concerning ethical problems. Each psychologist supplements, but does not violate, the Ethics Code's values and rules on the basis of guidance drawn from personal values, culture, and experience.

General Principles

Principle A: Competence

Psychologists strive to maintain high standards of competence in their work. They recognize the boundaries of their particular competencies and the limitations of their expertise. They provide only those services and use only those techniques for which they are qualified by education, training, or experience. Psychologists are cognizant of the fact that the competencies required in serving, teaching, and/or studying groups of people vary with the distinctive characteristics of those groups. In those areas in which recognized professional standards do not yet exist, psychologists exercise careful judgment and take appropriate precautions to protect the welfare of those with whom they work. They maintain knowledge of relevant scientific and professional information related to the services they render, and they recognize the need for ongoing education. Psychologists make appropriate use of scientific, professional, technical, and administrative resources.

Principle B: Integrity

Psychologists seek to promote integrity in the science, teaching, and practice of psychology. In these activities psychologists are honest, fair, and respectful of others. In describing or reporting their qualifications, services, products, fees, research, or teaching, they do not make statements that are false, misleading, or deceptive. Psychologists strive to be aware of their own belief systems, values, needs, and limitations and the effect of these on their work. To the extent feasible, they attempt to clarify for relevant parties the roles they are performing and to function appropriately in accordance with those roles. Psychologists avoid improper and potentially harmful dual relationships.

Principle C: Professional and Scientific Responsibility

Psychologists uphold professional standards of conduct, clarify their professional roles and obligations, accept appropriate responsibility for their behavior, and adapt their methods to the needs of different populations. Psychologists consult with, refer to, or cooperate with other professionals and institutions to the extent needed to serve the best interests of their patients, clients, or other recipients of their services. Psychologists' moral standards and conduct are personal matters to the same degree as is true for any other person, except as psychologists' conduct may compromise their professional responsibilities or reduce the public's trust in psychology and psychologists. Psychologists are concerned about the ethical compliance of their colleagues' scientific and professional conduct. When appropriate, they consult with colleagues in order to prevent or avoid unethical conduct.

Principle D: Respect for People's Rights and Dignity

Psychologists accord appropriate respect to the fundamental rights, dignity, and worth of all people. They respect the rights of individuals to privacy, confidentiality, self-determination, and autonomy, mindful that legal and other obligations may lead to inconsistency and conflict with the exercise of these rights. Psychologists are aware of cultural, individual, and role differences, including those due to age, gender, race, ethnicity, national origin, religion, sexual orientation, disability, language, and socioeconomic status. Psychologists try to eliminate the effect on their work of biases based on those factors, and they do not knowingly participate in or condone unfair discriminatory practices.

Principle E: Concern for Others' Welfare

Psychologists seek to contribute to the welfare of those with whom they interact professionally. In their professional actions, psychologists weigh the welfare and rights of their patients or clients, students, supervisees, human research participants, and other affected persons, and the welfare of animal subjects of research. When conflicts occur among psychologists' obligations or concerns, they attempt to resolve these conflicts and to perform their roles in a responsible fashion that avoids or minimizes harm. Psychologists are sensitive to real and ascribed differences in power between themselves and others, and they do not exploit or mislead other people during or after professional relationships.

Principle F: Social Responsibility

Psychologists are aware of their professional and scientific responsibilities to the community and the society in which they work and live. They apply and make public their knowledge of psychology in order to contribute to human welfare. Psychologists are concerned about and work to mitigate the causes of human suffering. When undertaking research, they strive to advance human welfare and the science of psychology. Psychologists try to avoid misuse of their work. Psychologists comply with the law and encourage the development of law and social policy that serve the interests of their patients and clients and the public. They are encouraged to contribute a portion of their professional time for little or no personal advantage.

Ethical Standards

1. *General Standards*

These General Standards are potentially applicable to the professional and scientific activities of all psychologists.

1.01 Applicability of the Ethics Code

The activity of a psychologist subject to the Ethics Code may be reviewed under these Ethical Standards only if the activity is part of his or her work-related functions or the activity is psychological in nature. Personal activities having no connection to or effect on psychological roles are not subject to the Ethics Code.

1.02 Relationship of Ethics and Law

If psychologists' ethical responsibilities conflict with law, psychologists make known their commitment to the Ethics Code and take steps to resolve the conflict in a responsible manner.

1.03 Professional and Scientific Relationship

Psychologists provide diagnostic, therapeutic, teaching, research, supervisory, consultative, or other psychological services only in the context of a defined professional or scientific relationship or role. (See also Standards 2.01, Evaluation, Diagnosis, and Interventions in Professional Context, and 7.02, Forensic Assessments.)

1.04 Boundaries of Competence

(a) Psychologists provide services, teach, and conduct research only within the boundaries of their competence, based on their education, training, supervised experience, or appropriate professional experience.

(b) Psychologists provide services, teach, or conduct research in new areas or involving new techniques only after first undertaking appropriate study, training, supervision, and/or consultation from persons who are competent in those areas or techniques.

(c) In those emerging areas in which generally recognized standards for preparatory training do not yet exist, psychologists nevertheless take reasonable steps to ensure the competence of their work and to protect patients, clients, students, research participants, and others from harm.

1.05 Maintaining Expertise

Psychologists who engage in assessment, therapy, teaching, research, organizational consulting, or other professional activities maintain a reasonable level of awareness of current scientific and professional information in their fields of activity, and undertake ongoing efforts to maintain competence in the skills they use.

1.06 Basis for Scientific and Professional Judgments

Psychologists rely on scientifically and professionally derived knowledge when making scientific or professional judgments or when engaging in scholarly or professional endeavors.

1.07 Describing the Nature and Results of Psychological Services

(a) When psychologists provide assessment, evaluation, treatment, counseling, supervision, teaching, consultation, research, or other psychological services to an individual, a group, or an organization, they provide, using language that is reasonably understandable to the recipient of those services, appropriate information beforehand about the nature of such services and appropriate information later about results and consultations. (See also Standard 2.09, Explaining Assessment Results.)

(b) If psychologists will be precluded by law or by organizational roles from providing such information to particular individuals or groups, they so inform those individuals or groups at the outset of the service.

1.08 Human Differences

Where differences of age, gender, race, ethnicity, national origin, religion, sexual orientation, disability, language, or socioeconomic status significantly affect psychologists' work concerning particular individuals or groups, psychologists obtain the training, experience, consultation, or supervision necessary to ensure the competence of their services, or they make appropriate referrals.

1.09 Respecting Others

In their work-related activities, psychologists respect the rights of others to hold values, attitudes, and opinions that differ from their own.

1.10 Nondiscrimination

In their work-related activities, psychologists do not engage in unfair discrimination based on age, gender, race, ethnicity, national origin, religion, sexual orientation, disability, socioeconomic status, or any basis proscribed by law.

1.11 Sexual Harassment

(a) Psychologists do not engage in sexual harassment. Sexual harassment is sexual solicitation, physical advances, or verbal or nonverbal conduct that is sexual in nature, that occurs in connection with the psychologist's activities or roles as a psychologist, and that either: (1) is unwelcome, is offensive, or creates a hostile workplace environment, and the psychologist knows or is told this; or (2) is sufficiently severe or intense to be abusive to a reasonable person in the context. Sexual harassment can consist of a single intense or severe act or of multiple persistent or pervasive acts.

(b) Psychologists accord sexual-harassment complaints and respondents dignity and respect. Psychologists do not participate in denying a person academic admittance or advancement, employment, tenure, or promotion, based solely upon their having made, or their being the subject of, sexual-harassment charges. This does not preclude taking action based upon the outcome of such proceedings or consideration of other appropriate information.

1.12 Other Harassment

Psychologists do not knowingly engage in behavior that is harassing or demeaning to persons with whom they interact in their work based on factors such as those persons' age, gender, race, ethnicity, national origin, religion, sexual orientation, disability, language, or socioeconomic status.

1.13 Personal Problems and Conflicts

(a) Psychologists recognize that their personal problems and conflicts may interfere with their effectiveness. Accordingly, they refrain from undertaking an activity when they know or should know that their personal problems are likely to lead to harm to a patient, client, colleague, student, research participant, or other person to whom they may owe a professional or scientific obligation.

(b) In addition, psychologists have an obligation to be alert to signs of, and to obtain assistance for, their personal problems at an early stage, in order to prevent significantly impaired performance.

(c) When psychologists become aware of personal problems that may interfere with their performing work-related duties adequately, they take appropriate measures, such as obtaining professional consultation or assistance, and determine whether they should limit, suspend, or terminate their work-related duties.

1.14 Avoiding Harm

Psychologists take reasonable steps to avoid harming their patients or clients, research participants, students, and others with whom they work, and to minimize harm where it is foreseeable and unavoidable.

1.15 Misuse of Psychologists' Influence

Because psychologists' scientific and professional judgments and actions may affect the lives of others, they are alert to and guard against personal, financial, social, organizational, or political factors that might lead to misuse of their influence.

1.16 Misuse of Psychologists' Work

(a) Psychologists do not participate in activities in which it appears likely that their skills or data will be misused by others, unless corrective mechanisms are available. (See also Standard 7.04, Truthfulness and Candor.)

(b) If psychologists learn of misuse or misrepresentation of their work, they take reasonable steps to correct or minimize the misuse or misrepresentation.

1.17 Multiple Relationships

(a) In many communities and situations, it may not be feasible or reasonable for psychologists to avoid social or other nonprofessional contacts with persons such as patients, clients, students, supervisees, or research participants. Psychologists must always be sensitive to the potential harmful effects of other contacts on their work and on those persons with whom they deal. A psychologist refrains from entering into or promising another personal, scientific, professional, financial, or other relationship with such persons if it appears likely that such a relationship reasonably might impair the psychologist's objectivity or otherwise interfere with the psychologist's effectively performing his or her function as a psychologist, or might harm or exploit the other party.

(b) Likewise, whenever feasible, a psychologist refrains from taking on professional or scientific obligations when preexisting relationships would create a risk of such harm.

(c) If a psychologist finds that, due to unforeseen factors, a potentially harmful multiple relationship has arisen, the psychologist attempts to resolve it with due regard for the best interests of the affected person and maximal compliance with the Ethics Code.

1.18 Barter (With Patients or Clients)

Psychologists ordinarily refrain from accepting goods, services, or other nonmonetary remuneration from patients or clients in return for psychological services because such arrangements create inherent potential for conflicts, exploitation, and distortion of the professional relationship. A psychologist may participate in bartering only if (1) it is not clinically contraindicated, and (2) the relationship is not exploitative. (See also

Standards 1.17, Multiple Relationships, and 1.25, Fees and Financial Arrangements.)

1.19 Exploitative Relationships

(a) Psychologists do not exploit persons over whom they have supervisory, evaluative, or other authority such as students, supervisees, employees, research participants, and clients or patients. (See also Standards 4.05–4.07 regarding sexual involvement with clients or patients.)

(b) Psychologists do not engage in sexual relationships with students or supervisees in training over whom the psychologist has evaluative or direct authority, because such relationships are so likely to impair judgment or be exploitative.

1.20 Consultations and Referrals

(a) Psychologists arrange for appropriate consultations and referrals based principally on the best interests of their patients or clients, with appropriate consent, and subject to other relevant considerations, including applicable law and contractual obligations. (See also Standards 5.01, Discussing the Limits of Confidentiality, and 5.06, Consultations.)

(b) When indicated and professionally appropriate, psychologists cooperate with other professionals in order to serve their patients or clients effectively and appropriately.

(c) Psychologists' referral practices are consistent with law.

1.21 Third-Party Requests for Services

(a) When a psychologist agrees to provide services to a person or entity at the request of a third party, the psychologist clarifies to the extent feasible, at the outset of the service, the nature of the relationship with each party. This clarification includes the role of the psychologist (such as therapist, organizational consultant, diagnostician, or expert witness), the probable uses of the services provided or the information obtained, and the fact that there may be limits to confidentiality.

(b) If there is a foreseeable risk of the psychologist's being called upon to perform conflicting roles because of the involvement of a third party, the psychologist clarifies the nature and direction of his or her responsibilities, keeps all parties appropriately informed as matters develop, and resolves the situation in accordance with this Ethics Code.

1.22 Delegation to and Supervision of Subordinates

(a) Psychologists delegate to their employees, supervisees, and research assistants only those responsibilities that such persons can reasonably be expected to perform competently, on the basis of their education, training, or experience, either independently or with the level of supervision being provided.

(b) Psychologists provide proper training and supervision to their employees or supervisees and take reasonable steps to see that such persons perform services responsibly, competently, and ethically.

(c) If institutional policies, procedures, or practices prevent fulfillment of this obligation, psychologists attempt to modify their role or to correct the situation to the extent feasible.

1.23 Documentation of Professional and Scientific Work

(a) Psychologists appropriately document their professional and scientific work in order to facilitate provision of services later by them or by other professionals, to ensure accountability, and to meet other requirements of institutions or the law.

(b) When psychologists have reason to believe that records of their professional services will be used in legal proceedings involving recipients of or participants in their work, they have a responsibility to create and maintain documentation in the kind of detail and quality that would be consistent with reasonable scrutiny in an adjudicative forum. (See also Standard 7.01, Professionalism, under Forensic Activities.)

1.24 Records and Data

Psychologists create, maintain, disseminate, store, retain, and dispose of records and data relating to their research, practice, and other work in accordance with law and in a manner that permits compliance with the requirements of this Ethics Code. (See also Standard 5.04, Maintenance of Records.)

1.25 Fees and Financial Arrangements

(a) As early as is feasible in a professional or scientific relationship, the psychologist and the patient, client, or other appropriate recipient of psychological services reach an agreement specifying the compensation and the billing arrangements.

(b) Psychologists do not exploit recipients of services or payors with respect to fees.

(c) Psychologists' fee practices are consistent with law.

(d) Psychologists do not misrepresent their fees.

(e) If limitations to services can be anticipated because of limitations in financing, this is discussed with the patient, client, or other appropriate recipient of services as early as is feasible. (See also Standard 4.08, Interruption of Services.)

(f) If the patient, client, or other recipient of services does not pay for services as agreed, and if the psychologist wishes to use collection agencies or legal measures to collect the fees, the psychologist first informs the person that such measures will be taken and provides that person an opportunity to make prompt payment. (See also Standard 5.11, Withholding Records for Nonpayment.)

1.26 Accuracy in Reports to Payors and Funding Sources

In their reports to payors for services or sources of research funding, psychologists accurately state the nature of the research or service provided, the fees or charges, and where applicable, the identity of the provider, the findings, and the diagnosis. (See also Standard 5.05, Disclosures.)

1.27 Referrals and Fees

When a psychologist pays, receives payment from, or divides fees with another professional other than in an employer–employee relationship, the payment to each is based on the services (clinical, consultative, administrative, or other) provided and is not based on the referral itself.

2. *Evaluative, Assessment, or Intervention*

2.01 Evaluation, Diagnosis, and Interventions in Professional Context

(a) Psychologists perform evaluations, diagnosis services, or interventions only within the context of a defined professional relationship. (See also Standard 1.03, Professional and Scientific Relationship.)

(b) Psychologists' assessments, recommendations, reports, and psychological diagnostic or evaluative statements are based on information and techniques (including personal interviews of the individual when appropriate) sufficient to provide appropriate substantiation for their findings. (See also Standard 7.02, Forensic Assessments.)

2.02 Competence and Appropriate Use of Assessments and Interventions

(a) Psychologists who develop, administer, score, interpret, or use psychological assessment techniques, interviews, tests, or instruments do so in a manner and for purposes that are appropriate in light of the research on or evidence of the usefulness and proper application of the techniques.

(b) Psychologists refrain from misuse of assessment techniques, interventions, results, and interpretations and take reasonable steps to prevent others from misusing the information these techniques provide. This includes refraining from releasing raw test results or raw data to persons, other than to patients or clients as appropriate, who are not qualified to use such information. (See also Standards 1.02, Relationship of Ethics and Law, and 1.04, Boundaries of Competence.)

2.03 Test Construction

Psychologists who develop and conduct research with tests and other assessment techniques use specific procedures and current professional knowledge for test design, standardization, validation, reduction or elimination of bias, and recommendations for use.

2.04 Use of Assessment in General and With Special Populations

(a) Psychologists who perform interventions or administer, score, interpret, or use assessment techniques are familiar with the reliability, validation, and related standardization or outcome studies of, and proper applications and uses of, the techniques they use.

(b) Psychologists recognize limits to the certainty with which diagnoses, judgments, or predictions can be made about individuals.

(c) Psychologists attempt to identify situations in which particular interventions or assessment techniques or norms may not be applicable or may require adjustment in administration or interpretation because of factors such as individuals' gender, age, race, ethnicity, national origin, religion, sexual orientation, disability, language, or socioeconomic status.

2.05 Interpreting Assessment Results

When interpreting assessment results, including automated interpretations, psychologists take into account the various test factors and characteristics of the person being assessed that might affect psychologists' judgments or reduce the accuracy of their interpretations. They indicate any significant reservations they have about the accuracy or limitations of their interpretations.

2.06 Unqualified Persons

Psychologists do not promote the use of psychological assessment techniques by unqualified persons. (See also Standard 1.22, Delegation to and Supervision of Subordinates.)

2.07 Obsolete Tests and Outdated Test Results

(a) Psychologists do not base their assessment or intervention decisions or recommendations on data or test results that are outdated for the current purpose.

(b) Similarly, psychologists do not base such decisions or recommendations on tests and measures that are obsolete and not useful for the current purpose.

2.08 Test Scoring and Interpretation Services

(a) Psychologists who offer assessment or scoring procedures to other professionals accurately describe the purpose, norms, validity, reliability, and applications of the procedures and any special qualifications applicable to their use.

(b) Psychologists select scoring and interpretation services (including automated services) on the basis of evidence of the validity of the program and procedures as well as on other appropriate considerations.

(c) Psychologists retain appropriate responsibility for the appropriate application, interpretation, and use of assessment instruments, whether they score and interpret such tests themselves or use automated or other services.

2.09 Explaining Assessment Results

Unless the nature of the relationship is clearly explained to the person being assessed in advance and precludes provision of an explanation of results (such as in some organizational consulting, preemployment or security screenings, and forensic evaluations), psychologists ensure that an explanation of the results is provided using language that is reasonably understandable to the person assessed or to another legally authorized person on behalf of the client. Regardless of whether the scoring and interpretation are done by the psychologist, by assistants, or by automated or other outside services, psychologists take reasonable steps to ensure that appropriate explanations of results are given.

2.10 Maintaining Test Security

Psychologists make reasonable efforts to maintain the integrity and security of tests and other assessment techniques consistent with law, contractual obligations, and in a manner that permits compliance with the requirements of this Ethics Code. (See also Standard 1.02, Relationship of Ethics and Law.)

3. *Advertising and Other Public Statements*

3.01 Definition of Public Statements

Psychologists comply with this Ethics Code in public statements relating to their professional services, products, or publications or to the field of psychology. Public statements include but are not limited to paid or unpaid advertising, brochures, printed matter, directory listings, personal resumes or curricula vitae, interviews or comments for use in media, statements in legal proceedings, lectures and public oral presentations, and published materials.

3.02 Statements by Others

(a) Psychologists who engage others to create or place public statements that promote their professional practice, products, or activities retain professional responsibility for such statements.

(b) In addition, psychologists make reasonable efforts to prevent others whom they do not control (such as employers, publishers, sponsors, organizational clients, and representatives of the print or broadcast media) from making deceptive statements concerning psychologists' practice or professional or scientific activities.

(c) If psychologists learn of deceptive statements about their work made by others, psychologists make reasonable efforts to correct such statements.

(d) Psychologists do not compensate employees of press, radio, television, or other communication media in return for publicity in a news item.

(e) A paid advertisement relating to the psychologist's activities must be identified as such, unless it is already apparent from the context.

3.03 Avoidance of False or Deceptive Statements

(a) Psychologists do not make public statements that are false, deceptive, misleading, or fraudulent, either because of what they state, convey, or suggest or because of what they omit, concerning their research, practice, or other work activities or those of persons or organizations with which they are affiliated. As examples (and not in limitation) of this standard, psychologists do not make false or deceptive statements concerning (1) their training, experience, or competence; (2) their academic degrees; (3) their credentials; (4) their institutional or association affiliations; (5) their services; (6) the scientific or clinical basis for, or results or degree of success of, their services; (7) their fees; or (8) their publications or research findings. (See also Standards 6.15, Deception in Research, and 6.18, Providing Participants With Information About the Study.)

(b) Psychologists claim as credentials for their psychological work, only degrees that (1) were earned from a regionally accredited educational institution or (2) were the basis for psychology licensure by the state in which they practice.

3.04 Media Presentations

When psychologists provide advice or comment by means of public lectures, demonstrations, radio or television programs, prerecorded tapes, printed articles, mailed material, or other media, they take reasonable precautions to ensure that (1) the statements are based on appropriate psychological literature and practice, (2) the statements are otherwise consistent with this Ethics Code, and (3) the recipients of the information are not encouraged to infer that a relationship has been established with them personally.

3.05 Testimonials

Psychologists do not solicit testimonials from current psychotherapy clients or patients or other persons who because of their particular circumstances are vulnerable to undue influence.

3.06 In-Person Solicitation

Psychologists do not engage, directly or through agents, in uninvited in-person solicitation of business from actual or potential psychotherapy patients or clients or other persons who because of their particular circumstances are vulnerable to undue influence. However, this does not preclude attempting to implement appropriate collateral contacts with significant others for the purpose of benefiting an already engaged therapy patient.

4. Therapy

4.01 Structuring the Relationship

(a) Psychologists discuss with clients or patients as early as is feasible in the therapeutic relationship appropriate issues, such as the nature and anticipated course of therapy, fees, and confidentiality. (See also Standards 1.25, Fees and Financial Arrangements, and 5.01, Discussing the Limits of Confidentiality.)

(b) When the psychologist's work with clients or patients will be supervised, the above discussion includes that fact, and the name of the supervisor, when the supervisor has legal responsibility for the case.

(c) When the therapist is a student intern, the client or patient is informed of that fact.

(d) Psychologists make reasonable efforts to answer patients' questions and to avoid apparent misunderstandings about therapy. Whenever possible, psychologists provide oral and/or written information, using language that is reasonably understandable to the patient or client.

4.02 Informed Consent to Therapy

(a) Psychologists obtain appropriate informed consent to therapy or related procedures, using language that is reasonably understanding to participants. The content of informed consent will vary depending on many circumstances; however, informed consent generally implies that the person (1) has the capacity to consent, (2) has been informed of significant information concerning the procedure, (3) has freely and without undue influence expressed consent, and (4) consent has been appropriately documented.

(b) When persons are legally incapable of giving informed consent, psychologists obtain informed permission from a legally authorized person, if such substitute consent is permitted by law.

(c) In addition, psychologists (1) inform those persons who are legally incapable of giving informed consent about the proposed interventions in a manner commensurate with the persons' psychological capacities, (2) seek their assent to those interventions, and (3) consider such persons' preferences and best interests.

4.03 Couple and Family Relationships

(a) When a psychologist agrees to provide services to several persons who have a relationship (such as husband and wife or parents and children), the psychologist attempts to clarify at the outset (1) which of the individuals are patients or clients and (2) the relationship the psychologist will have with each person. This clarification includes the role of the psychologist and the probable uses of the services provided or the information obtained. (See also Standard 5.01, Discussing the Limits of Confidentiality.)

(b) As soon as it becomes apparent that the psychologist may be called on to perform potentially conflicting roles (such as marital counselor to husband and wife, and then witness for one party in a divorce proceeding), the psychologist attempts to clarify and adjust, or withdraw from, roles appropriately. (See also Standard 7.03, Clarification of Role, under Forensic Activities.)

4.04 Providing Mental Health Services to Those Served by Others

In deciding whether to offer or provide services to those already receiving mental health services elsewhere, psychologists carefully consider the treatment issues and the potential patient's or client's welfare. The psychologist discusses these issues with the patient or client, or another legally authorized person on behalf of the client, in order to minimize the risk of confusion and conflict, consults with the other service providers when appropriate, and proceeds with caution and sensitivity to the therapeutic issues.

4.05 Sexual Intimacies With Current Patients or Clients

Psychologists do not engage in sexual intimacies with current patients or clients.

4.06 Therapy With Former Sexual Partners

Psychologists do not accept as therapy patients or clients persons with whom they have engaged in sexual intimacies.

4.07 Sexual Intimacies With Former Therapy Patients

(a) Psychologists do not engage in sexual intimacies with a former therapy patient or client for at least two years after cessation or termination of professional services.

(b) Because sexual intimacies with a former therapy patient or client are so frequently harmful to the patient or client, and because such intimacies undermine public confidence in the psychology profession and thereby deter the public's use of needed services, psychologists do not engage in sexual intimacies with former therapy patients and clients even after a two-year interval except in the most unusual circumstances. The psychologist who engages in such activity after the two years following cessation or termination of treatment bears the burden of demonstrating that there has been no exploitation, in light of all relevant factors, including (1) the amount of time that has passed since therapy terminated, (2) the nature and duration of the therapy, (3) the circumstances of termination, (4) the patient's or client's personal history, (5) the patient's or client's current mental status, (6) the likelihood of adverse impact on the patient or client and others, and (7) any statements or actions made by the therapist during the course of therapy suggesting or inviting the possibility of a posttermination sexual or romantic relationship with the patient or client. (See also Standard 1.17, Multiple Relationships.)

4.08 Interruption of Services

(a) Psychologists make reasonable efforts to plan for facilitating care in the event that psychological services are interrupted by factors such as the psychologist's illness, death, unavailability, or relocation or by the client's relocation or financial limitations. (See also Standard 5.09, Preserving Records and Data.)

(b) When entering into employment or contractual relationships, psychologists provide for orderly and appropriate resolution of responsibility for patient or client care in the event that the employment or contractual relationship ends, with paramount consideration given to the welfare of the patient or client.

4.09 Terminating the Professional Relationship

(a) Psychologists do not abandon patients or clients. (See also Standard 1.25e, under Fees and Financial Arrangements.)

(b) Psychologists terminate a professional relationship when it becomes reasonably clear that the patient or client no longer needs the service, is not benefiting, or is being harmed by continued service.

(c) Prior to termination for whatever reason, except where precluded by the patient's or client's conduct, the psychologist discusses the patient's or client's views and needs, provides appropriate pretermination counseling, suggests alternative service providers as appropriate, and takes other reasonable steps to facilitate transfer of responsibility to another provider if the patient or client needs one immediately.

5. *Privacy and Confidentiality*

These Standards are potentially applicable to the professional and scientific activities of all psychologists.

5.01 Discussing the Limits of Confidentiality

(a) Psychologists discuss with persons and organizations with whom they establish a scientific, or professional relationship (including, to the extent feasible, minors and their legal representatives) (1) the relevant limitations on confidentiality, including limitations where applicable in group, marital, and family therapy or in organizational consulting, and (2) the foreseeable uses of the information generated through their services.

(b) Unless it is not feasible or is contraindicated, the discussion of confidentiality occurs at the outset of the relationship and thereafter as new circumstances may warrant.

(c) Permission for electronic recording of interviews is secured from clients and patients.

5.02 Maintaining Confidentiality

Psychologists have a primary obligation and take reasonable precautions to respect the confidentiality rights of those with whom they work or consult, recognizing that confidentiality may be established by law, institutional rules, or professional or scientific relationships. (See also Standard 6.26, Professional Reviewers.)

5.03 Minimizing Intrusions on Privacy

(a) In order to minimize intrusions on privacy, psychologists include in written and oral reports, consultations, and the like, only information germane to the purpose for which the communication is made.

(b) Psychologists discuss confidential information obtained in clinical or consulting relationships, or evaluative data concerning patients, individual or organizational clients, students, research participants, supervisees, and employees, only for appropriate scientific or professional purposes and only with persons clearly concerned with such matters.

5.04 Maintenance of Records

Psychologists maintain appropriate confidentiality in creating, storing, accessing, transferring, and disposing of records under their control, whether these are written, automated, or in any other medium. Psychologists maintain and dispose of records in accordance with law and in a manner that permits compliance with the requirements of this Ethics Code.

5.05 Disclosures

(a) Psychologists disclose confidential information without the consent of the individual only as mandated by law, or where permitted by law for a valid purpose, such as (1) to provide needed professional services to the patient or the individual or organizational client, (2) to obtain appropriate professional consultations, (3) to protect the patient or client or others from harm, or (4) to obtain payment for services, in which instance disclosure is limited to the minimum that is necessary to achieve the purpose.

(b) Psychologists also may disclose confidential information with the appropriate consent of the patient or the individual or organizational client (or of another legally authorized person on behalf of the patient or client), unless prohibited by law.

5.06 Consultations

When consulting with colleagues, (1) psychologists do not share confidential information that reasonably could lead to the identification of a patient, client, research participant, or other person or organization with whom they have a confidential relationship unless they have obtained the prior consent of the person or organization or the disclosure cannot be avoided, and (2) they share information only to the extent necessary to achieve the purposes of the consultation. (See also Standard 5.02, Maintaining Confidentiality.)

5.07 Confidential Information in Databases

(a) If confidential information concerning recipients of psychological services is to be entered into databases or systems of records available to persons whose access has not been consented to by the recipient, then psychologists use coding or other techniques to avoid the inclusion of personal identifiers.

(b) If a research protocol approved by an institutional review board or similar body requires the inclusion of personal identifiers, such identifiers are deleted before the information is made accessible to persons other than those of whom the subject was advised.

(c) If such deletion is not feasible, then before psychologists transfer such data to others or review such data collected by others, they take reasonable steps to determine that appropriate consent of personally identifiable individuals has been obtained.

5.08 Use of Confidential Information for Didactic or Other Purposes

(a) Psychologists do not disclose in their writings, lectures, or other public media, confidential, personally identifiable information concerning their patients, individual or organizational clients, students, research participants, or other recipients of their services that they obtained during the course of their work, unless the person or organization has consented in writing or unless there is other ethical or legal authorization for doing so.

(b) Ordinarily, in such scientific and professional presentations, psychologists disguise confidential information concerning such persons or organizations so that they are not individually identifiable to others and so that discussions do not cause harm to subjects who might identify themselves.

5.09 Preserving Records and Data

A psychologist makes plans in advance so that confidentiality of records and data is protected in the event of the psychologist's death, incapacity, or withdrawal from the position or practice.

5.10 Ownership of Records and Data

Recognizing that ownership of records and data is governed by legal principles, psychologists take reasonable and lawful steps so that records and data remain available to the extent needed to serve the best interests of patients, individual or organizational clients, research participants, or appropriate others.

5.11 Withholding Records for Nonpayment

Psychologists may not withhold records under their control that are requested and imminently needed for a patient's or client's treatment solely because payment has not been received, except as otherwise provided by law.

6. Teaching, Training Supervision, Research, and Publishing

6.01 Design of Education and Training Programs

Psychologists who are responsible for education and training programs seek to ensure that the programs are competently designed, provide the proper experiences, and meet the requirements for licensure, certification, or other goals for which claims are made by the program.

6.02 Descriptions of Education and Training Programs

(a) Psychologists responsible for education and training programs seek to ensure that there is a current and accurate description of the program content, training goals and objectives, and requirements that must be met for satisfactory completion of the program. This information must be made readily available to all interested parties.

(b) Psychologists seek to ensure that statements concerning their course outlines are accurate and not misleading, particularly regarding the subject matter to be covered, bases for evaluating progress, and the nature of course experiences. (See also Standard 3.03, Avoidance of False or Deceptive Statements.)

(c) To the degree to which they exercise control, psychologists responsible for announcements, catalogs, brochures, or advertisements describing workshops, seminars, or other non-degree-granting educational programs ensure that they accurately describe the audience for which the program is intended, the educational objectives, the presenters, and the fees involved.

6.03 Accuracy and Objectivity in Teaching

(a) When engaged in teaching or training, psychologists present psychological information accurately and with a reasonable degree of objectivity.

(b) When engaged in teaching or training, psychologists recognize the power they hold over students or supervisees and therefore make reasonable efforts to avoid engaging in conduct that is personally demeaning to students or supervisees. (See also Standards 1.09, Respecting Others, and 1.12, Other Harassment.)

6.04 Limitation on Teaching

Psychologists do not teach the use of techniques or procedures that require specialized training, licensure, or expertise, including but not limited to hypnosis, biofeedback, and projective techniques, to individuals who lack the prerequisite training, legal scope of practice, or expertise.

6.05 Assessing Student and Supervisee Performance

(a) In academic and supervisory relationships, psychologists establish an appropriate process for providing feedback to students and supervisees.

(b) Psychologists evaluate students and supervisees on the basis of their actual performance on relevant and established program requirements.

6.06 Planning Research

(a) Psychologists design, conduct, and report research in accordance with recognized standards of scientific competence and ethical research.

(b) Psychologists plan their research so as to minimize the possibility that results will be misleading.

(c) In planning research, psychologists consider its ethical acceptability under the Ethics Code. If an ethical issue is unclear, psychologists seek to resolve the issue through consultation with institutional review boards, animal care and use committees, peer consultations, or other proper mechanisms.

(d) Psychologists take responsible steps to implement appropriate protections for the rights and welfare of human participants, other persons affected by the research, and the welfare of animal subjects.

6.07 Responsibility

(a) Psychologists conduct research competently and with due concern for the dignity and welfare of the participants.

(b) Psychologists are responsible for the ethical conduct of research conducted by them or by others under their supervision or control.

(c) Researchers and assistants are permitted to perform only those tasks for which they are appropriately trained and prepared.

(d) As part of the process of development and implementation of research projects, psychologists consult those with expertise concerning any special population under investigation or most likely to be affected.

6.08 Compliance With Law and Standards

Psychologists plan and conduct research in a manner consistent with federal and state law and regulations, as well as professional standards governing the conduct of research, and particularly those standards governing research with human participants and animal subjects.

6.09 Institutional Approval

Psychologists obtain from host institutions or organizations appropriate approval prior to conducting research, and they provide accurate information about their research proposals. They conduct the research in accordance with the approved research protocol.

6.10 Research Responsibilities

Prior to conducting research (except research involving only anonymous surveys, naturalistic observations, or similar research), psychologists enter into an agreement with participants that clarifies the nature of the research and the responsibilities of each party.

6.11 Informed Consent to Research

(a) Psychologists use language that is reasonably understandable to research participants in obtaining their appropriate informed consent (except as provided in Standard 6.12, Dispensing With Informed Consent). Such informed consent is appropriately documented.

(b) Using language that is reasonably understandable to participants, psychologists inform participants of the nature of the research; they inform participants that they are free to participate or to decline to participate or to withdraw from the research; they explain the foreseeable consequences of declining or withdrawing; they inform participants of significant factors that may be expected to influence their willingness to participate (such as risks, discomfort, adverse effects, or limitations on confidentiality, except as provided in Standard 6.15, Deception in Research); and they explain other aspects about which the prospective participants inquire.

(c) When psychologists conduct research with individuals such as students or subordinates, psychologists take special care to protect the prospective participants from adverse consequences of declining or withdrawing from participation.

(d) When research participation is a course requirement or opportunity for extra credit, the prospective participant is given the choice of equitable alternative activities.

(e) For persons who are legally incapable of giving informed consent, psychologists nevertheless (1) provide an appropriate explanation, (2) obtain the participant's assent, and (3) obtain appropriate permission from a legally authorized person, if such substitute consent is permitted by law.

6.12 Dispensing With Informed Consent

Before determining that planned research (such as research involving only anonymous questionnaires, naturalistic observations, or certain kinds of archival research) does not require the informed consent of research participants, psychologists consider applicable regulations and institutional review board requirements, and they consult with colleagues as appropriate.

6.13 Informed Consent in Research Filming or Recording

Psychologists obtain informed consent from research participants prior to filming or recording them in any form, unless the research involves simply naturalistic observations in public places and it is not anticipated that the recording will be used in a manner that could cause personal identification or harm.

6.14 Offering Inducement for Research Participants

(a) In offering professional services as an inducement to obtain research participants, psychologists make clear the nature of the services, as well as the risks, obligations, and limitations. (See also Standard 1.18 Barter [With Patients or Clients].)

(b) Psychologists do not offer excessive or inappropriate financial or other inducements to obtain research participants, particularly when it might tend to coerce participation.

6.15 Deception in Research

(a) Psychologists do not conduct a study involving deception unless they have determined that the use of deceptive techniques is justified by the study's prospective scientific, educational, or applied value and that equally effective alternative procedures that do not use deception are not feasible.

(b) Psychologists never deceive research participants about significant aspects that would affect their willingness to participate, such as physical risks, discomfort, or unpleasant emotional experiences.

(c) Any other deception that is an integral feature of the design and conduct of an experiment must be explained to participants as early as is feasible, preferably at the conclusion of their participation, but no later than at the conclusion of the research. (See also Standard 6.18, Providing Participants With Information About the Study.)

6.16 Sharing and Utilizing Data

Psychologists inform research participants of their anticipated sharing or further use of personally identifiable research data and of the possibility of unanticipated future uses.

6.17 Minimizing Invasiveness

In conducting research, psychologists interfere with the participants or milieu from which data are collected only in a manner that is warranted by an appropriate research design and that is consistent with psychologists' roles as scientific investigators.

6.18 Providing Participants With Information About the Study

(a) Psychologists provide a prompt opportunity for participants to obtain appropriate information about the nature, results, and conclusions of the research, and psychologists attempt to correct any misconceptions that participants may have.

(b) If scientific or humane values justify delaying or withholding this information, psychologists take reasonable measures to reduce the risk of harm.

6.19 Honoring Commitments

Psychologists take reasonable measures to honor all commitments they have made to research participants.

6.20 Care and Use of Animals in Research

(a) Psychologists who conduct research involving animals treat them humanely.

(b) Psychologists acquire, care for, use, and dispose of animals in compliance with current federal, state, and local laws and regulations, and with professional standards.

(c) Psychologists trained in research methods and experienced in the care of laboratory animals supervise all procedures involving animals and are responsible for ensuring appropriate consideration of their comfort, health, and humane treatment.

(d) Psychologists ensure that all individuals using animals under their supervision have received instruction in research methods and in the care, maintenance, and handling of the species being used, to the extent appropriate to their role.

(e) Responsibilities and activities of individuals assisting in a research project are consistent with their respective competencies.

(f) Psychologists make reasonable efforts to minimize the discomfort, infection, illness, and pain of animal subjects.

(g) A procedure subjecting animals to pain, stress, or privation is used only when an alternative procedure is unavailable and the goal is justified by its prospective scientific, educational, or applied value.

(h) Surgical procedures are performed under appropriate anesthesia; techniques to avoid infection and minimize pain are followed during and after surgery.

(i) When it is appropriate that the animal's life be terminated, it is done rapidly, with an effort to minimize pain, and in accordance with accepted procedures.

6.21 Reporting of Results

(a) Psychologists do not fabricate data or falsify results in their publications.

(b) If psychologists discover significant errors in their published data, they take reasonable steps to correct such errors in a correction, retraction, erratum, or other appropriate publication means.

6.22 Plagiarism

Psychologists do not present substantial portions or elements of another's work or data as their own, even if the other work or data source is cited occasionally.

6.23 Publication Credit

(a) Psychologists take responsibility and credit, including authorship credit, only for work they have actually performed or to which they have contributed.

(b) Principal authorship and other publication credits accurately reflect the relative scientific or professional contributions of the individuals involved, regardless of their relative status. Mere possession of an institutional position, such as Department Chair, does not justify authorship credit. Minor contributions to the research or to the writing for publications are appropriately acknowledged, such as in footnotes or in an introductory statement.

(c) A student is usually listed as principal author on any multiple-authored article that is substantially based on the student's dissertation or thesis.

6.24 Duplicate Publication of Data

Psychologists do not publish, as original data, data that have been previously published. This does not preclude republishing data when they are accompanied by proper acknowledgment.

6.25 Sharing Data

After research results are published, psychologists do not withhold the data on which their conclusions are based from other competent professionals who seek to verify the substantive claims through reanalysis and who intend to use such data only for that purpose, provided that the confidentiality of the participants can be protected and unless legal rights concerning proprietary data preclude their release.

6.26 Professional Reviewers

Psychologists who review material submitted for publication, grant, or other research proposal review respect the confidentiality of and the proprietary rights in such information of those who submitted it.

7. *Forensic Activities*

7.01 Professionalism

Psychologists who perform forensic functions, such as assessments, interviews, consultations, reports, or expert testimony, must comply with all other provisions of this Ethics Code to the extent that they apply to such activities. In addition, psychologists base their forensic work on appropriate knowledge of and competence in the areas underlying such work, including specialized knowledge concerning special populations. (See also Standards 1.06, Basis for Scientific and Professional Judgments; 1.08, Human Differences; 1.15, Misuse of Psychologists' Influence; and 1.23, Documentation of Professional and Scientific Work.)

7.02 Forensic Assessments

(a) Psychologists' forensic assessments, recommendations, and reports are based on information and techniques (including personal interviews of the individual, when appropriate) sufficient to provide appropriate substantiation for their findings. (See also Standards 1.03, Professional and Scientific Relationship; 1.23, Documentation of Professional and Scientific Work; 2.01, Evaluation, Diagnosis, and Interventions in Professional Context; and 2.05, Interpreting Assessment Results.)

(b) Except as noted in (c), below, psychologists provide written or oral forensic reports or testimony of the psychological characteristics of an individual only after they have conducted an examination of the individual adequate to support their statements or conclusions.

(c) When, despite reasonable efforts, such an examination is not feasible, psychologists clarify the impact of their limited information on the reliability and validity of their reports and testimony, and they appropriately limit the nature and extent of their conclusions or recommendations.

7.03 Clarification of Role

In most circumstances, psychologists avoid performing multiple and potentially conflicting roles in forensic matters. When psychologists may be called on to serve in more than one role in a legal proceeding—for example, as consultant or expert for one party or for the court and as a fact witness—they clarify role expectations and the extent of confidentiality in advance to the extent feasible, and thereafter as changes occur, in order to avoid compromising their professional judgment and objectivity and in order to avoid misleading others regarding their role.

7.04 *Truthfulness and Candor*

(a) In forensic testimony and reports, psychologists testify truthfully, honestly, and candidly and, consistent with applicable legal procedures, describe fairly the bases for their testimony and conclusions.

(b) Whenever necessary to avoid misleading, psychologists acknowledge the limits of their data or conclusions.

7.05 *Prior Relationships*

A prior professional relationship with a party does not preclude psychologists from testifying as fact witnesses or from testifying to their services to the extent permitted by applicable law. Psychologists appropriately take into account ways in which the prior relationship might affect their professional objectivity or opinions and disclose the potential conflict to the relevant parties.

7.06 *Compliance With Law and Rules*

In performing forensic roles, psychologists are reasonably familiar with the rules governing their roles. Psychologists are aware of the occasionally competing demands placed upon them by these principles and the requirements of the court system, and attempt to resolve these conflicts by making known their commitment to this Ethics Code and taking steps to resolve the conflict in a responsible manner. (See also Standard 1.02, Relationship of Ethics and Law.)

8. *Resolving Ethical Issues*

8.01 *Familiarity With Ethics Code*

Psychologists have an obligation to be familiar with this Ethics Code, other applicable ethics codes, and their application to psychologists' work. Lack of awareness or misunderstanding of an ethical standard is not itself a defense to a charge of unethical conduct.

8.02 *Confronting Ethical Issues*

When a psychologist is uncertain whether a particular situation or course of action would violate this Ethics Code, the psychologist ordinarily consults with other psychologists knowledgeable about ethical issues, with state or national psychology ethics committees, or with other appropriate authorities in order to choose a proper response.

8.03 Conflicts Between Ethics and Organizational Demands

If the demands of an organization with which psychologists are affiliated conflict with this Ethics Code, psychologists clarify the nature of the conflict, make known their commitment to the Ethics Code, and to the extent feasible, seek to resolve the conflict in a way that permits the fullest adherence to the Ethics Code.

8.04 Informal Resolution of Ethical Violations

When psychologists believe that there may have been an ethical violation by another psychologist, they attempt to resolve the issue by bringing it to the attention of that individual if an informal resolution appears appropriate and the intervention does not violate any confidentiality rights that may be involved.

8.05 Reporting Ethical Violations

If an apparent ethical violation is not appropriate for informal resolution under Standard 8.04 or is not resolved properly in that fashion, psychologists take further action appropriate to the situation, unless such action conflicts with confidentiality rights in ways that cannot be resolved. Such action might include referral to state or national committees on professional ethics or to state licensing boards.

8.06 Cooperating With Ethics Committees

Psychologists cooperate in ethics investigations, proceedings, and resulting requirements of the APA or any affiliated state psychological association to which they belong. In doing so, they make reasonable efforts to resolve any issues as to confidentiality. Failure to cooperate is itself an ethics violation.

8.07 Improper Complaints

Psychologists do not file or encourage the filing of ethics complaints that are frivolous and are intended to harm the respondent rather than to protect the public.

Appendix F

Canadian Code of Ethics for Psychologists

Revised, 1991

TABLE OF CONTENTS

Preamble

Introduction

Every discipline that has relatively autonomous control over its entry requirements, training, development of knowledge, standards, methods, and practices does so only within the context of a contract with the society in which it functions. This social contract is based on attitudes of mutual respect and trust, with society granting support for the autonomy of a discipline in exchange for a commitment by the discipline to do everything it can to assure that its members act ethically in conducting the affairs of the discipline within society; in particular, a commitment to try to assure that each member will place the welfare of the society and individual members of that society above the welfare of the discipline and its own members.

The Canadian Psychological Association recognizes its responsibility to help assure ethical behaviour and attitudes on the part of psychologists. Attempts to assure ethical behaviour and attitudes include articulating ethical principles, values, and standards; promoting those principles, values, and standards through education, peer modelling, and consultation; developing and implementing methods to help psychologists monitor the ethics of their behaviour and attitudes; adjudicating complaints of unethical behaviour; and, taking corrective action when warranted.

This Code articulates ethical principles, values, and standards to guide all members of the Canadian Psychological Association, whether scientists, practitioners, or scientist practitioners, or whether acting in a research, direct service, teaching, student, administrative, supervisory, consultative, peer review, editorial, expert witness, social policy, or any other role related to the discipline of psychology.

Structure and Derivation of Code

Structure. Four ethical principles, to be considered and balanced in ethical decision-making, are presented. Each principle is followed by a statement of those values which are included in and give definition to the principle. Each values statement is followed by a list of ethical standards which illustrate the application of the specific principle and values to the activities of psychologists. The standards range from minimal behavioural expectations (e.g., Standards I.14, II.34, III.1, IV.24) to more idealized, but achievable, attitudinal and behavioural expectations (e.g., Standards I.16, II.10, III.10, IV.5). In the margin, to the left of the standards, key words are placed to guide the reader through the standards and to illustrate the relationship of the specific standards to the values statement.

Derivation. The four principles represent those ethical principles used most consistently by Canadian psychologists to resolve hypothetical ethical dilemmas sent to them by the CPA Committee on Ethics during the initial development of the Code. In addition to the responses provided by Canadian psychologists, the values statements and ethical standards have been derived from interdisciplinary and international ethics codes, provincial and specialty codes of conduct, and ethics literature.

When Principles Conflict

All four principles are to be taken into account and balanced in ethical decision-making. However, there are circumstances in which ethical principles will conflict and it will not be possible to give each principle equal weight.

The complexity of ethical conflicts precludes a firm ordering of the principles. However, the four principles have been ordered according to the weight each generally should be given when they conflict, namely:

Principle I: respect for the dignity of persons. This principle, with its emphasis on moral rights, generally should be given the highest weight, except in circumstances in which there is a clear and imminent danger to the physical safety of any individual.

Principle II: responsible caring. This principle generally should be given the second highest weight. Responsible caring requires competence and should be carried out only in ways that respect the dignity of persons.

Principle III: integrity in relationships. This principle generally should be given the third highest weight. Psychologists are expected to demonstrate the highest integrity in all of their relationships. However, in rare circumstances, values such as openness and straightforwardness may need to be subordinated to the values contained in the Principles of Respect for the Dignity of Persons and Responsible Caring.

Principle IV: responsibility to society. This principle generally should be given the lowest weight of the four principles when it conflicts with one or more of them. Although it is necessary and important to consider responsibility to society in every ethical decision, adherence to this principle must be subject to and guided by Respect for the Dignity of Persons, Responsible Caring, and Integrity in Relationships. When individual welfare appears to conflict with benefits to society, it is often possible to find ways of working for the benefit of society which do not violate respect and responsible caring for individuals. However, if this is not possible, then greater weight must be given to individual welfare.

Even with the above ordering of the principles, psychologists will be faced with ethical dilemmas which are difficult to resolve. In these circumstances, psychologists are expected to engage in an ethical decision-making process that is explicit enough to bear public scrutiny. In some cases, resolution may be a matter of personal conscience. However, decisions of personal conscience are also expected to be the result of a decision-making process which is based on a reasonably coherent set of ethical principles and which can bear public scrutiny. If the psychologist can demonstrate that every reasonable effort was made to apply the ethical principles of this Code and resolution of the conflict has had to depend on the personal conscience of the psychologist, such a psychologist would be deemed to have followed this Code.

The Ethical Decision-Making Process

The ethical decision-making process may occur very rapidly, leading to an easy resolution of an ethical issue. This is particularly true of issues for which clear-cut guidelines or standards exist and for which there is no conflict between principles. On the other hand, some ethical issues (particularly those in which ethical principles conflict) are not easily resolved and might require time-consuming deliberation. The following basic steps typify approaches to ethical decision-making:

1. Identification of ethically relevant issues and practices.
2. Development of alternative courses of action.
3. Analysis of likely short-term, ongoing, and long-term risks and benefits of each course of action on the individual(s)/group(s) involved or likely to be affected (e.g., client, client's family or employees, employing institution, students, research participants, colleagues, the discipline, society, self).
4. Choice of course of action after conscientious application of existing principles, values, and standards.
5. Action, with a commitment to assume responsibility for the consequences of the action.
6. Evaluation of the results of the course of action.
7. Assumption of responsibility for consequences of action, including correction of negative consequences, if any, or re-engaging in the decision-making process if the ethical issue is not resolved.

Psychologists engaged in time-consuming deliberation are encouraged and expected to consult with colleagues and/or advisory bodies when such persons can add knowledge and/or objectivity to the decision-making process. Although the decision for action remains with the individual psychologist, the seeking and consideration of such assistance reflects an ethical decision-making.

Uses of the Code

This Code is intended to guide psychologists in their everyday conduct, thinking and planning, and in the resolution of ethical dilemmas; that is, it advocates the practice of both proactive and reactive ethics.

The Code is also intended to serve as an umbrella document for the development of the codes of conduct or other more specific codes. For example, the Code could be used as an ethical framework for the identification of behaviours which would be considered enforceable in a certain jurisdiction, the violation of which would constitute misconduct; and/or, certain jurisdictions could identify those standards in the Code that would be considered of a more serious nature and, therefore, reportable and subject to possible discipline. Also, the principles and values could be used to help specialty areas develop standards which are specific to those areas. Some work in this direction has already occurred within CPA (e.g., use of animals in research, therapy and counselling with women, practice guidelines for providers of psychological services). The principles and values incorporated into this Code, insofar as they come to be reflected in other documents guiding the behaviour of psychologists, will reduce inconsistency and conflict between documents.

A third use of the Code is to assist in the adjudication of complaints against psychologists. A body charged with this responsibility is required to investigate allegations, judge whether unacceptable behaviour has occurred, and determine what corrective action should be taken. In determining corrective action, one of the judgements the adjudicating body needs to make is whether an individual conscientiously engaged in an ethical decision-making process and acted in good faith, or whether there was a negligent or willful disregard of ethical principles. The articulation of the ethical decision-making process contained in this Code provides guidance for making such judgements.

Responsibility of the Individual Psychologist

Responsibility for ethical action by psychologists depends foremost on the integrity of each individual psychologist; that is, on each psychologist's commitment to behave as ethically as possible in every situation. This commitment is essential to the fulfillment of any discipline's contract with society. Acceptance to membership in the Canadian Psychological Association, a scientific and professional association of psychologists, commits members:

1. To adhere to the ethical Code adopted by the Association.
2. To assess and discuss ethical issues and practices with colleagues on a regular basis.
3. To bring concerns about possible unethical actions by a psychologist directly to the psychologist, when appropriate, and to attempt to reach an agreement on the issue and, if needed, on the appropriate action to be taken.
4. To consider seriously others' concerns about one's own possibly unethical actions and attempt to reach an agreement on the issue and, if needed, take appropriate action.
5. To cooperate with duly constituted committees of the Association which are concerned with ethics and ethical conduct.

6. To bring to the attention of the Association ethical issues which require clarification or the development of new guidelines or standards.

Relationship of Code to Personal Behaviour

This Code is intended to guide and regulate only those activities a psychologist engages in by virtue of being a psychologist. There is no intention to guide or regulate a psychologist's activities outside of this context. Personal behaviour becomes a concern of the discipline only if it is of such a nature that it undermines public trust in the discipline as a whole or if it raises questions about the psychologist's ability to carry out appropriately his/her responsibilities as a psychologist.

Relationship of Code to Provincial Regulatory Bodies

In exercising its responsibility to articulate ethical principles, values, and standards for those who wish to become and remain members in good standing, the Canadian Psychological Association recognizes the multiple membership that some psychologists have (both regulatory and voluntary). The Code has attempted to encompass and incorporate those ethical principles most prevalent in the discipline as a whole, thereby minimizing the possibility of variance with provincial/territorial regulations and guidelines. Psychologists are expected to respect the requirements of their provincial/territorial regulatory bodies. Such requirements may define particular behaviours which constitute misconduct, are reportable to the regulatory body, and/or which are subject to discipline.

Definitions of Terms

For the purposes of this Code:

a) "Psychologist" means any person who is a Fellow, Member, Student Affiliate or Foreign Affiliate of the Canadian Psychological Association, or a member of any psychology voluntary association or regulatory body adopting this Code. (Readers are reminded that provincial/territorial jurisdictions may restrict the legal use of the term "psychologist" in their jurisdiction and that such restrictions are to be honoured.)
b) "Client" means a person, family, or group (including an organization or community) receiving service from a psychologist.
c) Clients, research participants, students and any other persons with whom psychologists come in contact in the course of their work, are "independent" if they can independently contract or give informed consent. Such persons are "partially dependent" if the decision to contract or give informed consent is shared between two or more parties (e.g., parents and school boards, workers and Worker Com-

pensation Boards, adult members of a family). Such persons are considered to be "fully dependent" if they have little or no choice about whether or not to receive service or participate in an activity (e.g., patients who have been involuntarily committed to a psychiatric facility, or very young children involved in a research project).

d) "Others" means any individual or group with whom psychologists come in contact in the course of their work. It may include, but is not limited to: research participants; clients seeking help with personal, family, organizational, industrial or community issues; students; supervisees; employees; colleagues; employers; third party payers; and, members of the general public.

e) "Legal or civil rights" mean those rights protected under laws and statutes recognized by the province in which the psychologist is working.

f) "Moral rights" means fundamental and inalienable human rights which may or may not be fully protected by existing laws and statutes. Of particular significance to psychologists, for example, are rights to: equal justice; fairness and due process; and, developmentally appropriate privacy, self-determination, and personal liberty. Protection of some aspects of these rights may involve practices which are not contained or controlled within current laws and statutes. Moral rights are not limited to those mentioned in this definition.

g) "Unjust discrimination" or "unjustly discriminatory" means activities which are prejudicial or promote prejudice to persons because of their culture, nationality, ethnicity, colour, race, religion, gender, marital status, sexual orientation, physical or mental abilities, age, socioeconomic status, and/or any other preference or personal characteristic, condition, or status.

h) "Sexual harassment" includes either or both of the following: (i) The use of power or authority in an attempt to coerce another person to engage in or tolerate sexual activity. Such uses include explicit or implicit threats of reprisal for noncompliance or promises of reward for compliance. (ii) Engaging in deliberate and/or repeated unsolicited sexually oriented comments, anecdotes, gestures, or touching, if such behaviours: are offensive and unwelcome; create an offensive, hostile or intimidating working environment; or, can be expected to be harmful to the recipient.[1]

i) The "discipline of psychology" refers to the scientific and applied methods and knowledge of psychology, and to the structures and procedures used by its members for conducting their work in relationship to society, to members of the public, to students, and to each other.

---

[1]From: Canadian Psychological Association. (1985). *Guidelines for the elimination of sexual harassment*. Old Chelsea, Quebec, Canada: Author.

Review Schedule

In order to maintain the relevance and responsiveness of this Code, it will be reviewed by the CPA Board of Directors in three years, and revised as needed. You are invited to forward comments and suggestions, at any time, to the CPA office. In addition to psychologists, this invitation is extended to all readers, including members of other disciplines and the public.

Principle I: Respect for the Dignity of Persons

Values Statement

In the course of their work as scientists, practitioners, or scientist–practitioners, psychologists come into contact with many different individuals and groups, including: research participants; clients seeking help with personal, family, organizational, industrial or community issues; students; supervisees; employees; colleagues; employers; third-party payers; and, the general public.

In these contacts, psychologists accept as fundamental the principle of respect for the dignity of persons; that is, the belief that each person should be treated primarily as a person or an end in him/herself, not as an object or a means to an end. In so doing, psychologists acknowledge that all persons have a right to have their innate worth as human beings appreciated and that this worth is not enhanced or reduced by their culture, nationality, ethnicity, colour, race, religion, gender, marital status, sexual orientation, physical or mental abilities, age, socioeconomic status, and/or any other preference or personal characteristic, condition, or status.

Although psychologists have a responsibility to respect the dignity of all persons with whom they come in contact in their role as psychologists, the nature of their contract with society demands that their greatest responsibility be to those persons directly receiving or involved in the psychologist's activities and, therefore, normally in a more vulnerable position (e.g., research participants, clients, students). This responsibility is almost always greater than their responsibility to those indirectly involved (e.g., employers, third-party payers, the general public).

Adherence to the concept of moral rights is an essential component of respect for the dignity of persons. Rights to privacy, self-determination, personal liberty, and natural justice are of particular importance to psychologists, and they have a responsibility to protect and promote these rights in all of their activities. As such, psychologists have a responsibility to develop and follow procedures for informed consent, confidentiality, fair treatment, and due process that are consistent with those rights.

As individual rights exist within the context of the rights of others and of responsible caring (see Principle II), there may be circumstances in which the possibility of serious detrimental consequences to themselves or others, a diminished capacity to be autonomous, or a court order, might disallow some aspects of the rights to privacy, self-determination, and personal liberty. Indeed, such circumstances might be serious enough to create a duty to warn others (see Standards I.40 and II.36). However, psychologists still have a responsibility to respect the rights of the person(s) involved to the greatest extent possible under the circumstances, and to do what is necessary and reasonable to reduce the need for future disallowances.

In addition, psychologists recognize that as individual, family, group or community vulnerabilities increase and/or as the power of persons to control their environment or their lives decreases, psychologists have an increasing responsibility to seek ethical advice and to establish safeguards to protect the rights of the persons involved. For this reason, psychologists consider it their responsibility to increase safeguards to protect and promote the rights of fully dependent persons than partially dependent persons, and more safeguards for partially-dependent than independent persons.

Respect for the dignity of persons also includes the concept of equal justice. With respect to psychologists, this concept implies that all persons are entitled to benefit equally from the contributions of psychology and to equal quality in the processes, procedures, and services being conducted by psychologists. Although individual psychologists might specialize and direct their activities to particular populations, psychologists must not exclude persons on a capricious or unjustly discriminatory basis.

Ethical Standards

In adhering to the Principle of Respect for the Dignity of Persons, psychologists would:

General Respect	I.1	Demonstrate appropriate respect for the knowledge, insight, experience, and areas of expertise of others.
	I.2	Not engage publicly (e.g., in public statements, presentations, research reports, or with clients) in demeaning descriptions of others, including jokes based on culture, nationality, ethnicity, colour, race, religion, gender, etc., or other remarks which reflect adversely on the dignity of others.
	I.3	Use language that conveys respect for the dignity of others (e.g., gender-neutral terms) in all written or verbal communication.
	I.4	Abstain from all forms of harassment, including sexual harassment.
General Rights	I.5	Avoid or refuse to participate in practices disrespectful of the legal, civil, or moral rights of others.

I.6 Refuse to advise, train, or supply information to anyone who, in the psychologist's judgement, will use the knowledge or skills to infringe on human rights.

I.7 Make every reasonable effort to ensure that psychological knowledge is not misused, intentionally or unintentionally, to infringe on human rights.

I.8 Respect the right of recipients of service, research participants, employees, supervisees, students, and others, to safeguard their own dignity.

Non-Discrimination

I.9 Not practice, condone, facilitate, or collaborate with any form of unjust discrimination.

I.10 Act to prevent or correct practices that are unjustly discriminatory.

Informed Consent

I.11 Seek as full and active participation as possible from others in decisions which affect them.

I.12 Respect and integrate as much as possible the opinions and wishes of others regarding decisions which affect them.

I.13 Obtain informed consent from all independent and partially dependent persons for any psychological services provided to them except in circumstances of urgent need (e.g., suicidal gesture). In such circumstances, psychologists would proceed with the assent of such persons, but fully informed consent would be obtained as soon as possible. (Also see Standard I.22.)

I.14 Obtain informed consent for all research activities which involve obtrusive measures, invasion into the private lives of research participants, risks to the participants, or any attempt to change the behaviour of research participants.

I.15 Establish and use signed consent forms which specify the dimensions of informed consent or which acknowledge that such dimensions have been explained and are understood, if such forms are required by law or if such forms are desired by the psychologist, the person(s) giving consent, or the organization for whom the psychologist works.

I.16 Recognize that informed consent is the result of a process of reaching an agreement to work collaboratively, rather than of simply having a consent form signed.

I.17 Provide, in obtaining informed consent, as much information as a reasonable or prudent person, family, group, or community would want to know before making a decision or consenting to an activity. The psychologist would relay this information in language which the persons understand (including providing translation into another language, if necessary) and would take whatever reasonable steps are necessary to assure that the information was, in fact, understood.

I.18 Assure, in the process of obtaining informed consent, that at least the following points are understood: purpose and nature of the activity; mutual responsibilities; likely benefits and risks; alternatives; the likely consequences of non-action; the option to refuse or withdraw at any time, without prejudice; over what period of time the consent applies; and, how to rescind consent if desired.

I.19 Clarify the nature of multiple relationships to all concerned parties before obtaining consent, if providing services to or conducting research with individuals, families, groups, or communities at the request or for the use of third parties. This would include, but not be limited to: the purpose of the service or research; the use that will be made of information collected; and, the limits on confidentiality. Third parties may include schools, courts, government agencies, insurance companies, police, and special funding bodies.

Freedom of Consent

I.20 Take all reasonable steps to ensure that consent is not given under conditions of coercion or undue pressure. (Also see Standard III.31.)

I.21 Not proceed with any research activity, if consent is given under any condition of coercion or undue pressure. (Also see Standard III.31.)

I.22 Take all reasonable steps to confirm or re-establish freedom of consent, if consent for service is given under conditions of duress or conditions of extreme need.

I.23 Respect the right of individuals to discontinue participation or service at any time, and be responsive to nonverbal indications of a desire to discontinue if the individual has difficulty with verbally communicating such a desire (e.g., young children, verbally disabled persons).

Fair Treatment/ Due Process

I.24 Work and act in a spirit of fair treatment to others.

I.25 Help to establish and abide by due process or other natural justice procedures for employment, evaluation, adjudication, editorial, and peer review activities.

I.26 Compensate others justly for the use of their time, energy, and intelligence, unless such compensation is refused in advance.

Vulnerabilities

I.27 Seek an independent and adequate ethical review of human rights issues and protections for any research involving vulnerable groups and/or persons of diminished capacity to give informed consent, before making a decision to proceed.

I.28 Not use persons of diminished capacity to give informed consent in research studies, if the research involved might equally well be carried out with persons who have a fuller capacity to give informed consent.

I.29 Carry out informed consent processes with those persons who are legally responsible or appointed to give informed consent on behalf of individuals who are not competent to consent on their own behalf.

I.30 Seek willing and adequately informed participation from any person of diminished capacity to give informed consent, and proceed without this assent only if the service or research activity is considered to be of direct benefit to that person.

I.31 Be particularly cautious in establishing the freedom of consent of any individual who is in a dependent relationship to the psychologist (e.g., student, employee). This may include, but is not limited to, offering that person an alternative activity to fulfill their educational or employment goals, or offering a range of research studies or experience opportunities from which the person can select.

Privacy

I.32 Explore and collect only that information which is germane to the purpose(s) for which consent has been obtained.

I.33 Take care not to infringe, in research or service activities, on the personally or culturally defined private space of individuals or groups unless clear permission is granted to do so.

I.34 Record only that private information necessary for the provision of continuous, coordinated service, or for the goals of the particular research study being conducted, or which is required by law (see Standards IV.15 and IV.16).

I.35 Respect the right of employees, supervisees, students, or psychologists-in-training to reasonable personal privacy.

I.36 Store, handle, and transfer all records, both written and unwritten (e.g., computer files, videotapes), in a way that attends to the needs for privacy and security. This would include having adequate plans for records in circumstances of one's own serious illness or death.

I.37 Take all reasonable steps to ensure that records over which they have control remain personally identifiable only as long as is necessary in the interests of those to whom they refer and/or to the research project for which they were collected, or as required by law, and render anonymous or destroy any records under their control that no longer need to be personally identifiable.

Confidentiality

I.38 Be careful not to relay information which they have gained about colleagues, colleagues' clients, students, and members of organizations gained in the process of their activities as psychologists and which the psychologist has reason to believe is considered confidential by those persons, except as required or justified by law (see Standards IV.15 and IV.16).

I.39 Clarify what measures will be taken to protect confidentiality, and what responsibilities family, group, and community members have for the protection of each other's confidentiality, when engaged in services to or research with individuals, families, groups, or communities.

I.40 Share confidential information with others only with the informed consent of those involved, or in a manner that the individuals involved cannot be identified, except as required or justified by law, or in circumstances of actual or possible serious physical harm or death (see Standard II.36).

Extended Responsibility	I.41	Encourage others, if appropriate, to respect the dignity of persons and to expect respect for their own dignity.
	I.42	Assume overall responsibility for the scientific and professional activities of their assistants, students, supervisees, and employees with regard to Respect for the Dignity of Persons, all of whom, however, incur similar obligations.

Principle II: Responsible Caring

Values Statement

A basic ethical expectation of any discipline is that its activities will benefit members of society or, at least, do no harm. Therefore, psychologists demonstrate an active concern for the welfare of any individual, family, group, or community with whom they relate in their role as psychologists. This concern includes both those directly involved and those indirectly involved in their activities. However, as with Principle I, psychologists' greatest responsibility is to protect the welfare of those directly involved in their activities and, therefore, normally in a more vulnerable position (e.g., research participants, clients, students). Their responsibility to those indirectly involved (e.g., employers, third-party payers, the general public) is secondary.

As individuals are usually concerned about their own welfare, obtaining informed consent (see Principle I) is one of the best methods for ensuring that their welfare will be protected. However, it is only when informed consent is combined with the responsible caring of the psychologist that there is considerable ethical protection of the welfare of the person(s) involved.

Responsible caring leads psychologists to "take care" to discern the potential harm and benefits involved, to predict the likelihood of their occurrence, to proceed only if the potential benefits outweigh the potential harms, to develop and use methods that will minimize harms and maximize benefits, and to take responsibility for correcting any harmful effects that have occurred as a result of their activities.

In order to carry out these steps, psychologists recognize the need for competence and self-knowledge. They consider incompetent action to be unethical *per se*, as it is unlikely to be of benefit and likely to be harmful. They engage only in those activities in which they have competence, and they perform their activities as competently as possible. They acquire, contribute to, and use the existing knowledge most relevant to the best interests of those concerned. They also engage in self-reflection regarding how their own values, attitudes, experiences, and social context (e.g., culture, ethnicity, colour, religion, gender, sexual orientation, physical and mental ability level, age, and socioeconomic status) influence their actions, interpretations, choices, and recommendations. This is done with the intent of increasing the probability that their activities will benefit and not harm the individuals, families, groups and communities to whom they relate in their role as psychologists. Psychologists define harm and benefit in terms of both physical and psychological dimensions. They are concerned about such factors as feelings of self-worth, fear, humiliation, interpersonal trust, cynicism, self-knowledge and general knowledge, as well as such factors as physical safety, comfort, pain, and injury. They are concerned about immediate, short-term, and long-term effects.

Responsible caring recognizes and acknowledges (e.g., through obtaining informed consent) the ability of individuals, families, groups, and communities to care for themselves and each other. It does not replace or undermine such ability. However, psychologists recognize that as vulnerabilities increase and/or as power to control one's own life decreases, they have an increasing responsibility to protect the well-being of the individual, family, group, or community involved. For this reason, as in Principle I, psychologists consider it their responsibility to increase safeguards proportionate to the degree of dependency and lack of voluntary initiation on the part of the persons involved. However, for Principle II, the safeguards are for the well-being of persons rather than for the rights of persons.

Psychologists' treatment and use of animals in their research and teaching activities are also a component of responsible caring. Although animals do not have the same rights as persons (e.g., informed consent), they do have the right to be treated humanely and not to be exposed to unnecessary discomfort, pain, or disruption.

Ethical Standards

In adhering to the Principle of Responsible Caring, psychologists would:

General Caring	II.1	Protect and promote the welfare of clients, students, research participants, colleagues, and others.
	II.2	Avoid doing harm to clients, students, research participants, colleagues, and others.
	II.3	Accept responsibility for the consequence of their actions.
	II.4	Refuse to advise, train, or supply information to anyone who, in the psychologist's judgement, will use the knowledge or skills to harm others.
	II.5	Make every reasonable effort to ensure that psychological knowledge is not misused, intentionally or unintentionally, to harm others.

Competence and Self-Knowledge

II.6 Offer or carry out (without supervision) only those activities for which they have established their competence to carry them out to the benefit of others.

II.7 Not delegate activities to persons not competent to carry them out to the benefit of others.

II.8 Take immediate steps to obtain consultation or to refer a client to a colleague or other appropriate professional, whichever is more likely to result in providing the client with competent service, if it becomes apparent that a client's problems are beyond their competence.

II.9 Keep themselves up-to-date with relevant knowledge, research methods, and techniques, through the reading of relevant literature, peer consultation, and continuing education activities, in order that their service or research activities and conclusions will benefit and not harm others.

II.10 Evaluate how their own experiences, attitudes, culture, beliefs, values, social context, individual differences, and stresses influence their interactions with others, and integrate this awareness into all efforts to benefit and not harm others.

II.11 Seek appropriate help and/or discontinue scientific or professional activity for an appropriate period of time, if a physical or psychological condition reduces their ability to benefit and not harm others.

II.12 Engage in self-care activities which help to avoid conditions (e.g., burnout, addictions) which could result in impaired judgement and interfere with their ability to benefit and not harm others.

Risk/Benefit Analysis

II.13 Assess the individuals, families, groups, and communities involved in their activities adequately enough to ensure that they will be able to discern what will benefit and not harm those persons.

II.14 Be sufficiently sensitive to and knowledgeable about individual differences and vulnerabilities to discern what will benefit and not harm persons involved in their activities.

II.15 Carry out pilot studies to determine the effects of all new procedures and techniques which might carry some risks, before considering their use on a broader scale.

II.16 Seek an independent and adequate ethical review of the balance of risks and potential benefits of all research which involves procedures of unknown consequence, or where pain, discomfort, or harm are possible, before making a decision to proceed.

II.17 Not carry out any scientific or professional activity unless the probable benefit is proportionately greater than the risk involved.

Maximize Benefit

II.18 Provide services which are coordinated over time and with other service providers, in order to avoid duplication or working at cross purposes. Such coordination would be promoted by the maintenance of adequate records and communication with other service providers.

II.19 Make themselves aware of the knowledge and skills of other disciplines (e.g., law, medicine) and advise the use of such knowledge and skills, where relevant to the benefit of others.

II.20 Strive to obtain the best possible service for those needing and seeking psychological service. This includes recommending professionals other than psychologists, if appropriate.

II.21 Monitor and evaluate the effect of their activities, record their findings and, if appropriate, communicate new knowledge to others in the field.

II.22 Debrief research participants in such a way that the participants' knowledge is enhanced and the participants have a sense of contribution to knowledge.

II.23 Perform their teaching duties on the basis of careful preparation, so that their instruction is current and scholarly.

II.24 Act on their obligation to facilitate the professional and scientific development of their students, trainees, employees, and supervisees by assuring that these persons understand the values and ethical prescriptions of the discipline, and by providing or arranging for adequate working conditions, timely evaluations, and constructive consultation and experience opportunities.

II.25 Encourage and assist students in publication of worthy student papers.

Minimize Harm

II.26 Be acutely aware of the power relationship in therapy and, therefore, not encourage or engage in sexual intimacy with therapy clients, neither during therapy, nor for that period of time following therapy during which the power relationship reasonably could be expected to influence the client's personal decision-making.

II.27 Be careful not to engage in activities in a way that could place incidentally involved individuals at risk.

II.28 Be acutely aware of the need for discretion in the recording and communication of information, in order that the information not be interpreted or used to the detriment of others. This includes, but is not limited to: not recording information which could lead to misinterpretation and misuse; avoiding conjecture; clearly labelling opinion; and, communicating information in language that can be understood clearly by the particular recipient of the information.

II.29 Give reasonable assistance to secure needed psychological services or activities, if personally unable to meet requests for needed psychological services or activities.

II.30 Maintain appropriate contact, support, and responsibility for caring until a colleague or other professional begins service, if referring a client to a colleague or other professional.

II.31 Give reasonable notice and be reasonably assured that discontinuation will cause no harm to the client, before discontinuing services.

II.32 Screen appropriate research participants and select those not likely to be harmed, if risk or harm to some research participants is possible.

II.33 Act to minimize the impact of their research activities on research participants' personality or their physical or mental integrity.

Offset/ Correct Harm

II.34 Terminate an activity when it is clear that the activity is more harmful than beneficial, or when the activity is no longer needed.

II.35 Refuse to help individuals, families, groups, or communities to carry out or submit to activities which, according to current knowledge and/or legal and professional guidelines, would cause serious physical or psychological harm to themselves or others.

II.36 Do everything reasonably possible to stop or offset the consequence of actions by others when these actions are likely to cause serious physical harm or death. This may include reporting to appropriate authorities (e.g., the police) or an intended victim, and would be done even when a confidential relationship is involved. (See Standard I.40.)

II.37 Act to stop or offset the consequences of clearly harmful activities being carried out by another psychologist or member of another discipline, when these activities have come to their attention outside of a confidential client relationship with that psychologist or member of another discipline. Depending on the nature of the harmful activities, this may include talking informally with the psychologist or member of the other discipline, obtaining objective information and, if possible, the assurance that the harm will discontinue and be corrected. However, if the harm is serious and/or continues to persist, the situation would be reported to the appropriate regulatory body, authority, and/or committee for action.

II.38 Not place an individual, group, family, or community needing service at a serious disadvantage by offering them no service over an unreasonable period of time in order to fulfill the conditions of a control condition in a research study and, where resources allow, offer such person(s) the service found to be most effective after the research study is completed.

II.39 Debrief research participants in such a way that any harm caused can be discerned, and act to correct any resultant harm.

Care of Animals

II.40 Not use animals in their research unless there is a reasonable expectation that the research will increase understanding of the structures and processes underlying behaviour, or increase understanding of the particular animal species used in the study, or result eventually in benefits to the health and welfare of humans or other animals.

II.41 Use a procedure subjecting animals to pain, stress, or privation only if an alternative procedure is unavailable and the goal is justified by its prospective scientific, educational, or applied value.

II.42 Make every effort to minimize the discomfort, illness, and pain of animals. This would include performing surgical procedures only under appropriate anaesthesia, using techniques to avoid infection and minimize pain during and after surgery and, if disposing of experimental animals is carried out at the termination of study, doing so in a humane way.

II.43 Use animals in classroom demonstrations only if the instructional objectives cannot be achieved through the use of videotapes, films, or other methods, and if the type of demonstration is warranted by the anticipated instructional gain.

Extended Responsibility

II.44 Encourage others, if appropriate, to care responsibly.

II.45 Assume overall responsibility for the scientific and professional activities of their assistants, students, supervisees, and employees with regard to the Principle of Responsible Caring, all of whom, however, incur similar obligations.

Principle III: Integrity in Relationships

Values Statement

The relationships formed by psychologists in the course of their work embody explicit and implicit mutual expectations of integrity that are vital to the advancement of scientific knowledge and to the maintenance of public confidence in the discipline of psychology. These expectations include: accuracy and honesty; straightforwardness and openness; the maximization of objectivity and minimization of bias; and, avoidance of conflicts of interest. Psychologists have a responsibility to meet these expectations and to encourage reciprocity.

In addition to accuracy, honesty, and the obvious prohibitions of fraud or misrepresentation, meeting expectations of integrity is enhanced by self-knowledge and the use of critical analysis. Although it can be argued that science is value-free, scientists are not. Personal values can affect the questions psychologists ask, how they ask those questions, what assumptions they make, their selection of methods, what they observe and what they fail to observe, and how they interpret their data.

Psychologists are not expected to be value-free in conducting their activities. However, they are expected to understand how their backgrounds and values interact with their activities, to be open and honest about the influence of such factors, and to be as objective and unbiased as possible under the circumstances.

The values of openness and straightforwardness exist within the context of Respect for the Dignity of Persons (Principle I) and Responsible Caring (Principle II). As such, there will be circumstances in which openness and straightforwardness will need to be tempered. Full disclosure may not be needed or desired by others, and in some circumstances, may be a risk to their dignity or well-being. In such circumstances, however, psychologists have a responsibility to ensure that their decision not to be fully open or straightforward is justified by higher-order values.

Of special concern to psychologists is the use of deception in research, or the use of any technique (e.g., temporary withholding of information) which could be interpreted as deception by research participants or clients. Although research which uses such techniques can lead to knowledge which is beneficial, and service which uses techniques which might be interpreted as deception can lead to beneficial changes for the client, such benefits must be weighed against the individual's right to self-determination and the importance of public and individual trust in psychology. Psychologists have a serious obligation never to use deception in service activities, and to avoid as much as possible the use of deception in research or the use of any technique which could be interpreted as deception in either research or service activities. They also have a serious obligation to consider the need for, the possible consequences of, and their responsibility to correct any resulting mistrust or other harmful effects from the use of such techniques.

As public trust in the discipline of psychology includes trusting that psychologists will act in the best interests of members of the public, situations which present real or potential conflicts of interest are of concern to psychologists. Conflict-of-interest situations can readily motivate psychologists to act in ways which meet their own personal, political, or business interests at the expense of the best interests of members of the public. Although avoidance of all situations which present a conflict of interest is not possible, it is the responsibility of psychologists to avoid as many as possible and, when such situations cannot be avoided, to ensure that the best interests of the members of the public are protected.

Integrity in relationships implies that psychologists, as a matter of honesty, have a responsibility to maintain competence in any specialty area for which they declare competence, whether or not they are currently practising in that area. It also requires that psychologists, in as much as they present themselves as members and representatives of a specific discipline, have a responsibility to actively rely on and be guided by that discipline and its guidelines and requirements.

Ethical Standards

In adhering to the Principle of Integrity in Relationships, psychologists would:

Accuracy/ Honesty

III.1 Not participate in, condone, or be associated with dishonesty, fraud, or misrepresentation.

III.2 Accurately represent their own and their associates' qualifications, education, experience, competence, and affiliations, in all spoken, written, or printed communications, being careful not to use descriptions or information which could be misinterpreted.

III.3 Carefully protect their own and their associates' credentials from being misrepresented by others, and act quickly to correct any such misrepresentation.

III.4 Maintain competence in their declared area(s) of psychological competence, as well as in their current area(s) of activity. (See Standard II.9.)

III.5 Accurately represent their activities, functions, and likely or actual outcomes of their work, in all spoken, written, or printed communication. This includes, but is not limited to: advertisements of services; course and workshop descriptions; academic grading requirements; and research reports.

III.6 Ensure that their activities, functions, and likely or actual outcomes of their activities are not misrepresented by others, and act quickly to correct any such misrepresentation.

III.7 Take credit only for the work and ideas that they have actually done or generated, and give credit for work done or ideas contributed by others (including students) in proportion to their contribution.

III.8 Acknowledge the limitations of their knowledge, methods, findings, interventions, and views.

III.9 Not suppress disconfirming evidence of their findings and views, acknowledging alternative hypotheses and explanations.

Objectivity/Lack of Bias	III.10	Evaluate how their personal experiences, attitudes, values, social context, individual differences, and stress influence their activities and thinking, integrating this awareness into all attempts to be objective and unbiased in their research, service and other activities.
	III.11	Take care to communicate as completely and objectively as possible, and to clearly differentiate facts, opinions, theories, hypotheses, and ideas, if communicating their knowledge, findings, and views.
	III.12	Present instructional information accurately, avoiding bias in the selection and presentation of information, and publicly acknowledge any personal values or bias which influence the selection and presentation of information.
	III.13	Act quickly to clarify any distortion by a sponsor, client, or other persons, of the findings of their research.
Straight-forwardness/ Openness	III.14	Be clear and straightforward about all information needed to establish informed consent or any other valid written or unwritten agreement (for example: fees; concerns; mutual responsibilities; ethical responsibilities of psychologists; purpose and nature of the relationship; alternatives; likely experiences; possible conflicts; possible outcomes; and expectations for processing, using, and sharing any information generated).
	III.15	Provide suitable information about the results of assessments, evaluations, or research findings to the persons involved, if appropriate and/or if asked. This information would be communicated in understandable language.
	III.16	Fully explain reasons for their actions to persons who have been affected by their actions, if appropriate and/or if asked.
	III.17	Honour all promises and commitments included in any written or verbal agreement unless serious and unexpected circumstances (e.g., illness) intervene. If such circumstances occur, then the psychologist would make a full and honest explanation to other parties involved.

III.18 Make clear whether they are acting as private citizens, as members of specific organizations or groups, or as representatives of the discipline of psychology, when making statements or when involved in public activities.

III.19 Conduct research in a way that is consistent with a commitment to honest, open inquiry, and to clear communication of any research aims, sponsorship, social context, personal values, or financial interests that may affect or appear to affect their research.

III.20 Submit their research, in some accurate form and within the limits of confidentiality, to independent colleagues with expertise in the research area, for their comments and evaluations.

III.21 Encourage the free exchange of ideas between themselves and their students.

III.22 Make no attempt to conceal the status of a trainee.

Avoidance of Deception

III.23 Not engage in deception in any service activity.

III.24 Not engage in deception in research or the use of techniques which might be interpreted as deception, in research or service activities, if there are alternative procedures available and/or if the negative effects cannot be predicated or offset.

III.25 Not engage in deception in research or the use of techniques which might be interpreted as deception in research or service activities, if it would interfere with the individual's understanding of facts which clearly might influence a decision to give informed consent.

III.26 Use the minimum necessary deception in research or techniques which might be interpreted as deception in research, or service activities.

III.27 Provide research participants, during debriefing, with a clarification of the nature of the study, if deception or the use of techniques which could be interpreted as deception has occurred. In such circumstances, psychologists would seek to remove any misconceptions which might have arisen and to re-establish any trust which might have been lost, assuring the participant during debriefing that the real or apparent deception was neither arbitrary nor capricious. (Also see Standard II.22.)

III.28 Act to re-establish with clients any trust which might have been lost due to the use of techniques which might be interpreted as deception.

III.29 Seek an independent and adequate ethical review of the risks to public or individual trust and of safeguards to protect such trust for any research which uses deception or techniques which might be interpreted as deception, before making a decision to proceed.

Avoidance of Conflict of Interest

III.30 Not exploit any relationship established as a psychologist to further personal, political, or business interests at the expense of the best interests of their clients, research participants, students, employees, or others. This includes, but is not limited to: soliciting clients of one's employing agency for private practice; taking advantage of trust or dependency to engage in sexual activities or to frighten clients into receiving services; appropriating student's ideas, research or work; using the resources of one's employing institution for purposes not agreed to; securing or accepting significant financial or material benefit for activities which are already awarded by salary or other compensation; and prejudicing others against a colleague for reasons of personal gain.

III.31 Not offer rewards sufficient to motivate an individual or group to participate in an activity that has possible or known risks to themselves or others. (See Standards I.20; I.21; II.2; and II.44.)

III.32 Avoid dual relationships (e.g., with students, employees, or clients) and other situations which might present a conflict of interest or which might reduce their ability to be objective and unbiased in their determinations of what might be in the best interests of others.

III.33 Inform all parties, if a real or potential conflict of interest arises, of the need to resolve the situation in a manner that is consistent with Respect for the Dignity of Persons (Principle I) and Responsible Caring (Principle II), and take all reasonable steps to resolve the issue in such a manner.

Reliance on the Discipline

III.34 Familiarize themselves with their discipline's rules and regulations, and abide by them, unless abiding by them would be seriously detrimental to the rights or well-being of others as demonstrated in the Principles of Respect for the Dignity of Persons or Responsible Caring. (See Standard IV.16 for guidelines regarding the resolution of such conflicts.)

III.35 Familiarize themselves with and demonstrate a commitment to maintaining the standards of their discipline.

III.36 Seek consultation from colleagues and/or appropriate groups and committees, and give due regard to their advice in arriving at a responsible decision, if faced with difficult situations.

Extended Responsibility

III.37 Encourage others, if appropriate, to relate with integrity.

III.38 Assume overall responsibility for the scientific and professional activities of their assistants, students, supervisors, and employees with regard to the Principle of Integrity in Relationships, all of whom, however, incur similar obligations.

Principle IV: Responsibility to Society

Values Statement

Psychology functions as a discipline within the context of human society.[2] Psychologists, both in their work and as private citizens, have responsibilities to the societies in which they live and work, such as the neighbourhood or city, and to the welfare of all human beings in those societies.

Two of the legitimate expectations of psychology as a science and a profession are that it will increase knowledge and that it will conduct its affairs in such ways that it will promote the welfare of all human beings.

In the context of society, the above expectations imply that scientific freedom will be balanced by scientific responsibility; that is, psychologists will actively increase knowledge only through the use of activities and methods that are consistent with ethical requirements, and be willing to demonstrate that such requirements have been met.

The expectations also imply that psychologists will do whatever they can to ensure that psychological knowledge, when used in the development of social structures and policies, will be used for beneficial purposes, and that the discipline's own structures and policies will support those beneficial purposes. Within the context of this document, social structures and policies which have beneficial purposes are defined as those which more readily support and reflect respect for the dignity of person, responsible caring, integrity in relationships, and responsibility to society. If psychological knowledge or structures are used against these purposes, psychologists have an ethical responsibility to try to draw attention to and correct the misuse. Although this is a collective responsibility, those psychologists having direct involvement in the structures of the discipline, in social development, and/or in the theoretical or research data base that is being used (e.g., through research, expert testimony, or policy advice) have the greatest responsibility to act. Other psychologists must decide for themselves the most appropriate and beneficial use of their time and talents to help meet this collective responsibility.

In carrying out their work, psychologists acknowledge that many social structures have evolved slowly over time in response to human need, are valued by society, and are primarily beneficial. In such circumstances, psychologists convey respect for these social structures and avoid unwarranted or unnecessary disruption. Suggestions for and action toward changes or enhancement of such structures are carried out only through processes which seek to achieve a consensus within society through democratic means.

On the other hand, if structures or policies seriously ignore or oppose the principles of respect for the dignity of the person, responsible caring, integrity in relationships, or responsibility to society, psychologists in-

---

[2]Society is used here in the broad sense of a body of individuals living as members of one or more human communities, rather than in the limited sense of state or government.

volved have a responsibility to be critical and advocate for change to occur as quickly as possible.

In order to be responsible to society and to contribute constructively to its ongoing evolution, psychologists need to be self-reflective about the place of the discipline of psychology in society. They need to engage in even-tempered observation and interpretation of the effects of societal structures and policies, and their process of change, developing the ability of psychologists to increase the beneficial use of psychological knowledge and structures, and avoid their misuse. The discipline needs to be willing to set high standards for its members, to do what it can to assure that such standards are met, and to support its members in their attempts to maintain the standards. Once again, individual psychologists must decide for themselves the most appropriate and beneficial use of their time and talents in helping to meet these collective responsibilities.

Ethical Standards

In adhering to the Principle of Responsibility to Society, psychologists would:

Development of Knowledge	IV.1	Contribute to the discipline of psychology and of society's understanding of itself and human beings generally, through a free pursuit and sharing of knowledge, unless such activity conflicts with other basic ethical requirements.
	IV.2	Keep informed of progress in their area(s) of psychological activity, take this progress into account in their work, and try to make their own contributions to this progress.
Beneficial Activities	IV.3	Participate in and contribute to continuing education and the professional and scientific growth of self and colleagues.
	IV.4	Assist in the development of those who enter the discipline of psychology by helping them to acquire a full understanding of the ethics, responsibilities, and needed competencies of their chosen area(s), including an understanding of critical analysis and of the variations, uses, and possible misuses of the scientific paradigm.

IV.5 Participate in the process of critical self-evaluation of the discipline's place in society and in the development and implementation of structures and procedures which help the discipline to contribute to beneficial societal functioning and changes.

IV.6 Engage in regular monitoring, assessment, and reporting (e.g., through peer review, and in program reviews, case management reviews, and reports of one's own research) of their ethical practices and safeguards.

IV.7 Help develop, promote, and participate in accountability processes and procedures related to their work.

IV.8 Uphold the discipline's responsibility to society by promoting and maintaining the highest standards of the discipline.

IV.9 Protect the skills, knowledge, and interpretation of psychology from being misused, used incompetently, or made useless (e.g., loss of security of assessment techniques) by others.

IV.10 Contribute to the general welfare of society (e.g., improving accessibility of services, regardless of ability to pay) and/or to the general welfare of their discipline by offering a portion of their time to work for which they receive little or no financial return.

IV.11 Uphold the discipline's responsibility to society by bringing incompetent or unethical behaviour, including misuses of psychological knowledge and techniques, to the attention of appropriate regulatory bodies, authorities, and/or committees, in a manner consistent with the ethical principles of this Code, if informal resolution or correction of the situation is not appropriate or possible.

IV.12 Only enter into agreements or contracts which allow them to act in accordance with the ethical principles and standards of this Code.

Respect for Society

IV.13 Acquire an adequate knowledge of the culture, social structure, and customs of a community before beginning any major work there.

IV.14 Convey respect for and abide by prevailing community mores, social customs, and cultural expectations in their scientific and professional activities, provided that this does not contravene any of the ethical principles of this Code.

IV.15 Abide by the laws of the society in which they work. If those laws seriously conflict with the ethical principles contained herein, psychologists would do whatever they could to uphold the ethical principles. If upholding the ethical principles could result in serious personal consequences (e.g., jail or physical harm), decision for final action would be considered a matter of personal conscience.

IV.16 Consult with colleagues, if faced with an apparent conflict between keeping a law and following an ethical principle, unless in an emergency, and seek consensus as to the most ethical course of action and the most responsible, knowledgeable, effective, and respectful way to carry it out.

Development of Society

IV.17 Act to change those aspects of the discipline of psychology which detract from beneficial societal changes, where appropriate and possible.

IV.18 Be sensitive to the needs, current issues, and problems of society, if determining research questions to be asked, services to be developed, information to be collected, or the interpretation of results or findings.

IV.19 Be especially careful to keep well informed through relevant reading, peer consultation and continuing education, if their work is related to societal issues.

IV.20 Speak out, in a manner consistent with the four principles of this Code, when they possess expert knowledge that bears on important societal issues being studied or discussed.

IV.21 Provide thorough discussion of the limits of their data, if their work touches on social policy and structure.

IV.22 Make themselves aware of the current social and political climate and of previous and possible future societal misuses of psychological knowledge, and exercise due discretion in communicating psychological information (e.g., research results, theoretical knowledge) in order to discourage any further misuse.

IV.23 Exercise particular care when reporting the results of any work regarding vulnerable groups, ensuring that results are not likely to be misinterpreted or misused in the development of social policy, attitudes, and practices (e.g., encouraging manipulation of vulnerable persons or reinforcing discrimination against any specific population).

IV.24 Not contribute to nor engage in research or any other activity which promotes or is intended for use in the torture of persons, the development of prohibited weapons, destruction of the environment, or any other act which contravenes international law.

IV.25 Provide the public with any psychological knowledge relevant to the public's informed participation in the shaping of social policies and structures, if involved in public policy issues.

IV.26 Speak out and/or act, in a manner consistent with the four principles of this Code, if the policies, practices or regulations of the social structure within which they work seriously ignore or oppose any of the principles of this Code.

Extended Responsibility

IV.27 Encourage others, if appropriate, to exercise responsibility to society.

IV.28 Assume overall responsibility for the scientific and professional activities of their assistants, students, supervisees, and employees with regard to the Principle of Responsibility to Society, all of whom, however, incur similar obligations.

Appendix G

Comparison of ASPPB Code Requirements With Requirements of APA and CPA Codes

Main content of each rule of conduct of ASPPB Code (1991)	Excerpts from and/or commentary regarding comparative ethical standards of APA Code (1992)	Excerpts from and/or commentary regarding comparative ethical standards of CPA Code (1991)
A. Competence		
A.1. ". . . shall limit practice and supervision to the areas of competence in which proficiency has been gained through education, training, and experience."	1.04(a). ". . . provide services, teach, and conduct research only within the boundaries of their competence, based on their education, training, supervised experience, or appropriate professional experience."	II.6. "Offer or carry out (without supervision) only those activities for which they have established their competence to carry them out to the benefit of others."
	2.04(a). "Psychologists who perform interventions or administer, score, interpret, or use assessment techniques are familiar with the reliability, validation, and related standardization or outcome studies of, and proper applications and uses of, the techniques they use."	II.14. "Be sufficiently sensitive to and knowledgeable about individual differences and vulnerabilities to discern what will benefit and not harm persons involved in their activities."
		II.19 "Make themselves aware of the knowledge and skills of other disciplines (e.g., law, medicine) and advise the use of such knowledge and skills, where relevant to the benefit of others."
		IV.13. "Acquire an adequate knowledge of the culture, social structure, and customs of a community before beginning any major work there."

continues

Appendix G *(Continued)*

Main content of each rule of conduct of ASPPB Code (1991)	Excerpts from and/or commentary regarding comparative ethical standards of APA Code (1992)	Excerpts from and/or commentary regarding comparative ethical standards of CPA Code (1991)
A.2. ". . . shall maintain current competency in the areas in which he/she practices, through continuing education, consultation, and/or other procedures, in conformance with current standards of scientific and professional knowledge."	1.05. ". . . maintain . . . level of awareness of current scientific and professional information in their fields of activity, and undertake ongoing efforts to maintain competence in the skills they use."	II.9. "Keep themselves up to date with relevant knowledge, research methods, and techniques, through the reading of relevant literature, peer consultation, and continuing education activities, in order that their service or research activities and conclusions will benefit and not harm others." IV.19. "Be especially careful to keep well informed through relevant reading, peer consultation and continuing education, if their work is related to societal issues."
A.3. ". . . when developing competency in a service or technique that is either new to the psychologist or new to the profession, shall engage in ongoing consultation with other psychologists or other professionals and shall seek appropriate education and training in the new area. The psychologist shall inform clients of the innovative nature and the known risks associated with the services, so that the client can exercise freedom of choice regarding such services."	1.04(b). ". . . provide services, teach, or conduct research in new areas or involving new techniques only after first undertaking appropriate study, training, supervision, and/or consultation from persons who are competent in these areas or techniques." 1.04(c). "In those emerging areas in which generally recognized standards for preparatory training do not yet exist, . . . nevertheless take reasonable steps to ensure the competence of their work and to protect patients, clients, students, research participants, and others from harm." (Comment: No specific mention of new services or techniques in context of obtaining informed consent.)	(Comment: No specific mention of new or emerging services or techniques in context of either competence or informed consent.)

A.4. ". . . shall make or recommend referral to other professional, technical, or administrative resources when such referral is clearly in the best interests of the clients."	1.08. "Where differences of age, gender, race, ethnicity, national origin, religion, sexual orientation, disability, language, or socioeconomic status significantly affect psychologists' work concerning particular individuals or groups, psychologists obtain the training, experience, consultation, or supervision necessary to ensure the competence of their services, or they make appropriate referrals." 1.20(a). ". . . arrange for appropriate consultations and referrals based principally on the best interests of their patients or clients, with appropriate consent, and subject to other relevant considerations, including applicable law and contractual obligations."	II.8. "Take immediate steps to obtain consultation or to refer a client to a colleague or other appropriate professional, whichever is more likely to result in providing the client with competent service, if it becomes apparent that a client's problems are beyond their competence."
A.5. "A psychologist rendering a formal professional opinion about a person, for example about the fitness of a parent in a custody hearing, shall not do so without direct and substantial professional contact with or a formal assessment of that person."	2.01(a). ". . . perform evaluations, diagnostic services, or interventions only within the context of a defined professional relationship." 2.01(b). "Psychologists' assessments, recommendations, reports, and psychological diagnostic or evaluative statements are based on information and techniques (including personal interviews of the individual when appropriate) sufficient to provide appropriate substantiation for their findings." (See also Standard 7.02, Forensic Assessments.)	II.13. "Assess the individuals, families, groups, and communities involved in their activities adequately enough to ensure that they will be able to discern what will benefit and not harm those persons."

continues

Appendix G *(Continued)*

Main content of each rule of conduct of ASPPB Code (1991)	Excerpts from and/or commentary regarding comparative ethical standards of APA Code (1992)	Excerpts from and/or commentary regarding comparative ethical standards of CPA Code (1991)
	7.02(a). ". . . forensic assessments . . . are based on information and techniques (including personal interviews of the individual, when appropriate) sufficient to provide substantiation for their findings."	
	7.02(b). ". . . except as noted in (c), below . . . provide written or oral forensic reports or testimony of the psychological characteristics of an individual only after they have conducted an examination of the individual adequate to support their statements or conclusions."	
	7.02(c). "When, despite reasonable efforts, such an examination is not feasible, psychologists clarify the impact of their limited information on the reliability and validity of their reports and testimony, and they appropriately limit the nature and extent of their conclusions or recommendations."	
A.6.a. ". . . shall maintain professional records that include: 1) the presenting problem(s) or purpose or diagnosis, 2) the fee arrangement, 3) the date and substance of each billed or service-count contact or service, 4) any test results or other evaluative results	1.23(a). ". . . appropriately document their professional and scientific work in order to facilitate provision of services later by them or by other professionals, to ensure accountability, and to meet other requirements of institutions or the law."	II.18. "Provide services which are coordinated over time and with other service providers, in order to avoid duplication or working at cross purposes. Such coordination would be promoted by the maintenance of adequate records and communication with other service providers."

obtained and any basic test data from which they were derived, 5) notation and results of formal consulting with other providers, 6) a copy of all test or other evaluative reports prepared as part of the professional relationship."		III.34. "Familiarize themselves with their discipline's rules and regulations, and abide by them unless abiding by them would be seriously detrimental to the rights or well-being of others as demonstrated in the Principles of Respect for the Dignity of Persons or Responsible Caring. (See Standard IV.16 for guidelines regarding the resolution of such conflicts.)"
A.6.b. ". . . shall assure that all data entries in the professional records are maintained for a period of not less than five years after the last date that service was rendered. The psychologist shall also abide by other legal requirements for record retention, even if longer periods of retention are required for other purposes."	1.24. ". . . create, maintain, disseminate, store, retain and dispose of records and data relating to their research, practice, and other work in accordance with law and in a manner that permits compliance with the requirements of this Ethics Code." 5.10. ". . . take reasonable and lawful steps so that records and data remain available to the extent needed to serve the best interests of patients . . . clients . . . or appropriate others."	I.37. "Take all reasonable steps to ensure that records over which they have control remain identifiable only as long as is necessary in the interests of those to whom they refer and/or to the research project for which they were collected or as required by law. . . ." (Comment: No specific time period mentioned. However, see III.34 above.)
A.6.c. ". . . shall store and dispose of written, electronic and other records in such a manner as to insure their confidentiality."	See 1.24 above.	I.36. "Store, handle, and transfer all records, both written and unwritten (e.g., computer files, videotapes), in a way that attends to the needs for privacy and security. This would include having adequate plans for records in circumstances of one's own serious illness or death."

continues

Appendix G *(Continued)*

Main content of each rule of conduct of ASPPB Code (1991)	Excerpts from and/or commentary regarding comparative ethical standards of APA Code (1992)	Excerpts from and/or commentary regarding comparative ethical standards of CPA Code (1991)
		I.37. "... and render anonymous or destroy any records ... that no longer need to be personally identifiable." (Comment: See above for first part of this Standard.)
A.6.d. "For each person professionally supervised ... shall maintain for a period of not less than five years ... a record of the supervisory session that shall include, among other information, the type, place, and general content of the session."	(Comment: No specific requirement that records of professional supervision be kept.)	(Comment: No specific requirement that records of professional supervision be kept.)
A.7. "... shall make arrangements for another appropriate professional or professionals to deal with emergency needs of his/her clients ... during periods of his/her foreseeable absences from professional availability."	4.08(a). "... make reasonable efforts to plan for facilitating care in the event that psychological services are interrupted by factors such as the psychologist's illness, death, unavailability, or relocation or by the client's relocation or financial limitations."	II.29. "Give reasonable assistance to secure needed psychological services or activities, if personally unable to meet requests for needed psychological services or activities." (Comment: No specific requirement that plans be made in advance.)
B. Impaired Objectivity and Dual Relationships B.1. "... shall not undertake or continue a professional relationship with a client when the psychologist is, or could reasonably be expected by the Board to be, impaired due to mental, emotional, pharmacologic, or substance abuse conditions. If such a condition	1.13(a). "... refrain from undertaking an activity when they know or should know that their personal problems are likely to lead to harm to a patient, client, colleague, student, research participant, or other person to whom they may owe a professional or scientific obligation."	II.11. "Seek appropriate help and/or discontinue scientific or professional activity for an appropriate period of time, if a physical or psychological condition reduces their ability to benefit and not harm others."

develops after a professional relationship has been initiated . . . shall terminate the relationship in an appropriate manner, shall notify the client in writing of the termination, and shall assist the client in obtaining services from another professional."	1.13(b). ". . . be alert to signs of, and to obtain assistance for, their personal problems at an early stage, in order to prebvent significantly impaired performance." 1.13(c). "When psychologists become aware of personal problems that might interfere with their performing work-related duties adequately, they take appropriate measures such as obtaining professional consultation or assistance, and determine whether they should limit, suspend, or terminate their work-related duties." Also see 4.08(a) above.	II.12. "Engage in self-care activities which help avoid conditions (e.g., burnout, addictions) which could result in impaired judgment and interfere with their ability to benefit and not harm others." Also see II.29 above.
B.2.a. ". . . shall not undertake or continue a professional relationship with a client when the objectivity or competency of the psychologist is, or could reasonably be expected by the Board to be, impaired because of the psychologist's present or previous familial, social, sexual, emotional, financial, supervisory, political, administrative, or legal relationship with the client or a relevant person associated with or related to the client."	1.17(a). ". . . it may not be feasible or reasonable for psychologists to avoid social or other nonprofessional contacts with persons such as patients, clients, students, supervisees, or research participants. . . . A psychologist . . . refrains from entering into or promising another personal, scientific, professional, financial, or other relationship with such persons if it appears likely that such a relationship reasonably might impair the psychologist's objectivity or otherwise interfere with the psychologist's effectively performing his or her functions as a psychologist, or might harm or exploit the other party."	III.32. "Avoid dual relationships (e.g., with students, employees, or clients) and other situations which might present a conflict of interest or which might reduce their ability to be objective and unbiased in their determinations of what might be in the best interests of others." III.33. "Inform all parties, if a real or potential conflict of interest arises, of the need to resolve the situation in a manner that is consistent with Respect for the Dignity of Persons . . . and Responsible Caring . . . and take all reasonable steps to resolve the issue in such a manner."

continues

Appendix G *(Continued)*

Main content of each rule of conduct of ASPPB Code (1991)	Excerpts from and/or commentary regarding comparative ethical standards of APA Code (1992)	Excerpts from and/or commentary regarding comparative ethical standards of CPA Code (1991)
	1.17(b). "... refrains from taking on professional or scientific obligations when pre-existing relationships would create a risk of such harm."	
	4.06 "... do not accept as therapy patients or clients persons with whom they have engaged in sexual intimacies."	
	7.03. "... when psychologists may be called on to serve in more than one role in a legal proceeding ... they clarify role expectations ... to the extent feasible ... in order to avoid compromising their professional judgment and objectivity. ..."	
	7.05. "A prior professional relationship ... does not preclude psychologists from testifying as fact witnesses ... appropriately take into account ways in which the prior relationship might affect their ... objectivity and disclose the potential conflict to the relevant parties."	
B.2.b. "... in interacting with a client or former client to whom the psychologist has at any time within the previous 24 months rendered counseling, psychotherapeutic, or other professional psychological services for the treatment or amelioration of emotional	1.11.(a). "... do not engage in sexual harassment. ..." 1.19(a). "... do not exploit persons over whom they have supervisory, evaluative, or other authority such as students, supervisees, employees, research partici-	I.4. "Abstain from all forms of harassment, including sexual harassment." II.26. "... not encourage or engage in sexual intimacy with therapy clients, neither during therapy, nor for that period of time following therapy during which the

distress or behavioral inadequacy, shall not 1) engage in any verbal or physical behaviour toward him/her which is sexually seductive, demeaning, or harassing; or 2) engage in sexual intercourse or other physical intimacies with him/her; or 3) enter into a financial or other potentially exploitive relationship with him/her."	pants, and clients or patients." 4.05. ". . . do not engage in sexual intimacies with current patients or clients." 4.07(a). ". . . do not engage in sexual intimacies with a former therapy patient or client for at least two years after cessation or termination of professional services."	power relationship reasonably could be expected to influence the client's personal decision making." III.30. "Not exploit any relationship established as a psychologist to further personal, political, or business interests at the expense of their clients, research participants, students, employers, or others. This includes, but is not limited to: taking advantage of trust or dependency to engage in sexual activities or to frighten clients into receiving services. . . ."
B.2.c. "The prohibitions set out in (b) above shall extend indefinitely if the client is proven to be clearly vulnerable, by reason of emotional or cognitive disorder, to exploitive influence by the psychologist."	4.07(b). ". . . the psychologist who engages in such activity after two years following cessation or termination of treatment bears the burden of demonstrating that there has been no exploitation, in light of all relevant factors, including (1) the amount of time that has passed since therapy terminated, (2) the nature and duration of the therapy, (3) the circumstances of termination, (4) the patient's or client's personal history, (5) the patient's or client's current mental status, (6) the likelihood of adverse impact on the patient or client and others, and (7) any statements or actions made by the therapist during the course of therapy suggesting or inviting the possibility of a post-termination sexual or romantic relationship with the patient or client."	See I.4, II.26 and III.30 above.

continues

Appendix G *(Continued)*

Main content of each rule of conduct of ASPPB Code (1991)	Excerpts from and/or commentary regarding comparative ethical standards of APA Code (1992)	Excerpts from and/or commentary regarding comparative ethical standards of CPA Code (1991)
C. Client Welfare C.1. ". . . shall give a truthful, understandable, and appropriate account of the client's condition to the client or to those responsible for the care of the client. The psychologist shall keep the client fully informed as to the purpose and nature of any evaluation, treatment, or other procedures, and of the client's right to freedom of choice regarding services provided." (Comment: The term *informed consent* is not used, although the concept of "mutually agreed upon relationship" is used in this Code's definition of a "professional relationship," and the concept of "informed written consent" appears under E. Protecting Confidentiality of Clients.)	1.07(a). "When psychologists provide assessment, evaluation, treatment, counseling, supervision, teaching, consultation, research, or other psychological services to an individual, a group, or an organization, they provide, using language that is reasonably understandable to the recipient of those services, appropriate information beforehand about the nature of such services and appropriate information later, about results and conclusions." 1.07(b). "If psychologists will be precluded by law or by organizational rules from providing such information to particular individuals or groups, they so inform those individuals or groups at the outset of the service."	(Comment: Ethical Standards I.11-19 and I.29-31 cover informed consent for all forms of service and research activities. The requirements include ensuring maximization of involvement in decision making, the circumstances in which informed consent is needed, exceptions regarding emergencies, the use of consent forms, kinds of information to be covered, understandability of language, involvement of multiple parties, assent from those without capacity, obtaining substitute consent for those without capacity, special care for vulnerable persons and alternative options for students. Due to the number and length of these standards, readers are referred to the original for more detail.)
	2.09. "Unless the nature of the relationship is clearly explained to the person being assessed in advance and precludes provision of an explanation of results (such as in some organizational consulting, pre-employment or security screenings, and forensic evaluations), psychologists ensure that an explanation of the	I.20. Take all reasonable steps to ensure that consent is not given under conditions of coercion or undue pressure." I.21. "Not proceed with any research activity, if consent is given under any condition of coercion or undue pressure."

	results is provided using language that is reasonably understandable to the person assessed or to another legally authorized person on behalf of the client. . . ." (Comment: Ethical Standards 4.01[a], 4.01[d], 4.02[a]–[c], and 4.03[a] cover informed consent for therapy; and, Standards 5.01[a] and 5.01[b] cover informed consent regarding confidentiality. The requirements in these standards include necessary conditions for informed consent; the kinds of information to be provided; obtaining assent from those without capacity; obtaining substitute consent for those without capacity; informing persons/organizations, at the outset, about limitations on confidentiality; and keeping clients informed of any changes in the limits of confidentiality. Due to the number and length of these Standards, readers are referred to the original for further detail.)	I.22. "Take all reasonable steps to confirm or reestablish freedom of consent, if consent for service is given under conditions of duress or conditions of extreme need." I.23. "Respect the right of individuals to discontinue participation or service at any time, and be responsive to nonverbal indications of a desire to discontinue if the individual has difficulty with verbally communicating such a desire (e.g., young children, verbally disabled persons)." III.15. "Provide suitable information about the results of assessments, evaluations or research findings to the persons involved, if appropriate and/or if asked. This information would be communicated in understandable language."
	6.09. ". . . obtain from host institutions or organizations appropriate approval prior to conducting research. . . ." (Comment: Ethical Standards 6.11[a]–[e] cover informed consent for research. The requirements include: using understandable language; the kinds of information to be provided; special care with vulnerable	III.16. "Fully explain reasons for their actions to persons who have been affected by their actions, if appropriate and/or if asked." III.31. "Not offer rewards sufficient to motivate an individual or group to participate in an activity that has possible or known risks to themselves or others."

continues

Appendix G *(Continued)*

Main content of each rule of conduct of ASPPB Code (1991)	Excerpts from and/or commentary regarding comparative ethical standards of APA Code (1992)	Excerpts from and/or commentary regarding comparative ethical standards of CPA Code (1991)
	populations; alternative options for students; obtaining assent from those without capacity; and, obtaining substitute consent for those without capacity. Readers are referred to the original for more detail.)	
C.2. "Whenever professional services are terminated . . . shall offer to help locate alternative sources of professional services or assistance if indicated . . . shall terminate a professional relationship when it is reasonably clear that the client is not benefiting from the relationship, and shall prepare the client appropriately for such termination."	4.09(a). ". . . do not abandon patients or clients." 4.09(b). ". . . terminate a professional relationship when it becomes reasonably clear that the patient or client no longer needs the service, is not benefiting, or is being harmed by continued service." 4.09(c). "Prior to termination for whatever reason, except where precluded by the patient's or client's conduct, the psychologist discusses the patient's or client's views and needs, provides appropriate pretermination counseling, suggests alternative service providers as appropriate, and takes other reasonable steps to facilitate transfer of responsibility to another provider if the patient or client needs one immediately."	See II.29 above. II.30. "Maintain appropriate contact, support and responsibility for caring until a colleague or other professional begins service, if referring a client to a colleague or other professional." II.31. "Give reasonable notice and be reasonably assured that discontinuation will cause no harm to the client before discontinuing services." II.34. "Terminate an activity when it is clear that the activity is more harmful than beneficial, or when the activity is no longer needed."

C.3. "... shall not impose on the client any stereotypes of behaviour, values, or roles related to age, gender, religion, race, disability, nationality, sexual preference, or diagnosis which would interfere with objective provision of psychological services to the client."	1.10. "... do not engage in unfair discrimination based on age, gender, race, ethnicity, national origin, religion, sexual orientation, disability, socioeconomic status, or any basis prescribed by law." 1.12. "... do not knowingly engage in behavior that is harassing or demeaning to persons with whom they interact in their work based on factors such as those persons' age, gender, race, ethnicity, national origin, religion, sexual orientation, disability, language, or socioeconomic status."	I.9. "Not practice, condone, facilitate, or collaborate with any form of unjust discrimination." II.10. Evaluate how their own experiences, attitudes, culture, beliefs, values, social context, individual differences, and stresses influence their interactions with others, and integrate this awareness into all efforts to benefit and not harm others." III.10. "Evaluate how their own experiences, attitudes, culture, beliefs, values, social context, individual differences, and stress influence their activities and thinking, integrating this awareness into all attempts to be objective and unbiased in their research, service, and other activities."
C.4. "... shall not enter into a sexual or other dual relationship with a client, as specified in Section III, B. of this Code of Conduct."	See above for comparison of ASPPB III.B.2 with APA Standards.	See above for comparison of ASPPB III.B.2 with CPA Standards.
C.5. "The psychologist providing services to an individual client shall not induce that client(s) to solicit business on behalf of the psychologist."	See 1.19(a) above. (Comment: No specific mention of solicitation of business.)	III.30. "Not exploit any relationship established as a psychologist to further personal, political, or business interests at the expense of the best interests of their clients, research participants, students, employers, or others. . . ." (Comment: No specific mention of solicitation of business.)

continues

Appendix G *(Continued)*

Main content of each rule of conduct of ASPPB Code (1991)	Excerpts from and/or commentary regarding comparative ethical standards of APA Code (1992)	Excerpts from and/or commentary regarding comparative ethical standards of CPA Code (1991)
C.6. "The psychologist providing services to a client shall make an appropriate referral of the client to another professional when requested to do so by the client."	(Comment: No specific requirement to make an appropriate referral when requested to do so by the client. However, see 1.20(a) above regarding referrals.)	I.12. "Respect and integrate as much as possible the opinions and wishes of others regarding decisions which affect them." (Comment: No specific requirement to make an appropriate referral when requested to do so by the client. However, see II.8 above regarding referrals.)
D. Welfare of Supervisees and Research Subjects		
D.1. ". . . shall not exploit a supervisee in any way—sexually, financially or otherwise.	1.19(a). ". . . do not exploit persons over whom they have supervisory, evaluative, or other authority such as students, supervisees, employees, research participants, and clients or patients." 1.19(b) ". . . do not engage in sexual relationships with students or supervisees in training over whom the psychologist has evaluative or direct authority, because such relationships are so likely to impair judgment or be exploitative." (Comment: Several other APA Ethical Standards outline ways to protect the "welfare of supervisees." Requirements include: to "respect the rights of others to hold values, attitudes, and opinions that differ from their own" [1.09]; to avoid harming [1.14]; to refrain from dual rela-	III.30. "Not exploit any relationship . . . to further personal, political, or business interests at the expense of the best interests of their . . . students . . . or others. This includes but is not limited to: taking advantage of trust or dependency to engage in sexual activities . . . appropriating student's ideas, research, or work. . . ." (Comment: Several other CPA Standards outline ways to protect the "welfare of supervisees." Requirements include to "respect the right of . . . supervisees . . . to safeguard their own dignity" [1.8]; to "respect the right of . . . supervisees . . . to reasonable personal privacy" [I.35]; to protect information that students would consider confidential [I.38]; to encourage students to publish "worthy" papers [II.25]; to provide or arrange for "adequate

	tionships with students [1.17]; to not engage in sexual relationships [1.19.b]; to provide "proper training and supervision to their employees or supervisees" [1.22.b]; to ensure that training programs are "competently designed, provide the proper experiences, and meet the requirements for licensure" [6.01]; to "make reasonable efforts to avoid . . . conduct that is personally demeaning to students or supervisees" [6.03.b]; to "establish an appropriate process for providing feedback [6.05.a]; to "evaluate students and supervisees on the basis of their actual performance on relevant and established program requirements" [6.05.b]. Due to the number and length of these Standards, readers are referred to the original for further detail.)	working conditions, timely evaluations, and constructive consultation and experience opportunities" [II.24]; to encourage a free exchange of ideas [III.21]; and to help students acquire an understanding of the ethics, responsibilities, and needed competencies of their area[s] [IV.4]. Due to the number and length of these standards, readers are referred to the original for further detail.)
D.2. ". . . shall respect the dignity and protect the welfare or his/her research subjects, and shall comply with all relevant statutes and administrative rules concerning treatment of research subjects."	(Comment: There are several APA Ethical Standards that outline ways to protect the "welfare of research subjects." Requirements include to avoid harm [1.14]; to not exploit research participants [1.19a]; to protect confidentiality [5.07.b and 5.07.c]; to evaluate the ethical acceptability of research studies [6.06.c]; to take reasonable steps to implement appropriate protections for the rights and welfare of participants [6.06.d]; to conduct research competently and with due concern for dignity and welfare [6.07.a]; to comply with law and standards [6.08]; to obtain institutional approval and conduct re-	(Comment: There are several CPA Ethical Standards that outline ways to protect the "welfare of research subjects." Requirements include to respect the right of participants to safeguard own dignity [I.8]; to obtain informed consent [I.14]; to seek review of ethical issues [I.27]; to protect vulnerable participants [I.28, 30, 31]; to protect and promote welfare [II.1]; to avoid doing harm [II.2]; to carry out pilot studies of new procedures and techniques before using [II.15]; to seek independent ethical review if using techniques of unknown consequence [II.16]; to debrief [II.22, 39]; to avoid keeping those needing

continues

Appendix G *(Continued)*

Main content of each rule of conduct of ASPPB Code (1991)	Excerpts from and/or commentary regardPing comparative ethical standards of APA Code (1992)	Excerpts from and/or commentary regarding comparative ethical standards of CPA Code (1991)
	search in accordance with approved protocol [6.09]; to obtain informed consent [6.10–13, 6.16]; to take special care when participants are students or subordinates [6.11]; to not use excessive inducements [6.14]; to use deception only under certain conditions [6.15]; and to provide feedback [6.18]. Due to the number and length of these Standards, readers are referred to the original for further detail.)	treatment in control groups [II.38]; to screen to avoid harm [II.32]; to minimize impact [II.33]; to use deception only under certain conditions [III.24–29]; to follow discipline's rules and regulations [III.34]; and to adhere to law [IV.15]. Due to the number and length of these Standards, readers are referred to the original for further detail.)
E. Protecting Confidentiality of Clients E.1. ". . . shall safeguard the confidential information obtained in the course of practice, teaching, research, or other professional services. With the exceptions set forth below, the psychologist shall disclose confidential information to others only with the informed written consent of the client."	5.02. ". . . take reasonable precautions to respect the confidentiality rights of those with whom they work or consult, recognizing that confidentiality may be established by law, institutional rules, or professional or scientific relationships. (See also Standard 6.26, Professional Reviewers.)"	I.38. "Be careful not to relay information which they have gained about colleagues, colleagues' clients, students, and members of organizations gained in the process of their activities as psychologists and which the psychologist has reason to believe is considered confidential by those persons, except as required or justified by law. (See Standards IV.15 and IV.16)."
	5.06. "When consulting with colleagues, (1) psychologists do not share confidential information that reasonably could lead to the identification of a patient, client, research participant, or other person or organization unless they have obtained the prior consent of the person or organization or the disclosure cannot be avoided, and (2) they share information only to the	I.40. "Share confidential information with others only with the informed consent of those involved, or in a manner that the individuals involved cannot be identified, except as required or justified by law, or in circumstances of actual or possible serious harm or death. (See Standard II.36)."

	extent necessary to achieve the purposes of the consultation." 5.08(a). ". . . do not disclose in their writings, lectures, or other public media, confidential, personally identifiable information concerning their patients, individual or organizational clients, students, research participants, or other recipients of their services . . . unless the person or organization has consented in writing or unless there is other ethical or legal authorization for doing so." 6.26. "Psychologists who review material submitted for publication, grant, or other research proposal review respect the confidentiality of and the proprietary rights of those who submitted it."	
E.2. ". . . may disclose confidential information without the informed consent of the client when the psychologist judges that disclosure is necessary to protect against a clear and substantial risk of imminent harm being inrPPflicted by the client on the client or another person. In such case, the psychologist shall limit disclosure . . . to only those persons and only that content which would be consistent with the standards of the profession. . . . When the client is an organi-	5.05(a). ". . . disclose confidential information without the consent of the individual only as mandated by law, or where permitted by law for a valid purpose, such as (1) to provide needed professional services to the patient or the individual or organizational client, (2) to obtain appropriate professional consultations, (3) to protect the patient or client from harm, or (4) to obtain payment for services, in which instance disclosure is limited to the minimum that is necessary to achieve the purpose."	II.36. "Do everything reasonably possible to stop or offset the consequences of actions by others when these actions are likely to cause serious physical harm or death. This may include reporting to appropriate authorities (e.g., the police), or an intended victim, and would be done even when a confidential relationship is involved. (See Standard I.40.)"

continues

Appendix G *(Continued)*

Main content of each rule of conduct of ASPPB Code (1991)	Excerpts from and/or commentary regarding comparative ethical standards of APA Code (1992)	Excerpts from and/or commentary regarding comparative ethical standards of CPA Code (1991)
zation, disclosure shall be made only after the psychologist has made a reasonable and unsuccessful attempt to have the problems corrected within the organization."	5.05(b). ". . . may disclose confidential information with the appropriate consent of the . . . client (or of another legally authorized person . . .), unless prohibited by law."	
E.3. "In a situation in which more than one party has an appropriate interest, . . . shall, to the extent possible, clarify to all parties prior to rendering the services the dimensions of confidentiality and professional responsibility that shall pertain. . . . Such clarification is specifically indicated, among other circumstances, when the client is an organization."	1.21(a). "When a psychologist agrees to provide services to a person or entity at the request of a third party . . . clarifies to the extent feasible, at the outset of the service, the nature of the relationship with each party. This clarification includes the role of the psychologist (such as therapist, organizational consultant, diagnostician, or expert witness), the probable uses of the services provided or the information obtained, and the fact that there may be limits to confidentiality." 1.21(b). "If there is a foreseeable risk of . . . being called upon to perform conflicting roles . . . clarifies nature and direction of his or her responsibilities, keeps all parties appropriately informed . . . and resolves the situation in accordance with this Ethics Code."	1.19. "Clarify the nature of multiple relationships to all concerned parties before obtaining consent, if providing services to or conducting research with individuals, families, groups, or communities at the request of or for the use of third parties. This would include but not be limited to the purpose of the service or research, the use that will be made of the information collected, and the limits on confidentiality. . . ." III.14. "Be clear and straightforward about all information needed to establish informed consent or any other valid written or unwritten agreement (for example: . . . mutual responsibilities; . . . purpose and nature of the relationship; . . . expectations for processing, using, and sharing any information generated)."

E.4. "When service is rendered to more than one client during a joint session . . . shall at the beginning of the professional relationship clarify to all parties the manner in which confidentiality will be handled. All parties shall be given opportunity to discuss and to accept whatever limitations to confidentiality adhere in the situation."	4.03(a). "When a psychologist agrees to provide services to several persons who have a relationship . . . the psychologist attempts to clarify at the outset (1) which of the individuals are patients or clients and (2) the relationship the psychologist will have with each person. This clarification includes the role of the psychologist and the probable uses of the services provided or information obtained."	I.39. "Clarify what measures will be taken to protect confidentiality, and what responsibilities family, group, and community members have for the protection of each other's confidentiality, when engaged in services to or research with individuals, families, groups, or communities."
E.5. "At the beginning of a professional relationship, to the extent that the client can understand, the psychologist shall inform a client who is below the age of majority or who has a legal guardian, of the limit the law imposes on the right of confidentiality. . . ."	4.02(c). ". . . (1) inform those persons who are legally incapable of giving informed consent about the proposed interventions in a manner commensurate with the person's psychological capacities, (2) seek their assent to these interventions, and (3) consider such persons' preferences and best interests." (Comment: Applies to *4. Therapy* only.)	I.30. "Seek willing and adequately informed participation from any person of diminished capacity to give informed consent, and proceed without this assent only if the research or service activity is considered to be of direct benefit to that person." (Comment: Applies to all activities, not just release of confidential information.)
	6.11(e). "For persons who are legally incapable of giving informed consent, psychologists nevertheless (1) provide an appropriate explanation, (2) obtain the participant's assent. . . ." (Comment: Applies to research only.)	
E.6. ". . . shall limit access to client records to preserve their confidentiality and shall assure that all persons working under the psychologist's authority comply with the requirements for confidentiality of client material."	1.22(b). ". . . provide proper training and supervision to their employees or supervisees and take reasonable steps to see that such persons perform services responsibly, competently, and ethically."	I.36. "Store, handle, and transfer all records . . . in a way that attends to the needs for privacy and security. This would include having adequate plans for records in circumstances of one's own serious illness or death."

continues

Appendix G *(Continued)*

Main content of each rule of conduct of ASPPB Code (1991)	Excerpts from and/or commentary regarding comparative ethical standards of APA Code (1992)	Excerpts from and/or commentary regarding comparative ethical standards of CPA Code (1991)
	See 1.24 above.	I.41. "Encourage others, if appropriate, to respect the dignity of persons. . . ." (Comment: This would include confidentiality and goes beyond those under the psychologist's direct authority.)
	5.04. ". . . maintain appropriate confidentiality in creating, storing, accessing, transferring, and disposing of records under their control, whether these are written, automated, or in any other medium. Psychologists maintain and dispose of records in accordance with law and in a manner that permits compliance with the requirements of this Ethics Code."	I.42. "Assume overall responsibility for the scientific and professional activities of their assistants, students, supervisees, and employees with regard to Respect for the Dignity of Persons, all of whom, however, incur similar obligations."
	5.07(a). "If confidential information . . . to be entered into databases or systems of records available to persons whose access has not been consented to by the recipient, then . . . use coding or other techniques to avoid the inclusion of personal identifiers."	
	5.09. ". . . plans in advance so that confidentiality of records and data is protected in the event of the psychologist's death, incapacity, or withdrawal from the position or practice."	
E.7. ". . . may release confidential information upon court order, as defined in Section II of this Code, or to conform with state, federal or provincial law, rule, or regulation."	1.02. "If psychologists' ethical responsibilities conflict with the law, psychologists make known their commitment to the Ethics Code and take steps to resolve the conflict in a reasonable manner."	See I.38 and I.40 above. IV.15. "Abide by the laws of the society in which they work. If those laws seriously conflict with the ethical principles con-

	See 5.05(a) above.	tained herein, psychologists would do whatever they could to uphold the ethical principles. If upholding the ethical principles could result in serious personal consequences (e.g., jail or physical harm), decision for final action would be considered a matter of personal conscience." IV.16. "Consult with colleagues, if faced with an apparent conflict between keeping a law and following an ethical principle, unless in an emergency, and seek consensus as to the most ethical course of action and the most responsible, knowledgeable, effective, and respectful way to carry it out."
E.8. ". . . shall be familiar with any relevant law concerning the reporting of abuse of children and vulnerable adults, and shall comply with such laws."	See 1.02 and 5.05(a) above.	See I.38, I.40, IV.15, and IV.16 above.
E.9. "When rendering professional services as part of a team or when interacting with other appropriate professionals concerning the welfare of the client . . . may share confidential information about the client provided the psychologist takes reasonable steps to assure that all persons receiving the information are informed about the confidential nature of the information and abide by the rules of confidentiality."	See 1.22(b) above. 5.03(b). ". . . discuss confidential information obtained in clinical or consulting relationships, or evaluative data concerning patients, individual or organizational clients, students, research participants, supervisees, and employees, only for appropriate scientific or professional purposes and only with persons clearly concerned with such matters."	See I.40, I.41, and I.42 above. (Comment: No specific mention of team members or "other appropriate professionals;" however, both categories would be covered under concept "justified by law" in Standard 1.40.)

continues

Appendix G *(Continued)*

Main content of each rule of conduct of ASPPB Code (1991)	Excerpts from and/or commentary regarding comparative ethical standards of APA Code (1992)	Excerpts from and/or commentary regarding comparative ethical standards of CPA Code (1991)
	See 5.05(a) above.	
E.10. When case reports or other confidential information is used as the basis of teaching, research, or other published reports . . . shall exercise reasonable care to ensure that the reported material is appropriately disguised to prevent client identification."	See 5.08(a) above. 5.08(b). "Ordinarily, in such scientific and professional presentations, psychologists disguise confidential information concerning such persons or organizations so that they are not individually identifiable to others and so that discussions do not cause harm to subjects who might identify themselves."	See I.40 above.
E.11. ". . . shall ensure that diagnostic interviews or therapeutic sessions with a client are observed or electronically recorded only with the informed written consent of the client."	5.01(c). "Permission for electronic recording of interviews is secured from clients and patients." (Comment: Note absence of phrase *informed consent* or phrase *written*, as well as no mention of *observation*.)	(Comment: No specific requirement to obtain such consent; however, standards on informed consent [I.11–19] would imply that informed consent would be required, although the consent would need to be written only if the institution, client, or psychologist wished it to be written or if such written consent was required by law.)
E.12. ". . . shall continue to treat as confidential information regarding a client after the professional relationship between the psychologist and the client has ceased."	(Comment: No specific statement that confidential information about a client remains confidential after termination; however, can be inferred from APA Code.)	(Comment: No specific statement that confidential information about a client remains confidential after termination; however, can be inferred from CPA Code.)

F. Representation of Services F.1. ". . . shall display his/her current (name of jurisdiction) license to practice psychology, on the premises of his/her professional office."	(Comment: No such requirement.)	(Comment: No such requirement.)
F.2. ". . . shall not misrepresent directly or by implication his/her professional qualifications such as education, experience, or areas of competence."	3.03(a). ". . . do not make public statements that are false, deceptive, misleading, or fraudulent, either because of what they state, convey, or suggest or because of what they omit. . . . As examples . . . false or deceptive statements concerning (1) their training, experience, or competence; (2) their academic degrees; (3) their credentials; (4) their institutional or association affiliations; (5) their services; (6) the scientific or clinical basis for, or results or degree of success of, their services; (7) their fees; or (8) their publications or research findings." 3.03(b). ". . . claim as credentials for their psychological work, only degrees that (1) were earned from a regionally accredited educational institution or (2) were the basis for psychology licensure by the state in which they practice."	III.1. "Not participate in, condone, or be associated with dishonesty, fraud, or misrepresentation." III.2. "Accurately represent their own and their associates' qualifications, education, experience, competence and affiliations, in all spoken, written, or printed communications, being careful not to use descriptions or information which could be misinterpreted." III.4. "Maintain competence in their declared area(s) of psychological competence, as well as their current area(s) of activity."
F.3. ". . . shall not misrepresent directly or by implication his/her affiliations, or the purposes or characteristics of institutions and organizations with which the psychologist is associated."	See 3.03(a) above.	See III.1. and III.2. above.

continues

Appendix G *(Continued)*

Main content of each rule of conduct of ASPPB Code (1991)	Excerpts from and/or commentary regarding comparative ethical standards of APA Code (1992)	Excerpts from and/or commentary regarding comparative ethical standards of CPA Code (1991)
F.4. ". . . shall not include false or misleading information in public statements concerning professional services offered."	1.26. "In their reports to payors for services or sources of research funding . . . accurately state the nature of the research or service provided, the fees or charges, and where applicable, the identity of the provider, the findings, and the diagnosis." See 3.03(a) above. 6.02(a). "Psychologists responsible for education and training programs seek to ensure that there is a current and accurate description. . . ." 6.02(b). ". . . seek to ensure that statements concerning their course outlines are accurate and not misleading. . . ." 6.02(c). "To the degree to which they exercise control . . . for announcements, catalogs, brochures or advertisements . . . ensure that they accurately describe. . . ."	See III.1 above. III.5. "Accurately represent their activities, functions, and likely or actual outcomes of their work, in all spoken, written, or printed communication. This includes, but is not limited to: advertisements of services; course and workshop descriptions; academic grading requirements; and research reports."
F.5. ". . . shall not associate with or permit his/her name to be used in connection with any services or products in such a way as to misrepresent (a) the services or products, (b) the degree	3.02(a). "Psychologists who engage others to create or place public statements that promote their professional practice, products, or activities retain professional responsibility for such statements."	III.3. "Carefully protect their own and their associates' credentials from being misrepresented by others, and act quickly to correct any such misrepresentation."

of his/her responsibility for the services or products, (c) the nature of his/her association with the services or products."	3.02(b). ". . . make reasonable efforts to prevent others whom they do not control (such as employers, publishers, sponsors, organizational clients, and representatives of the print or broadcast media) from making deceptive statements concerning psychologists' practice or professional or scientific activities."	III.6. "Ensure that their activities, functions, and likely or actual outcomes of their activities are not misrepresented by others, and act quickly to correct any such misrepresentation."
F.6. ". . . shall correct others who misrepresent the psychologist's professional qualifications or affiliations." (Comment: Note limitation to qualifications or affiliations.)	1.16(b). "If psychologists learn of misuse or misrepresentation of their work, they take reasonable steps to correct or minimize the misuse or misrepresentation." 3.02(c). "If psychologists learn of deceptive statements about their work made by others, psychologists make reasonable efforts to correct such statements."	See III.3 and III.6 above. III.13. "Act quickly to clarify any distortion by a sponsor, client, or other persons, of the findings of their research."
G. Fees and Statements G.1. ". . . shall not mislead or withhold from the client, a prospective client, or third party payor, information about the cost of his/her professional services.	1.25(a). "As early as is feasible in a professional or scientific relationship . . . reach an agreement specifying the compensation and the billing arrangements." 1.25(d). ". . . do not misrepresent their fees." 1.25(f). ". . . if the psychologist wishes to use collection agencies or legal measures to collect the fees, the psychologist first informs the person that such measures will be taken and provides that person an opportunity to make prompt payment."	See III.1 and III.5 above. III.14. "Be clear and straightforward about all information needed to establish informed consent or any other valid written or unwritten agreement (for example: fees . . .)."

continues

Appendix G *(Continued)*

Main content of each rule of conduct of ASPPB Code (1991)	Excerpts from and/or commentary regarding comparative ethical standards of APA Code (1992)	Excerpts from and/or commentary regarding comparative ethical standards of CPA Code (1991)
	See 3.03(a) above.	
G.2. "... shall not exploit the client or responsible payor by charging a fee that is excessive for the services performed or by entering into an exploitive bartering arrangement in lieu of a fee."	1.18. "... ordinarily refrain from accepting goods, services, or other nonmonetary remuneration from patients or clients in return for psychological services because such arrangements create inherent potential for conflicts, exploitation, and distortion of the professional relationship. A psychologist may participate in bartering *only* if (1) it is not clinically contraindicated, *and* (2) the relationship is not exploitative.	See III.30 and III.32 above. (Comment: No specific mention of bartering.)
	1.25(b). "... do not exploit recipients of services or payors with respect to fees."	
H. Assessment Procedures		
H.1. "... shall treat an assessment result or interpretation regarding an individual as confidential information."	See APA Standards corresponding to ASPPB Rules E.1, E.2, E.4, E.7–10, and E.12 above. (Comment: The APA Code does not differentiate assessment results or interpretations from other forms of confidential information.)	See I.38–40 above. (Comment: The CPA Code does not differentiate assessment results or interpretations from other forms of confidential information.)
H.2. "... shall accompany communication of results of assessment procedures to the client, parents, legal guardians or other agents of the client by adequate interpretive aids or explanations."	See 1.07(a) above. See 2.09 above.	See III.15 above.

H.3. ". . . shall include in his/her report of the results of a formal assessment procedure . . . any deficiencies of the assessment norms for the individual assessed and any relevant reservations or qualifications which affect the validity, reliability, or other interpretation of results."	2.04(b). ". . . recognize limits to the certainty with which diagnoses, judgments, or predictions can be made about individuals." 2.05. "When interpreting assessment results . . . indicate any significant reservations they have about the accuracy or limitations of their interpretations." See 7.02(c) above. 7.04(b). "Whenever necessary to avoid misleading, psychologists acknowledge the limits of their data or conclusions." (Comments: This requirement appears only under 7. *Forensic Activities*.)	III.8. "Acknowledge the limitations of their knowledge, methods, findings, interventions, and views." III.9. "Not suppress disconfirming evidence of their findings and views, acknowledging alternative hypotheses and explanations." III.11. "Take care to communicate as completely and objectively as possible, and to clearly differentiate facts, opinions, theories, hypotheses, and ideas, if communicating their knowledge, findings, and views."
H.4. ". . . shall not reproduce or describe in popular publications, lectures, or public presentations psychological tests or other assessment devices in ways that might invalidate them."	2.10. ". . . make reasonable efforts to maintain the integrity and security of tests and other assessment techniques consistent with law, contractual obligations, and in a manner that permits compliance with the requirements of this Ethics Code."	IV.9. "Protect the skills, knowledge, and interpretation of psychology from being misused, used incompetently, or made useless (e.g., loss of security of assessment techniques) by others."
H5. "The psychologist offering an assessment procedure or automated interpretation service to other professionals shall accompany this offering by a manual or other printed material which fully describes the development of the assessment procedure or service, the rationale, evidence of validity and relia-	2.08(a). "Psychologists who offer assessment or scoring procedures to other professionals accurately describe the purpose, norms, validity, reliability, and applications of the procedures and any special qualifications applicable to their use."	(Comment: No specific requirements regarding offering an assessment procedure or automated interpretation service. General requirement to accurately represent their work [III.5], and to take care to communicate as completely and objectively as possible [III.11].)

continues

Appendix G *(Continued)*

Main content of each rule of conduct of ASPPB Code (1991)	Excerpts from and/or commentary regarding comparative ethical standards of APA Code (1992)	Excerpts from and/or commentary regarding comparative ethical standards of CPA Code (1991)
bility, and characteristics of the normative population . . . shall explicitly state the purpose and application for which the procedure is recommended and identify special qualifications required to administer and interpret it properly . . . shall ensure that advertisements for the assessment procedure or interpretive service are factual and descriptive."		
I. Violations of Law		
I.1. ". . . shall not violate any applicable statute or administrative rule regulating the practice of psychology."	(Comment: No specific requirement to abide by any statute or administrative rule regulating the practice of psychology. However, there are standards that refer to referral practices being consistent with "the law" [1.20.c]; fee practices being consistent with "the law" [1.25.c]; research being consistent with "federal and state law and regulations" [6.08]; practices with animals being "in compliance with current federal, state, and local laws and regulations" [6.20]; and, being familiar with "rules governing their roles" in forensic activities [7.06].)	See III.34 and IV.15 above.
I.2. ". . . shall not use fraud, misrepresentation, or deception in obtaining a	(Comment: The APA Code contains several standards with requirements to not	See III.1 above.

psychology license, in passing a psychology licensing examination, in assisting another to obtain a psychology license or to pass a psychology licensing examination, in billing clients or third party payors, in providing psychological service, in reporting the results of psychological evaluations or services, or in conducting any other activity related to the practice of psychology."	misrepresent their fees [1.25, 1.26]; not make public statements that are "false, deceptive, misleading or fraudulent" [3.03.a]; not fabricate data or falsify results in their publications [6.21.a]; not "present substantial proportion or elements of another's work or data as their own" [6.22]; "not publish, as original data, data that have been previously published" [6.24]. Excerpts from some of these standards appear above. Due to the number and length of the standards, readers are referred to the original for further details.)	III.23. "Not engage in deception in any service activity."
J. Aiding Illegal Practice J.1. ". . . shall not aid or abet another person in misrepresenting his/her professional credentials or in illegally engaging in the practice of psychology."	See 3.03(a) above.	See III.1 and III.2 above. See IV. 15 above.
J.2. ". . . shall not delegate professional responsibilities to a person not appropriately credentialed or otherwise appropriately qualified to provide such services."	1.22(a). ". . . delegate to their employees, supervisees, and research assistants only those responsibilities that such persons can reasonably be expected to perform competently. . . ." 6.04. ". . . do not teach the use of techniques or procedures that require specialized training, licensure, or expertise . . . to individuals who lack the prerequisite training, legal scope of practice, or expertise."	II.7. "Not delegate activities to persons not competent to carry them out to the benefit of others."

continues

Appendix G *(Continued)*

Main content of each rule of conduct of ASPPB Code (1991)	Excerpts from and/or commentary regarding comparative ethical standards of APA Code (1992)	Excerpts from and/or commentary regarding comparative ethical standards of CPA Code (1991)
	6.07(c). "Researchers and assistants are permitted to perform only those tasks for which they are appropriately trained and prepared." 6.20(e). "Responsibilities and activities of individuals assisting in a research project are consistent with their respective competencies." (Comment: This standard applies only to research in which animals are used.)	
J.3. ". . . shall exercise appropriate supervision over supervisees, as set forth in the rules and regulations of the Board."	See 1.22(b) above. 6.07(b). ". . . responsible for the ethical conduct of research conducted by them or any others under their supervision and control."	(Comment: In the CPA Code, there is one ethical standard under each of the four Ethical Principles, as follows: "Assume overall responsibility for the scientific and professional activities of their assistants, students, supervisees, and employees with regard to the Principle of ______, all of whom, however, incur similar obligations." The blank is filled in with the particular Ethical Principle [I.42, II.45, III.38, IV.28].) See III.34 above.
J.4. "The psychologist who has substantial reason to believe that there has been a violation of the statutes or rules of the Board shall so inform the	See 1.02, 5.02, and 5.05 above. 8.05. "If an apparent ethical violation is not appropriate for informal resolution	See I.38 and I.40 above. IV.11. "Uphold the discipline's responsibility to society by bringing incompetent

Board in writing, except that when the information regarding such violation is obtained in a professional relationship with a client, the psychologist shall report it only with the written permission of the client. Nothing in this Code shall relieve a psychologist of the duty to file any report required by applicable statutes."	under Standard 8.04 or is not resolved properly in that fashion, psychologists take further action appropriate to the situation, unless such action conflicts with confidentiality rights in ways that cannot be resolved.	or unethical behaviour, including misuses of psychological knowledge and techniques, to the attention of appropriate regulatory bodies, authorities, and/or committees, in a manner consistent with the ethical principles of this Code, if informal resolution or correction of the situation is not appropriate or possible." See IV.15 above.

Appendix H

Record Keeping Guidelines

Drafted by the Committee on Professional Practice & Standards, A Committee of the Board of Professional Affairs
Adopted by the Council of Representatives, February 1993

Introduction[1]

The guidelines that follow are based on the General Guidelines, adopted by the American Psychological Association (APA) in July 1987 (APA, 1987). The guidelines receive their inspirational guidance from specific APA *Ethical Principles of Psychologists and Code of Conduct* (APA, 1992).

These guidelines are aspirational and professional judgment must be used in specific applications. They are intended for use by providers of

---

[1]In 1988 the Board of Professional Affairs (BPA) directed the Committee on Professional Practice and Standards (COPPS) to determine whether record keeping guidelines would be appropriate. COPPS was informed that these guidelines would supplement the provisions contained in the *General Guidelines for Providers of Psychological Services*, which had been amended two years earlier. The Council of Representatives approved the General Guidelines records provisions after extended debate on the minimum recordation concerning the nature and contents of psychological services. The General Guidelines reflect a compromise position that psychologists hold widely varying views on the wisdom of recording the content of the psychotherapeutic relationship. In light of the Council debate on the content of psychological records and the absence of an integrated document, BPA instructed COPPS to assess the need for such guidelines, and, if necessary, the likely content.

COPPS undertook a series of interviews with psychologists experienced in this area. The consensus of the respondents indicated that practicing psychologists could benefit from guidance in this area. In addition, an APA legal intern undertook a 50-state review of laws governing psychologists with respect to record keeping provisions. The survey demonstrated that while some states have relatively clear provisions governing certain types of records, many questions are often left unclear. In addition, there is a great deal of variability among the states, so that consistent treatment of records as people move from state to state, or as records are sought from other states, may not be easy to achieve.

Based on COPPS' survey and legal research, BPA in 1989 directed COPPS to prepare an initial set of record keeping guidelines. This document resulted.

health care services.[2,3] The language of these guidelines must be interpreted in light of their aspirational intent, advancements in psychology and the technology of record keeping, and the professional judgment of the individual psychologist. It is important to highlight that professional judgment is not preempted by these guidelines: rather, the intent is to enhance it.

Underlying Principles and Purpose

Psychologists maintain records for a variety of reasons, the most important of which is the benefit of the client. Records allow a psychologist to document and review the delivery of psychological services. The nature and extent of the record will vary depending upon the type and purpose of psychological services. Records can provide a history and current status in the event that a user seeks psychological services from another psychologist or mental health professional.

Conscientious record keeping may also benefit psychologists themselves, by guiding them to plan and implement an appropriate course of psychological services, to review work as a whole, and to self-monitor more precisely.

Maintenance of appropriate records may also be relevant for a variety of other institutional, financial, and legal purposes. State and federal laws in many cases require maintenance of appropriate records of certain kinds of psychological services. Adequate records may be a requirement for receipt of third party payment for psychological services.

In addition, well documented records may help protect psychologists from professional liability, if they become the subject of legal or ethical proceedings. In these circumstances, the principal issue will be the professional action of the psychologist, as reflected in part by the records.

At times, there may be conflicts between the federal, state or local laws governing record keeping, the requirements of institutional rules, and these guidelines. In these circumstances, psychologists bear in mind their obligations to conform to applicable law. When laws or institutional rules appear to conflict with the principles of these guidelines, psychologists use their education, skills and training to identify the relevant issues, and to attempt to resolve it in a way that, to the maximum extent feasible, conforms both to law and to professional practice, as required by ethical principles.

Psychologists are justifiably concerned that, at times, record keeping information will be required to be disclosed against the wishes of the psy-

---

[2]These guidelines apply to Industrial/Organizational psychologists providing health care services but generally not to those providing non-health care I/O services. For instance, in I/O psychology, written records may constitute the primary work product, such as a test instrument or a job analysis, while psychologists providing health care services may principally use records to document non-written services and to maintain continuity.

[3]Rather than keeping their own record system, psychologists practicing in institutional settings comply with the institution's policies on record keeping, so long as they are consistent with legal and ethical standards.

chologist or client, and may be released to persons unqualified to interpret such records. These guidelines assume that no record is free from disclosure all of the time, regardless of the wishes of the client or the psychologist.

1. Content of Records

a. Records include any information (including information stored in a computer) that may be used to document the nature, delivery, progress, or results of psychological services. Records can be reviewed and duplicated.

b. Records of psychological services minimally include (a) identifying data, (b) dates of services, (c) types of services, (d) fees, (e) any assessment, plan for intervention, consultation, summary reports, and/or testing reports and supporting data as may be appropriate, and (f) any release of information obtained.

c. As may be required by their jurisdiction and circumstances, psychologists maintain to a reasonable degree accurate, current, and pertinent records of psychological services. The detail is sufficient to permit planning for continuity in the event that another psychologist takes over delivery of services, including, in the event of death, disability, and retirement. In addition, psychologists maintain records in sufficient detail for regulatory and administrative review of psychological service delivery.

d. Records kept beyond the minimum requirements are a matter of professional judgment for the psychologist. The psychologist takes into account the nature of the psychological services, the source of the information recorded, the intended use of the records, and his or her professional obligation.

e. Psychologists make reasonable efforts to protect against the misuse of records. They take into account the anticipated use by the intended or anticipated recipients when preparing records. Psychologists adequately identify impressions and tentative conclusions as such.

2. Construction and Control of Records

a. Psychologists maintain a system that protects the confidentiality of records. They must take reasonable steps to establish and maintain the confidentiality of information arising from their own delivery of psychological services, or the services provided by others working under their supervision.

b. Psychologists have ultimate responsibility for the content of their records and the records of those under their supervision. Where appropriate, this requires that the psychologist oversee the design and implementation of record keeping procedures, and monitor their observance.

c. Psychologists maintain control over their clients' records, taking into account the policies of the institutions in which they practice. In situations where psychologists have control over their clients' records and where circumstances change such that it is no longer feasible to maintain control over such records, psychologists seek to make appropriate arrangements for transfer.

d. Records are organized in a manner that facilitates their use by the psychologist and other authorized persons. Psychologists strive to assure that record entries are legible. Records are to be completed in a timely manner.

e. Records may be maintained in a variety of media, so long as their utility, confidentiality and durability are assured.

3. Retention of Records

a. The psychologist is aware of relevant federal, state and local laws and regulations governing record retention. Such laws and regulations supersede the requirements of these guidelines. In the absence of such laws and regulations, complete records are maintained for a minimum of 3 years after the last contact with the client. Records, or a summary, are then maintained for an additional 12 years before disposal.[4] If the client is a minor, the record period is extended until 3 years after the age of majority.

b. All records, active and inactive, are maintained safely, with properly limited access, and from which timely retrieval is possible.

4. Outdated Records

a. Psychologists are attentive to situations in which record information has become outdated, and may therefore be invalid, particularly in circumstances where disclosure might cause adverse effects. Psychologists ensure that when disclosing such information that its outdated nature and limited utility are noted using professional judgment and complying with applicable law.

b. When records are to be disposed of, this is done in an appropriate manner that ensures nondisclosure (or preserves confidentiality) (see Section 3a).

5. Disclosure of Record Keeping Procedures

a. When appropriate, psychologists may inform their clients of the nature and extent of their record keeping procedures. This information includes a statement on the limitations of the confidentiality of the records.

b. Psychologists may charge a reasonable fee for review and reproduction of records. Psychologists do not withhold records that are needed for valid healthcare purposes solely because the client has not paid for prior services.

---

[4]These time limits follow the APA's specialty guidelines. If the specialty guidelines should be revised, a simple 7 year requirement for the retention of the complete record is preferred, which would be a more stringent requirement than any existing state statute.

Appendix I

Professional Conduct and Discipline in Psychology Self-Evaluation

I. PROFESSIONAL OFFICE PRACTICES

A. Record Keeping	Y	NI	N	NA	ASPPB Code of Conduct	APA Principles and Code of Conduct	CPA Code of Ethics
1. Do I maintain records for each client?					III A6a	1.24	Guide V.1
2. Do client records for which I am responsible contain the following information? a) identifying data of clients (e.g., names, addresses, telephone numbers, dates of birth, sex). b) problems for which the service was sought. c) any assessments undertaken and the interventions recommended (if appropriate). Psychologist's formulation and goals of intervention. d) description of the types of services provided and the date on which they were delivered. e) periodic description of client progress. f) if a service contract has been established between the client and the psychologist, include this contract in the records.					III A6a	1.24a	Guide V.1.a Ethics II.18 Ethics II.21

Note. Y = Yes, NI = Needs Improvement, N = No, NA = Not Applicable. Guide = Practice Guidelines for Providers of Psychological Services, Canadian Psychological Association, 1989. Ethics = Canadian Code of Ethics for Psychologists, 1991. Adapted by Christa Peterson from *The Professional Practice of Psychology: Self-Evaluation,* prepared by Jean L. Pettifor, Barry Bultz, Marilyn Samuels, Richard Griffin, and George Lucki for the Practice Review Committee of the Psychologists Association of Alberta. Copyright 1994 by the Psychologists Association of Alberta. Adapted with permission of the publisher.

I. PROFESSIONAL OFFICE PRACTICES (*Continued*)

A. Record Keeping (*Continued*)	Y	NI	N	NA	ASPPB Code of Conduct	APA Principles and Code of Conduct	CPA Code of Ethics
g) signature of the psychologist who has placed information into the file, if the origin of the information is in doubt. h) signed authorization for release of information sent to third parties as well as a summary of the information sent.							
3. Do I maintain client records for at least five years from date of last service provided or longer as needed or as required by law?					III A6b	1.24, 5.04	Ethics I.37
4. Do I keep records secure so that unauthorized persons cannot gain access to them?					III A6c	5.09	Ethics I.36 Guide V.2 Guide V.2.a
B. Service Fees							
1. Do I have a schedule of fees charged for my services?						1.25	Ethics III.30 Ethics III.3
2. Do I inform my clients of fees and billing practices prior to providing services?					III G1	1.25, 4.01	Guide III.3 Ethics III.14
3. Do I ensure that my clients are billed for services received in a manner which ensures client dignity and privacy?					III E6	1.25, 5.05	Guide III.3
4. Do I provide accurate, consistent information when billing 3rd party payors?					III G1	1.26 1.25	III.23 III.1
C. Service Environment							
1. Does my work environment ensure privacy between the client and myself?					III E1	2.04	

2. Is my work environment accessible to clients?						Principle F	
3. Is my work environment designed to meet the special needs of clients and of any special services provided?						Principle D 1.10	
D. Liability Coverage							
1. Do I carry liability insurance coverage?						1.14	
E. Representation							
1. Do I provide accurate information about my a) academic credentials? b) professional experience? c) status in the profession?					III F2–3	3.03	Ethics III.2
2. Do I provide accurate information about the status of supervisees, registrants, and any other non-chartered psychological staff with whom I work?					III F4 III A6D		Ethics III.2 Ethics III.22
3. Do I submit accurate and reasonable information about assessments, interventions, and other services which I provide?					III F4, 5	1.26, 2.02, 2.05, 2.09, 3.02, 3.03, 3.04	Ethics III.5 Ethics III.8
F. Professional Services							
1. Do I provide relevant information promptly and without cost to the person to whom a client is referred?					III C1	1.20 5.10 5.11	
2. Do I refrain from giving or accepting a commission, rebate or remuneration for referrals made to or accepted from other professional service providers?					III B2	1.27	

continues

I. PROFESSIONAL OFFICE PRACTICES (*Continued*)

G. Confidentiality	Y	NI	N	NA	ASPPB Code of Conduct	APA Principles and Code of Conduct	CPA Code of Ethics
1. Do I appropriately inform the client of the conclusions and recommendations resulting from a formal psychological assessment, when requested to do so by the client, unless release of the information is prohibited by law?					III H2 III C1	5.05 5.10 5.11 2.09	Ethics III.15
2. Do I release information concerning a client to another person only with the consent of the client unless otherwise required to do so by law?					III E1	5.02 5.05 5.07	Code 9.1 Ethics I.40
3. Do I take steps to protect others from foreseeable serious harm or death (e.g., by warning or police notification) even when a confidential relationship is involved?					III E2	Principle E 1.14 5.05	Ethics II.36 Ethics I.40
H. Supervision							
1. As a supervising psychologist, do I monitor my supervisees' work by: a) being available for emergencies b) ensuring that the supervisee's clients are informed of the supervisee's role and status c) Being available for periodic meetings with the clients at their or the supervisee's request d) countersigning supervisees' reports.					III J2	1.22 2.08 4.01	Ethics I.42 Ethics II.45 Ethics III.38 Guide I.2.c
2. As a supervising psychologist, do I maintain ongoing written record of the supervision?					III J2	1.23	Ethics III.3

II. PROFESSIONAL CLIENT SERVICES

A. Informed Consent	Y	NI	N	NA	ASPPB Code of Conduct	APA Principles and Code of Conduct	CPA Code of Ethics
1. Do I fully explain the purposes, methods and possible benefits of the services I propose to provide?					III C1	2.09 4.02 1.07	Ethics I.11
2. Do I ensure that clients have the capacity and information necessary to provide an informed consent to the services proposed and that a free and informed consent is obtained?					III C1	4.02	Ethics I.13, I.16, I.17, I.18
3. If I use experimental interventions do I inform the client and seek consultation from colleagues?					III C1	1.04	II.8 II.16
4. Do I document the informed consent process?						4.02	I.15
5. Do I inform the client about office hours, access drug emergencies, and billing policies?					III C1	1.25 4.01	I.13
6. Do I inform the client about the limits of confidentiality in certain circumstances (i.e., child abuse) and in certain treatment modalities (i.e., marital therapy)?					III C1	5.01	I.40
B. Assessment Procedures							
1. Do I use assessment procedures that are appropriate to the client and to the client's problems?						2.04[a] 2.05	Ethics II.13 Ethics II.14 Guide I.1.b
2. In formulating and implementing assessments, do I use approaches which are logical and theoretically sound?						2.02 2.08 2.07	

[a]See also *Standards for Educational and Psychological Testing*, 1985, American Educational Research Association, APA, and National Council on Measurement in Education, *Guidelines for Computer-Based Assessment and Interpretation*, 1986, APA, *Guidelines for the Control of Psychological Tests by Psychologists*, 1987, PAA.

continues

II. PROFESSIONAL CLIENT SERVICES (*Continued*)

B. Assessment Procedures (*Continued*)	Y	NI	N	NA	ASPPB Code of Conduct	APA Principles and Code of Conduct	CPA Code of Ethics
3. Do I only use assessment procedures for which I am adequately trained and in which I have demonstrated my competence?					III A1	2.02 2.06	Ethics II.6 Ethics II.8 Guide I.2 Guide I.3.a
4. If I am conducting an assessment at the direction of a third party (e.g., employer, the court) do I clarify with the patient issues of confidentiality and access to records?					III E3	1.21	I.19
5. Do I avoid even the appearance of conflict of interest (personal involvement, socializing, accepting gifts)?						1.17	
C. Intervention Procedures							
1. Are my interventions appropriate to the client and to the client's problems?						1.04	Ethics II.13 Ethics II.14 Guide I.1.b
2. Are my interventions reasoned, thought out and consistent with a defined theoretical approach?						1.06	
3. Do I periodically evaluate my interventions in terms of intervention goal?							Ethics II.21 Guide I.3.c Guide I.3.d
4. Do I only use interventions for which I am adequately trained and at which I am competent?					III A2, 3	1.04	Ethics II.6 Ethics II.8 Guide I.2 Guide I.3.a

5. Do I ensure that there are effective provisions made for client care when transferring or discontinuing services?					III A7	4.08 4.09	Ethics II.29 Ethics II.30 Ethics II.31
6. Do I prepare clients when it is necessary for me to interrupt therapy (i.e., illness, vacation)?							
7. Do I arrange for adequate supervision of my clients and practice in my absence?					III C2	4.08	III.29
D. Use of Other Professional Services							
1. Do I make referrals to appropriate resources when clients' service needs extend beyond those I can meet?					III A4 III C2	1.20	Ethics II.8
2. When a client is concurrently receiving services from another professional practitioner for the same concern, do I attempt to collaborate appropriately with that practitioner and advise the client of the potential risks involved in receiving services from more than one service provider?						4.04	Ethics II.18
E. Service Evaluation							
1. Do I monitor and evaluate the effect of my service, and where appropriate, take remedial steps to improve the quality of my practice (i.e., peer consultation, supervision and continuing education)?					III A2, 3	1.05	Ethics II.21 Guide I.3.c Guide I.3.d
F. Supervision of Provisional Chartered Psychologists, Registrants, Interns, Practicum Students and Psychological Assistants							
1. Do I limit my supervision and the practices of my supervisees to my demonstrated areas of professional competence?					III J3	1.22	Ethics I.42 Ethics II.45 Ethics III.38

continues

II. PROFESSIONAL CLIENT SERVICES (*Continued*)

F. Supervision of Provisional Chartered Psychologists, Registrants, Interns, Practicum Students and Psychological Assistants (*Continued*)	Y	NI	N	NA	ASPPB Code of Conduct	APA Principles and Code of Conduct	CPA Code of Ethics
2. As a supervising psychologist, do I provide training and work experience which is commensurate with the supervisee's level of ability and which allow for growth?					III J3	1.22	Ethics I.42 Ethics II.45 Ethics III.38
3. As a supervising psychologist, do I ensure that issues of professional conduct, ethics and confidentiality are addressed as part of the supervision process?						1.22	Ethics I.42 Ethics II.45 Ethics III.38
4. As a supervising psychologist, do I provide the supervisee and designated others with feedback pertaining to the supervisee's level of skill and limits of competency, at the end of the training period?					III J3	1.22 6.05	
G. Administration							
1. As an administrator of service units, do I perform the following functions: a) recruit qualified staff b) direct the unit's treatment and research activities c) ensure that a high level of professional practice is maintained d) coordinate the unit's services with those of the larger organization e) periodically evaluate the unit's services.							Guide I.2 Guide II.1 Guide II.2 Guide II.3 Guide II.3.a
H. Professional and Employer Relationships							
1. When functioning as an employee, am I aware of the multiple relationships and potentially conflicting expectations which I may face (e.g., employer/institutional procedures, client needs, third party interests, professional standards, personal conscience)?						8.03 1.17	Ethics I.19 Ethics II.33

2. Am I able to understand the expectations of each of the parties to whom I am responsible?							
3. Am I able to prioritize and balance these competing interests in ways which do not jeopardize the well-being of the client–recipient of services?						8.03	
4. Do I monitor and resolve any feelings of sexual attraction toward clients in the course of therapy, referring the client to another professional, if necessary?					III B1, 2	4.07	II.26
5. Do I monitor potential conflicts of interest between my status as an employee and as a member of a profession with defined standards for ethical and competent practice?							Ethics III.30
6. Do I carefully review my contractual obligations (conditions, limits being set for my professional work by employers or other third parties who pay for the services I provide)?							Ethics III.30
7. Am I able to resolve differences between employer or third party expectations and professional standards when they arise?							Ethics III.30
8. Do I refuse to ignore or condone activities of other professionals which are clearly harmful?						8.04	Ethics III.37 Ethics IV.11 Ethics IV.15 Ethics IV.26
9. Do I maintain respectful and collaborative relations with other professions including employment in multidisciplinary terms and programs?						4.04 1.20	Ethics I.1 Ethics II.8 Ethics II.30
10. Do I consult respected colleagues in my own and other professions when faced with difficult ethical dilemmas (including problems in interdisciplinary relations)?						8.02	Ethics III.36

continues

II. PROFESSIONAL CLIENT SERVICES (*Continued*)

H. Professional and Employer Relationships (*Continued*)	Y	NI	N	NA	ASPPB Code of Conduct	APA Principles and Code of Conduct	CPA Code of Ethics
11. Do I recognize that my employer has a legitimate need to review and evaluate my performance?							Guide I.3.d
12. Do I recognize that my profession or regulatory body is established in law to protect the public?							
13. Do I participate collaboratively with my employer and my professional body to carry out the procedures established for accountability?							
I. Continuing Education							
1. Do I take steps to ensure my continuing competence in the areas of psychological practice I engage in?					III A2	1.05	Ethics III.4 Ethics II.9
2. For example, do I: a) review the relevant literature? b) participate in continuing education activities and workshops? c) have established mechanisms for peer consultation? d) systematic study? e) other?					III A2	1.05	Ethics IV.19
3. Do I participate in the professional development and continuing education of colleagues and students?						1.05	Ethics IV.3
J. Self-Care							
1. Do I take steps in my own self-care to maintain my health and prevent burnout?						1.13	Ethics II.24

2. Do I monitor my own psychological and physical health?						1.13	Ethics II.12 Guide IV.5
3. Have I established a relationship(s) with an appropriate person(s) who can assist me in monitoring and providing feedback on my psychological and physical health? For example: a) am I in therapy to monitor and maintain my own mental health? b) do I schedule regular physical checkups? c) do I invite my colleagues to give me personal feedback?						1.13	
4. Do I regularly take action for my own self-care, for example: a) schedule regular opportunities for such activities as reading, social contact, or doing nothing? b) limit the hours worked to a level which can be maintained over time? c) take breaks away from work? d) seek help and/or nurturing from others outside the professional setting when needed? e) pay attention to my nutrition, exercise and rest? f) pay attention to relationships, social life and outside interests? g) other						1.13	
5. Do I refrain from practice if under the influence of alcohol and/or drugs?					III B1	1.14	
6. Do I withdraw from practice if my health is impaired?					III B1	1.14	
K. General							
1. Am I able to define the scope and limitations of my practice?					III A1	1.04	Ethics II.6 Ethics II.8–10 Guide IV.1 Guide IV.5

continues

III. SELF-EVALUATION GUIDELINES FOR RESEARCH ACTIVITIES

A. Research Plan	Y	NI	N	NA	ASPPB Code of Conduct	APA Principles and Code of Conduct	CPA Code of Ethics
1. Do I have a written research plan?						6.06	Ethics III.19 Ethics III.29 Ethics II.15 Ethics II.16
2. Does it include: a) rationale for research b) questions being investigated c) subjects involved d) methodology for research e) type of data to be collected f) plan for data analysis g) consideration of ethical issues						6.06	
3. Do I use only research procedures for which I am adequately trained and in which I have demonstrated my competence?						1.04	Code 15 Ethics II.6 Ethics II.8 Guide I.2 Guide I.3.a
4. Do I submit my research plans for review by an ethics committee?					III D2	1.14 6.09	Ethics II.16
B. Risks							
1. Do I consider all possible risks involved in the research, including the possibility of unforeseen risks?							Ethics II.13 Ethics II.14

2. Do I consider risks to: a) subjects involved b) third parties c) researcher and staff involved d) society or any segment thereof						6.06	Ethics IV.23
3. Are the following types of risk considered a) physical harm b) psychological harm c) injury to reputation or privacy d) breach of any relevant laws						6.06	Ethics II.32 Ethics II.15 Ethics II.16
C. Benefits							
1. Do I assess all of the possible benefits from the research?						6.06	Ethics II.21 Ethics II.22
2. Do I consider the specific advantages for: a) subjects involved b) third parties c) researcher and staff involved d) society or any segment thereof						6.06	
3. Do I consider alternative methodologies to better balance risks and benefits?					III D2	6.07	
D. Informed Consent							
1. Do I inform research participants and/or those giving consent about the proposed research?					III C1	6.11	Ethics I.13 Ethics I.14 Ethics I.18 Ethics I.39 Ethics II.3

continues

III. SELF-EVALUATION GUIDELINES FOR RESEARCH ACTIVITIES (*Continued*)

D. Informed Consent (*Continued*)	Y	NI	N	N A	ASPPB Code of Conduct	APA Principles and Code of Conduct	CPA Code of Ethics
2. Do I include the following information: a) that research is involved b) description of topic being researched c) description of methodology including time commitment d) description of possible benefits e) description of possible risks f) where benefit is involved, description of alternative means for obtaining the same benefit g) description of the extent to which privacy and confidentiality will be protected h) description of the available means of compensation should a risk materialize						6.11	
3. Do I provide sufficient time and opportunity for involved persons to consider the information?						6.11	
4. Do I take steps to ensure that information is clearly understood?					III C1	6.11	Ethics I.16
5. Do I clearly state that: a) participation in or consent to the research is fully voluntary b) consent may be withdrawn without penalty c) exemplary care will be taken to safeguard the subject						6.11	Ethics I.20 Ethics I.18 Ethics I.23 Ethics II.1
6. Do I consider the special circumstances involved in obtaining informed consent (e.g., from children, mentally incompetent persons, prisoners, other captive groups such as students, employees, legal wards or therapeutically dependent persons)?						6.11	Ethics I.28–31
7. Do I document that informed consent has been given?						6.11	Ethics I.15

E. Deception							
1. Do I obtain an independent ethical review to consider the risks involved in deliberately withholding relevant information as part of the research methodology?						6.12	Ethics III.29
2. Is there a reasonably available alternative methodology that would avoid the use of deception of: a) subjects involved b) third parties c) researcher and staff involved d) society or any segment thereof						6.15	Ethics III.24
3. Would the research be invalid without the use of deception?						6.15	
4. Can the effects of deception be predicted and offset?							Ethics III.28
5. Do the benefits anticipated from the research justify the use of deception?						6.15	Ethics II.17
6. Is the information being withheld such that if revealed the client would likely still give consent to participate?						6.15	Ethics III.25
7. Do I have a plan for immediate debriefing of the participants following the study?						6.18	Ethics II.22 Ethics II.3
8. Can I do a meaningful debriefing given the nature of the subjects (e.g., children, mentally handicapped) or size of sample (e.g., very large)?							Ethics III.27
F. Privacy and Confidentiality							
1. Do I consider how privacy (i.e., personal information not already in the public domain) of subjects will be protected?					III E1	3.04	Ethics I.32 Ethics I.33
2. Do I consider the confidentiality (anonymity) of subjects will be preserved?					III E1	5.03	

continues

III. SELF-EVALUATION GUIDELINES FOR RESEARCH ACTIVITIES (*Continued*)

F. Privacy and Confidentiality (*Continued*)	Y	NI	N	NA	ASPPB Code of Conduct	APA Principles and Code of Conduct	CPA Code of Ethics
3. Do I take steps to guard against unintended breaches of confidentiality during data collection and analysis?					III E1	5.03	
4. Upon completion of data analysis, do I consider what will be done with the data (e.g., destroyed, kept in secure storage)?						1.24 5.04	Ethics I.36 Ethics I.37
5. Are all matters of privacy and confidentiality and any anticipated breaches thereof, clearly explained during the informed consent process?						6.11	
G. Supervision							
1. Do I monitor the work of research assistants, students and others who may be involved in the research project?					III J3	6.07	Ethics I.42 Ethics II.45 Ethics III.38

IV. SELF-EVALUATION GUIDELINES FOR TEACHING

A. Information Taught	Y	NI	N	NA	ASPPB Code of Conduct	APA Principles and Code of Conduct	CPA Code of Ethics
1. Do I teach only in areas in which I am competent?						1.04	Ethics II.6
2. Do I present information accurately, clarifying what information is supported by objective evidence and what are my personal views?						6.03	Ethics III.11 Ethics III.12 Ethics III.9 Ethics II.10
3. Am I careful in my choice of examples, jokes, case studies, etc. to ensure that they could not be construed as demeaning or discriminatory to others?						1.09 1.08 6.04	Ethics I.2

4. Do I take precautions to ensure that the information being taught will be used appropriately by the learner?						6.01	Ethics I.6 Ethics II.5
B. Relationship with Students							
1. Do I respect the knowledge and experience of my students?						6.04	Ethics I.1
2. Do I encourage a free exchange of ideas?							Ethics III.21
3. Do I abstain from all forms of harassment, including sexual harassment?						1.11	Ethics I.3 Ethics II.2
4. Do I avoid becoming involved in personal or other dual relationships with my students?						1.17	Ethics III.30 Ethics III.32
5. Do I respect the rights of my students to personal privacy?							Ethics I.29
6. Do I have procedures in place to ensure that students' grades and other information about their performance is kept confidential?							Ethics I.32
7. Do I provide adequate feedback to students so that they are aware of the limits of their knowledge and skills?						6.05	Ethics III.8 Ethics III.16
8. Do I encourage and assist students to publish worthy papers and do I give appropriate credit to them?						6.23	Ethics II.25 Ethics III.7
9. Do I provide adequate supervision of my students to ensure that they are behaving in an ethical fashion?					III J3	1.22	Ethics I.42 Ethics II.45 Ethics III.38 Ethics II.24

Appendix J

Guidelines for the Practice of Psychology: An Annotated Bibliography

This annotated bibliography provides a listing of major standards documents guiding the practice of psychology today on this continent. Psychologists need to pay special attention to standards which are adopted by their state or provincial regulatory bodies, as well as to other standards which address their specialty areas of practice. It is not possible or necessary to have detailed knowledge of every standards document. Standards are living documents continually in a process of change and therefore it is necessary to keep up-to-date. This bibliography should be revised at least every two years in order to keep it current and relevant.

A. General Standards for Competent and Ethical Practice

1) *A Canadian Code of Ethics for Psychologists.* (1991). Canadian Psychological Association. Adopted by the majority of provincial jurisdictions. Available from CPA Office, in CPA Directory (1992), and in the Companion Manual to the Canadian Code of Ethics for Psychologists 1991 (1992). The principles are placed in order of priority: 1. Respect for the Dignity of Persons, 2. Responsible Caring, 3. Integrity in Relationships, 4. Responsibility to Society. An ethical framework is provided for a process of decision making. Conflict between principles is recognized. Vulnerability of clients, consultation, conscience, and public scrutiny are addressed.

2) *Companion Manual to the Canadian Code of Ethics for Psychologists, 1991.* (1992). Canadian Psychological Association. Available from CPA Office. The manual describes how the Code was developed, reprints the code with explanatory comments, demonstrates the ethical decision making process, provides numerous vignettes of ethical dilemmas, provides extensive bibliography, and reprints other ethics documents adopted by CPA. It is an excellent resource for teaching ethics.

3) Ethical Principles of Psychologists and Code of Conduct. (1992). American Psychological Association. Available from APA Order Depart-

---

Prepared in 1990 by Jean L. Pettifor, Barry Bultz, Marilyn Samuels, Richard Griffin and George Lucki for the Psychologists Association of Alberta. Adapted by the authors in 1992 for presentation at the annual meeting of the American Psychological Association. Used with permission of the Psychologists Association of Alberta.

ment. Published in *American Psychologist* (1992) *47*, 1597–1611. The first section, General Principles, presents 6 aspirational principles or ideal concepts. The second section, Ethical Standards, uses eight topic areas to present the minimum standards with which every psychologist must comply. There are significant changes from the *Ethical Principles of Psychologists* (1981) in areas of sexual intimacies, forensic psychology, bartering, continuity of service, informed consent and advertising.

4) *ASPPB Code of Conduct*. (1991). Association of State and Provincial Psychology Boards. Available from ASPPB Central Office. This document attempts to translate codes of ethics (which tend to be aspirational) into statements of minimal required behaviours which can be included in licensing acts. Codes of conduct are often considered more useful in adjudicating violations of ethical behaviour. The document is intended to be a model for jurisdictions wishing to include definitions of misconduct in their regulations.

5) *General Guidelines for Providers of Psychological Services*. (1987). American Psychological Association. Available from APA Order Department. Published in *American Psychologist*, *42*, 712–723. These guidelines replace the 1977 APA Standards for Providers of Psychological Services. While there are no major changes in content, the Guidelines are described as a set of aspirational statements, while the 1977 Standards were described as specifying minimally acceptable levels of quality assurance and performance that providers must reach or exceed. "Providers" appear to refer to both individual psychologists and to organized service units.

6) *Practice Guidelines for Providers of Psychological Services*. (1989). Canadian Psychological Association. Available from CPA Office. This document has sections on 1) Provision of Service, 2) Organization of Services, 3) Client Relationships, 4) Training, Qualifications and Competence, and 5) Record Keeping and Confidentiality. The three levels of "providers" are the larger organization or employer, the psychologist administrator or supervisor, and the individual psychologist service provider. For the individual psychologist needing to know the basic practice requirements, it is important to distinguish between minimal and aspirational, and to differentiate between individual and organizational responsibility.

7a) *Specialty Guidelines for the Delivery of Services by Clinical Psychologists*

7b) *Specialty Guidelines for the Delivery of Services by Counseling Psychologists*

7c) *Specialty Guidelines for the Delivery of Services by Industrial and Organizational Psychologists*

7d) *Specialty Guidelines for the Delivery of Services by School Psychologists*

All of these specialty guidelines were approved in 1980 by the American Psychological Association. Available from APA Order Department. Published in *American Psychologist* (1981), *36*, 639–681. These specialty guidelines follow the same format and principles as the 1977 Standards and the 1987 Guidelines for Providers of Psychological Services by specifying the specialty area to replace the generic "professional psychologist."

8) *Specialty Guidelines for Forensic Psychologists*. (1991). Division 41 of the American Psychological Association and the American Psychology–Law Society. Available from the Department of Psychology, University of Utah. The Guidelines provide an aspirational model of professional practice by psychologists engaged in activities to provide professional expertise to the judicial system, such as assistance to courts, parties to legal proceedings, correctional and forensic mental health facilities, and legislative agencies.

9) *A Code of Ethics for the Canadian Association of School Psychologists*. (1992). Canadian Association of School Psychologists. CASP has adapted the Canadian Code of Ethics for Psychologists to be consistent with CASP's standards and bylaws. It has retained the four major principles of I. Respect for the Dignity of Persons, II. Responsible Caring, III. Integrity in Relationships, and IV. Responsibility to Society. It recognizes conflict between principles and it provides the steps for an ethical decision-making process.

10) *Principles for Professional Ethics*. (1985). National Association of School Psychologists. These principles address Professional Competency, Professional Relationships and Responsibilities, and Professional Practices. "The most basic ethical principle is to perform only those services for which that person has acquired a recognized level of competency."

11) *Guidelines for Ethical Behaviour*. (1989 Revision). Canadian Guidance and Counselling Association. These Guidelines are intended to guide counsellors in their everyday conduct and to demonstrate respect for the dignity and integrity of persons, responsible caring and responsibility to society. They include sections on Resolving Ethical Conflicts; General; Individual and Group Counselling Relationships; Testing; Research and Publication; Consulting and Private Practice; and Counsellor Preparation Standards.

12) *Guidelines for Conditions of Employment of Psychologists*. (1986). American Psychological Association. Available from APA Order Department. Published in *American Psychologist* (1987), *42*, 724–729. This revision of 1971 guidelines addresses Entry to the Profession, Recruitment, The Interview, Job Offers and Employment Agreements, Evaluation, Renewal, Promotion, Tenure, and Salary Increases; and Rights and Responsibilities of Employees and Employers. Psychologists are responsible for carrying out the full functions and obligations of their positions, as well as resisting the encroachment of influences on their work that would distort or prevent the scientific and professional development of psychology.

B. Psychological Testing

Educational and psychological testing significantly affects individuals, institutions, and often society as a whole, and therefore, it is essential that well constructed tests be developed and used correctly.

1) *Standards for Educational and Psychological Testing*. (1985). Jointly sponsored by American Educational Research Association, Amer-

ican Psychological Association, and the National Council on Measurement in Education. Available from APA Order Department. This document covers I. Technical Standards for Test Construction and Evaluation, II. Professional Standards for Test Use, III. Standards for Particular Applications, and IV. Standards for Administrative Procedures.

2) *Guidelines for Educational and Psychological Testing*. (1987). Canadian Psychological Association. Available from CPA Office. These Guidelines are consistent with the APA Standards for Educational and Psychological Testing (1985) and have been modified in order to ground them within the Canadian legal and social context. This document covers I. Test Instrumentation, II. Test Use (General principles, testing persons with handicapping conditions, testing and the two official languages of Canada, educational and psychological testing in schools, test use in clinical assessment and counselling, employment testing, professional and occupational licensure and certification, program evaluation, and III. Administrative Procedures.

3) *Guidelines for Computer-Based Assessment and Interpretation*. (1985). American Association of State and Provincial Psychology Boards. Available from ASPPB Office. This 6 page document addresses ethical principles of responsibility, competence, public statements, and assessment techniques.

4) *Guidelines for Computer-Based Tests and Interpretations*. (1986). American Psychological Association. Available from APA Order Department. This document is intended for users, developers, and distributors of computer-based test services.

5) *Code of Fair-Testing Practice in Education*. (1988). Joint Committee on Testing Practices with representation from American Education Research Association, American Psychological Association, National Council of Measurement in Education, American Association for Counselling and Development, Association for Measurement and Evaluation in Counselling and Development, and American Speech–Language–Hearing Association. Available from the National Council on Measurement in Education. Published in an article by J. Fremer, E. Diamond, & W. Camara, (1989), Developing a code of fair testing practices in education, *American Psychologist*, *44*, 1062–1067.

6) *Principles for Fair Student Assessment Practice for Education in Canada*. (1993). The Joint Advisory Committee consisted of representatives from Canadian Education Association, Canadian School Boards Association, Canadian Association for School Administrators, Canadian Teachers Federation, Canadian Guidance and Counselling Association, Canadian Association of School Psychologists, Canadian Council for Exceptional Children, Canadian Psychological Association, and Canadian Society for the Study of Education. Available from Centre for Research in Applied Measurement and Evaluation. The principles and their related guidelines are organized in two parts. Part A is directed at assessments carried out by teachers at the elementary and secondary school levels, and, with some modifications, is applicable at the postsecondary level. Part B is directed at standardized assessments developed external to the class-

room by commercial test publishers, provincial and territorial ministries and departments of education, and local school jurisdictions.

7) *Guidelines for Assessing Sex Bias and Sex Fairness in Career Interest Inventories.* (1978). Canadian Psychological Association. Available from CPA Office and in Companion Manual to the Canadian Code of Ethics for Psychologists 1991 (1992). These 15 statements provide guidance on how to avoid bias and discrimination in the use of interest inventories.

8) *National Institute of Education Guidelines for Assessment of Sex Bias and Sex Fairness in Career Interest Inventories.* In C.K. Tittle & D.G. Zytowski (Eds.). *Sex-Fair Interest Measurement: Research and Implications.* (1978). Washington, DC: National Institute of Education. These guidelines address the diverse concerns of inventory users, respondents, authors and publishers under the three sections of I. The Inventory Itself, II. Technical Information, and III. Interpretive Information.

C. Special Treatment Interventions

No one can master all the hundreds of types of therapies and interventions which are recorded in the literature for the treatment of psychological and educational problems. However, each professional should be competent in the practice of those therapies which he or she uses, and should be able to choose treatment modalities which are appropriate for the individual client. Organizations which develop guidelines for special treatment modalities tend to be multidisciplinary and to develop standards which address their common interests.

A representative list of guidelines for special treatment interventions is provided. It is not intended to be an exhaustive list. All contain common themes of respect, competence, integrity and social responsibility, while each has some unique applications.

1) *Ethical Issues for Human Services.* (1977). Association for the Advancement of Behavior Therapy. Available from AABT. The focus of this statement is on critical issues of central importance to human services, such as, treatment goals, treatment methods, voluntary participation, interest of "subordinate" (vulnerable and dependent) clients, evaluation of treatment, confidentiality, referrals and therapist qualifications. The issues are relevant to all types of interventions.

2) *Ethical Principles of Biofeedback.* (1985). Biofeedback Certification Institute of America. Available from BCIA. The format is similar to the APA 1981 Ethical Principles of Psychologists. The following principles are addressed: A. Responsibility, B. Competence, C. Standards, D. Public Statements, E. Confidentiality, F. Welfare to the Consumer, G. Professional Relationships, and H. Research.

3) *Code of Ethics.* (1983). The American Society of Clinical Hypnosis. The first statement requires members to observe the professional and ethical standards of their respective clinical professions. The remaining statements are short and address the specific practice of hypnosis.

4) *ASSECT Code of Ethics for Sex Therapists.* (1980). American As-

sociation of Sex Educators, Counselors and Therapists. Available from ASSECT. This 19 page document addresses I. Competence and Integrity of Sex Therapists, II. Confidentiality in Sex Therapy, III. Welfare of the Client, IV. Welfare of Students and Trainees, V. Welfare of the Research Subject, and VI. Competence and Integrity of Sex Educators.

5) *Feminist Therapy Ethical Code.* (1987). Feminist Therapy Institute. Available from FTI. This 2 page document addresses I. Cultural Diversities and Oppressions, II. Power Differentials, III. Overlapping Relationships, IV. Therapist Accountability, and V. Social Change. Most of these principles are relevant for disadvantaged populations such as ethnic minorities and persons with disabilities.

6) *Guidelines for Psychologists Conducting Growth Groups.* (1973). American Psychological Association. Available from APA Order Department. Published in *American Psychologist* (1973), *28*, 933. These guidelines are intended to aid psychologists who conduct growth or encounter groups to present themselves in a manner that is ethically sound and protects participants. While it was anticipated that the document would be subject to modification in the light of new knowledge and practice, it appears to have stood the test of time and is referenced in the 1987 General Guidelines for Providers of Psychological Services as one of the documents which guide the practice of psychologists.

7) *Code of Ethical Principles for Marriage and Family Therapists.* (1988). American Association for Marriage and Family Therapy. Available from AAMFT. Sections are included on 1. Responsibility to Clients, 2. Confidentiality, 3. Professional Competence and Integrity, 4. Responsibility to Students, Employees, and Supervisees, 5. Responsibility to the Profession, 6. Financial Arrangements, and 7. Advertising.

D. Special Populations

Concerns for special populations arise when there is real or perceived unfair discrimination against vulnerable groups. These groups may include the mentally disabled, physically disabled, mentally ill, prisoners, ethnic minorities, refugees, natives, the poor, children, women, the elderly, students, and employees. Books and articles may be written to draw attention to the issues, or new professional standards may be adopted for the purpose of correcting abuses. Such documents usually apply the generic principles of respect, caring, integrity and social responsibility to the area of concern.

Women's groups have been outstanding in obtaining formal approval by professional associations for special practice standards. It is interesting to note that many of the principles enunciated for services for women are equally relevant for other special populations. They deal with respect and empowerment for the disadvantaged and with advocacy to change the negative conditions in society which result in discrimination. Those who provide professional services for a special population should know the characteristics and vulnerabilities of that population, and should have the special knowledge, skills and attitudes to serve their needs.

1) *Guidelines for Therapy and Counselling with Women.* (1980). Canadian Psychological Association. Available from CPA Office. Is included in *CPA Therapy and Counselling with Women: A Handbook of Educational Materials* (1984). The ten guidelines are cross-referenced to principles in *Ethical Standards of Psychologists* (CPA 1977) and *Standards for Providers of Psychological Services* (CPA 1978), and violations are illustrated by actual case examples. The cross-referencing needs to be updated to current codes.

2) *Guidelines for Therapy with Women.* (1978). APA Task Force on Sex Bias and Sex Role Stereotyping in Psychotherapeutic Practice. Available in *CPA Therapy and Counselling with Women: A Handbook of Educational Materials* (1984). Published in *American Psychologist* (1978), *13*, 1122–1123. The thirteen principles address the four general categories of sex bias in therapeutic practice, e.g., 1. fostering traditional sex roles, 2. bias in expectations and devaluation of women, 3. sexist use of psychoanalytic concepts, and 4. responding to women as sex objects including seduction of female clients.

3) *Principles Concerning the Counseling and Therapy of Women.* (1978). American Psychological Association Division 17 Counseling Psychology. Available in *CPA Therapy and Counselling with Women: A Handbook of Educational Materials.* Published in *The Counseling Psychologist* (1979), *8*, 21.

4) *Therapy and Counselling with Women: A Handbook of Educational Materials.* (1984). Canadian Psychological Association. Available from CPA Office. The purpose of the Handbook is to assist professionals and consumers to conduct sex-fair therapy and counselling with women. The following topics are addressed: 1. Guidelines, 2. Education in the Psychology of Women, 3. Resources and Techniques for Continuing Education Workshops, 4. Additional Case Studies, 5. Listing of Resources. The bibliography needs to be updated.

5) *Guidelines for the Elimination of Sexual Harassment.* (1985). Canadian Psychological Association. Available from CPA Office. Published in *Companion Manual to the Canadian Code of Ethics for Psychologists 1991* (1992). An abbreviated version was published in *Canadian Psychology* (1986), *27*(4), 371. This document provides definitions, guidelines for psychologists, and examples of violations. It deals with prohibitions, prevention, and procedures to deal with complaints.

6) *Guidelines to Reduce Bias in Language.* (1994). American Psychological Association. Published in *Publication Manual of the American Psychological Association* (4th Ed.), (1994), pp. 46–60. The guidelines assist in rephrasing language so that communication is accurate and unbiased.

7) *Guidelines for Providers of Psychological Services to Ethnic, Linguistic, and Culturally Diverse Populations.* (1990). American Psychological Association Office of Ethnic Minority Affairs. Available from APA Order Department. The guidelines represent general principles that are intended to be aspirational in nature and are designed to provide suggestions to

psychologists in working with ethnic, linguistic, and culturally diverse populations.

8) *Guidelines for Child Custody Evaluations and Divorce Proceedings.* (1994). American Psychological Association. Available from APA Order Department. Published in *American Psychologist* (1994), *49*, 677–680. These 16 guidelines assist psychologists in focusing on the purpose, the preparation and the procedures for conducting a child custody evaluation, and in avoiding the pitfalls often involved in dealing with parental conflict.

E. Research With Human Subjects

Federally and provincially funded research must be approved by an institutional ethics review committee prior to receiving funding. Universities and other institutions establish ethics committees to review research proposals. When a clinician wishes to do some research in addition to direct services, there may be no formal proposal for external funding and no requirement for formal review. However, there are several specific documents on ethical principles for research with human subjects. Note that American sources of research funding have not been included.

1) *Ethical Guidelines—Research with Human Subjects.* (1988). Social Sciences and Humanities Research Council (SSHRC). Also endorsed by National Sciences and Engineering Research Council (NSERC). This document addresses the Rights of Individuals, Informed Consent, Deception, Risk and Benefit, Privacy, Confidentiality and Anonymity, and Research on Captive and Dependent Populations. Research on Children, Research in the Humanities, Acquisition and Use of Cultural Properties, and Research on Other Cultures, Countries, and Ethnic Groups are special areas for which guidelines are provided.

2) *Guidelines on Research Involving Human Subjects.* (1988). Medical Research Council of Canada (MRC). Also recommended by Natural Sciences and Engineering Research Council (NSERC). MRC will fund psychological research which has a clear and direct relevance to human health, including behavioral aspects of physical health and disease, or mental health and its disorders.

3) *The Declaration of Helsinki.* (as revised 1975). *Recommendation Guiding Medical Doctors in Biomedical Research Involving Human Subjects.* Medical Research Council of Canada (MRC). These 22 principles are basic guidelines for all types of research with human subjects. Respect and caring for the well-being of subjects and patients must take precedence over other considerations.

4) *Ethical Principles in the Conduct of Research with Human Participants.* (1982). American Psychological Association. Available from APA Order Department. The document presents "APA Ethical Principle #9, Research With Human Participants," from *APA Ethical Principles of Psychologists* (1981), and addresses its applications to ethical dilemmas, and decision-making in conducting research.

5) *Research with Children.* (1989). Society for Research in Child De-

velopment. Published in SRCD Newsletter. The following principles are applied to the use of children as research subjects and are intended to give special consideration to their vulnerable status. 1. Non-Harmful Procedures, 2. Informed Consent, 3. Parental Consent, 4. Additional Consent, 5. Incentives, 6. Deception, 7. Anonymity, 8. Mutual Responsibilities, 9. Jeopardy, 10. Unforeseen Consequences, 11. Confidentiality, and 12. Informing Participants.

6) *Science Free of Sexism: A Psychologist's Guide to the Conduct of Nonsexist Research*. (1983). Canadian Psychological Association. Published in *Canadian Psychology* (1984) *25*(1), 23–33. Discussion and detailed guidelines are provided under the major headings of I. Review of the Background Literature, II. Formulation of the Research Questions, III. Design and Conduct of Research, and IV. Interpretation of Findings.

7) *Issues to Consider in Promoting Nonsexist Psychology: A Guide for Researchers*. (1981). American Psychological Association Division 35 Task Force Report on *Guidelines for Nonsexist Research*. Available from APA. For further development of this material see M. McHugh, R. Koeske, & I. Frieze. (1986). Issues to consider in conducting nonsexist research. *American Psychologist, 41*, 879–890. Discussion and recommendations are provided under each of the major headings of: I. Excessive Confidence in Traditional Methods of Research, II. Conceptualization and Labelling of Variables, III. Using Precise Conceptual Models and Explanatory Systems, IV. Choosing Research Topics and Participants, V. The Role of Context Upon Behavior, VI. Research Examining Sex Related Differences, and VII. Special Problems with Animal Research.

8) *Ethical Principles for the Conduct of Research in the North*. (1982). Available from the Association of Canadian Universities for Northern Studies. The issues of research in northern communities in Canada are relevant to working in any ethnic community. The general principles of informed consent, risks and benefits, anonymity of subjects, and the ability to withdraw from research without penalty are addressed. In addition, the principle of community involvement and respect for the language, traditions, standards, knowledge and experience of the people is emphasized.

References and Addresses

American Association for Marriage and Family Therapy, 10th Flr, 1100 17th Street N.W., Washington, DC 20036 USA

American Association of Sex Educators, Counselors and Therapists, 435 North Michigan Avenue, Suite 1717, Chicago, IL 60611 USA

American Psychological Association, Order Department, P.O. Box 2710, Hyattsville, MD 20784 USA

American Society of Clinical Hypnosis, 2250 East Devon Avenue, Suite 336, Des Plaines, Illinois 60018 USA

Association for the Advancement of Behavior Therapy, 420 Lexington Avenue, New York, NY 10017 USA

Association of Canadian Universities for Northern Studies, 130 Albert, Suite 1915, Ottawa, Ontario K1P 5G4

Association of State and Provincial Psychology Boards, Central Office, P.O. Box 4389, 400 S. Union Street, Suite 295, Montgomery, AL 36103 USA

Biofeedback Certification Institute of America, 10200 W. 44th Avenue, #304, Wheat Ridge, CO 80033 USA

Canadian Association of School Psychologists—Ste. 252, 162-2025 l'avenue Corydon, Winnipeg, Manitoba R3P 0N5 Canada

Canadian Guidance and Counselling Association, 651 Cumberland, Room 212, Ottawa, ON K1N 6N5 Canada

Canadian Psychological Association, Suite 205, 151 Rue Slater, Ottawa, ON K1P 5H3 Canada

Centre for Research in Applied Measurement and Evaluation, 3-104 Education Building North, University of Alberta, Edmonton, AB T6G 2G5 Canada

Feminist Therapy Institute, Corporate Office, 50 South Steele, #850, Denver, CO 80209 USA

Medical Research Council of Canada (MRC), 20th Flr, Jeanne Mance Building, Tunney's Pasture, Ottawa, Ontario K1A 0W9 Canada

National Association of School Psychologists, Box 1295, Laurel, MD 20725-1295 USA

National Council on Measurement in Education, 1230 Seventeenth Street N.W., Washington, DC 20036 USA

Natural Sciences and Engineering Research Council (NSERC), Centennial Towers, 200 Kent Street, Ottawa, Ontario K1A 1H5 Canada

Social Sciences and Humanities Research Council of Canada (SSHRC), 255 Albert Street, P.O. Box 1610, Ottawa, ON K1P 6G4 Canada

Society for Research in Child Development Newsletter, Barbara Rogoff, Editor, Department of Psychology, University of Utah, Salt Lake City, UT 84112 USA

University of Utah, Department of Psychology, Salt Lake, UT 84103 USA

Appendix K

Ethical Decision Making Using the Canadian Code of Ethics for Psychologists

Ethical Dilemma

A psychologist working for a school board carried out an assessment of a nine year old girl who presented considerable behavioral difficulties since kindergarten. Results of intellectual and perceptual testing indicated average skills in these areas, although her academic skills were a year below grade level. Projective testing indicated that the child was anxious, confused, and insecure. Two interviews, one with the parents alone and one with the entire family, suggested a dysfunctional family system with many disruptions in the child's life. The psychologist had suggested a course of treatment at a local mental health clinic. The parents agreed to this recommendation and a referral was made.

Five months later, the psychologist is approached by the principal of the girl's school and is shown a psychological report on the same child which was prepared by a psychologist employed by a hospital clinic. The report states that the child is learning disabled and requires placement in a special education class. In studying the report, the psychologist finds that the assessment had been very brief, did not include any family contact, and that the instruments used did not include any specifically designed to assess the presence of learning disabilities. This is the second such report that the psychologist has seen in the past year written by the same professional. On checking with the mental health clinic to which the family was referred, the psychologist discovers that the family did not keep its appointment. The psychologist is of the opinion that the second evaluation obtained by the parents is incorrect, if not incompetent. The psychologist wonders what his responsibilities are in the situation and how he can best meet them.

STEP 1. IDENTIFICATION OF ETHICALLY RELEVANT ISSUES AND PRACTICES.

The initial reaction of the psychologist will probably include anger, concern and some feeling of guilt: anger at the psychologist who appears to have

---

From "Ethical Decision Making Using the Canadian Code of Ethics for Psychologists." In *Companion Manual to the Canadian Code of Ethics for Psychologists*, by C. Sinclair & J. Pettifor, 1991, Ottawa, ON: Canadian Psychological Association.

carried out an inadequate and misleading assessment; concern for the welfare of the child and her parents; and, guilt about not having followed up on the referral earlier or not having recognized the apparent resistance and denial of the parents. The task for the psychologist, however, is to determine the most ethical course of action, with the first step being to identify ethically relevant issues and practices. . . .

STEP 2. DEVELOPMENT OF ALTERNATIVE COURSES OF ACTION.

Principle or Value	Possible Thoughts of Psychologist About Course of Action
PRINCIPLE I: RESPECT FOR THE DIGNITY OF PERSONS	
Value: General Respect I.1. Demonstrate appropriate respect for the knowledge, insight, experience, and areas of expertise of others.	Whatever I decide to do, I need to convey appropriate respect for the parents and the other psychologist in my contacts with them around this issue.
Value: Informed Consent I.11. Seek as full and active participation as possible from others in decisions which affect them.	This Standard implies that I should involve the parents in working out this issue.
Value: Vulnerabilities No specific standard. Values statement: ". . . psychologists recognized that as individual, family, group or community vulnerabilities increase or as the power of persons to control their environment or their lives decreases, psychologists have an increasing responsibility to seek ethical advice and to establish safeguards to protect the rights of the persons involved."	I need to do what I can to ensure that this child's "right to treatment" is dealt with in whatever resolution we come to.
Value: Confidentiality I.40. Share confidential information with others only with the informed consent of those involved, or in a manner that the individuals involved cannot be identified, except as required or justified by law, or in circumstances of actual or possible serious physical harm or death.	The hospital report has been sent to us with the parents' permission, so I may call the other psychologist to discuss it. However, I need to determine whether the hospital knows about our assessment and if the parents have given them informed consent to obtain details of the assessment. If yes, I could discuss the discrepancies with the psychologist. If no, I am required to seek informed consent from the parents before calling. If they refuse, I can only discuss the hospital report with the hospital psychologist.

continues

Step 2. (*Continued*)

Principle or Value	Possible Thoughts of Psychologist About Course of Action
PRINCIPLE II: RESPONSIBLE CARING	
Value: General Caring II.1. Protect and promote the welfare of clients, students, research participants, colleagues, and others.	I need to be concerned about protecting the welfare of the child, the family, and the other psychologist.
No specific Standard. Values Statement "... psychologists recognize that as vulnerabilities increase and/or as power to control one's own life decreases, they have an increasing responsibility to protect the well-being of the individual, family, group, or community involved."	However, the child is the most vulnerable person in this situation, and my course of action should be designed to protect the child first and foremost.
Value: Competence and Self-Knowledge II.10. Evaluate how their own experiences, attitudes, culture, beliefs, values, social context, individual differences, and stresses influence their interactions with others, and integrate this awareness into all efforts to benefit and not harm others.	I am sometimes unsympathetic to the stress and difficulties of parenting. This may be related to my never having been a parent myself. I tend to want to rescue the child from the family instead of working with the family to the child's benefit.
Value: Maximize Benefit II.18. Provide services which are coordinated over time and with other service providers, in order to avoid duplication or working at cross purposes. Such coordination would be promoted by the maintenance of adequate records and communication with other service providers.	I know about the hospital service and, therefore, have a responsibility to coordinate by exploring the discrepancy between the reports. I need to determine if the hospital knows about our assessment.
Value: Minimize Harm II.30. Maintain appropriate contact, support, and responsibility for caring until a colleague or other professional begins service, if referring a client to a colleague or other professional.	In the future, I will need to play a more active role in helping clients to follow through on agreed-to referrals or, at least, more thoroughly explore their objections or reservations about a referral.

continues

Step 2. (*Continued*)

Principle or Value	Possible Thoughts of Psychologist About Course of Action
Value: Offset/Correct Harm II.37. Act to stop or offset the consequences of clearly harmful activities being carried out by another psychologist or member of another discipline, when these activities have come to their attention outside of a confidential client relationship. . . . Depending on the nature of the harmful activities, this may include talking informally with the psychologist or member of the other discipline, obtaining objective information and, if possible, the assurance that the harm will discontinue and be corrected. However, if the harm is serious and/or continues to persist, the situation would be reported to the appropriate regulatory body, authority, and/or committee for action.	I need to speak to the other psychologist directly about my concerns. Because the intent and the degree of harm are debatable at this point, I should not take it any further unless I am convinced that there is "clear harm" and that this or the possibility of future situations cannot be resolved. Even then, the psychologist's supervisor might be the most appropriate "authority" with whom to start, since this might offset future potential harm more quickly than using our professional regulatory body. However, I cannot rule out the possibility of having to go to the regulatory body and being prepared to substantiate my complaint formally.
Value: Extended Responsibility II.44. Encourage others, if appropriate, to care responsibly.	I need to help the parents to understand my perception of their child's needs in the situation and enable them to act primarily in the interest of their child's welfare.
PRINCIPLE III: INTEGRITY IN RELATIONSHIPS	
Value: Objectivity/Lack of Bias III.10. Evaluate how their personal experiences, attitudes, values, social context, individual differences, and stresses influence their activities and thinking, integrating this awareness into all attempts to be objective and unbiased in their research, service and other activities.	I highly value competence and intelligence, and can be a little self-righteous about others' failings. Although I think I'm right about the incompetence of this report, I need to obtain further information and not jump to conclusions.
Value: Straightforwardness/Openness III.16. Fully explain reasons for their actions to persons who have been affected by their actions, if appropriate and/or if asked.	In contacts with the family and the other psychologist, I need to be straightforward about the reasons for the previous referral, about the Board's requirements for special class placement, about my own views on the situation, and about discrepancies between the reports.

continues

Step 2. (*Continued*)

Principle or Value	Possible Thoughts of Psychologist About Course of Action
Value: Reliance on the Discipline III.36. Seek consultation from colleagues and/or appropriate groups and committees, and give due regard to their advice in arriving at a responsible decision, if faced with difficult situations.	I have the time and available resources to check my perceptions of the situation and possible course of action with colleagues, including a colleague outside my own Board (to better ensure objectivity).
PRINCIPLE IV: RESPONSIBILITY TO SOCIETY	
Value: Respect for Society IV.14. Convey respect for and abide by prevailing community mores, social customs, and cultural expectation in their scientific and professional activities, provided that this does not contravene any of the ethical principles of this Code.	The role of parents in our society includes the legal right to control decisions regarding their child. I need to convey respect for this role and become more insistent only if it is clear to me that the child's welfare could be harmed significantly by their choices.

The above analysis would seem to rule out some possible courses of action: a) For the psychologist to do nothing, assuming that the Board's placement committee will turn down the request for placement and that the parents and other psychologist will "learn from the experience"; b) For the psychologist to report the hospital psychologist to the regulatory body immediately, using the two reports as evidence of incompetence.

On the other hand, there are several courses of action which could be planned and which would be consistent with the psychologist's application of the code to his decision making. For present purposes, two alternatives considered by psychologists resolving this dilemma during the development phase of the Code will be used to demonstrate the remaining steps in the ethical decision-making process.

Alternative I

i) First, phone the parents, acknowledging receipt of the report and the difference in the evaluations. Ask to meet with them, and ask their permission to speak with the hospital psychologist before that meeting to clarify the differences. Invite them to form a partnership with me (and perhaps the special education resource team) to explore the best plan for their child in school. Not share my opinion that the hospital psychologist report reflects incompetence, only that the specific assessment tools considered by the Board in their decision about special class placement have not been used. If appropriate, offer to help arrange for the appropriate assessment to be carried out. Once again, refer to the mental health clinic if, in my opinion, it is still required.

ii) Next, phone the hospital psychologist to determine the circumstances of the assessment and the psychologist's understanding of the overall situation. Point out the difficulty of accepting the child into a special class placement with so little background work having been done. If permission has been obtained from the parents, inform the hospital psychologist of the nature of my earlier involvement and my assessment of the family. Ask for the other psychologist's perspective now that the psychologist has a more complete picture. Offer to make a list of the instruments that the Board considers necessary for special class placement.

iii) In future, be more supportive of clients in the referral process, following up to explore any reservations or difficulties the client might be having with the referral.

Alternative II

i) First, phone the psychologist at the hospital. Determine whether the psychologist was aware of the school assessment and whether the psychologist has permission from the parents to receive the school report. If so, proceed as in Alternative I, but add that I wish the psychologist had called me in order to better coordinate our efforts. If there is no permission from the parents, discuss only the hospital assessment as outlined in Alternative I. State that I have difficulty with the label "learning disability" being applied to a child without more specialized instruments being used for assessment. Also say that, in any case, the more specialized instruments would have to be used before the Board would consider the child for special class placement. Ask the psychologist to join me in deciding what we should do about the problem.

ii) Then phone the parents, letting them know that there is a problem with the hospital assessment, but that I have spoken to the psychologist and that we would suggest doing "X." Enquire about the previously suggested referral and offer to meet with the parents to discuss their concerns.

iii) In future, be more supportive of the client in the referral process, following up to explore any reservations or difficulties the client might be having with the referral.

STEP 3. ANALYSIS OF LIKELY SHORT-TERM, ONGOING, AND LONG-TERM RISKS AND BENEFITS OF EACH COURSE OF ACTION ON THE INDIVIDUAL(S) / GROUP(S) LIKELY TO BE AFFECTED.

While it is not possible to list all possible consequences, some can be predicted:

Possible Positive Consequences	Possible Negative Consequences
ALTERNATIVE I.	
Bringing the issues out into the open for discussion may lead to a quick resolution conducive to the child's welfare.	Bringing issues into the open might frighten parents, making them more defensive and resistant.
Give parents a sense of maximum control, leading to a greater willingness to collaborate.	Give parents the control to make what I consider to be harmful choices for their daughter.
Offer the hospital psychologist enough "face-saving" that the psychologist is less defensive and more likely to change.	Tactful communication may be too indirect for the hospital psychologist to understand the seriousness of the situation.
ALTERNATIVE II.	
In the short-term, present a unified front to the parents, making harmful choices less likely.	In the long-term, undermine the parents' perception of the importance of their role, resulting in more resistance.
Get more quickly to the need for follow-through on the mental health clinic referral.	Get to the need for mental health clinic referral more quickly than the parents can handle, making it less likely that they will agree.
Psychologist will have clear understanding of issues and concerns, which is more likely to result in quick changes to practice.	Psychologist will become angry and defensive and less likely to change.

STEP 4. CHOICE OF ACTION AFTER CONSCIENTIOUS APPLICATION OF EXISTING PRINCIPLES, VALUES, AND STANDARDS.

The psychologist resolving this dilemma would likely find the actions and consequences for Alternative I to be oriented to more clearly supporting the values included in Principle I (Respect for the Dignity of Persons). On the other hand, the actions and consequences for Alternative II are oriented more clearly to the values included in Principle II (Responsible Caring). Both alternatives are clearly oriented to Principle III (Integrity in Relationships). In the first alternative, however, the emphasis is on the application of Principle III to contacts with the parents; in the second alternative, the emphasis is on the application of Principle III to contact with the other psychologist. Although either course of action could be considered reasonably ethical, Alternative I would appear to reflect more closely the spirit of the Code, with its heavier emphasis on Principle I and its application of Principle III more to the parent than the other psychologist.

STEP 5. ACTION WITH A COMMITMENT TO ASSUME RESPONSIBILITY FOR THE CONSEQUENCES OF THE ACTION.

This step is self-evident; there is no possible resolution of the dilemma unless the psychologist implements the chosen course of action.

STEP 6. EVALUATION OF THE RESULTS OF THE COURSE OF ACTION.

Evaluation of this complex situation would need to be ongoing. There may be a need to revise the course of action depending on further information received, or on the reactions of the parents, child, or other psychologist.

STEP 7. ASSUMPTION OF RESPONSIBILITY FOR THE CONSEQUENCES OF ACTION, INCLUDING CORRECTION OF NEGATIVE CONSEQUENCES, IF ANY, OR RE-ENGAGING IN THE DECISION-MAKING PROCESS IF ETHICAL ISSUE IS NOT RESOLVED.

In spite of our best efforts to anticipate and plan ways to maximize positive and minimize negative consequences, it is always possible to misjudge what is likely to happen. Ethical responsibility includes correction, as much as possible, of negative consequences. In the above situation, for instance, it is possible that the parents might decide to remove the child from her current school system and transfer her to a new system, refusing consent for the school psychologist's report to be sent to the new Board. This final step in the ethical decision-making process assumes that the psychologist will accept the responsibility to try to resolve this new ethical dilemma. Deciding that "the problem is no longer mine, but belongs to the new school board" would be considered unethical.

Appendix L

Ethical Decision Making Using the APA Ethical Principles of Psychologists and Code of Conduct

Ethical Dilemma

Dr. James is providing therapy for a depressed client, Mr. Hines, who is in the process of recalling memories of childhood abuse. Mr. Hines comes to the therapist to either discontinue therapy or negotiate a barter agreement because he has just lost his job and his young son has been diagnosed with leukemia. He wishes to do carpentry work or painting to renovate Dr. James's offices and/or his home in return for further therapy sessions.

Dr. James does not wish to abandon or refer his client at this stage of therapy. He also does not need any work done on the office or the home. Neither does he wish to do the amount of pro bono work that he believes this client requires.

Dr. James consults a trusted colleague, Dr. Sharp, both on the clinical dynamics of the case and on the ethical implications and potential pitfalls of entering into a barter arrangement. After some discussion, Dr. Sharp says, "You know, you are telling me about young Murray Hines, that ne'er-do-well who married my granddaughter. I'm sure glad you are seeing him because the family has been worried about him for some time. You have given me some fascinating insights though. . . . That marriage may not be worth saving. I might just have a chat with Susie. . . . Of course, I won't mention that you and I have been talking." Dr. James has confidence that his colleague will respect the confidentiality of the consultation, and he arranges with Mr. Hines to continue therapy with a greatly reduced fee to be reviewed in 3 months' time.

Dr. Sharp talks to his granddaughter to persuade her to divorce Murray. When she resists doing so, he lets her know that he has access to personal information of a therapeutic nature that justifies his position. Susie talks to Murray. Mr. Hines discontinues therapy with Dr. James and files a complaint against him for breach of confidentiality of personal information.

From "Ethical Decision Making Using the Canadian Code of Ethics for Psychologists." In *Companion Manual to the Canadian Code of Ethics for Psychologists,* by C. Sinclair & J. Pettifor, 1991, Ottawa, ON: Canadian Psychological Association. Copyright 1991 by the Canadian Psychological Association. Adapted with permission.

STEP 1. IDENTIFICATION OF ETHICALLY RELEVANT ISSUES AND PRACTICES.

The initial reaction of the psychologist will probably include anger, concern, and some feelings of guilt: anger at the colleague who appears to have violated his trust and confidentiality, concern for the welfare of the client who has discontinued needed therapy and whose marriage may be in jeopardy, and guilt for not having taken sufficient precautions to protect his client's confidentiality. He appears to have three tasks at hand (a) making amends for harm to the client, (b) protecting himself against allegations of professional misconduct, and (c) determining how he might avoid such a breach of confidentiality in the future.

STEP 2. DEVELOPMENT OF ALTERNATIVE COURSES OF ACTION.

Principles and Standards from the APA's Ethical Principles of Psychologists and Code of Conduct	Possible Thoughts of the Psychologist About Courses of Action
Principle D: Respect for People's Rights and Dignity. . . . They respect the rights of individuals to privacy, confidentiality, self-determination, and autonomy. . . .	I have always tried to respect client confidentiality. I wonder if I should have emphasized more strongly to Dr. Sharp that the content of this discussion must be strictly confidential. But he must have known that. I wonder if I should have asked Mr. Hines permission to consult confidentially with Dr. Sharp, and then I might have known ahead of time they were related by marriage.
Principle E: Concern for Others' Welfare. Psychologists seek to contribute to the welfare of those with whom they interact professionally. . . .	The only reason I consulted Dr. Sharp was to do the best for my client . . . and I suppose also how to do so without sacrificing my income.
Standard 1.18 Barter. Psychologists ordinarily refrain from accepting goods, services, or other nonmonetary remuneration from patients or clients in return for psychological services because such arrangements create inherent potential for conflicts, exploitation, and distortion of the professional relationship. A psychologist may participate in bartering *only* if (1) it is not clinically contraindicated, *and* (2) the relationship is not exploitative.	I think we resolved the barter issue for the present, but I worry about the confidentiality issue. What would I do if Dr. Sharp offered to pay for his grandson-in-law's therapy with me and wanted progress reports to boot? No, that would never happen.

continues

Step 2. (*Continued*)

Principles and Standards from the APA's Ethical Principles of Psychologists and Code of Conduct	Possible Thoughts of the Psychologist About Courses of Action
Standard 4.08 Interruption of Services.	
(a) Psychologists make reasonable efforts to plan for facilitating care in the event that psychological services are interrupted by factors such as the psychologist's illness, death, unavailability, or relocation or by the client's relocation or financial limitations.	I would like to facilitate Mr. Hines's obtaining treatment from someone else if he does not wish to see me anymore, which he obviously does not. Since he has laid a formal complaint against me, though, my lawyer says under no circumstance may I speak to him until the case is adjudicated.
(b) When entering into employment or contractual relationships, psychologists provide for orderly and appropriate resolution of responsibility for patient or client care in the event that the employment or contractual relationship ends, with paramount consideration given to the welfare of the patient or client.	The client wants nothing further to do with me, and the lawyer wants me to have nothing further to do with him.
Standard 4.09 Terminating the Professional Relationship.	
(a) Psychologists do not abandon patients or clients.	I did not abandon him. He abandoned me. But I unintentionally precipitated the abrupt termination of therapy.
Standard 5.02 Maintaining Confidentiality.	
Psychologists have a primary obligation and take reasonable precautions to respect the confidentiality rights of those with whom they work or consult, recognizing that confidentiality may be established by law, institutional rules, or professional or scientific relationships.	I respected confidentiality by not giving any names of parties involved. I did acknowledge that Dr. Sharp had recognized the client.
5.03 Minimizing Intrusions on Privacy.	
(a) In order to minimize intrusions on privacy, psychologists include . . . only information germane to the purpose for which the communication is made.	I wonder if I provided more detailed information to Dr. Sharp than was necessary because I was too involved in the situation. I should review what would be minimal information for a valid consultation.
(b) Psychologists discuss confidential information . . . only for appropriate scientific or professional purposes and only with persons clearly concerned with such matters.	Dr. Sharp is(was) a trusted and eminent colleague whose advice is frequently sought by younger professionals. I have always considered him an appropriate person to consult. I must reconsider this perception, too.
	continues

Step 2. (*Continued*)

Principles and Standards from the APA's Ethical Principles of Psychologists and Code of Conduct	Possible Thoughts of the Psychologist About Courses of Action
Standard 5.05 Disclosures (a) Psychologists disclose confidential information without the consent of the individual only as mandated by law, or where permitted by law for a valid purpose, such as (1) to provide needed professional services to the patient or the individual or organizational client, (2) to obtain appropriate professional consultations, (3) to protect the patient or client or others from harm, or (4) to obtain payment for services, in which instance disclosure is limited to the minimum that is necessary to achieve the purpose.	I was seeking appropriate professional consultation for the benefit of the client, so I do not think I required client consent, although in hindsight it might have been a good idea. I also wanted advice on how I could be remunerated under these special circumstances.
Standard 5.06 Consultations When consulting with colleagues, (1) psychologists do not share confidential information that reasonably could lead to the identification of a patient, client, research participant or other person or organization with whom they have a confidential relationship unless they have obtained the prior consent of the person or organization or the disclosure cannot be avoided, and (2) they share information only to the extent necessary to achieve the purposes of the consultation.	I think I was reasonable in my sharing of information only for the purpose of obtaining professional guidance. However, perhaps I could have been more careful. I am being charged, but I think that my good friend and colleague, Dr. Sharp, is more guilty than I am of breaching confidentiality. Perhaps I should have another chat with him.

Alternative 1

The psychologist might believe that he must insist on meeting with Mr. Hines again to explain the misunderstandings and to express his good intentions and desire to continue therapy. He also hopes that Mr. Hines will understand and withdraw the charges against him of professional misconduct. He is not sure what the consequences of this action might be for all the concerned parties.

Alternative 2

The psychologist might consult with Dr. Sharp about the current dilemma, especially since he plays an important role in it and Dr. James still respects his judgment. Maybe Dr. Sharp can advise the client to continue to receive professional help from someone, and/or Dr. Sharp might give evidence to defend Dr. James if a formal hearing is held (although he might incriminate himself in doing so), or maybe Dr. Sharp can persuade Mr. Hines to withdraw the charges (although it seems doubtful that they are on friendly terms).

Alternative 3

Dr. James retains a lawyer to defend himself against the complaints laid against him, discusses his situation with nobody else, and takes no actions unless so directed by his lawyer.

The reader is left with the task of following through on the remaining steps in the ethical decision-making process.

STEP 3. ANALYSIS OF LIKELY SHORT-TERM, ONGOING, AND LONG-TERM RISKS AND BENEFITS OF EACH COURSE OF ACTION ON THE INDIVIDUAL(S)/GROUP(S) LIKELY TO BE AFFECTED.

There are many possibilities, both positive and negative.

STEP 4. CHOICE OF COURSE OF ACTION AFTER CONSCIENTIOUS APPLICATION OF EXISTING PRINCIPLES, VALUES, AND STANDARDS.

STEP 5. ACTION WITH A COMMITMENT TO ASSUME RESPONSIBILITY FOR THE CONSEQUENCES OF THE ACTION.

STEP 6. EVALUATION OF THE RESULTS OF THE COURSE OF ACTION.

STEP 7. ASSUMPTION OF RESPONSIBILITY FOR THE CONSEQUENCES OF ACTION, INCLUDING CORRECTION OF NEGATIVE CONSEQUENCES, IF ANY, OR REENGAGING IN THE DECISION-MAKING PROCESS IF THE ETHICAL ISSUE IS NOT RESOLVED.

Index